"Being of Sound Mind..."
An Index to the Probate Records

in the Fauquier County, Virginia
Clerk's Loose Papers and
Superior and Circuit Court Records
1759-1919

Compiled by
Joan W. Peters, C.G.R.S.

Heritage Books
2008

HERITAGE BOOKS
AN IMPRINT OF HERITAGE BOOKS, INC.

Books, CDs, and more—Worldwide

For our listing of thousands of titles see our website
at
www.HeritageBooks.com

Published 2008 by
HERITAGE BOOKS, INC.
Publishing Division
100 Railroad Ave. #104
Westminster, Maryland 21157

Copyright © 2001 Joan W. Peters

Other books by the author:

Abstracts of Fauquier County, Virginia Birth Records, 1853-1896

Fauquier County, Virginia's Clerk's Loose Papers: A Guide to the Records, 1759-1919

Military Records, Certificates of Service, Discharge, Heirs, and Pensions Declarations and Schedules from the Fauquier County, Virginia Court Minute Books, 1784-1840

Military Records, Patriotic Service, and Public Service Claims from the Fauquier County, Virginia Court Minute Books, 1759-1784

Military Records, Pension Applications, Heirs at Law and Civil War Military Records from the Fauquier County, Virginia Court Minute Books, 1840-1904

Neglected and Forgotten: Fauquier County, Virginia, French & Indian War, Revolutionary War and War of 1812 Veterans

Prince William County, Virginia General Index to Wills, 1734-1951

The Tax Man Cometh—Land and Property in Colonial Fauquier County, Virginia: Tax List from the Fauquier County Court Clerk's Loose Papers, 1759-1782

All rights reserved. No part of this book may be reproduced or transmitted in any form or by any means, electronic or mechanical, including photocopying, recording or by any information storage and retrieval system without written permission from the author, except for the inclusion of brief quotations in a review.

International Standard Book Numbers
Paperbound: 978-1-58549-690-7
Clothbound: 978-0-7884-7343-2

ACKNOWLEDGMENTS

I would like to thank Mrs. Gail Barb, the Clerk of the Fauquier County Circuit Court for her care, diligence and interest in preserving Fauquier County's earliest records. It was under her stewardship, as the Chief Deputy Clerk under Mr. William Harris, and then as Clerk of the Court, that the Clerks Loose Papers were preserved, arranged and indexed. Without her encouragement and interest, this index could not have been completed. Thanks go too to the staff of the Fauquier County Circuit Court: Kathy, Wilma, Carolyn, Nancy and Phyllis. Both Phyllis and Kathy made helpful suggestions that were incorporated into the format of this index.

COVER ILLUSTRATIONS

The Front Cover Illustration is a scanned image from Box 39, Wills, Sales &c. 1793-006. Page 1 of Peter Waggoner's Will. The Back Cover Illustration is a scanned image from Box 50, Clerks Copies/Unrecorded Wills. 1779-001 James Scott's Will.

Foreword

In 1993, the Fauquier County Circuit Court applied for and received a grant from the State Library of Virginia to organize, arrange and preserve the contents of the 520 Woodruff drawers in the basement vault known as the Clerks Loose Papers of the Fauquier County Court. These drawers contained diverse records of the day –to-day activities of the county court.

Among the probate records in these drawers were wills, inventories, sales, divisions, relinquishments, administrator and executor bonds, guardian bonds and a drawer labeled unrecorded wills. These "unrecorded" wills were really proven or certified copies of wills, made by the clerk, for Court use.

Four of the record series in the Clerks Loose papers had probate records associated with them. Chancery records had wills, inventories and appraisements, sales, guardianships and accounts, administrator bonds and accounts, executor bonds and accounts, divisions and plats & surveys of divisions, division of slaves among heirs and the like.

Land Records and Disputes had wills and other probate records filed as exhibits in land controversies. Military records contained information regarding heirs of deceased soldiers. Finally the probate records, themselves, contained enough records to have several sub-series associated with them. There were wills and sales and the traditional probate records along with the administrator, executor and guardian bonds, found in separate drawers, and given separate designations to retain the integrity of the record base.

The Superior and Circuit Court files from 1832-1910 contained enough probate to fill six document boxes. None of these probate records appear in the Circuit Court's General Index to Wills.

Here, then, was an opportunity to put together an index of all of the probate records found in the Clerks Loose Papers between 1759-1919 along with the probate records in the Superior/Circuit Courts between 1832-1910.

This "consolidated" probate index has several advantages.

    1) When researchers visit the Fauquier Circuit Court record room, they have access to *all* the probate records preserved in the Clerks Loose Papers *and* the probate records in the Superior and Circuit Court records.

    2) The previous separate indexes for probate sub-series like the Administrator and Executor Bonds and for Guardian Bonds have been consolidated into one index. The remaining probate records in this series, previously unindexed, are now part of this index.

    3) The probate records from the "Unrecorded Wills" are found in this Index. These are part of Box 50 Clerks Copies/Unrecorded Wills.

    4) Any probate record found in Chancery Record Series of the Clerks Loose Papers is in this index.

    5) The 25 Land Disputes from the Land Records & Disputes Record Series of the Clerk Loose Papers that have probate records are found in this index.

    6) The seven men who left heirs listed in the Military Records are found in this index.

7) At the suggestion of a member of the staff, box numbers for the probate sub-series were added to the index for easier accessibility. The Superior/Circuit Court probate records were designated as such in the index and identified by box number.

This "consolidated" probate index provides the researcher with an entirely new set of records to examine. For the first time, **all** of the probate records in the Clerks Loose Papers are together in one index. For the first time, **all** of the probate records in the Superior/Circuit Court to 1910 can now be found in the same index. This index is easy to use and easy to understand.

Family historians, genealogists, and historical researchers will benefit alike from this index and the accessibility of the probate records in both the Clerks Loose Papers and the Superior/Circuit Court records.

                                                Joan W. Peters, C.G.R.S.
                                                    Broad Run, VA.
                                                         June 2001

TABLE OF CONTENTS

	PAGES
Foreword	
Introduction	i - iii
Abbot through Ayres	1 - 7
Bailey through Byrne	7a - 26
Calaghan through Curry	27 - 42
Dagg through Duncan	43 – 52
Eaton through Ewell	53 – 58
Fairfax through Furr	59 – 73
Plate # 1. Scanned Image from Box 39 *1771-001 Ann Green's Dower Allotment.*	74
Gabby through Gutridge	75 – 84
Haddux through Hutchison	85 – 106
Iden through Ivey	106
Jackman through Julius	107 – 113
Plate # 2. Scanned Image from Box 39 *1779-002 Peggy Norris' Relinquishment.*	114
Kamper through Knox	115 – 121

Plate # 3. Scanned Image from Box 39
     1810-002 William Smith's Inventory & Appraisement.
     (pg 1)
	122

TABLE OF CONTENTS

	PAGES
Lacey through Luttrell	123 – 128
MacNeil through Murry	129 – 148
Nalle through Nutt	149 – 152
Obanion through Owens	153 – 155
Plate # 4. Scanned Image from Box 44 Admr. & Exor Bonds. 1759-005 John Shadrack's Extrx. Bond.	156
Padgett through Putnam	157 – 168
Quesenberry through Quisenberry	168
Raley through Rust	169 – 179
Plate # 5. Scanned Image from Box 49. Guardian Bonds. 1807-002 Margaret & Elizabeth Mauzey's Guardian Bond.	180
Saffell through Sweeny	181 – 201
Plate # 6. Scanned Image from Box 45. Admr. & Exor. Bonds 1778-004. John Squire's Admtrx. Bond.	202
Talbert through Tyson	203 – 210
Ullman through Utterback	211
Vanhorn through Vowles	211
Plate # 7. Scanned Image from Box 50. Clerks Copies/Unrecorded Deeds. 1779-001 James Scott's Will.	212
Waddell through Wykoff	213 – 230
Yates	230

INTRODUCTION

1. The Clerks Loose Papers

The Clerks Loose Papers is the term given to the records in the 520 metal Woodruff drawers in the Fauquier County Circuit Court basement vault. The papers were tri-folded, jacketed and tied, with red string, into bundles arranged by Court dates.

The contents chronicle the day-to-day activities of the County court. To a great extent, the activity centered around civil law and criminal suits. Much of the civil process had to do with the recovery of debts owed by promissory notes, bonds or overdue accounts. Slander, Breach of the close, Trespass and Breach of Contract and Covenant suits were of common occurrence.

There were land disputes over boundary lines, ejectment suits, suits for back rent. There were grand jury presentments and indictments. There were criminal suits for theft, grand larceny, brawling, and even a murder or two. Slaves and their owners were brought to court routinely for various breaches of the Black Codes.

While the legal process formed an important part of the Clerks Loose Papers of the County Court, there were other important records found in these drawers as well. Sandwiched among these "official" records were bonds of public officials; information relating to the building and repair of the Courthouse, Clerks Office and the Jail; applications for roads, mills, and ordinaries; military appointments, pension applications and court-martials; Church warden and Overseer of the Poor Apprenticeships and other records relating to the maintenance and upkeep for the poor of the county; personal property and land tax records; and 34 previously unknown and unindexed 1784 marriage bonds.

Also housed within these drawers were probate records. So many probate records, in fact, that sub-series were necessary to retain the integrity of the record base. Wills, sales and the traditional probate records formed one sub-series. Administrator and Executor Bonds, found separately, formed another. Guardian Bonds, also found in a separate drawer, formed a third sub-series. Finally, the "Unrecorded Wills" (in reality copies of proven or certified copies of wills made by the Clerk for Court use) made up the last sub-series.

2. Probate Records in the Clerks Loose Papers

- **Chancery Records**

Many of the probate records in the Clerks Loose Papers are found in the Chancery suits. Chancery was a court of equity. This meant that suits were decided on what was fair to the parties rather than through the strict application of law.

Chancery suits could be brought for any number of reasons. Those suits having probate records in them were likely to have been brought to effect a division of an estate. Sometimes they would be brought to force the sale of real estate to pay off a debt or creditors to the estate. Other suits could be brought to sell real estate or slaves for the benefits of minor children.

- **Retrieving a Chancery Record in the Probate Index**

    Whatever the reason, the Chancery suits appear to have the widest variety of probate records in this index. Follow these steps to retrieve a Chancery suit with a probate record you wish to examine:

    1. The index will tell you the record series in the "CLP Record Series" column. (CLP is the abbreviation used for the Clerks Loose Papers). If it says "Chancery", that means this record is a Chancery record.

    2. Then look at the index number. This index number will tell you where the record is in the Chancery record series.

    For example, Edward Burgess left an Inventory + Sales in 1789 in one of the county Chancery suits from the Clerks Loose Papers. This suit, 1789-012, can be found in the box housing the 1789 Chancery suits.

    3. Give **all** the information found in the index, the name, the instrument, the date, the County, the CLP record series and the index number, to one of the staff and they will pull the suit for you.

    Members of the research public do not have access to the court records housed in the vault. If your suit is found in a document box housed upstairs in the record room proper, please ask the staff for assistance.

    4. Sign the sign-out sheet for the suit. When you finish looking at the suit, return it to one of the staff members who will sign the suit back in. When looking at Chancery records, please remember to keep the records in the order they are found in the folders.

- **Land Records & Disputes in the Clerks Loose Papers**

    There are 25 people named in the Land Records and Disputes in the Clerks Loose Papers who left a probate record. Nineteen of the twenty-five left wills filed within the Land Disputes. Follow the same steps for retrieving a Land Dispute as you would for retrieval of Chancery records, outlined above.

- **Military Records in the Clerks Loose Papers**

    There are seven men in the Military Records who have any kind of record specifically related to heirs. Captain William Blackwell, Joshua Jenkins, Captain George Kemper, Dempsey Padgett, Captain Richard H. Peyton, Captain Thomas Ransdell and Thomas Wiser all left heirs named in the Military Records Series of the Clerks Loose Papers. However, many of the pension applications have family information, which may prove helpful. The pension applications are not found in this index.

    If you are interested in the heirs of one of the men in the list above, copy the information from this index and give it to a staff member. Follow the steps as given for the retrieval of a Chancery record.

- **The Probate Record Series and Sub-Series in the Clerks Loose Papers**

    The Probate Record series and its sub-series make up the largest bloc of records in this index. You will need to make sure you give **all** the information in the index, including the Box number. Be sure to give the member of the staff the **box number** of the Probate Record series.

    For example, you may be looking for Joshua Owen's 1776 Guardian Bond, indexed as 1776-001. If you do not give the staff the right box number, they must look through several boxes in order to find the guardian bond. Box number 48 will identify the whereabouts of this particular guardian bond.

    If you are not specific, you could end up with John Weedon's Administrator Bond, which also has the 1776-001 Index number. Its box number, however, is Box 44.

    When looking at any of the Clerks Loose Papers identified as Probate Records, be sure to copy *all* of the information in that column for the staff.

2. **Probate Records in the Superior and Circuit Court Records**

    There are a variety of probate records found in the boxes labeled Superior/Circuit Court records. These records date from 1832-1910.

    When retrieving a probate record from the Superior/Circuit Court boxes, be sure to note on the retrieval sheet that the index states this is a Superior/Circuit Court record along with the box number. Otherwise, you follow the same steps for retrieving these records as you would for the probate records in the Clerks Loose Papers.

3. **Abbreviations**

    Below is a list of commonly used abbreviations found in this index.

Abbreviation	**for**	**Abbreviation**	**for**
Admr.	Administrator	CA	California
Admtrx.	Administratrix	GA	Georgia
Acct.	Account	KY	Kentucky
Appt.	Appointment	LA	Louisiana
CLP	Clerks Loose Papers	MD	Maryland
Co.	County	NC	North Carolina
Comr.	Commissioner	OH	Ohio
Exor.	Executor	PA	Pennsylvania
Extrx.	Executrix	TN	Tennessee
Gdn	Guardian	VA	Virginia
Gdnship	Guardianship	WV	West Virginia
OS	Oversize	+/&c	and
Rapphk.	Rappahannock		

iii

Consolidated Probate Index from the Clerks Loose Papers & the Superior Court/Circuit Court Records 1759-1919

Surname	Given Name	Instrument	Date	County	CLP Record Series	Index #
ABBOT						
Abbot	Clarence	Guardian Account	8/10/1897	Holt Co. MO	Chancery	1897-051
Abbot	Grover S.	Guardian Account	8/10/1897	Holt Co. MO.	Chancery	1897-051
Abbot	Myrtle B.	Guardian Account	8/10/1897	Holt Co. MO.	Chancery	1897-051
Abbot	Pearl M.	Guardian Account	8/10/1897	Holt Co. MO.	Chancery	1897-051
ABELL						
Abell	James H.	Guardian Bond	1812	Fauquier Co.	Probate, Box 49	1812-003
Abell	Polley	Guardian Bond	1812	Fauquier Co.	Probate, Box 49	1812-003
Abell	Robert	Guardian Bond	1812	Fauquier Co.	Probate, Box 49	1812-003
Abell	Thornton	Guardian Bond	1812	Fauquier Co.	Probate, Box 49	1812-003
ABLES						
Ables	Ephraim	Exor. Bond	1810	Fauquier Co.	Probate, Box 47	1810-003
ADAMS						
Adams	James	Heirs	4/22/1851	Fauquier Co.	Chancery	1861-004
Adams	James	Appraisement	4/22/1851	Fauquier Co.	Chancery	1861-004
Adams	John	Admtrx. Bond	1781	Fauquier Co.	Probate, Box 45	1781-011
Adams	John	Admr. Bond	1813	Fauquier Co.	Probate, Box 47	1813-015
Adams	Littleton	Report of Division Of Slaves	10/16/1834	Fauquier Co.	Chancery	1839-060
Adams	Littleton	Division of Slaves	2/23/1835	Fauquier Co.	Chancery	1839-060
Adams	Littleton	Report of Division	10/29/1839	Fauquier Co.	Chancery	1839-060
Adams	Littleton	Plat & Survey of Division	10/29/1839	Fauquier Co.	Chancery	1839-060
Adams	Peter	Sales List	3/24/1845	Fauquier Co.	Chancery	1846-047
Adams	Sarah	Exor. Bond	1806	Fauquier Co.	Probate, Box 47	1806-006
Adams	Thomas T.	Will	9/22/1856	Fauquier Co.	Chancery	1859-017
Adams	Virginia	Heirs	Undated	Fauquier Co.	Chancery	1855-012
Adams	Willis	Admr. Bond	11/25/1852	Fauquier Co.	Chancery	1860-047
Adams	Willis	Division	2/6/1854	Fauquier Co.	Chancery	1860-047
AISQUITH						
Aisquith	Virginia	Guardian Bond	9/6/1832	Fauquier Co.	Chancery	1832-010

Consolidated Probate Index from the Clerks Loose Papers & the Superior Court/Circuit Court Records 1759-1919

Surname	Given Name	Instrument	Date	County	CLP Record Series	Index #
ALLASON						
Allason	William	Will	5/24/1793	Fauquier Co.	Chancery	1814-004
Allason	William	Sales	Undated	Fauquier Co.	Chancery	1814-004
Allason	William	Inventory + Appraisement	1/26/1802	Fauquier Co.	Chancery	1824-035
Allason	William	Will	8/29/1939	Fauquier Co.	Chancery	1843-028
Allason	William	Will	4/28/1800	Fauquier Co.	Chancery	1854-018
ALLEN						
Allen	Elizabeth S.	Will	3/22/1858	Fauquier Co.	Chancery	1880-042
Allen	Fielding S.	Will	8/24/1857	Fauquier Co.	Chancery	1880-042
Allen	Henry	Admtrx. Bond	1775	Fauquier Co.	Probate, Box 44	1775-004
Allen	Joanna	Guardian Bond	1797	Fauquier Co.	Probate, Box 48	1797-008
Allen	John	Exors. Bond	1761	Fauquier Co.	Probate, Box 44	1761-009
Allen	John	Admr. Bond	1774	Fauquier Co.	Probate, Box 44	1774-011
Allen	William	Will	5/12/1741	Stafford Co. VA	Land Records & Disputes	1809-010
Allen	William	Guardian Bond	1797	Fauquier Co.	Probate, Box 48	1797-008
AMBLER						
Ambler	Charles E.	Will	2/4/1876	Charlestown, WV	Chancery	1903-060
Ambler	Charles Marshall	Guardian Appt.	11/22/1909	Fauquier Co.	Probate, Box 56 Superior/Circuit Ct.	1909-021
Ambler	John (Rev.)	Admr. Account	6/8/1895	Fauquier Co.	Probate, Box 55 Superior/Circuit Ct.	1895-005
Ambler	Lucy H.	Dower Allotment In Report of Division	9/19/1876	Fauquier Co.	Chancery	1903-060
Ambler	Mary Morris	Guardian Appt.	11/22/1909	Fauquier Co.	Probate, Box 56 Superior/Circuit Ct.	1909-021
Ambler	R. Jacqueline	Will	3/27/1876	Fauquier Co.	Chancery	1893-034
Ambler	Thomas M.	Report of Division	9/19/1876	Fauquier Co.	Chancery	1903-060
AMISS						
Amiss	Dolly	Guardian Account	1783	Fauquier Co.	Chancery	1791-012
Amiss	Gabriel	Will	2/26/1770	Frederick Co. VA	Chancery	1791-012

Consolidated Probate Index from the Clerks Loose Papers & the Superior Court/Circuit Court Records 1759-1919

Surname	Given Name	Instrument	Date	County	CLP Record Series	Index #
ANDERSON						
Anderson	Eli	Will	2/24/1854	Fauquier Co.	Chancery	1880-061
Anderson	Eli	Will	2/28/1854	Fauquier Co.	Chancery	1887-010
Anderson	Eli	Will	2/28/1854	Fauquier Co.	Chancery	1887-020
Anderson	Elizabeth	Dower Allotment	9/10/1856	Fauquier Co.	Chancery	1873-045
Anderson	Harrison	Appraisement	11/11/1861	Fauquier Co.	Chancery	1898-040
Anderson	Lulah	Guardian Appt.	6/24/1872	Fauquier Co.	Chancery	1887-020
Anderson	Marshall K.	Plat & Survey Of Division	Undated	Fauquier Co.	Chancery	1900-027
Anderson	Martha A.	Survey of Dower Allotment	4/1872	Fauquier Co.	Chancery	1880-061
Anderson	Nancy	Admr. Appt.	10/23/1865	Fauquier Co.	Chancery	1887-020
Anderson	Nancy	Will	6/24/1872	Fauquier Co.	Chancery	1887-020
Anderson	Nannie E.	Gdn. Appt.	6/24/1872	Fauquier Co.	Chancery	1887-020
Anderson	Susan Hope	Report of Division	3/25/1890	Fauquier Co.	Chancery	1892-043
Anderson	Susan Hope	Plat & Survey Of Division	3/25/1890	Fauquier Co.	Chancery	1892-043
Anderson	Thomas	Admtrx. Bond	10/23/1865	Fauquier Co.	Chancery	1880-061
Anderson	Thomas	Plat & Survey Of Division	12/21/1882	Fauquier Co.	Chancery	1882-035
Anderson	Thomas	Admr. Appt.	10/23/1865	Fauquier Co.	Chancery	1887-010
Anderson	Thomas E.	Guardian Appt.	6/24/1872	Fauquier Co.	Chancery	1887-020
Anderson	Thomas R.	Committee Bond	12/13/1857	Fauquier Co.	Probate, Box 53 Superior/Circuit Ct.	1875-009
Anderson	William	Admr. Appt.	2/28/1905	Fauquier Co.	Probate, Box 55 Superior/Circuit Ct.	1905-004

Consolidated Probate Index from the Clerks Loose Papers & the Superior Court/Circuit Court Records 1759-1919

Surname	Given Name	Instrument	Date	County	CLP Record Series	Index #
ARMISTEAD						
Armistead	Ann B.	Plat & Survey Of Division	10/1831	Fauquier Co.	Chancery	1832-055
Armistead	John	Will	3/24/1788	Caroline Co. VA.	Chancery	1815-048
Armistead	John	Will	7/21/1788	Philadelphia PA.	Chancery	1816-008
Armistead	John B.	Admr. Bond	5/23/1815	Fauquier Co.	Probate, Box 47	1815-001
Armistead	John C.	Admr. Bond	5/14/1846	Fauquier Co.	Probate, Box 51 Superior/Circuit Ct.	1846-001
Armistead	Lewis G. A.	Admr. Bond	1815	Fauquier Co.	Probate, Box 51 Superior/Circuit Ct.	1846-001
Armistead	Walker K.	Will	1/27/1846	Fauquier Co.	Chancery	1873-003
ARMSTRONG						
Armstrong	George W.	Admr. Appt.	8/3/1910	Fauquier Co.	Probate, Box 56 Superior/Circuit Ct.	1910-008
ARNOLD						
Arnold	Ann	Relinquishment	12/1804	Fauquier Co.	Probate, Box 39	1804-002
Arnold	John	Admr. Bond	1780	Fauquier Co.	Probate, Box 45	1780-003
ASBURY						
Asbury	Susan W.	Guardian Chosen	3/1818	Fauquier Co.	Probate, Box 39	1818-012
ASH						
Ash	Francis	Exor. Bond	1774	Fauquier Co.	Probate, Box 44	1774-016
Ash	George	Exors. Bond	1807	Fauquier Co.	Probate, Box 46	1807-036
Ash	George	Exors. Bond	1807	Fauquier Co.	Probate, Box 46	1807-047
Ash	George	Will	10/26/1807	Fauquier Co.	Chancery	1858-050
Ash	Mary	Will	1/24/1814	Fauquier Co.	Chancery	1837-010
Ash	Mary	Exor. Bond	1814	Fauquier Co.	Probate, Box 47	1814-002
Ash	William	Court order to Appraise Estate	1/1820	Fauquier Co.	Probate, Box 40	1822-002
ASHBY						
Ashby	Bryan Martin	Guardian Bond	1764	Fauquier Co.	Probate, Box 48	1764-001
Ashby	Caroline	Guardian Bond	5/20/1835	Fauquier Co.	Chancery	1858-043
Ashby	Elizabeth T.	Will	11/28/1864	Fauquier Co.	Chancery	1870-052
Ashby	Elizabeth T.	Will	11/24/1864	Fauquier Co.	Chancery	1878-011
Ashby	Elizabeth T.	Will	11/28/1864	Fauquier Co.	Chancery	1894-022
Ashby	Henry A.	Admr. Appt.	9/25/1909	Fauquier Co.	Probate, Box 56 Superior/Circuit Ct.	1909-013

Consolidated Probate Index from the Clerks Loose Papers & the Superior Court/Circuit Court Records 1759-1919

Surname	Given Name	Instrument	Date	County	CLP Record Series	Index #
ASHBY (Cont.)						
Ashby	John	Exors. Bond	1815	Fauquier Co.	Probate, Box 47	1815-012
Ashby	John	Will	4/26/1831	Fauquier Co.	Chancery	1845-035
Ashby	John	Will	8/28/1815	Fauquier Co.	Chancery	1859-030
Ashby	John	Plat & Survey Of Division	8/12/1836	Fauquier Co.	Chancery	1860-021
Ashby	John Henry	Will	4/19/1834	Fauquier Co.	Probate, Box 50	1834-002
Ashby	John Henry	Will	6/28/1834	Fauquier Co.	Chancery	1842-016
Ashby	John Henry	Will	7/28/1834	Fauquier Co.	Chancery	1852-024
Ashby	John Henry	Will	4/19/1834 Made	Fauquier Co.	Chancery	1858-043
Ashby	John Henry	Will	6/28/1831	Fauquier Co.	Chancery	1889-045
Ashby	Joseph E.	Guardian Bond	12/14/1876	Fauquier Co.	Chancery	1876-083
Ashby	Joseph E.	Guardian Acct.	4/8/1879	Fauquier Co.	Probate, Box 54 Superior/Circuit Ct.	1879-001
Ashby	Mariah	Guardian Bond	1818	Fauquier Co.	Probate, Box 49	1818-001
Ashby	Martha	Admr. Acct.	9/28/1831	Fauquier Co.	Probate, Box 50	1831-002
Ashby	Martha	Admr. Acct. Settled	9/28/1831	Fauquier Co.	Probate, Box 50	1831-002
Ashby	Martha	Report of Division Of Land + Slaves	7/28/1829	Fauquier Co.	Chancery	1838-039
Ashby	Martha	Court order to Adjust Admr. Acct.	5/1846	Fauquier Co.	Probate, Box 40	1846-001
Ashby	Martha	Guardian Acct.	5/20/1835	Fauquier Co.	Chancery	1858-043
Ashby	Mary T.	Estate Account	10/5/1842	Fauquier Co.	Probate, Box 51 Superior/Circuit Ct.	1842-005
Ashby	Mary T.	Exor. Acct.	10/1/1844	Fauquier Co.	Probate, Box 51 Superior/Circuit Ct.	1844-002
Ashby	Mary T.	Estate Account	5/4/1847	Fauquier Co.	Probate, Box 51 Superior/Circuit Ct.	1847-001
Ashby	Mary T.	Estate Account	10/3/1848	Fauquier Co.	Probate, Box 51 Superior/Circuit Ct.	1848-001
Ashby	Mary T.	Memo from R. S. Ashby to settle .Exor. Acct.	4/24/1850	Fauquier Co.	Probate, Box 52 Superior/Circuit Ct.	1850-004
Ashby	Mary T.	Exor. Acct.	10/8/1851	Fauquier Co.	Probate, Box 52 Superior/Circuit Ct.	1851-009

Consolidated Probate Index from the Clerks Loose Papers & the Superior Court/Circuit Court Records 1759-1919

Surname	**Given Name**	**Instrument**	**Date**	**County**	**CLP Record Series**	**Index #**
ASHBY (Cont.)						
Ashby	Nimrod	Admrs. Bond	1764	Fauquier Co.	Probate, Box 44	1764-001
Ashby	Nimrod	Shew cause order To revoke gdnship	7/1766	Fauquier Co.	Probate, Box 39	1766-001
Ashby	Nimrod	Will	3/4/1830	Fauquier Co.	Chancery	1847-015
Ashby	Nimrod	Will	3/4/1830	Fauquier Co.	Chancery	1847-017
Ashby	Nimrod T.	Plat & Survey Of Division	8/1876	Fauquier Co.	Chancery	1883-005
Ashby	Nimrod T.	Report of Division	8/1876	Fauquier Co.	Chancery	1883-005
Ashby	R. S.	Memo to settle Mary T. Ashby Exor. Acct.	5/24/1850	Fauquier Co.	Probate, Box 52	1850-002
Ashby	Rebecca A.	Guardian Bond	9/15/1877	Fauquier Co.	Probate, Box 54 Superior/Circuit Ct.	1877-005
Ashby	Samuel	Report of Division Of Land + Slaves	7/28/1829	Fauquier Co.	Chancery	1838-039
Ashby	Samuel	Will	2/26/1816	Fauquier Co.	Chancery	1858-043
Ashby	Sarah	Guardian Bond	1817	Fauquier Co.	Probate, Box 49	1809-003
Ashby	Turner	Admr. Acct.	10/10/1846	Fauquier Co.	Chancery	1869-030
Ashby	Turner	Division of Slaves	10/13/1848	Fauquier Co.	Chancery	1869-030
ASHTON						
Ashton	Ann A	Will	3/27/1876	Fauquier Co.	Chancery	1888-069
Ashton	J. G.	Sales	12/15/1815	Fauquier Co.	Probate, Box 40	1823-006
Ashton	Lawrence	Will	9/23/1811	Fauquier Co.	Chancery	1884-022
ATHEY						
Athey	William L.	Admr. Bond	4/12/1879	Fauquier Co.	Probate, Box 54 Superior/Circuit Ct.	1879-002
AYRES						
Ayres	C. R.	Exor. Report	4/24/1879	Fauquier Co.	Chancery	1897-002
Ayres	C. R.	Admr. Acct.	4/6/1894	Fauquier Co.	Chancery	1897-002
Ayres	Charles	Will	7/28/1829	Fauquier Co.	Chancery	1832-057
Ayres	Charles	Division of Slaves	1831	Fauquier Co.	Chancery	1832-057
Ayres	Charles	Will	12/28/1830	Fauquier Co.	Chancery	1837-018

Consolidated Probate Index from the Clerks Loose Papers & the Superior Court/Circuit Court Records 1759-1919

Surname	Given Name	Instrument	Date	County	CLP Record Series	Index #
AYRES (Cont.)						
Ayres	Charles	Admr. Bond	1/24/1831	Fauquier Co.	Chancery	1837-018
Ayres	Charles	Admr. Bond	1/25/1831	Fauquier Co.	Chancery	1837-018
Ayres	Charles	Admr. Bond	4/28/1834	Fauquier Co.	Chancery	1837-018
Ayres	Charles R.	Will	12/03/1859	Fauquier Co.	Chancery	1897-002
Ayres	Mary W.	Admr. Bond	2/26/1850	Fauquier Co.	Chancery	1852-045
Ayres	Mary W.	Admr. Bond	2/26/1850	Fauquier Co.	Chancery	1869-010
Ayres	Vianna	Exor. Certificates	6/29/1880	Cayuga Co. NY	Chancery	1897-002

Consolidated Probate Index from the Clerks Loose Papers & the Superior Court/Circuit Court Records 1759-1919

Surname	Given Name	Instrument	Date	County	CLP Record Series	Index #
BAILEY (See also Bayley)						
Bailey	Ann	Renunciation	1812	Fauquier Co.	Probate, Box 39	1812-001
Bailey	Carr	Will	10/7/1770	Fauquier Co.	Chancery	1809-056
Bailey	Carr	Exors. Bond	1771	Fauquier Co.	Probate, Box 44	1771-002
Bailey	James	Admtrx. Bond	1771	Fauquier Co.	Probate, Box 44	1771-005
Bailey	James	Division	1777	Fauquier Co.	Chancery	1808-024
Bailey	James	Sales	1/10/177	Fauquier Co.	Chancery	1808-024
Bailey	James W.	Will	10/24/1865	Fauquier Co.	Chancery	1879-004
Bailey	James W.	Sales	12/15/1865	Fauquier Co.	Chancery	1879-004
Bailey	James W.	Admr. Appt.	11/27/1865	Fauquier Co.	Chancery	1879-004
Bailey	John	Exor. Bond	1777	Fauquier Co.	Probate, box 44	1777-014
Bailey	Joseph	Will	3/27/1826	Fauquier Co.	Chancery	1833-007
Bailey	Joseph	Will	3/27/1826	Fauquier Co.	Chancery	1834-020
Bailey	Molly	Guardian Bond	1777	Fauquier Co.	Probate, Box 48	1777-003
Bailey	Moses	Admr. Bond	1812	Fauquier Co.	Probate, Box 47	1812-012
Bailey	Nanny	Guardian Bond	1777	Fauquier Co.	Probate, Box 48	1777-003
Bailey	Thomas	Guardian Bond	1777	Fauquier Co.	Probate, Box 48	1777-003
Bailey	William	Guardian Bond	1777	Fauquier Co.	Probate, Box 48	1777-003
BAKER						
Baker	John	Will	9/5/1878	Fauquier Co.	Probate, Box 54 Superior/Circuit Ct.	1878-009
Baker	John	Admr. Bond	9/9/1878	Fauquier Co.	Probate, Box 54 Superior/Circuit Ct.	1878-009

Consolidated Probate Index from the Clerks Loose Papers & the Superior Court/Circuit Court Records 1759-1919

Surname	**Given Name**	**Instrument**	**Date**	**County**	**CLP Record Series**	**Index #**
BAKER (Cont.)						
Baker	John	Appraisement	10/28/1878	Fauquier Co.	Probate, Box 54 Superior/Circuit Ct.	1878-010
Baker	John	Sales	11/26/1880	Fauquier Co.	Probate, Box 54 Superior/Circuit Ct.	1880-007
Baker	Lucy A.	Will	9/24/1870	Fauquier Co.	Chancery	1875-075
Baker	Lucy A.	Will	10/25/1870	Fauquier Co.	Chancery	1893-001
BALL						
Ball	Ann	Exor. Bond	1813	Fauquier Co.	Probate, Box 47	1813-002
Ball	Benjamin	Admr. Bond	1807	Fauquier Co.	Probate, Box 48	1807-030
Ball	Burges	Court action re: 6200 acres in Fauqr.	11/7/1767	Fauquier Co.	Probate, Box 39	1767-002
Ball	Charity	Will	1/28/1883	Fauquier Co.	Chancery	1903-058
Ball	Edward	Inventory + Appraisement	2/28/1742	Pr. Wm. Co. VA.	Land Records & Disputes	1767-003
Ball	Edward	Admr. Acct.	3/1745	Prince Wm. Co. VA.	Land Records & Disputes	1767-003
Ball	George Lewis	Guardian Bond	1806	Fauquier Co.	Probate, Box 49	1806-005
Ball	James	Plat & Survey Of 1759 Division	11/21/1759	Fauquier Co.	Chancery	1851-002
Ball	James	Court Action re: 6200 acres in Fauqr.	11/7/1767	Fauquier Co.	Probate, Box 39	1767-002
Ball	James	Commonwealth Cause Against	11/7/1767	Fauquier Co.	Probate, Box 39	1767-002
Ball	James	Guardian Bond	1773	Fauquier Co.	Probate, Box 48	1773-003
Ball	John	Admtrx. Bond	1773	Fauquier Co.	Probate, Box 44	1773-009
Ball	John	Will	12/22/1804	Fauquier Co.	Chancery	1842-056
Ball	John	Exor. Bond	1806	Fauquier Co.	Probate, Box 46	1806-019
Ball	Judith	Guardian Bond	1780	Fauquier Co.	Probate, Box 48	1780-002
Ball	Letty	Motion to appoint Committee	9/20/1858	Fauquier Co.	Probate, Box 52 Superior/Circuit Ct.	1858-001
Ball	Mary Bland	Guardian Bond	1780	Fauquier Co.	Probate, Box 48	1780-002
Ball	Mottram	Guardian Bond	1773	Fauquier Co.	Probate, Box 48	1773-003

Consolidated Probate Index from the Clerks Loose Papers & the Superior Court/Circuit Court Records 1759-1919

Surname	Given Name	Instrument	Date	County	CLP Record Series	Index #
BALL (Cont.)						
Ball	Nancy	Renunciation	1807	Fauquier Co.	Probate, Box 39	1807-030
Ball	Nancy	Guardian Bond	1817	Fauquier Co.	Probate, Box 49	1817-004
Ball	Richard	Guardian Bond	1773	Fauquier Co.	Probate, Box 48	1773-003
Ball	Sarah R.	Guardian Bond	1815	Fauquier Co.	Probate, Box 49	1815-016
Ball	Tacy	Guardian Bond	1815	Fauquier Co.	Probate, Box 49	1815-013
Ball	Taliaferro	Estate Papers	1845	Fauquier Co.	Probate, Box 40	1845-004
Ball	William	Admr. Bond	1773	Fauquier Co.	Probate, Box 44	1773-001
Ball	William	Admr. Acct.	5/1783	Fauquier Co.	Probate, Box 39	1783-001
Ball	William	Will	12/1807	Fauquier Co.	Land Records & Disputes	1824-011
Ball	William	Exors. Bond	1807	Fauquier Co.	Probate, Box 49	1807-031
Ball	William	Exor. Bond	1815	Fauquier Co.	Probate, Box 49	1815-023
BALTHROPE						
Balthrope	Charles A.	Will	3/26/1850	Fauquier Co.	Chancery	1872-015
Balthrope	Jeremiah	Admr. Bond	10/9/1849	Fauquier Co.	Probate, Box 51 Superior/Circuit Ct.	1849-003
Balthrope	Jeremiah	Appraisement	5/7/1850	Fauquier Co.	Probate, Box 52 Superior/Circuit Ct.	1850-003
Balthrope	Jeremiah	Plat & Survey Of Division	2/1/1859	Fauquier Co.	Chancery	1872-015
Balthrope	Jeremiah	Report of Division	5/5/1851	Fauquier Co.	Chancery	1878-054
Balthrope	Sarah	Comr. Report about	2/1851	Fauquier Co.	Probate, Box 50	1851-001
Balthrope	Sarah	Plat & Survey of Dower Allotment	3/24/1870	Fauquier Co.	Chancery	1872-015
BANGER						
Banger	George	Guardian Bond	1794	Fauquier Co.	Probate, Box 46	1794-002
BANKHEAD						
Bankhead	John	Will	6/13/1836	Caroline Co. VA.	Chancery	1846-001
BARBEE						
Barbee	Andrew R.	Guardian Bond	1801	Fauquier Co.	Probate, Box 46	1801-012
Barbee	Charlotte	Guardian Bond	1801	Fauquier Co.	Probate, Box 46	1801-012
Barbee	Elizabeth	Guardian Bond	1800	Fauquier Co.	Probate, Box 46	1800-001

Consolidated Probate Index from the Clerks Loose Papers & the Superior Court/Circuit Court Records 1759-1919

Surname	Given Name	Instrument	Date	County	CLP Record Series	Index #
BARBEE (Cont.)						
Barbee	James	Guardian Bond	1800	Fauquier Co.	Probate, Box 46	1800-001
Barbee	Jemmerson	Admtrx. Bond	7/28/1834	Fauquier Co.	Probate, Box 50	1834-001
Barbee	John	Will	11/22/1835	Fauquier Co.	Chancery	1838-033
Barbee	John	Will	11/23/1835	Fauquier Co.	Chancery	1849-002
Barbee	John	Division of Slaves	11/20/1846	Fauquier Co.	Chancery	1849-002
Barbee	John J.	Admr. Bond	8/26/1833	Fauquier Co.	Probate, Box 50	1833-004
Barbee	John J.	Admr. Bond	8/26/1833	Fauquier Co.	Chancery	1860-027
Barbee	John J.	Admr. Bond	7/28/1834	Fauquier Co.	Chancery	1860-027
Barbee	Joseph	Admr. Account	Undated	Fauquier Co.	Probate, Box 39	Undated-002
Barbee	Joseph	Guardian Bond	1802	Fauquier Co.	Probate, Box 49	1802-008
Barbee	Joseph A.	Division	1/1902	Fauquier Co.	Chancery	1904-022
Barbee	Joseph A.	Plat & Survey Of Division at Hume	1/1902	Fauquier Co.	Chancery	1904-022
Barbee	Lucy	Guardian Bond	1800	Fauquier Co.	Probate, Box 48	1800-001
Barbee	Nimrod A.	Admr. Bond	6/24/1839	Fauquier Co.	Probate, Box 50	1839-002
Barbee	Owen	Guardian Bond	1800	Fauquier Co.	Probate, Box 48	1800-001
Barbee	Russell	Guardian Bond	1805	Fauquier Co.	Probate, Box 48	1805-005
Barbee	Thom	Guardian Bond	1800	Fauquier Co.	Probate, Box 47	1800-001
Barbee	Thomas	Admr. Bond	1775	Fauquier Co.	Probate, Box 44	1775-015
Barbee	Thomas	Court Summons	1805	Fauquier Co.	Probate, Box 39	1805-005
Barbee	Turner D.	Admr. Bond	7/24/1834	Fauquier Co.	Chancery	1860-027
Barbee	Turner D.	Inventory + Appraisement	3/23/1836	Fauquier Co.	Chancery	1860-027
Barbee	William	Guardian Bond	1801	Fauquier Co.	Probate, Box 48	1801-013

Consolidated Probate Index from the Clerks Loose Papers & the Superior Court/Circuit Court Records 1759-1919

Surname	Given Name	Instrument	Date	County	CLP Record Series	Index #
BARBER (See also Barbour)						
Barber	Bathsheba	Will	9/25/1848	Fauquier Co.	Chancery	1899-028
Barber	Bathsheba	Inventory + Appraisement	10/1/1848	Fauquier Co.	Chancery	1899-028
Barber	Bathsheba	Sales	10/13/1848	Fauquier Co.	Chancery	1899-028
Barber	John E.	Will	3/31/1914	Fauquier Co.	Probate, Box 50 Addendum Folder	1914-002
BARBOUR (See also Barber)						
Barbour	Eliza A.	Admr. Appt.	2/11/1879	Culpeper Co. VA.	Chancery	1885-013
BARKER						
Barker	Cloe	Guardian Bond	1797	Fauquier Co.	Probate, Box 48	1797-011
Barker	Jemima	Plat & Survey Of Dower	6/1787	Fauquier Co.	Land Records & Disputes	1793-011
Barker	John	Admrs. Bond	1784	Fauquier Co.	Probate, Box 45	1784-001
Barker	Mary	Guardian Bond	1797	Fauquier Co.	Probate, Box 48	1797-011
Barker	Milley	Guardian Bond	1797	Fauquier Co.	Probate, Box 48	1797-009
Barker	Nancy	Guardian Bond	1797	Fauquier Co.	Probate, Box 48	1797-009
BARNETT						
Barnett	Ambrose	Admr. Account	7/24/1815	Fauquier Co.	Probate, Box 50	1815-002
Barnett	Ambrose	Admr. Account Settled	11/28/1826	Fauquier Co.	Probate, Box 50	1819-001
Barnett	Ambrose Jr.	Guardian Bond	1808	Fauquier Co.	Probate, Box 49	1808-002
Barnett	George	Admr. Bond	1814	Fauquier Co.	Probate, Box 47	1814-022
BARTLETT						
Bartlett	Thomas	Will	1/22/1783	Fauquier Co.	Probate, Box 39	1783-002
BASHAW						
Bashaw	James	Admr. Bond	1778	Fauquier Co.	Probate, Box 45	1778-003
Bashaw	Peter	Extrx. Bond	1780	Fauquier Co.	Probate, Box 45	1780-007
BASYE						
Basye	Josiah	Admr. Bond	1814	Fauquier Co.	Probate, Box 47	1814-019
Basye	Sarah	Relinquishment	1814	Fauquier Co.	Probate, Box 39	1814-019
Basye	Sary	Relinquishment	2/1814	Fauquier Co.	Probate, Box 39	1814-003
BATTAILE (See also Battaley)						
Battaile	Caroline	Will	4/5/1853	Fauquier Co.	Chancery	1872-041

Consolidated Probate Index from the Clerks Loose Papers & the Superior Court/Circuit Court Records 1759-1919

Surname	Given Name	Instrument	Date	County	CLP Record Series	Index #
BATTALEY (See also Battaile)						
Battaley	Ann	Exors. Bond	1783	Fauquier Co.	Probate, Box 45	1783-017
BAXLEY						
Baxley	Emilie H.	Will	8/22/1901	Fauquier Co.	Chancery	1901-029
BAYLEY (See also Bailey, Bayly)						
Bayley	Mary	Dower Allotment	6/21/1858	Fauquier Co.	Chancery	1900-036
Bayley	Mary	Sale of Dower Tract	8/23/1869	Fauquier Co.	Chancery	1900-036
Bayley	Mary B.	Dower Allotment	8/5/1858	Fauquier Co.	Chancery	1883-066
BAYLISS						
Bayliss	Martha C. G.	Will	1/26/1852	Fauquier Co.	Chancery	1883-066
Bayliss	William Sr.	Will	8/29/1834	Fauquier Co.	Chancery	1841-040
BAYLOR						
Baylor	Ann	Will	12/24/1860	Fauquier Co.	Chancery	1877-039
Baylor	Ann D.	Will	5/5/1860	Fauquier Co.	Chancery	1865-005
Baylor	Ann D.	Will	12/24/1860	Fauquier Co.	Chancery	1881-054
BAYLY (See also Bayley, Bailey)						
Bayly	Elise C.	Will	4/15/1890	Fauquier Co.	Probate, Box 54 Superior/Circuit Ct.	1890-001
BEACH						
Beach	Peter	Exor. Bond	1779	Fauquier Co.	Probate, Box 45	1779-008
BEALE						
Beale	James A.	Admr. Bond	9/29/1836	Fauquier Co.	Chancery	1853-005
Beale	James A.	Admr. Acct.	4/1839	Fauquier Co.	Chancery	1853-005
BEARD						
Beard	Andrew	Admr. Appt.	1761	Fauquier Co.	Probate, Box 39	1761-001
Beard	Andrew	Admr. Bond	1761	Fauquier Co.	Probate, Box 44	1761-001
Beard	George	Admr. Bond	1764	Fauquier Co.	Probate, Box 44	1764-003
BECKHAM						
Beckham	John	Will	11/23/1831	Culpeper Co. VA.	Chancery	1866-076
Beckham	John	Inventory	7/28/1837	Fauquier Co.	Chancery	1866-076
Beckham	John	Admr. Bond	5/2/1842	Fauquier Co.	Chancery	1866-076
Beckham	John	Admr. Account	5/2/1842	Fauquier Co.	Chancery	1866-076

Consolidated Probate Index from the Clerks Loose Papers & the Superior Court/Circuit Court Records 1759-1919

Surname	Given Name	Instrument	Date	County	CLP Record Series	Index #
BECKWITH						
Beckwith	Marmaduke	Admr. Account	5/1827	Fauquier Co.	Chancery	1888-030
Beckwith	Marmaduke	Admr. Account	7/21/1829	Fauquier Co.	Chancery	1888-030
Beckwith	Marmaduke	Admr. Account	10/9/1837	Fauquier Co.	Chancery	1888-030
Beckwith	Sybill	Dower Allotment	12/1800	Fauquier Co.	Chancery	1888-030
BEDIENT						
Bedient	Fannie A.	Will	4/1/1911	Fauquier Co.	Probate, Box 50 Addendum Folder	1911-001
BELL						
Bell	Bailey	Admr. Bond	1814	Fauquier Co.	Probate, Box 47	1814-015
Bell	James	Exors. Bond	1812	Fauquier Co.	Probate, Box 47	1812-006
Bell	James B.	Will	5/31/1814	Fauquier Co.	Probate, Box 50	1814-001
Bell	John	Will	6/10/1743	Lancaster Co. VA.	Land Records & Disputes	1809-004
Bell	John	Will	6/10/1743	Lancaster Co. VA.	Land Records & Disputes	1815-008
Bell	Sarah	Will	11/28/1853	Fauquier Co.	Chancery	1859-066
Bell	Thomas	Division	7/29/1902	Fauquier Co.	Chancery	1904-007
Bell	Thomas	Plat & Survey Of Division	7/29/1902	Fauquier Co.	Chancery	1904-007
BELT						
Belt	William	Inventory + Appraisement	1/23/1845	Fauquier Co.	Chancery	1850-003
Belt	William	Admr. Account	3/26/1846	Fauquier Co.	Chancery	1850-003
BERNARD						
Bernard	Richard	Will	5/1/1783	King Geo. Co. VA.	Land Records & Disputes	1813-013
Bernard	William	Will	5/1/1783	King Geo. Co. VA.	Land Records & Disputes	1813-013
BERRYMAN						
Berryman	George	Guardian Bond	1815	Fauquier Co.	Probate, Box 49	1815-003
Berryman	Hannah	Admr. Bond	1815	Fauquier Co.	Probate, Box 47	1815-031
Berryman	Maximilian	Exor. Bond	1812	Fauquier Co.	Probate, Box 47	1812-004

Consolidated Probate Index from the Clerks Loose Papers & the Superior Court/Circuit Court Records 1759-1919

Surname	Given Name	Instrument	Date	County	CLP Record Series	Index #
BERRYMAN (Cont.)						
Berryman	Taliaferro M.	Plat & Survey of Division to Heirs	6/2/1898	Fauquier Co.	Chancery	1903-062
Berryman	Zachariah	Admr. Bond	1815	Fauquier Co.	Probate, Box 47	1815-030
BEVERIDGE						
Beveridge	Noble	Will	3/1842	Loudoun Co. VA.	Chancery	1855-057
BEVERLEY						
Beverley	Benjamin Sloane	Guardian Bond	2/28/1902	Fauquier Co.	Chancery	1902-011
Beverley	William B.	Will	12/17/1866	Essex Co. VA.	Chancery	1898-050
BIGGS						
Biggs	John H.	Guardian Appt.	4/6/1835	Licking Co. OH.	Chancery	1836-054
Biggs	Joseph C.	Guardian Appt.	4/6/1835	Licking Co. OH.	Chancery	1836-054
Biggs	Louisa	Guardian Appt.	4/6/1835	Licking Co. OH.	Chancery	1836-054
Biggs	Mary Ann	Guardian Appt.	4/6/1835	Licking Co. OH.	Chancery	1836-054
BILLINGSLEY						
Billingsley	Clement	Guardian Bond	1812	Fauquier Co.	Probate, Box 49	1812-002
Billingsley	Elizabeth	Guardian Bond	1803	Fauquier Co.	Probate, Box 49	1803-008
BISE						
Bise	Aaron	Will	8/22/1870	Fauquier Co.	Chancery	1883-036
Bise	Aaron	Will	8/22/1870	Fauquier Co.	Chancery	1900-001
Bise	Aaron	Inventory	9/30/1870	Fauquier Co.	Chancery	1900-001
Bise	Elizabeth	Plat & Survey of Dower Allotment	12/20/1871	Fauquier Co.	Chancery	1883-036
Bise	John	Admr. Bond	1815	Fauquier Co.	Probate, Box 47	1815-057
Bise	John	Sales	4/1831	Fauquier Co.	Probate, Box 40	1831-002
BISHOP						
Bishop	Annie	Admr. Appt. (death date in Appt.)	5/23/1905	Fauquier Co.	Probate, Box 55 Superior/Circuit Ct.	1905-006
BLACKMORE						
Blackmore	James	Report of Division Of Land + Slaves	1/24/1860	Fauquier Co.	Chancery	1883-086
Blackmore	Mary E.	Will	6/1882 Made	Fauquier Co.	Chancery	1903-056

Consolidated Probate Index from the Clerks Loose Papers & the Superior Court/Circuit Court Records 1759-1919

Surname	Given Name	Instrument	Date	County	CLP Record Series	Index #
BLACKWELL						
Blackwell	Ann Eliza	Guardian Bond	9/18/1855	Fauquier Co.	Chancery	1855-051
Blackwell	Armistead	Will	10/24/1836	Fauquier Co.	Chancery	1867-001
Blackwell	Armistead	Will	10/24/1836	Fauquier Co.	Chancery	1867-006
Blackwell	Dulaney	Guardian Bond	1809	Fauquier Co.	Probate, Box 49	1809-001
Blackwell	E.	Plat & Survey Of Dower	2/23/1871	Fauquier Co.	Chancery	1871-108
Blackwell	Elizabeth	Will	5/27/1859	Fauquier Co.	Chancery	1867-006
Blackwell	Elizabeth	Admr. Account	4/19/1861	Fauquier Co.	Chancery	1902-004
Blackwell	Elizabeth (Mrs.)	Plat & Survey of Dower Allotment	Undated	Fauquier Co.	Chancery	1911-002
Blackwell	Elizabeth	Estate Papers	1871	Fauquier Co.	Probate, Box 42 Blackwell &c Estate Papers	1871-001
Blackwell	Elizabeth P.	Will	5/27/1859	Fauquier Co.	Chancery	1867-001
Blackwell	Elizabeth P.	Will	5/27/1859	Fauquier Co.	Chancery	1898-001
Blackwell	Elizabeth P.	Inventory + Appraisement (Extract)	8/9/1857	Fauquier Co.	Chancery	1898-001
Blackwell	Elizabeth P.	Heirs	8/9/1857	Fauquier Co.	Chancery	1898-001
Blackwell	F. G.	Guardian Appt.	4/1889	Fauquier Co.	Chancery	1889-034
Blackwell	Hannah R.	Will	9/27/1858	Fauquier Co.	Chancery	1887-042
Blackwell	John	Will	6/23/1823	Fauquier Co.	Chancery	1868-053
Blackwell	John E.	Admr. Appt.	8/22/1870	Fauquier Co.	Chancery	1875-027
Blackwell	Joseph	Report of Division	11/24/1840	Fauquier Co.	Chancery	1840-069
Blackwell	Joseph	Plat & Survey Of Division	11/24/1840	Fauquier Co.	Chancery	1840-069
Blackwell	Joseph	Division of Slaves	11/24/1840	Fauquier Co.	Chancery	1840-069
Blackwell	Joseph	Guardian Bond	9/18/1855	Fauquier Co.	Chancery	1855-051
Blackwell	Joseph H.	Admr. Appt.	3/7/1905	Fauquier Co.	Probate, Box 55 Superior/Circuit Ct.	1905-033
Blackwell	Lucy	Plat & Survey of Dower Allotment	10/1898	Fauquier Co.	Chancery	1898-063
Blackwell	Samuel	Admr. Bond	1814	Fauquier Co.	Probate, Box 47	1814-012

Consolidated Probate Index from the Clerks Loose Papers & the Superior Court/Circuit Court Records 1759-1919

Surname	Given Name	Instrument	Date	County	CLP Record Series	Index #
BLACKWELL (Cont.)						
Blackwell	Sarah J.	Guardian Chosen	9/1823	Fauquier Co.	Probate, Box 40	1823-004
Blackwell	William	Extrx. Bond	1774	Fauquier Co.	Probate, Box 44	1774-010
Blackwell	William (Capt.)	Heirs	6/29/1931	Fauquier Co.	Military Records	1831-002
Blackwell	William	Trustee Account	8/5/1836	Fauquier Co.	Chancery	1838-011
BLAND						
Bland	Benjamin	Admtrx. Bond	1771	Fauquier Co.	Probate, Box 44	1771-006
Bland	Benjamin	Admr. Bond	1782	Fauquier Co.	Probate, Box 45	1782-007
Bland	Charles	Guardian Bond	1782	Fauquier Co.	Probate, Box 48	1782-003
Bland	John	Guardian Bond	1783	Fauquier Co.	Probate, Box 48	1783-004
Bland	Mary	Exor. Bond	1782	Fauquier Co.	Probate, Box 45	1782-001
Bland	Mildred	Guardian Bond	1771	Fauquier Co.	Probate, Box 48	1771-001
BLYTHE						
Blythe	James	Admr. Bond	1796	Fauquier Co.	Probate, Box 46	1796-001
BOARD						
Board	John	Will	5/19/1835	Fauquier Co.	Probate, Box 50	1835-002
BOGGESS						
Boggess	Thomas	Extrx. Bond	1772	Fauquier Co.	Probate, Box 44	1772-006
BOLING						
Boling	Jane W.	Admr. Bond	4/6/1853	Fauquier Co.	Probate, Box 52 Superior/Circuit Ct.	1853-001
BOROUGHS (See also Burroughs)						
Boroughs	Jemima	Relinquishment	8/1801	Fauquier Co.	Probate, Box 39	1812-001
BOSWELL						
Boswell	Lucy	Inventory	7/23/1853	Fauquier Co.	Chancery	1873-040
Boswell	Lucy A. S.	Report of Division Of Slaves	9/28/1859	Fauquier Co.	Chancery	1875-051
Boswell	William	Admr. Bond	1773	Fauquier Co.	Probate, Box 44	1773-004
BOTELER						
Boteler	Joseph	Will	9/25/1843	Fauquier Co.	Chancery	1881-051
Boteler	Joseph	Will	9/25/1843	Fauquier Co.	Chancery	1881-052
BOTTS						
Botts	Thomas	Admr. Bond	1771	Fauquier Co.	Probate, Box 44	1771-010

Consolidated Probate Index from the Clerks Loose Papers & the Superior Court/Circuit Court Records 1759-1919

Surname	Given Name	Instrument	Date	County	CLP Record Series	Index #
BOWEN						
Bowen	Catharine R.	Guardian Chosen	7/1828	Fauquier Co.	Probate, Box 40	1828-001
Bowen	Elizabeth	Guardian Bond	1801	Fauquier Co.	Probate, Box 48	1801-006
Bowen	Ellen D.	Will	3/31/1871	Fauquier Co.	Chancery	1887-043
Bowen	Ellen D.	Plat & Survey of Dower Allotment	9/1886	Fauquier Co.	Chancery	1908-014
Bowen	James	Exor. Bond	1815	Fauquier Co.	Probate, Box 47	1815-001
Bowen	Lucy	Guardian Bond	1806	Fauquier Co.	Probate, Box 49	1806-007
Bowen	Peter B.	Will	7/16/1860	Culpeper Co. VA.	Chancery	1891-030
Bowen	Peter B.	Exor. Account	5/30/1863	Culpeper Co. VA.	Chancery	1891-030
Bowen	Peter B.	Exor. Account	7/14/1869	Culpeper Co. VA.	Chancery	1891-030
Bowen	Peter B.	Exor. Account	11/15/1869	Culpeper Co. VA.	Chancery	1891-030
Bowen	Peter B.	Estate Account	1871	Fauquier Co.	Chancery	1891-030
Bowen	Peter B.	Estate Account	1888	Fauquier Co.	Chancery	1891-030
Bowen	Peter B.	Admr. Account	1889	Fauquier Co.	Chancery	1891-030
Bowen	William A.	Plat of Division	9/10/1874	Fauquier Co.	Chancery	1908-014
BOWER (See also Bowers)						
Bower	Peter	Will	12/22/1800	Fauquier Co.	Chancery	1894-019
Bower	Peter	Will	12/22/1800	Fauquier Co.	Chancery	1902-013
Bower	Peter	Exors Bond	1812	Fauquier Co.	Probate, Box 47	1812-005
BOWERS (See also Bower)						
Bowers	Peter	Will	12/22/1800	Fauquier Co.	Chancery	1884-019
Bowers	William	Plat & Survey Of Division	1/16/1866	Fauquier Co.	Probate, Box 50 Addendum Folder	1866-001
BOWERSETT						
Bowersett	John	Will	4/13/1867	Fauquier Col.	Probate, Box 53 Superior/Circuit Ct.	1867-001
BOWIE						
Bowie	John	Will	2/26/1839	Fauquier Co.	Chancery	1841-010
Bowie	John	Inventory + Appraisement	3/8/1839	Fauquier Co.	Chancery	1841-010
Bowie	John	Will	2/26/1839	Fauquier Co.	Chancery	1841-048
Bowie	John	Will	2/2/6/1839	Fauquier Co.	Chancery	1842-014

Consolidated Probate Index from the Clerks Loose Papers & the Superior Court/Circuit Court Records 1759-1919

Surname	Given Name	Instrument	Date	County	CLP Record Series	Index #
BOWIE (Cont.)						
Bowie	John	Will	2/26/1839	Fauquier Co.	Chancery	1854-008
Bowie	John	Exor. Bond	2/26/1839	Fauquier Co.	Chancery	1854-008
Bowie	John	Inventory	2/26/1839	Fauquier Co.	Chancery	1854-008
Bowie	John	Division of Slaves	5/26/1840	Fauquier Co.	Chancery	1854-008
Bowie	John	Exor. Account	1840-1847	Fauquier Co.	Chancery	1854-008
BOWLING						
Bowling	Elizabeth	Guardian Bond	1805	Fauquier Co.	Probate, Box 49	1802-006
BOWMAN						
Bowman	Lillie	Guardian Qualification	4/27/1905	Fauquier Co.	Chancery	1909-021
BOYD						
Boyd	Jane	Guardian Bond	1805	Fauquier Co.	Probate, Box 49	1805-007
Boyd	Samuel	Admr. Bond	1783	Fauquier Co.	Probate, Box 45	1783-012
Boyd	Thomas	Guardian Bond	1805	Fauquier Co.	Probate, Box 49	1805-007
BRADFORD						
Bradford	Catharine	Will	10/27/1851	Fauquier Co.	Chancery	1873-056
Bradford	Catharine	Division of Slaves	12/25/1854	Fauquier Co.	Chancery	1873-056
Bradford	Catharine	Admr. Account	4/13/1855	Fauquier Co.	Chancery	1873-056
Bradford	Catharine	Admr. Account	10/26/1858	Fauquier Co.	Chancery	1873-056
Bradford	Daniel	Court order for Division Of Estate according to Will	4/1802	Fauquier Co.	Probate, Box 39	1802-002
Bradford	James M.	Curator Appt.	4/12/1883	Fauquier Co.	Probate, Box 54 Superior/Circuit Ct.	1883-002
Bradford	James M.	Curator Bond	4/12/1883	Fauquier Co.	Probate, Box 54 Superior/Circuit Ct.	1883-002
Bradford	Joseph	Will	6/25/1812	Madison Co. VA.	Chancery	1815-046
Bradford	Joseph	Exor. Accounts	Undated	Fauquier Co.	Chancery	1815-046
Bradford	Mary	Exor. Bond	1783	Fauquier Co.	Probate, Box 45	1783-007
Bradford	Robert	Curator Appt.	4/12/1883	Fauquier Co.	Probate, Box 54 Superior/Circuit Ct.	1883-002
Bradford	Robert	Curator Bond	4/12/1883	Fauquier Co.	Probate, Box 54 Superior/Circuit Ct.	1883-002
Bradford	William	Extrx. Bond	1760	Fauquier Co.	Probate, Box 44	1760-010

Consolidated Probate Index from the Clerks Loose Papers & the Superior Court/Circuit Court Records 1759-1919

Surname	Given Name	Instrument	Date	County	CLP Record Series	Index #
BRADY						
Brady	Elizabeth	Guardian Chosen	1810	Fauquier Co.	Probate, Box 39	1810-003
Brady	Jane	Guardian Chosen	1817	Fauquier Co.	Probate, Box 39	1817-013
Brady	Joseph	Will	6/26/1809	Fauquier Co.	Probate, Box 50	1809-001
Brady	Joseph	Exor. Bond	1809	Fauquier Co.	Probate, Box 47	1809-024
BRAGG						
Bragg	William	Admtrx. Bond	1813	Fauquier Co.	Probate, Box 47	1813-025
BRAHAN						
Brahan	John	Exors. Bond	1775	Fauquier Co.	Probate, Box 44	1775-008
Brahan	Thomas	Will	8/24/1840	Fauquier Co.	Chancery	1894-018
BRAY						
Bray	William F.	Guardian Bond	1/27/1840	Fauquier Co.	Chancery	1845-005
BRENT						
Brent	Alexander	Admr. Bond	1806	Fauquier Co.	Probate, Box 46	1806-012
Brent	Alexander	Estate Account	Undated	Fauquier Co.	Chancery	1823-028
Brent	Christopher	Will	9/20/1831	Washington, DC	Chancery	1832-052
Brent	Christopher	Division of Slaves	1/25/1832	Fauquier Co.	Chancery	1832-052
Brent	Hugh	Will	11/22/1852	Fauquier Co.	Chancery	1861-016
Brent	Hugh	Admr. Account	7/27/1855	Fauquier Co.	Chancery	1873-041
Brent	Hugh	Admr. Account	2/6/1858	Fauquier Co.	Chancery	1873-041
Brent	William	Division	1/10/1802	Fauquier Co.	Chancery	1807-004
Brent	William	Plat & Survey Of Division	6/5/1807	Fauquier Co.	Chancery	1823-028
Brent	William	Will	7/27/1801	Fauquier Co.	Chancery	1832-052
BRIDGETT						
Bridgett	Burrell	Estate committed To Sheriff	10/1/1910	Fauquier Co.	Probate, Box 56 Superior/Circuit Ct.	1910-007
BRITT						
Britt	James W.	Admr. Appt.	9/14/1908	Fauquier Co.	Probate, Box 56 Superior/Circuit Ct.	1908-016
BRITTON						
Britton	---- (Mrs.)	Division of Slaves	10/27/1830	Fauquier Co.	Chancery	1842-002
Britton	George	Will	8/17/1818	Fairfax Co. VA.	Chancery	1848-040
Britton	George	Exor. Account	6/21/1819	Fairfax Co. VA.	Chancery	1848-040

Consolidated Probate Index from the Clerks Loose Papers & the Superior Court/Circuit Court Records 1759-1919

Surname	**Given Name**	**Instrument**	**Date**	**County**	**CLP Record Series**	**Index #**
BRITTON (Cont.)						
Britton	George	Heirs	Undated	Not Given	Chancery	1848-040
Britton	George	Exor. Account	10/19/1829	Fairfax Co. VA.	Chancery	1848-040
Britton	George	Will	8/17/1818	Fairfax Co. VA.	Chancery	1856-001
Britton	George	Inventory + Appraisement	1818	Fairfax Co. VA.	Chancery	1856-001
Britton	George	Sales	9/2/1818	Fairfax Co. VA.	Chancery	1856-001
Britton	George	Exor. Account	6/21/1819	Fauquier Co.	Chancery	1856-001
BROCK						
Brock	William	Admr. Appt.	9/1825	Fauquier Co.	Chancery	1835-028
Brock	William	Admr. Account	2/23/1830	Fauquier Co.	Chancery	1835-028
BRONAUGH						
Bronaugh	John	Extrx. Bond	1778	Fauquier Co.	Probate, Box 45	1778-014
Bronaugh	John	Exor. Bond	1786	Fauquier Co.	Probate, Box 45	1786-008
Bronaugh	John T.	Will	12/15/1880	Fauquier Co.	Probate, Box 54 Superior/Circuit Ct.	1880-010
Bronaugh	John T.	Exor. Bond	12/15/1880	Fauquier Co.	Probate, Box 54 Superior/Circuit Ct.	1880-010
Bronaugh	Thomas	Admr. Bond	1807	Fauquier Co.	Probate, Box 46	1807-004
BROOK (See also Brooke, Brooks)						
Brook	Elizabeth	Guardian Bond	1814	Fauquier Co.	Probate, Box 49	1814-006
BROOKE (See also Brook, Brooks)						
Brooke	Betty Whiting	Guardian Bond	12/16/1819	Fauquier Co.	Chancery	1866-008
Brooke	Cecilia	Dower Allotment	12/19/1819	Fauquier Co.	Chancery	1866-008
Brooke	Francis	Guardian Bond	1811	Fauquier Co.	Probate, Box 49	1811-013
Brooke	Francis W.	Admr. Appt.	8/25/1828	Fauquier Co.	Chancery	1866-009
Brooke	Francis W.	Admr. Bond	8/25/1828	Fauquier Co.	Chancery	1866-009
Brooke	M. W.	Will	2/24/1857	Fauquier Co.	Probate, Box 50	1857-001
Brooke	Martin	Guardian Bond	1811	Fauquier Co.	Probate, Box 49	1811-013
Brooke	Mary	Guardian Bond	1811	Fauquier Co.	Probate, Box 49	1811-016

Consolidated Probate Index from the Clerks Loose Papers & the Superior Court/Circuit Court Records 1759-1919

Surname	Given Name	Instrument	Date	County	CLP Record Series	Index #
BROOKE (Cont.)						
Brooke	Matthew W.	Will	12/3/1816	Pr. Wm. Co. VA.	Chancery	1866-008
Brooke	Matthew W.	Exor. Bond	12/3/1816	Pr. Wm. Co. VA.	Chancery	1866-008
Brooke	Matthew W.	Inventory + Appraisement	9/11/1818	Pr. Wm. Co. VA.	Chancery	1866-008
Brooke	Matthew	Exor. Account Settled	10/18/1823	Pr. Wm. Co. VA.	Chancery	1866-008
Brooke	Milly	Division of Slaves	9/23/1811	Fauquier Co.	Probate, Box 50	1811-002
Brooke	Robert H.	Will	8/26/1872	Fauquier Co.	Chancery	1880-011
Brooke	Robert H.	Will	8/26/1872	Fauquier Co.	Chancery	1888-032
Brooke	Whiting	Guardian Bond	1815	Fauquier Co.	Probate, Box 49	1815-027
BROOKS (See also Brook, Brooke)						
Brooks	Adolphus	Guardian Appt.	11/8/1910	Fauquier Co.	Probate, Box 56 Superior/Circuit Ct.	1910-003
Brooks	Emma	Guardian Appt.	11/8/1910	Fauquier Co.	Probate, Box 56 Superior/Circuit Ct.	1910-003
Brooks	Eveline	Guardian Appt.	11/8/1910	Fauquier Co.	Probate, Box 56 Superior/Circuit Ct.	1910-003
Brooks	Horton	Guardian Appt.	11/8/1910	Fauquier Co.	Probate, Box 56 Superior/Circuit Ct.	1910-003
Brooks	Joseph	Admr. Appt.	9/27/1858	Fauquier Co.	Chancery	1871-029
Brooks	Joseph	Sales	11/18/1858	Fauquier Co.	Chancery	1871-029
Brooks	Lucinday	Relinquishment	11/1830	Fauquier Co.	Probate, Box 40	1830-003
Brooks	Moses	Guardian Appt.	11/8/1910	Fauquier Co.	Probate, Box 56 Superior/Circuit Ct.	1910-003
Brooks	Ruby	Guardian Appt.	11/8/1910	Fauquier Co.	Probate, Box 56 Superior/Circuit Ct.	1910-003
BROWN (See also Browne)						
Brown	Ann	Relinquishment	6/23/1761	Fauquier Co.	Probate, Box 44	1761-006
Brown	Barbary	Guardian Bond	1805	Fauquier Co.	Probate, Box 49	1805-011
Brown	Betty	Guardian Appt.	1/27/1908	Fauquier Co.	Probate, Box 56 Superior/Circuit Ct.	1908-002
Brown	Catharine	Dower Allotment	12/20/1883	Fauquier Co.	Chancery	1898-014
Brown	Dixon	Admtrx. Bond	1780	Fauquier Co.	Probate, Box 45	1780-004

Consolidated Probate Index from the Clerks Loose Papers & the Superior Court/Circuit Court Records 1759-1919

Surname	Given Name	Instrument	Date	County	CLP Record Series	Index #
BROWN (Cont.)						
Brown	Elizabeth	Guardian Bond	1815	Fauquier Co.	Probate, Box 49	1815-023
Brown	Enoch J.	Admr. Bond	1807	Fauquier Co.	Probate, Box 46	1807-014
Brown	Henson	Admr. Appt.	7/29/1907	Fauquier Co.	Probate, Box 56 Superior/Circuit Ct.	1907-012
Brown	Jesse	Will	1/23/1837	Fauquier Co.	Chancery	1844-009
Brown	John	Admr. Bond	1761	Fauquier Co.	Probate, Box 44	1761-005
Brown	John	Admr. Bond	1761	Fauquier Co.	Probate, Box 44	1761-006
Brown	John	Will	1/3/1817	Jefferson Co. KY.	Probate, Box 39	1817-001
Brown	John	Will	6/25/1849	Fauquier Co.	Chancery	1852-057
Brown	John	Admr. Account	Undated	Fauquier Co.	Chancery	1908-053
Brown	Malcolm	Guardian Appt.	9/24/1907	Fauquier Co.	Probate, Box 56 Superior/Circuit Ct.	1907-017
Brown	Mary	Exors. Bond	1784	Fauquier Co.	Probate, Box 45	1784-014
Brown	Molly	Will	4/26/1796	Fauquier Co.	Chancery	1796-001
Brown	Nancy (Tulloss)	Heirs	Undated	Fauquier Co.	Chancery	1844-009
Brown	Peggy	Guardian Bond	1804	Fauquier Co.	Probate, Box 49	1804-009
Brown	Thomas	Guardian Bond	1808	Fauquier Co.	Probate, Box 49	1808-008
Brown	Thornton	Guardian Appt.	1/27/1908	Fauquier Co.	Probate, Box 56 Superior/Circuit Ct.	1908-002
BROWNE (See also Brown)						
Browne	Elizabeth W.	Guardian Chosen	1814	Fauquier Co.	Probate, Box 49	1814-002
BROWNING						
Browning	Caleb	Admtrx. Bond	1786	Fauquier Co.	Probate, Box 45	1786-009 OS Probate
Browning	Nicholas	Admr. Bond	1774	Fauquier Co.	Probate, Box 44	1774-001
BRUIN						
Bruin	Hiram	Admr. Account	9/27/1842	Fauquier Co.	Chancery	1857-010
Bruin	Hiram	Admr. Account	9/27/1842	Fauquier Co.	Chancery	1859-064
Bruin	Hiram	Heirs	Undated	Fauquier Co.	Chancery	1859-064
Bruin	John	Admtrx. Bond	1809	Fauquier Co.	Probate, Box 47	1809-013

Consolidated Probate Index from the Clerks Loose Papers & the Superior Court/Circuit Court Records 1759-1919

Surname	Given Name	Instrument	Date	County	CLP Record Series	Index #
BRYANT						
Bryant	G. G.	Committee Appt.	6/10/1910	Fauquier Co.	Probate, Box 56 Superior/Circuit Ct.	1910-011
BUCHANAN						
Buchanan	Michael	Will	6/24/1799	Fauquier Co.	Probate, Box 50	1799-001
BUCKHOLZ						
Buckholz	Bertha	Guardian Bond	6/16/1896	Fauquier Co.	Chancery	1896-024
BUCKNER						
Buckner	Ariss	Report of Division	9/12/1872	Fauquier Co.	Chancery	1882-013
Buckner	Ariss	Plat & Survey Of Division	9/12/1872	Fauquier Co.	Chancery	1882-013
Buckner	Eliza A.	Guardian Account	12/23/1839	Fauquier Co.	Probate, Box 50	1839-003
Buckner	Eliza A.	Guardian Account	12/26/1843	Fauquier Co.	Probate, Box 50	1843-002
Buckner	Ella	Guardian Account	12/23/1839	Fauquier Co.	Probate, Box 50	1839-003
Buckner	Ella	Guardian Account	12/26/1843	Fauquier Co.	Probate, Box 50	1843-003
Buckner	Louisa B.	Guardian Account	12/23/1839	Fauquier Co.	Probate, Box 50	1839-003
Buckner	Louisa B.	Guardian Account	12/26/1843	Fauquier Co.	Probate, Box 50	1843-003
Buckner	Lucy	Will	3/12/1855	Fauquier Co.	Chancery	1871-029
Buckner	Richard B.	Guardian Account	12/23/1839	Fauquier Co.	Probate, Box 50	1839-003
Buckner	Richard B.	Guardian Account	12/26/1843	Fauquier Co.	Probate, Box 50	1843-003
BULLITT						
Bullitt	Benjamin	Exors. Bond	1766	Fauquier Co.	Probate, Box 44	1766-001
Bullitt	Benoni	Guardian Bond	1767	Fauquier Co.	Probate, Box 48	1767-001
Bullitt	Benoni	Guardian Bond	1767	Fauquier Co.	Probate, Box 48	1767-002
Bullitt	Benoni	Guardian Bond	1774	Fauquier Co.	Probate, Box 48	1774-001
Bullitt	Burwell	Guardian Bond	1767	Fauquier Co.	Probate, Box 48	1767-001
Bullitt	Burwell	Guardian Bond	1767	Fauquier Co.	Probate, Box 48	1767-002
Bullitt	Burwell	Guardian Bond	1774	Fauquier Co.	Probate, Box 48	1774-001
Bullitt	Elizabeth	Guardian Bond	1767	Fauquier Co.	Probate, Box 48	1767-001
Bullitt	Elizabeth	Guardian Bond	1767	Fauquier Co.	Probate, Box 48	1767-002
Bullitt	Elizabeth	Guardian Bond	1767	Fauquier Co.	Probate, Box 48	1767-003

Consolidated Probate Index from the Clerks Loose Papers & the Superior Court/Circuit Court Records 1759-1919

Surname	**Given Name**	**Instrument**	**Date**	**County**	**CLP Record Series**	**Index #**
BULLITT (Cont.)						
Bullitt	George	Guardian Bond	1767	Fauquier Co.	Probate, Box 48	1767-001
Bullitt	George	Guardian Bond	1774	Fauquier Co.	Probate, Box 48	1774-001
Bullitt	John	Guardian Bond	1767	Fauquier Co.	Probate, Box 48	1767-001
Bullitt	John	Guardian Bond	1767	Fauquier Co.	Probate, Box 48	1767-002
Bullitt	Parmenous	Guardian Bond	1767	Fauquier Co.	Probate, Box 48	1767-001
Bullitt	Parminous	Guardian Bond	1767	Fauquier Co.	Probate, Box 48	1767-002
Bullitt	Parminas	Guardian Bond	1774	Fauquier Co.	Probate, Box 48	1774-001
Bullitt	Thomas	Exor. Bond	1778	Fauquier Co.	Probate, Box 45	1778-013
Bullitt	William	Guardian Bond	1767	Fauquier Co.	Probate, Box 48	1767-001
Bullitt	William	Guardian Bond	1767	Fauquier Co.	Probate, Box 48	1767-002
BULLOCK						
Bullock	Richard	Will	3/24/1739	Pr. Wm. Co. VA.	Land Records & Disputes	1796-010
BURGES (See also Burgess)						
Burges	Francis	Exor. Bond	1770	Fauquier Co.	Probate, Box 44	1770-003
BURGESS (See also Burges)						
Burgess	Alexander	Guardian Bond	1806	Fauquier Co.	Probate, Box 49	1806-016
Burgess	Catherine	Guardian Bond	1806	Fauquier Co.	Probate, Box 49	1806-016
Burgess	Dawson	Guardian Bond	1807	Fauquier Co.	Probate, Box 49	1806-016
Burgess	Edward	Will	5/18/1759	Stafford Co. VA.	Chancery	1783-004
Burgess	Edward	Will	5/18/1759	Stafford Co. VA.	Chancery	1789-012
Burgess	Edward	Inventory + Sales	5/1789	Stafford Co. VA.	Chancery	1789-012
Burgess	Edward	Sales	5/1789	Stafford Co. VA.	Chancery	1789-012
Burgess	Elizabeth	Guardian Bond	1806	Fauquier Co.	Probate, Box 49	1806-016
Burgess	Garner	Guardian Bond	1806	Fauquier Co.	Probate, Box 49	1806-016
Burgess	Garner	Sales	10/24/1803	Fauquier Co.	Chancery	1809-080
Burgess	Garner	Exor. Account	3/1809	Fauquier Co.	Chancery	1809-080
Burgess	James	Admr. Account	3/1809	Fauquier Co.	Chancery	1809-080
Burgess	Nancy	Guardian Bond	1806	Fauquier Co.	Probate, Box 49	1806-016

Consolidated Probate Index from the Clerks Loose Papers & the Superior Court/Circuit Court Records 1759-1919

Surname	Given Name	Instrument	Date	County	CLP Record Series	Index #
BURKE						
Burke	William	Will	12/26/1803	Fauquier Co.	Probate, Box 50	1803-001
BURROUGHS (See also Boroughs)						
Burroughs	Thomas	Admr. Bond	1812	Fauquier Co.	Probate, Box 47	1812-013
BUSSEY						
Bussey	Ann	Renunciation	7/18/1843	Fauquier Co.	Chancery	1847-001
Bussey	Ann	Admr. Appt.	4/21/1846	Fauquier Co.	Chancery	1847-001
Bussey	Henry	Will	3/27/1843	Fauquier Co.	Chancery	1847-001
Bussey	Henry	Inventory + Appraisement	4/3/1843	Fauquier Co.	Chancery	1847-001
Bussey	Henry	Sales	11/8/1843	Fauquier Co.	Chancery	1847-001
Bussey	Henry	Will	3/27/1843	Fauquier Co.	Chancery	1860-015
Bussey	Henry	Will	3/27/1843	Fauquier Co.	Chancery	1861-012
Bussey	Henry	Appraisement	Undated	Fauquier Co.	Chancery	1870-061
BUTLER						
Butler	Jesse	Will	5/28/1869	Fauquier Co.	Probate, Box 50 Addendum Folder	1869-001
Butler	Robert	Report of Division	11/1899	Fauquier Co.	Chancery	1900-011
Butler	Robert	Plat & Survey Of Division	11/1899	Fauquier Co.	Chancery	1900-011
Butler	Robert M.	Committee Appt.	7/30/1904	Fauquier Co.	Probate, Box 55 Superior/Circuit Ct.	1904-005
BYRNE						
Byrne	James	Will	11/10/1818	Petersburg, VA.	Chancery	1866-076
Byrne	James Sr.	Admr. Account	10/26/1825	Fauquier Co.	Chancery	1837-028
Byrne	James	Admr. Account	10/15/1834	Fauquier Co.	Chancery	1837-028
Byrne	James Sr.	Sales	5/12/1833	Fauquier Co.	Chancery	1837-028
Byrne	James	Admr. Account	7/1822	Pr. Geo. Co. VA.	Chancery	1866-076
Byrne	James	Estate Account	6/1823	Fauquier Co.	Chancery	1866-076
Byrne	James	Estate Account	7/11/1828	Culpeper Co. VA.	Chancery	1866-076
Byrne	James	Admr. Account	11/22/1828	Fredksburg, VA.	Chancery	1866-076
Byrne	James	Inventory	6/8/1830	Fauquier Co.	Chancery	1866-076
Byrne	James	Estate Account	2/8/1837	Fauquier Co.	Chancery	1866-076

Consolidated Probate Index from the Clerks Loose Papers & the Superior Court/Circuit Court Records 1759-1919

Surname	Given Name	Instrument	Date	County	CLP Record Series	Index #
BYRNE (Cont.)						
Byrne	James	Admr. Account	3/30/1837	Fauquier Co.	Chancery	1866-076
Byrne	James	Estate Account	1837	Fauquier Co.	Chancery	1866-076
Byrne	James	Estate Account	7/16/1840	Fauquier Co.	Chancery	1866-076
Byrne	James	Estate Account	1841	Fauquier Co.	Chancery	1866-076
Byrne	James	Estate Account	Undated	Fauquier Co.	Chancery	1866-076
Byrne	John S.	Inventory + Appraisement	4/9/1884	Fauquier Co.	Probate, Box 54 Superior/Circuit Ct.	1884-003
Byrne	Mahala	Relinquishment	10/1829	Fauquier Co.	Probate, Box 40	1829-001
Byrne	Sally	Survey of Property	10/9/1823	Fauquier Co.	Chancery	1866-076
Byrne	Uriah	Will	5/23/1836	Fauquier Co.	Chancery	1838-020
Byrne	William	Will	4/3/1861	Fauquier Co.	Probate, Box 52 Superior/Circuit Ct.	1861-003
Byrne	William	Exor. Bond	4/3/1861	Fauquier Co.	Probate, Box 52 Superior/Circuit Ct.	1861-003
Byrne	William	Will	4/3/1861	Baltimore, MD.	Chancery	1874-034
Byrne	William	Will	4/3/1861	Fauquier Co.	Chancery	1880-043

Consolidated Probate Index from the Clerks Loose Papers & the Superior Court/Circuit Court Records 1759-1919

Surname	**Given Name**	**Instrument**	**Date**	**County**	**CLP Record Series**	**Index #**
CALAGHAN						
Calaghan	John	Admr. Bond	1815	Fauquier Co.	Probate, Box 47	1815-040
CALVERT						
Calvert	C. C.	Stock Transfer	1882	Fauquier Co.	Probate, Box 54 Superior/Circuit Ct.	1882-002
Calvert	C. C.	Motion for Stock Transfer	12/16/1887	Fauquier Co.	Probate, Box 54 Superior/Circuit Ct.	1888-003
Calvert	C. C.	Admr. Appt.	10/21/1909	Fauquier Co.	Probate, Box 56 Superior/Circuit Ct.	1909-019
Calvert	E. L. (Mrs.)	Exor. Account	12/12/1887	Fauquier Co.	Probate, Box 54 Superior/Circuit Ct.	1887-004
Calvert	Elizabeth L.	Will	4/18/1874	Fauquier Co.	Probate, Box 53 Superior/Circuit Ct.	1874-005
Calvert	Elizabeth L.	Exor. Bond	9/9/1874	Fauquier Co.	Probate, Box 53 Superior/Circuit Ct.	1874-005
Calvert	Elizabeth L.	Appraisement	10/22/1875	Fauquier Co.	Probate, Box 53 Superior/Circuit Ct.	1875-006
Calvert	J. C.	Will	9/6/1892	Fauquier Co.	Probate Box 55 Superior/Circuit Ct.	1892-004
Calvert	J. C.	Exor. Qualification	9/6/1892	Fauquier Co.	Probate Box 55 Superior/Circuit Ct.	1892-004
CAMERAN						
Cameran	Angus	Admtrx. Bond	1809	Fauquier Co.	Probate, Box 47	1809-005
CAMPBELL						
Campbell	Alexander S.	Will	9/24/1890	Baltimore Co. MD.	Chancery	1893-021
Campbell	Hugh R.	Admtrx. Bond	1813	Fauquier Co.	Probate, Box 47	1813-016
Campbell	Nathaniel	Guardian Bond	1787	Fauquier Co.	Probate, Box 48	1797-006
CAREY						
Carey	J. O.	Plat & Resurvey Of Division	7/9/1906	Fauquier Co.	Chancery	1907-049
CARNALL						
Carnall	Annie L.	Guardian Appt.	10/30/1875	Fauquier Co.	Chancery	1875-069
Carnall	Ellen T.	Guardian Appt.	10/30/1875	Fauquier Co.	Chancery	1875-069

Consolidated Probate Index from the Clerks Loose Papers & the Superior Court/Circuit Court Records 1759-1919

Surname	Given Name	Instrument	Date	County	CLP Record Series	Index #
CARR						
Carr	Caldwell	Will	9/25/1855	Loudoun Co. VA.	Chancery	1860-053
Carr	Caldwell	Report of Division Of Land	4/20/1859	Fauquier Co.	Chancery	1860-053
Carr	Caldwell	Report of Division Of Slaves	4/20/1859	Fauquier Co.	Chancery	1860-053
Carr	Caldwell	Will	9/25/1855	Fauquier Co.	Chancery	1866-062
Carr	Caldwell	Will	9/25/1855	Fauquier Co.	Chancery	1877-028
Carr	Joseph	Admr. Account	1828	Fauquier Co.	Chancery	1830-126
Carr	Joseph	Plat & Survey Of Division	1/15/1828	Fauquier Co.	Chancery	1830-126
Carr	Joseph	Report of Division	3/27/1841	Fauquier Co.	Chancery	1841-046
Carr	Joseph	Plat & Survey Of Division	3/27/1841	Fauquier Co.	Chancery	1841-046
Carr	Joseph	Division of Slaves	10/4/1834	Fauquier Co.	Chancery	1847-002
Carr	Joseph's Estate	Memo of Negroes + ages for Henley Boggess as Gdn.	7/27/1840	Fauquier Co.	Chancery	1848-003
Carr	Joseph	Heirs	3/27/1845	Fauquier Co.	Chancery	1856-013
Carr	Peter	Heirs	3/27/1845	Fauquier Co.	Chancery	1856-013
Carr	William	Will	2/8/1791	Pr. Wm. Co. VA.	Chancery	1873-037
Carr	William	Admr. Account	11/2/1830	Fauquier Co.	Chancery	1873-037
Carr	William	Admr. Account	9/30/1834	Fauquier Co.	Chancery	1873-037
Carr	William	Estate Account	7/31/1830	Fauquier Co.	Chancery	1881-015
CARRELL						
Carrell	Sanford	Exors. Bond	1777	Fauquier Co.	Probate, Box 44	1777-016
CARTER						
Carter	Charles	Will	10/28/1816	Fauquier Co.	Chancery	1841-029
Carter	Charles	Exor. Account	4/1820	Fauquier Co.	Chancery	1841-029
Carter	Charles	Admr. Account	4/28/1829	Fauquier Co.	Chancery	1841-029
Carter,	Charles	Admr. Account	6/27/1836	Fauquier Co.	Chancery	1841-029
Carter	Charles L.	Admr. Account	3/20/1852	Fauquier Co.	Chancery	1853-027

Consolidated Probate Index from the Clerks Loose Papers & the Superior Court/Circuit Court Records 1759-1919

Surname	Given Name	Instrument	Date	County	CLP Record Series	Index #
CARTER (Cont.)						
Carter	Charles L.	Will	8/22/1842	Fauquier Co.	Chancery	1868-009
Carter	Charles L.	Plat & Survey Of Division	5/16/1849	Fauquier Co.	Chancery	1868-009
Carter	Edward	Guardian Bond	8/28/1858	Fauquier Co.	Probate Box 52 Superior/Circuit Ct.	1858-010
Carter	Edward	Guardian Bond	9/28/1858	Fauquier Co.	Chancery	1858-030
Carter	Edwin L.	Admtrx. Bond	4/11/1834	Fauquier Co.	Chancery	1836-001
Carter	Edwin L.	Inventory + Appraisement	4/11/1834	Fauquier Co.	Chancery	1836-001
Carter	Ellen	Guardian Acct.	9/13/1858	Fauquier Co.	Probate, Box 52 Superior/Circuit Ct.	1858-010
Carter	G. A.	Guardian Acct.	11/20/1844	Fauquier Co.	Chancery	1857-005
Carter	George	Guardian Bond	10/11/1837	Fauquier Co.	Chancery	1837-031
Carter	George	Will	10/28/1816	Fauquier Co.	Chancery	1846-002
Carter	George	Will	10/28/1816	Fauquier Co.	Probate, Box 50	1816-006
Carter	George	Will	10/26/1816	Fauquier Co.	Land Records & Disputes	1831-013
Carter	George	Appraisement	3/14/1816	Fauquier Co.	Probate, Box 50	1816-004
Carter	George	Will	2/28/1831	Fauquier Co.	Chancery	1840-006
Carter	George	Exor. Acct.	2/27/1833	Fauquier Co.	Chancery	1840-006
Carter	George	Will	2/28/1831	Fauquier Co.	Chancery	1866-026
Carter	Gertrude	Will	7/30/1872	Fauquier Co.	Chancery	1894-076
Carter	H. F.	Guardian Acct.	11/20/1844	Fauquier Co.	Chancery	1857-005
Carter	Helen	Guardian Chosen	5/25/1832	Fauquier Co.	Probate, Box 40	1832-002
Carter	John	Will	8/27/1828	Fauquier Co.	Chancery	1852-062
Carter	John	Plat & Survey Of Division	1838	Fauquier Co.	Chancery	1852-062
Carter	John	Will	8/27/1838	Fauquier Co.	Chancery	1842-021
Carter	John	Will	8/27/1838	Fauquier Co.	Chancery	1843-005

Consolidated Probate Index from the Clerks Loose Papers & the Superior Court/Circuit Court Records 1759-1919

Surname	Given Name	Instrument	Date	County	CLP Record Series	Index #
CARTER (Cont.)						
Carter	John	Exor. Acct.	6/30/1843	Fauquier Co.	Chancery	1843-005
Carter	John	Will	5/3/1838	Fauquier Co.	Chancery	1910-005
Carter	John	Will	5/29/1838	Fauquier Co.	Probate, Box 50	1836-002
Carter	John	Will	5/29/1838	Fauquier Co.	Chancery	1854-016
Carter	John	Will	5/29/1838	Fauquier Co.	Chancery	1868-001
Carter	John	Division of Slaves	9/1/1838	Fauquier Co.	Chancery	1868-001
Carter	John	Sales	9/4/1838	Fauquier Co.	Chancery	1868-001
Carter	John	Inventory + Appraisement	3/25/1840	Fauquier Co.	Chancery	1868-001
Carter	John B.	Will	5/5/1852	Fauquier Co.	Probate, Box 52 Superior/Circuit Ct.	1852-003
Carter	John B.	Appraisement	5/5/1853	Fauquier Co.	Probate, Box 52 Superior/Circuit Ct.	1853-002
Carter	John Brooke	Will	5/5/1852	Fauquier Co.	Chancery	1873-029
Carter	John Brooke	Inventory	4/11/1853	Fauquier Co.	Chancery	1873-029
Carter	Judith	Guardian Bond	10/11/1837	Fauquier Co.	Chancery	1837-031
Carter	Judith's Heirs	Plat & Survey of Dower Division	2/1847	Fauquier Co.	Chancery	1847-050
Carter	Landon	Guardian Chosen	1/1846	Roy Co. MO.	Chancery	1846-019
Carter	Landonia	Will	12/20/1868	Fauquier Co.	Chancery	1894-076
Carter	Mary Kossuth	Guardian Bond	9/28/1858	Fauquier Co.	Chancery	1858-030
Carter	Mary B.	Guardian Acct.	11/26/1828	Fauquier Co.	Chancery	1841-029
Carter	Mary K.	Guardian Acct.	9/13/1858	Fauquier Co.	Probate, Box 52 Superior/Circuit Ct.	1858-010
Carter	Mildred	Guardian Bond	10/11/1837	Fauquier Co.	Chancery	1837-031
Carter	Moore F.	Plat & Survey Of Division	10/18/1825	Fauquier Co.	Chancery	1855-063
Carter	Moore F.	Plat & Survey Of Division	8/30/1826	Fauquier Co.	Chancery	1830-134
Carter	Moore F.	Division of Slaves	4/27/1830	Fauquier Co.	Chancery	1844-001
Carter	Orra E.	Guardian Bond	9/28/1858	Fauquier Co.	Chancery	1858-030

Consolidated Probate Index from the Clerks Loose Papers & the Superior Court/Circuit Court Records 1759-1919

Surname	Given Name	Instrument	Date	County	CLP Record Series	Index #
CARTER (Cont.)						
Carter	Presley L.	Guardian Chosen	1/1846	Roy Co. MO.	Chancery	1846-019
Carter	Richard	Guardian Bond	10/11/1837	Fauquier Co.	Chancery	1837-031
Carter	Sally Ann	Guardian Bond	10/11/1837	Fauquier Co.	Chancery	1837-031
Carter	Sarah C.	Guardian Chosen	1/1846	Roy Co. MO.	Chancery	1846-019
Carter	Susan Catharine	Will	8/27/1838	Fauquier Co.	Chancery	1851-032
Carter	Susan Catharine	Will	8/27/1838	Fauquier Co.	Chancery	1868-009
Carter	Thomas L.	Guardian Appt.	5/9/1846	Fauquier Co.	Chancery	1846-019
Carter	Thomas O. B.	Will	1/25/1841	Fauquier Co.	Chancery	1869-025
Carter	Thomas O. B.	Exor. Bond	1/25/1841	Fauquier Co.	Chancery	1869-025
Carter	Thomas O.B.	Will	1/25/1841	Fauquier Co.	Chancery	1873-034
Carter	Virginia	Guardian Bond	10/11/1837	Fauquier Co.	Chancery	1837-031
Carter	W. L.	Guardian Account	9/13/1858	Fauquier Co.	Probate, Box 52 Superior/Circuit Ct.	1858-010
Carter	W. L.	Committee Report	9/17/1868	Fauquier Co.	Chancery	1911-002
Carter	Westward	Suit to revoke Guardianship	1/19/1827	Fauquier Co.	Probate, Box 40	1831-003
Carter	Westward M.	Guardian Acct.	6/27/1826	Fauquier Co.	Chancery	1841-029
Carter	Westward M.	Guardian Acct.	11/26/1828	Fauquier Co.	Chancery	1841-029
Carter	William H.	Guardian Acct.	11/20/1844	Fauquier Co.	Chancery	1857-005
CARTLICH						
Cartlich	Charles	Exors. Bond	1809	Fauquier Co.	Probate, Box 47	1809-021
Cartlich	Charles	Admr. Bond	1815	Fauquier Co.	Probate, Box 47	1815-026
Cartlich	Charlotte	Guardian Bond	1811	Fauquier Co.	Probate, Box 49	1811-017
CARVER						
Carver	William	Will	8/28/1846	Fauquier Co.	Chancery	1871-071
CASH						
Cash	John	Admtrx. Bond	12/2/1837	Fauquier Co.	Chancery	1847-004
Cash	Lucy	Report of Dower Allotment	10/19/1840	Fauquier Co.	Chancery	1847-004
CASKIE						
Caskie	James	Will	10/18/1866	Richmond, VA.	Chancery	1885-002

Consolidated Probate Index from the Clerks Loose Papers & the Superior Court/Circuit Court Records 1759-1919

Surname	Given Name	Instrument	Date	County	CLP Record Series	Index #
CATLETT						
Catlett	John	Exors. Bond	1778	Fauquier Co.	Probate, Box 45	1778-007
Catlett	Robert	Admtrx. Bond	1810	Fauquier Co.	Probate, Box 47	1810-005
CAVE						
Cave	Samuel	Admr. Bond	1807	Fauquier Co.	Probate, Box 46	1807-001
CAYNER (See also Caynor)						
Cayner	Celia	Guardian Bond	1808	Fauquier Co.	Probate, Box 49	1811-003
CAYNOR (See also Cayner)						
Caynor	Nancy	Guardian Bond	1808	Fauquier Co.	Probate, Box 49	1808-003
CHAMBERLAIN						
Chamberlain	James L.	Admr. Appt.	2/22/1908	Fauquier Co.	Probate, Box 56 Superior/Circuit Ct.	1908-005
CHANDLER						
Chandler	Henry	Report of Division Of Slaves	12/27/1840	Fauquier Co.	Chancery	1841-082
CHAPMAN						
Chapman	George	Will	11/02/1829	Pr. Wm. Co. VA.	Chancery	1838-045
Chapman	George	Division	11/1836	Fauquier Co.	Chancery	1838-045
CHAPPALEAR						
Chappalear	Armistead	Inventory	7/15/1839	Fauquier Co.	Chancery	1843-023
Chappalear	Armistead	Sales (Fragment)	Undated	Fauquier Co.	Chancery	1843-023
CHEW						
Chew	Richard	Admr. Acct. Settled	5/6/1828	Fauquier Co.	Probate, Box 50	1827-002
CHICHESTER						
Chichester	Richard	Sales	2/15/1830	Fauquier Co.	Chancery	1834-037
Chichester	Richard	Appraisement	4/26/1830	Fauquier Co.	Chancery	1834-037
Chichester	Richard	Exor. Acct.	11/1833	Fauquier Co.	Chancery	1834-037
Chichester	Richard	Exor. Acct.	1833	Fauquier Co.	Chancery	1834-037
Chichester	Richard	Inventory of Slaves	Undated	Fauquier Co.	Chancery	1832-059
Chichester	Richard	Division of Slaves	Undated	Fauquier Co.	Chancery	1832-059
Chichester	Richard	Exor. Acct.	6/23/1833	Fauquier Co.	Chancery	1832-059
Chichester	Richard	Plat & Survey Of Division	1/11/1843	Fauquier Co.	Chancery	1843-063
Chichester	Richard McCarty	Suit over Will	1830	Fauquier Co.	Probate, Box 40	1830-005
Chichester	Richard McCarty	Will	1/27/1830	Fauquier Co.	Probate, Box 40	1830-005

Consolidated Probate Index from the Clerks Loose Papers & the Superior Court/Circuit Court Records 1759-1919

Surname	Given Name	Instrument	Date	County	CLP Record Series	Index #
CHILTON						
Chilton	Catharine M.	Will	9/19/1885	Fauquier Co.	Probate, Box 54 Superior/Circuit Ct.	1885-007
Chilton	Charles B.	Will	11/15/1869	Culpeper Co. VA.	Chancery	1891-045
Chilton	Charles B.	Report of Division	4/4/1881	Fauquier Co.	Chancery	1891-045
Chilton	Charles B.	Plat & Survey Of Division	4/4/1881	Fauquier Co.	Chancery	1891-045
Chilton	George	Guardian Bond	1788	Fauquier Co.	Probate, Box 48	1788-001
Chilton	John	Exors. Bond	1778	Fauquier Co.	Probate, Box 45	1778-012
Chilton	Joseph	Guardian Bond	1788	Fauquier Co.	Probate, Box 48	1788-001
Chilton	Lucy	Guardian Bond	1781	Fauquier Co.	Probate, Box 48	1781-003
Chilton	Lucy	Guardian Bond	1788	Fauquier Co.	Probate, Box 48	1788-001
Chilton	Orrick	Guardian Bond	1778	Fauquier Co.	Probate, Box 48	1778-003
Chilton	Orrick	Guardian Bond	1781	Fauquier Co.	Probate, Box 48	1781-003
Chilton	Susanna	Guardian Bond	1778	Fauquier Co.	Probate, Box 48	1778-003
Chilton	William	Admrs. Bond	1775	Fauquier Co.	Probate, Box 44	1775-007
Chilton	William	Guardian Bond	1778	Fauquier Co.	Probate, Box 48	1778-003
CHINN (See also Chunn)						
Chinn	Agatha	Guardian Bond	1762	Fauquier Co.	Probate, Box 48	1762-001
Chinn	Charles	Will	7/22/1844	Fauquier Co.	Chancery	1849-011
Chinn	Charles	Inventory + Appraisement	8/31/1844	Fauquier Co.	Chancery	1849-011
Chinn	Charles	Plat & Survey Of Division	4/25/1845	Fauquier Co.	Chancery	1849-011
Chinn	Charles	Will	7/22/1844	Fauquier Co.	Chancery	1849-012
Chinn	Charles	Exor. Acct.	3/1846	Fauquier Co.	Chancery	1849-012
Chinn	Charles	Will	7/22/1844	Fauquier Co.	Chancery	1852-014
Chinn	Charles	Will	7/22/1844	Fauquier Co.	Chancery	1866-046
Chinn	Charles	Exor. Acct.	1844-1847	Fauquier Co.	Probate, Box 40	1847-001

Consolidated Probate Index from the Clerks Loose Papers & the Superior Court/Circuit Court Records 1759-1919

Surname	**Given Name**	**Instrument**	**Date**	**County**	**CLP Record Series**	**Index #**
CHINN (See also Chunn)						
Chinn	Elizabeth	Guardian Appt.	10/30/1863	Baton Rouge, LA.	Chancery	1897-039
Chinn	Horatio C.	Will	5/30/1840	Fauquier Co.	Chancery	1859-021
Chinn	Hugh	Exor. Bond	1817	Fauquier Co.	Probate, Box 47	1817-001
Chinn	Hugh	Admr. Acct	9/24/1821	Fauquier Co.	Probate, Box 50	1820-001
Chinn	Hugh	Exor. Acct.	9/24/1821	Fauquier Co.	Chancery	1837-010
Chinn	Martha	Will	4/25/1831	Fauquier Co.	Chancery	1852-024
Chinn	Thomas	Admr. Bond	10/14/1816	Fauquier Co.	Chancery	1837-021
Chinn	Thomas	Inventory	10/14/1816	Loudoun Co. VA.	Chancery	1837-021
Chinn	Thomas	Division of Slaves	5/26/1818	Fauquier Co.	Chancery	1837-021
Chinn	Thomas	Sales	12/8/1823	Loudoun Co. VA.	Chancery	1837-021
Chinn	Thomas	Division (Extract)	Undated	Fauquier Co.	Chancery	1856-024
CHRISTIAN						
Christian	Francis H.	Will	4/2/1788	Frederick Co. VA.	Chancery	1805-040
Christian	Francis H.	Inventory	4/2/1788	Frederick Co. VA.	Chancery	1805-040
CHUNN (See also Chinn)						
Chunn	Andrew	Admr. Bond	1813	Fauquier Co.	Probate, Box 47	1813-011
Chunn	Andrew	Will	9/28/1846	Fauquier Co.	Chancery	1847-015
Chunn	Andrew	Will	9/28/1846	Fauquier Co.	Chancery	1847-017
Chunn	Andrew	Will	9/1846	Fauquier Co.	Chancery	1853-044
Chunn	Andrew	Will	9/26/1846	Fauquier Co.	Chancery	1854-020
Chunn	Charles	Will	7/22/1844	Fauquier Co.	Chancery	1848-017
Chunn	Charles	Inventory + Appraisement	8/31/1844	Fauquier Co.	Chancery	1848-017
Chunn	Charles	Admr. Bond	4/27/1846	Fauquier Co.	Chancery	1848-017
Chunn	Charles	Exor. Acct.	7/29/1846	Fauquier Co.	Chancery	1848-017
Chunn	James T.	Guardian Bond	11/23/1846	Fauquier Co.	Chancery	1852-046
Chunn	Lucy M.	Guardian Bond	5/9/1840	Fauquier Co.	Chancery	1840-019
Chunn	Martha	Will	2/7/1820	Fauquier Co.	Probate, Box 50	1820-003

Consolidated Probate Index from the Clerks Loose Papers & the Superior Court/Circuit Court Records 1759-1919

Surname	Given Name	Instrument	Date	County	CLP Record Series	Index #
CHUNN (Cont.)						
Chunn	William S.	Guardian Bond	11/23/1846	Fauquier Co.	Chancery	1852-046
Chunn	William S.	Guardian Acct.	7/29/1848	Fauquier Co.	Probate, Box 50	1848-001
CHURCHHILL (See also Churchill)						
Churchhill	Henry	Admr. Bond	1761	Fauquier Co.	Probate, Box 44	1761-008
CHURCHILL (See also Churchhill)						
Churchill	Jane	Guardian Bond	1796	Fauquier Co.	Probate, Box 48	1796-006
CLAGGETT						
Claggett	Samuel	Inventory + Appraisement	10/1820	Fauquier Co.	Chancery	1837-037
Claggett	Samuel	Admr. Appt.	12/28/1846	Fauquier Co.	Chancery	1869-029
CLARK (See also Clarke)						
Clark	Benjamin	Admr. Bond	1813	Fauquier Co.	Probate, Box 47	1813-012
Clark	Polly	Renunciation	1813	Fauquier Co.	Probate, Box 39	1813-012
CLARKE (See also Clark)						
Clarke	Benjamin	Exor. Bond	1797	Fauquier Co.	Probate, Box 46	1797-009
Clarke	Patrick	Report of Division	5/17/1909	Fauquier Co.	Chancery	1909-023
Clarke	Patrick	Plat & Survey Of Division	5/17/1909	Fauquier Co.	Chancery	1909-023
Clarke	Susan	Will	8/26/1833	Fauquier Co.	Chancery	1847-027
Clarke	Susan	Exor. Bond	8/26/1833	Fauquier Co.	Chancery	1847-027
Clarke	Susan	Exor. Bond	1/1/1833	Fauquier Co.	Chancery	1847-027
Clarke	William	Admr. Bond	1807	Fauquier Co.	Probate, Box 46	1807-010
CLARKSON						
Clarkson	Henry	Admr. Bond	1806	Fauquier Co.	Probate, Box 46	1806-001
Clarkson	William	Admr. Acct.	9/24/1821	Fauquier Co.	Chancery	1824-030
CLATTERBACK						
Clatterback	Cora Lee	Guardian Appt.	8/18/1909	Fauquier Co.	Probate, Box 56 Superior/Circuit Ct.	1909-012
Clatterback	E. Blanche	Guardian Appt.	8/18/1909	Fauquier Co.	Probate, Box 56 Superior/Circuit Ct.	1909-012
CLAXTON						
Claxton	James	Guardian Bond	1810	Fauquier Co.	Probate, Box 49	1810-017
Claxton	Jeremiah	Exor. Bond	1808	Fauquier Co.	Probate, Box 46	1808-027
Claxton	John Peyton	Guardian Bond	1810	Fauquier Co.	Probate, Box 49	1810-018

Consolidated Probate Index from the Clerks Loose Papers & the Superior Court/Circuit Court Records 1759-1919

Surname	**Given Name**	**Instrument**	**Date**	**County**	**CLP Record Series**	**Index #**
CLAXTON (Cont.)						
Claxton	Pope	Admr. Bond	12/4/1827	Fauquier Co.	Chancery	1838-012
Claxton	Pope	Admr. Bond	3/25/1836	Fauquier Co.	Chancery	1838-012
Claxton	Richard	Guardian Chosen By Grandfather	1808	Fauquier Co.	Probate, Box 49	1808-014
Claxton	William	Guardian Bond	1810	Fauquier Co.	Probate, Box 49	1810-017
CLAYTOR						
Claytor	John	Admr. Bond	1773	Fauquier Co.	Probate, Box 44	1773-003
Claytor	John	Sales	1796	Fauquier Co.	Chancery	1796-006
CLEMENT						
Clement	Amelia Jane	Guardian Bond	4/19/1859	Fauquier Co.	Probate, Box 52 Superior/Circuit Ct.	1859-003
CLEMONS						
Clemons	Elizabeth	Relinquishment	1/1805	Fauquier Co.	Probate, Box 39	1805-002
CLOPTON						
Clopton	N. A.	Plat & Survey of Division of "Grassdale"	9/1886	Fauquier Co.	Chancery	1906-006
Clopton	Nathaniel V.	Heirs	10/27/1857	Fauquier Co.	Military Records	1857-001
COATES						
Coates	Elijah	Exor. Bond	1807	Fauquier Co.	Probate, Box 46	1807-017
COCHRAN						
Cochran	Catharine P.	Will	5/13/1895	Loudoun Co. VA.	Chancery	1903-055
Cochran	William L.	Will	2/11/1876	Albemarle Co. VA.	Chancery	1908-010
COCKE						
Cocke	Washington	Will	4/24/1848	Fauquier Co.	Chancery	1850-019
Cocke	Washington	Sales	10/26/1848	Fauquier Co.	Chancery	1850-019
COCKERILL (See also Cockrell, Cockrill, Cockrille)						
Cockerill	Thomas	Will	4/8/1885	Fauquier Co.	Probate, Box 54 Superior/Circuit Ct.	1885-001
Cockerill	Thomas	Exor. Bond	4/8/1885	Fauquier Co.	Probate, Box 54 Superior/Circuit Ct.	1885-001
Cockerill	Thomas	Admr. Acct.	12/13/1886	Fauquier Co.	Probate, Box 54 Superior/Circuit Ct.	1886-002
Cockerill	Thomas	Admr. Acct.	9/8/1887	Fauquier Co.	Probate, Box 54 Superior/Circuit Ct.	1887-006
COCKRELL (See also Cockerill, Cockrill, Cockrille)						
Cockrell	Joseph	Admr. Bond	1771	Fauquier Co.	Probate, Box 44	1771-007

Consolidated Probate Index from the Clerks Loose Papers & the Superior Court/Circuit Court Records 1759-1919

Surname	Given Name	Instrument	Date	County	CLP Record Series	Index #
COCKRILL (See also Cockerill, Cockrell, Cockrille)						
Cockrill	John	Evidence that Cockrill Left no wife or children; Mother was Mrs. Richards	1817	Fauquier Co.	Probate, Box 39	1817-003
COCKRILLE (See also Cockerill, Cockrell, Cockrill)						
Cockrille	Letitia	Admr. Appt.	1/21/1896	Fauquier Co.	Chancery	1904-033
Cockrille	Thomas	Will	4/8/1885	Fauquier Co.	Chancery	1904-033
Cockrille	Thomas	Appraisement	4/28/1885	Fauquier Co.	Probate, Box 54 Superior/Circuit Ct.	1885-004
COLBERT						
Colbert	Thornton B.	Inventory + Appraisement	3/19/1858	Fauquier Co.	Chancery	1860-041
Colbert	Thornton B.	Dower Allotment to widow in land and slaves	3/19/1858	Fauquier Co.	Chancery	1860-041
Colbert	William	Will	6/20/1864	Culpeper Co. VA.	Chancery	1890-033
Colbert	William	Exor. Acct.	7/1867	Culpeper Co. VA.	Chancery	1890-033
COLEMAN						
Coleman	William A. C.	Will	1/20/1906	Fauquier Co.	Probate, Box 50 Addendum Folder	1906-001
COLLINS						
Collins	John	Estate Papers	11/28/1846	Fauquier Co.	Probate, Box 50	1843-004
COLSTON						
Colston	Edward	Will	5/3/1850	Berkley Co. WV.	Chancery	1857-008
COLVIN						
Colvin	Richard	Report of Division	10/27/1828	Fauquier Co.	Chancery	1832-056
Colvin	Richard	Plat & Survey Of Division	10/27/1828	Fauquier Co.	Chancery	1832-056
Colvin	Sarah	Guardian Chosen	12/1831	Fauquier Co.	Probate, Box 40	1831-005
COMBS						
Combs	John	Will	5/28/1781	Fauquier Co.	Chancery	1852-013
Combs	K. E.	Estate Papers + Accounts	1762-1872	Fauquier Co.	Probate, Box 43 K. E. Combs Estate Papers	1762-001 to 1872-002
Combs	Sally	Will	8/28/1833	Fauquier Co.	Chancery	1836-015
COMPTON						
Compton	L. B.	Admr. Appt.	3/22/1909	Fauquier Co.	Probate, Box 56 Superior/Circuit Ct.	1909-006

Consolidated Probate Index from the Clerks Loose Papers & the Superior Court/Circuit Court Records 1759-1919

Surname	Given Name	Instrument	Date	County	CLP Record Series	Index #
CONNELLY						
Connelly	Grace	Petition to recover Estate inherited from her mother, Ella Green	8/20/1907	Fauquier Co.	Probate, Box 56 Superior/Circuit Ct.	1907-013
CONRAD						
Conrad	Ada Lewis	Guardian Bond	12/12/1882	Fauquier Co.	Chancery	1902-024
Conrad	Daniel Preston	Guardian Bond	12/12/1882	Fauquier Co.	Chancery	1902-024
Conrad	Lucy Edmond	Guardian Bond	1/2/12/1882	Fauquier Co.	Chancery	1902-024
CONWAY						
Conway	Peter	Sales	10/22/1827	Fauquier Co.	Probate, Box 50	1827-001
Conway	Peter	Will	2/25/1833	Fauquier Co.	Chancery	1834-023
Conway	Peter	Sales	4/1833	Fauquier Co.	Chancery	1834-023
Conway	Thomas	Exors. Bond	1784	Fauquier Co.	Probate, Box 45	1784-015
CONYERS						
Conyers	John	Admtrx. Bond	1817	Fauquier Co.	Probate, Box 47	1814-018
COOK (See also Cooke)						
Cook	John	Extrx. Bond	1760	Fauquier Co.	Probate, Box 44	1760-004
COOKE (See also Cook)						
Cooke	John	Court Order to Administer Estate	12/22/1817	Fauquier Co.	Probate, Box 39	1818-006
Cooke	Littleton	Exor. Bond	1782	Fauquier Co.	Probate, Box 49	1782-009
COOKSEY						
Cooksey	George	Guardian Bond	1817	Fauquier Co.	Probate, Box 49	1817-011
Cooksey	Maria	Guardian Bond	1817	Fauquier Co.	Probate, Box 49	1817-011
Cooksey	Philip	Admr. Acct.	11/15/1839	Fauquier Co.	Chancery	1860-024
Cooksey	Philip	Sales Account	5/1841	Fauquier Co.	Chancery	1860-024
Cooksey	Sally	Guardian Bond	1817	Fauquier Co.	Probate, Box 49	1817-011
COON						
Coon	Matthew	Will	4/14/1731	Stafford Co. VA.	Chancery	1789-011
Coon	Matthew	Inventory	5/10/1732	Stafford Co. VA.	Chancery	1789-011
COPPAGE (See also Coppedge, Coppege)						
Coppage	William	Guardian Bond	1760	Fauquier Co.	Probate, Box 48	1760-001
Coppage	William	Exor. Bond	1806	Fauquier Co.	Probate, Box 46	1806-018

Consolidated Probate Index from the Clerks Loose Papers & the Superior Court/Circuit Court Records 1759-1919

Surname	Given Name	Instrument	Date	County	CLP Record Series	Index #
COPPEDGE (See also Coppage, Coppege)						
Coppedge	Mary et als.	Indemnification	9/22/1817	Fauquier Co.	Probate, Box 50	1817-001
Coppedge	William	Will	12/22/1806	Fauquier Co.	Probate, Box 50	1806-001
Coppedge	William	Will	10/27/1806	Fauquier Co.	Chancery	1838-014
COPPEGE (See also Coppage, Coppedge)						
Coppege	William	Exor. Bond	3/29/1834	Fauquier Co.	Chancery	1838-014
Coppege	William	Exor. Acct.	3/19/1834	Fauquier Co.	Chancery	1838-014
CORAM						
Coram	Champe	Admr. Bond	1787	Fauquier Co.	Probate, Box 45	1787-001
CORBAN (See also Corbin)						
Corban	John	Admr. Appt.	9/22/1746	Fauquier Co.	Land Records & Disputes	1809-003
CORBIN (See also Corban)						
Corbin	Anderson	Admr. Appt.	1908	Fauquier Co.	Probate, Box 56 Superior/Circuit Ct.	1908-004
Corbin	Anderson's Estate	Waiver of Adm.	1908	Fauquier Co.	Probate, Box 56 Superior/Circuit Ct.	1908-004
Corbin	Jane	Guardian Bond	1792	Fauquier Co.	Probate, Box 48	1792-001
Corbin	John	Plat & Survey of Land Warrant	12/0/1727	Fauquier Co.	Land Records & Disputes	1809-003
Corbin	Priscilla	Will	6/11/1855	Stafford Co. VA.	Chancery	1877-009
Corbin	Priscilla	Inventory + Appraisement	6/11/1855	Fauquier Co.	Chancery	1877-009
Corbin	Priscilla	Sales	1855	Fauquier Co.	Chancery	1877-009
Corbin	Richard Henry	Certification of Death	6/12-13/1799	Fauquier Co.	Chancery	1868-108
CORDER						
Corder	John	Admtrx. Bond	1760	Fauquier Co.	Probate, Box 44	1760-007
CORLEY						
Corley	Minoah	Will	5/26/1823	Fauquier Co.	Chancery	1837-050
CORNWALL (See also Cornwell)						
Cornwall	Peter	Exors. Bond	1776	Fauquier Co.	Probate, Box 44	1776-003

Consolidated Probate Index from the Clerks Loose Papers & the Superior Court/Circuit Court Records 1759-1919

Surname	Given Name	Instrument	Date	County	CLP Record Series	Index #
CORNWELL (See also Cornwall)						
Cornwell	Jacob	Admr. Bond	12/10/1880	Fauquier Co.	Probate, Box 54 Superior/Circuit Ct.	1880-011
Cornwell	Jacob	Appraisement	12/10/1880	Fauquier Co.	Probate, Box 54 Superior/Circuit Ct.	1880-011
Cornwell	Jacob	Sales	8/20/1881	Fauquier Co.	Probate, Box 54 Superior/Circuit Ct.	1881-002
COURTNEY						
Courtney	John	Exor. Bond	1807	Fauquier Co.	Probate, Box 46	1807-022
COVERSTONE						
Coverstone	Lewis	Will	7/28/1902	Fauquier Co.	Chancery	1910-027
COWAN (See also Cowne)						
Cowan	Alexander	Admr. Bond	1811	Fauquier Co.	Probate, Box 47	1811-009
COWGILL						
Cowgill	Mary	Relinquishment	10/1802	Fauquier Co.	Probate, Box 39	1802-004
COWNE (See also Cowan)						
Cowne	Augustine	Admr. Bond	10/6/1841	Fauquier Co.	Probate, Box 51 Superior/Circuit Ct.	1841-003
COX						
Cox	Abram	Admr. Acct.	1/20/1827	Fauquier Co.	Chancery	1831-029
Cox	David Thomas	Guardian Appt.	9/27/1909	Fauquier Co.	Probate, Box 56 Superior/Circuit Ct.	1909-014
Cox	James William	Guardian Appt.	9/27/1909	Fauquier Co.	Probate, Box 56 Superior/Circuit Ct.	1909-014
Cox	Lucy	Guardian Bond	1799	Fauquier Co.	Probate, Box 48	1799-002
Cox	Marion Albert	Guardian Appt.	9/27/1909	Fauquier Co.	Probate, Box 56 Superior/Circuit Ct.	1909-014
CRAIG						
Craig	Alexander	Will	8/22/1859	Fauquier Co.	Chancery	1860-040
Craig	Alexander S.	Will	8/22/1859	Fauquier Co.	Chancery	1873-032
Craig	James	Admr. Bond	1806	Fauquier Co.	Probate, Box 46	1806-008
Craig	Mary	Will	3/24/1856	Fauquier Co.	Chancery	1857-019
Craig	Mary	Will	3/24/1856	Fauquier Co.	Chancery	1860-040
Craig	Mary	Exor. Acct.	11/11/1857	Fauquier Co.	Probate, Box 50 Addendum Folder	1857-002
Craig	Mary	Exor. Acct.	6/27/1859	Fauquier Co.	Probate, Box 50 Addendum Folder	1859-001
Craig	Mary	Will	3/24/1856	Fauquier Co.	Chancery	1860-022

Consolidated Probate Index from the Clerks Loose Papers & the Superior Court/Circuit Court Records 1759-1919

Surname	**Given Name**	**Instrument**	**Date**	**County**	**CLP Record Series**	**Index #**
CRAIN (See also Craine)						
Crain	Bailey	Will	9/26/1865	Fauquier Co.	Chancery	1875-057
Crain	Bailey	Will	9/26/1865	Fauquier Co.	Chancery	1890-032
Crain	Bailey	Appraisement	11/9/1865	Fauquier Co.	Chancery	1890-032
Crain	Bailey	Report of Division	4/1876	Fauquier Co.	Chancery	1890-032
Crain	Bailey	Plat & Survey Of Division	4/1876	Fauquier Co.	Chancery	1890-032
Crain	Huldah	Renunciation	5/28/1866	Fauquier Co.	Chancery	1890-032
Crain	Huldah	Plat & Survey Of Dower Allotment	11/25/1875	Fauquier Co.	Chancery	1890-032
Crain	James	Will	1/24/1859	Fauquier Co.	Chancery	1883-077
Crain	Mary	Will	5/25/1840	Fauquier Co.	Chancery	1846-004
Crain	Mary	Admr. Bond	5/25/1840	Fauquier Co.	Chancery	1846-004
CRAINE (See also Crain)						
Craine	John	Will	10/26/1829	Fauquier Co.	Chancery	1834-025
Craine	John	Will	10/26/1829	Fauquier Co.	Chancery	1853-004
Craine	John	Admr. Bond	7/27/1835	Fauquier Co.	Chancery	1853-004
Craine	John (Capt.)	Sales	2/26/1840	Fauquier Co.	Chancery	1853-004
CREEL						
Creel	John	Admtrx. Bond	1807	Fauquier Co.	Probate, Box 46	1807-033
Creel	Morris	Guardian Bond	1817	Fauquier Co.	Probate, Box 49	1817-021
Creel	William	Admr. Bond	7/26/1847	Fauquier Co.	Chancery	1870-016
Creel	William	Admr. Bond	10/15/1849	Fauquier Co.	Chancery	1870-016
Creel	William	Sales	11/04/1849	Fauquier Co.	Chancery	1870-016
CRIMM						
Crimm	Harman	Admtrx. Bond	1807	Fauquier Co.	Probate, Box 46	1807-032
Crimm	John	Admr. Bond	1772	Fauquier Co.	Probate, Box 44	1772-003
CRISENBERRY (See also Quesenberry)						
Crisenberry	John	Admtrx. Bond	1797	Fauquier Co.	Probate, Box 46	1797-004

Consolidated Probate Index from the Clerks Loose Papers & the Superior Court/Circuit Court Records 1759-1919

Surname	Given Name	Instrument	Date	County	CLP Record Series	Index #
CRITTENDEN						
Crittenden	John L.	Will	4/15/1905	Fauquier Co.	Chancery	1907-025
Crittenden	Lollie M.	Guardian Appt.	9/29/1905	Fauquier Co.	Chancery	1905-014
Crittenden	Merle B.	Guardian Appt.	9/29/1905	Fauquier Co.	Chancery	1905-014
Crittenden	Sallie W.	Guardian Appt.	9/29/1905	Fauquier Co.	Chancery	1905-014
Crittenden	William L.	Guardian Appt.	9/29/1905	Fauquier Co.	Chancery	1905-014
CROPP						
Cropp	James	Will	8/10/1832	Stafford Co. VA.	Chancery	1842-007
CROSBY						
Crosby	Francis Draper	Guardian Appt.	10/3/1909	Fauquier Co.	Probate, Box 56 Superior/Circuit Ct.	1909-020
CRUMP						
Crump	Benjamin	Will	6/23/1746	Pr. Wm. Co. VA.	Land Records & Disputes	1809-010
Crump	George	Suit over Estate	1790	Fauquier Co.	Probate, Box 39	1807-002
Crump	George	Will	8/25/1857	Fauquier Co.	Chancery	1860-063
Crump	Travers	Will	2/22/1830	Fauquier Co.	Probate, Box 50	1829-001
CULVERHOUSE						
Culverhouse	Elizabeth	Report of Division Of Slaves	12/28/1837	Fauquier Co.	Chancery	1868-181
CUMINS (See also Cummins)						
Cumins	Simon	Exor. Bond	1771	Fauquier Co.	Probate, Box 44	1771-008
CUMMINS (See also Cumins)						
Cummins	Alexander	Admr. Bond	1812	Fauquier Co.	Probate, Box 47	1812-016
Cummins	Daniel	Plat & Survey Of Division	2/28/1819	Fauquier Co.	Chancery	1824-020
Cummins	Malachia	Admtrx. Bond	1769	Fauquier Co.	Probate, Box 44	1769-006
CUNDIFF						
Cundiff	Lettice	Admr. Bond	1814	Fauquier Co.	Probate, Box 47	1814-008
CUNNINGHAM						
Cunningham	John	Admtrx. Bond	1786	Fauquier Co.	Probate, Box 45	1786-010 OS Probate
CURLETT/CURLETTE						
Curlett	Susan Qualls	Will	12/27/1877	Fauquier Co.	Chancery	1883-062
Curlette	Susan Qualls	Will	12/24/1877	Fauquier Co.	Chancery	1889-088
Curlette	Susan Qualls	Will	2/5/1870	Fauquier Co.	Chancery	1905-048
CURRY						
Curry	Elizabeth	Will	6/5/1911	Baltimore, MD.	Chancery	1911-001

Consolidated Probate Index from the Clerks Loose Papers & the Superior Court/Circuit Court Records 1759-1919

Surname	**Given Name**	**Instrument**	**Date**	**County**	**CLP Record Series**	**Index #**
DAGG						
Dagg	John	Will	3/5/1750/51	Pr. Wm. Co. VA.	Land Records & Disputes	1799-012
DANIEL						
Daniel	Charles	Admr. Appt.	12/2/1904	Fauquier Co.	Probate, Box 55 Superior/Circuit Ct.	1904-011
DARNALL						
Darnall	David	Exor. Bond	1786	Fauquier Co.	Probate, Box 45	1786-005
Darnall	Jeremiah	Admr. Acct.	1796	Fauquier Co.	Chancery	1803-066
Darnall	Morgan	Exor. Bond	1766	Fauquier Co.	Probate, Box 44	1766-012
Darnall	William	Exor. Bond	1771	Fauquier Co.	Probate, Box 44	1771-001
DAVIS						
Davis	Alexander	Extrx. Bond	1812	Fauquier Co.	Probate, Box 47	1812-003
Davis	Benjamin	Report of Division Of Slaves	3/30/1838	Fauquier Co.	Chancery	1838-047
Davis	John C.	Appraisement	11/26/1860	Fauquier Co.	Chancery	1875-062
Davis	Judith	Admr. Bond	1812	Fauquier Co.	Probate, Box 47	1812-018
Davis	Lucy	Admr. Bond	1807	Fauquier Co.	Probate, Box 46	1807-008
Davis	Malinda	Guardian Bond	1810	Fauquier Co.	Probate, Box 49	1810-013
Davis	Mary	Petition	1812	Fauquier Co.	Probate, Box 39	1812-010
Davis	Mary	Appraisement of Slaves	2/3/1844	Fauquier Co.	Probate, Box 50	1853-001
Davis	Thomas	Admtrx. Bond	1768	Fauquier Co.	Probate, Box 44	1768-005
Davis	Travis	Appraisement of Slaves	3/14/1853	Fauquier Co.	Probate, Box 50	1853-001
Davis	William	Admr. Bond	1810	Fauquier Co.	Probate, Box 47	1810-011
Davis	William	Admtrx. Bond	1812	Fauquier Co.	Probate, Box 47	1812-010
DAWSON						
Dawson	Lydia	Will	9/5/1914	Fauquier Co.	Probate, Box 50 Addendum Folder	1914-001
DAY						
Day	Baldwin	Guardian Acct.	1815	Fauquier Co.	Probate, Box 49	1815-024
Day	Baldwin	Will	12/28/1852	Fauquier Co.	Chancery	1887-062
Day	Baldwin	Will	12/28/1853	Fauquier Co.	Chancery	1889-018
Day	Baldwin	Inventory + Appraisement	4/1/1853	Fauquier Co.	Chancery	1889-018
Day	Baldwin	Will	12/28/1852	Fauquier Co.	Chancery	1872-060

Consolidated Probate Index from the Clerks Loose Papers & the Superior Court/Circuit Court Records 1759-1919

Surname	Given Name	Instrument	Date	County	CLP Record Series	Index #
DAY (Cont.)						
Day	Baldwin	Exor. Acct.	7/1/1869	Fauquier Co.	Chancery	1872-064
Day	Baldwin	Notice of Will Probate	12/28/1852	Fauquier Co.	Chancery	1883-026
Day	Baldwin	Will	12/28/1853	Fauquier Co.	Chancery	1889-018
Day	Cassandra	Will	1/24/1848	Fauquier Co.	Chancery	1883-026
Day	Cossom	Exor. Bond	1815	Fauquier Co.	Probate, Box 47	1815-005
Day	Jane	Will	4/25/1898	Fauquier Co.	Chancery	1900-040
Day	Paul	Admr. Appt.	1/25/1871	Fauquier Co.	Chancery	1883-026
Day	Paul (Mrs.)	Plat & Survey Of Division	12/23/1877	Fauquier Co.	Chancery	1883-026
DEAN						
Dean	Thomas	Relinquishment	12/23/1840	Fauquier Co.	Chancery	1849-046
Dean	Thomas	Affidavit proving Death (d. 9/1/1852)	9/17/1852	Parke Co. IN.	Chancery	1849-046
DeBUTTS						
DeButts,	--- Parson	Record Search for Lands devised by fraudulent Will	4/27/1801	Fauquier Co.	Land Records	1801-007
DeButts	Rosa E.	Admr. Appt.	11/19/1910	Fauquier Co.	Probate, Box 56 Superior/Circuit Ct.	1910-002
DeButts	S. M. M.	Trustee Acct.	4/6/1869	Fauquier Co.	Probate, Box 53 Superior/Circuit Ct.	1869-002
DeButts	Sarah	Trustee Acct.	4/21/1858	Fauquier Co.	Probate, Box 52 Superior/Circuit Ct.	1858-008
DENEALE						
Deneale	Elizabeth	Will	2/25/1858	Fauquier Co.	Chancery	1858-001
Deneale	Elizabeth	Guardian Bond	10/14/1846	Fauquier Co.	Chancery	1846-052
Deneale	Elizabeth	Guardian Acct.	10/8/1851	Fauquier Co.	Probate, Box 52 Superior/Circuit Ct.	1851-007
Deneale	Elizabeth	Guardian Acct.	1851-1852	Fauquier Co.	Chancery	1858-040
Deneale	Elizabeth	Guardian Acct.	9/21/1855	Fauquier Co.	Probate, Box 52 Superior/Circuit Ct.	1855-002
Deneale	George E.	Guardian Bond	1816	Fauquier Co.	Probate, Box 49	1816-005
Deneale	George E.	Guardian Bond	12/23/1816	Fauquier Co.	Chancery	1858-031
Deneale	Jane F.	Guardian Bond	1816	Fauquier Co.	Probate, Box 49	1816-005

Consolidated Probate Index from the Clerks Loose Papers & the Superior Court/Circuit Court Records 1759-1919

Surname	**Given Name**	**Instrument**	**Date**	**County**	**CLP Record Series**	**Index #**
DENEALE (Cont.)						
Deneale	Janet S.	Guardian Acct.	10/8/1851	Fauquier Co.	Probate, Box 52 Superior/Circuit Ct.	1851-005
Deneale	Jeannette S.	Guardian Acct.	9/21/1855	Fauquier Co.	Probate, Box 52 Superior/Circuit Ct.	1855-002
Deneale	Janette	Guardian Bond	10/14/1846	Fauquier Co.	Chancery	1846-052
Deneale	Janette	Guardian Acct.	1851-1852	Fauquier Co.	Chancery	1858-040
Deneale	Mary C.	Guardian Bond	1816	Fauquier Co.	Probate, Box 49	1816-005
Deneale	Mary C.	Guardian Bond	12/23/1816	Fauquier Co.	Chancery	1858-031
Deneale	Susan	Guardian Bond	10/14/1846	Fauquier Co.	Chancery	1846-052
Deneale	Susan	Guardian Acct.	10/8/1851	Fauquier Co.	Probate, Box 52 Superior/Circuit Ct.	1851-006
Deneale	Susan	Guardian Acct.	1851-1852	Fauquier Co.	Chancery	1858-040
Deneale	Susan	Guardian Acct.	9/21/1855	Fauquier Co.	Probate, Box 52 Superior/Circuit Ct.	1855-002
Deneale	William J.	Guardian Bond	1816	Fauquier Co.	Probate, Box 49	1816-005
Deneale	William S.	Guardian Bond	12/23/1816	Fauquier Co.	Chancery	1858-031
DENT						
Dent	George	Admr. Appt.	12/1/1838	Fauquier Co.	Chancery	1866-004
Dent	George	Will	11/25/1844	Fauquier Co.	Chancery	1859-003
Dent	George	Will	11/25/1844	Fauquier Co.	Chancery	1888-006
Dent	George	Admr. Bond	12/25/1844	Fauquier Co.	Chancery	1888-006
Dent	George	Appraisement	11/1844	Fauquier Co.	Chancery	1888-006
Dent	George	Sales	12/17/1844	Fauquier Co.	Chancery	1888-006
Dent	George	Admr. Bond	11/23/1880	Fauquier Co.	Chancery	1888-006
Dent	Grace	Guardian Bond	1803	Fauquier Co.	Probate, Box 49	1803-006
Dent	John H.	Will	4/17/1858	Fauquier Co.	Probate, Box 52 Superior/Circuit Ct.	1858-012
Dent	Judith A.	Guardian Bond	1812	Fauquier Co.	Probate, Box 49 Superior/Circuit Ct.	1812-005

Consolidated Probate Index from the Clerks Loose Papers & the Superior Court/Circuit Court Records 1759-1919

Surname	Given Name	Instrument	Date	County	CLP Record Series	Index #
DENT (Cont.)						
Dent	Warren	Admr. Bond	1807	Fauquier Co.	Probate, Box 46	1807-025
Dent	William	Admr. Bond	7/25/1836	Fauquier Co.	Chancery	1859-003
DERMONT						
Dermont	James	Admtrx. Bond	1786	Fauquier Co.	Probate, Box 45	1786-013 OS Probate
DIGGES (See also Diggs)						
Digges	Edward	Heirs	7/2/1902	Fauquier Co.	Chancery	1906-051
Digges	Jane E.	Will	6/23/1879	Fauquier Co.	Chancery	1906-051
Digges	Ludwell	Will	3/28/1836	Fauquier Co.	Chancery	1855-006
Digges	Ludwell	Exor. Acct.	10/10/1836	Fauquier Co.	Chancery	1855-006
Digges	Ludwell	Exor. Acct.	5/30/1838	Fauquier Co.	Probate, Box 50	1838-001
Digges	Ludwell	Exor. Acct.	1841	Fauquier Co.	Chancery	1854-001
Digges	Ludwell	Division of Slaves	5/13/1841	Fauquier Co.	Chancery	1855-006
Digges	Porcia L.	Will	6/23/1879	Fauquier Co.	Chancery	1906-01
Digges	Sarah	Guardian Bond	1777	Fauquier Co.	Probate, Box 48	1777-001
DIGGS (See also Digges)						
Diggs	Anna Elizabeth	Guardian Appt.	10/19/1888	Randolph Co. MO.	Chancery	1906-022
Diggs	Laura	Guardian Appt.	11/13/1885	New Macenia Co. MO.	Chancery	1906-022
DIXON						
Dixon	-----	Admr. Bond	1807	Fauquier Co.	Probate, Box 46	1807-013
Dixon	Alexander	Guardian Chosen	1/28/1833	Fauquier Co.	Chancery	1835-017
Dixon	Alexander	Guardian Appt.	1/28/1833	Fauquier Co.	Chancery	1844-013
Dixon	Alice	Guardian Chosen	1/28/1833	Fauquier Co.	Chancery	1835-017
Dixon	Alice	Guardian Appt.	1/28/1833	Fauquier Co.	Chancery	1844-013
Dixon	Charles C.	Guardian Chosen	1/28/1833	Fauquier Co.	Chancery	1835-017
Dixon	Charles C.	Guardian Appt.	1/28/1833	Fauquier Co.	Chancery	1844-013
Dixon	James	Admr. Acct.	4/15/1859	Fauquier Co.	Probate, Box 52 Superior/Circuit Ct.	1859-002
Dixon	James	Admr. Acct.	9/4/1877	Fauquier Co.	Probate, Box 54 Superior/Circuit Ct.	1877-002

Consolidated Probate Index from the Clerks Loose Papers & the Superior Court/Circuit Court Records 1759-1919

Surname	Given Name	Instrument	Date	County	CLP Record Series	Index #
DIXON (Cont.)						
Dixon	John	Guardian Chosen	1/28/1833	Fauquier Co.	Chancery	1835-017
Dixon	John	Guardian Appt.	1/28/1833	Fauquier Co.	Chancery	1844-013
Dixon	John	Guardian Acct.	11/24/1834	Fauquier Co.	Chancery	1844-013
Dixon	John	Guardian Acct.	9/21/1835	Fauquier Co.	Chancery	1844-013
Dixon	John	Guardian Acct.	9/28/1835	Fauquier Co.	Chancery	1844-013
Dixon	John	Admr. Appt.	3/29/1843	Fauquier Co.	Chancery	1844-013
Dixon	John	Plat & Survey of Estate	11/3/1843	Fauquier Co.	Chancery	1844-010
Dixon	John	Report of Division Of Slaves	12/28/1843	Fauquier Co.	Chancery	1844-010
Dixon	Lucius	Guardian Chosen	1/28/1833	Fauquier Co.	Chancery	1835-017
Dixon	Lucius	Guardian Appt.	1/28/1833	Fauquier Co.	Chancery	1844-013
Dixon	Maria	Committee Acct.	Undated	Fauquier Co.	Chancery	1835-017
Dixon	Turner	Estate Acct.	Undated	Fauquier Co.	Chancery	1830-129
Dixon	Turner	Division	1828	Fauquier Co.	Chancery	1831-030
Dixon	Turner	Estate Acct.	1823	Fauquier Co.	Chancery	1834-033
Dixon	Turner	Estate Acct.	11/26/1824	Fauquier Co.	Chancery	1834-033
Dixon	Turner	Admr. Acct.	1/25/1825	Fauquier Co.	Chancery	1834-033
Dixon	Turner	Act of Relief	Undated	Fauquier Co.	Chancery	1835-017
Dixon	Turner	Sales List of Slaves	8/26/1848	Fauquier Co.	Chancery	1848-052
DOBIE						
Dobie	Ann	Guardian Bond	1801	Fauquier Co.	Probate, Box 48	1801-010
Dobie	Eliza	Guardian Bond	1801	Fauquier Co.	Probate, Box 48	1801-010
Dobie	Hannah	Guardian Bond	1812	Fauquier Co.	Probate, Box 49	1812-009
Dobie	James	Guardian Bond	1801	Fauquier Co.	Probate, Box 48	1801-010
Dobie	Peggy	Guardian Bond	1801	Fauquier Co.	Probate, Box 48	1801-010
Dobie	Polly	Guardian Bond	1801	Fauquier Co.	Probate, Box 48	1801-002
Dobie	William	Guardian Bond	1801	Fauquier Co.	Probate, Box 48	1801-002
Dobie	William	Guardian Bond	1812	Fauquier Co.	Probate, Box 49	1812-004

Consolidated Probate Index from the Clerks Loose Papers & the Superior Court/Circuit Court Records 1759-1919

Surname	Given Name	Instrument	Date	County	CLP Record Series	Index #
DODD						
Dodd	Ann	Admr. Acct.	10/25/1825	Fauquier Co.	Chancery	1855-025
Dodd	Ann	Sales	2/22/1817	Fauquier Co.	Chancery	1859-057
Dodd	Benjamin	Guardian Acct.	1828	Fauquier Co.	Probate, Box 50	1828-001
Dodd	Benjamin	Will	7/24/1815	Fauquier Co.	Chancery	1849-046
Dodd	Benjamin	Exor. Bond	8/27/1821	Fauquier Co.	Chancery	1849-046
Dodd	Benjamin	Heirs	Undated	Fauquier Co.	Chancery	1849-046
Dodd	Benjamin	Sale of Slaves	2/23/1840	Fauquier Co.	Chancery	1849-046
Dodd	Benjamin	Report of Division	4/1/1842	Fauquier Co.	Chancery	1849-046
Dodd	Benjamin	Plat & Survey Of Division	4/1/1842	Fauquier Co.	Chancery	1849-046
Dodd	Bennett	Admr. Bond	10/27/1840	Fauquier Co.	Chancery	1854-052
Dodd	Bennett	Inventory + Appraisement	1/27/1841	Fauquier Co.	Probate, Box 50	1841-001
Dodd	Elizabeth	Inventory	11/30/1840	Fauquier Co.	Chancery	1849-046
Dodd	Elizabeth	Sales	12/10/1840	Fauquier Co.	Chancery	1849-046
Dodd	John	Exors. Bond	1815	Fauquier Co.	Probate, Box 47	1815-017
Dodd	Levi	Admr. Acct.	1823	Fauquier Co.	Chancery	1824-013
Dodd	Mahethalem	Dower Allotment	12/31/1813	Fauquier Co.	Probate, Box 50	1813-002
Dodd	Mahethalem	Plat & Survey of Dower Allotment	3/3/1819	Fauquier Co.	Chancery	1820-013
Dodd	Mahethalem	Will	4/2/1878	Fauquier Co.	Probate, Box 54 Superior/Circuit Ct.	1878-002
Dodd	Nathaniel	Exors. Bond	1784	Fauquier Co.	Probate, Box 45	1784-008
Dodd	Nathaniel	Admrs. Bond	1813	Fauquier Co.	Probate, Box 47	1813-020
Dodd	Nathaniel	Division	12/31/1813	Fauquier Co.	Probate, Box 39	1813-002
Dodd	Nathaniel	Division of Slaves	12/31/1813	Fauquier Co.	Probate, Box 50	1813-002
Dodd	Nathaniel	Admr. Acct.	2/23/1819	Fauquier Co.	Probate, Box 50	1819-003
Dodd	Nathaniel	Sales	12/13/1813	Fauquier Co.	Chancery	1855-025

Consolidated Probate Index from the Clerks Loose Papers & the Superior Court/Circuit Court Records 1759-1919

Surname	Given Name	Instrument	Date	County	CLP Record Series	Index #
DODD (Cont.)						
Dodd	Nathaniel	Admr. Acct.	1/25/1819	Fauquier Co.	Chancery	1855-025
Dodd	Nathaniel	Admr. Acct.	10/25/1825	Fauquier Co.	Chancery	1855-025
Dodd	Sarah E.	Plat & Survey Of Division	6/5/1873	Fauquier Co.	Chancery	1873-066
Dodd	Susan	Admr. Appt.	1/25/1871	Fauquier Co.	Chancery	1883-026
Dodd	Susan	Admr. Bond	12/19/1881	Fauquier Co.	Probate, Box 54 Superior/Circuit Ct.	1881-005
Dodd	William	Guardian Acct.	1828	Fauquier Co.	Probate, Box 50	1828-001
DODSON						
Dodson	Abraham	Exors. Bond	1768	Fauquier Co.	Probate, Box 44	1768-006
Dodson	Greenham	Exor. Bond	1777	Fauquier Co.	Probate, Box 44	1777-007
DOGETT (See also Doggett)						
Dogett	Benjamin	Admr. Bond	1778	Fauquier Co.	Probate, Box 45	1778-002
DOGGETT (See also Dogett)						
Doggett	Molly	Guardian Bond	1779	Fauquier Co.	Probate, Box 48	1779-005
Doggett	Sukey	Guardian Bond	1779	Fauquier Co.	Probate, Box 48	1779-005
Doggett	Thomas	Guardian Bond	1779	Fauquier Co.	Probate, Box 48	1779-005
DONALDSON						
Donaldson	Robert	Admr. Bond	1808	Fauquier Co.	Probate, Box 46	1808-023
Donaldson	Stephen	Admr. Bond	1777	Fauquier Co.	Probate, Box 44	1777-011
DOUGLAS						
Douglas	Evalyn D.	Guardian Appt.	1/23/1905	Fauquier Co.	Probate, Box 55 Superior/Circuit Ct.	1905-001
DOUTHAT						
Douthat	Mary	Report of Partition	8/1894	Fauquier Co.	Chancery	1898-022
Douthat	Mary	Plat & Survey Of Division	8/1894	Fauquier Co.	Chancery	1898-022
DOWDELL						
Dowdell	James G.	Will	4/9/1888	Loudoun Co. VA.	Chancery	1889-054

Consolidated Probate Index from the Clerks Loose Papers & the Superior Court/Circuit Court Records 1759-1919

Surname	**Given Name**	**Instrument**	**Date**	**County**	**CLP Record Series**	**Index #**
DOWELL						
Dowell	Ann	Will	9/12/1867	Fauquier Co.	Probate, Box 53 Superior/Circuit Ct.	1867-003
Dowell	Ann	Exor. Bond	9/12/1867	Fauquier Co.	Probate, Box 53 Superior/Circuit Ct.	1867-003
Dowell	Ann	Exor. Acct.	9/7/1870	Fauquier Co.	Probate, Box 53 Superior/Circuit Ct.	1870-005
Dowell	Nehemiah	Admr. Bond	1806	Fauquier Co.	Probate, Box 46	1806-010
Dowell	Octavia	Will	5/25/1879	Fauquier Co.	Chancery	1900-039
DOWNES (See also Downs)						
Downes	Henry	Will	5/23/1835	Fauquier Co.	Chancery	1841-009
DOWNING						
Downing	John H.	Will	8/28/1893	Fauquier Co.	Chancery	1900-023
Downing	John H.	Report of Division	8/16/1900	Fauquier Co.	Chancery	1900-023
Downing	John H.	Plat & Survey Of Division	1900	Fauquier Co.	Chancery	1900-023
DOWNS (See also Downes)						
Downs	James	Will	5/28/1894	Fauquier Co.	Chancery	1895-061
DRUMMOND						
Drummond	Aaron	Report of Division	11/25/1840	Fauquier Co.	Chancery	1878-022
Drummond	Aaron	Plat & Survey Of Division	11/25/1840	Fauquier Co.	Chancery	1878-022
Drummond	Aaron (Mrs.)	Dower Allotment	2/21/1872	Fauquier Co.	Chancery	1878-022
Drummond	Aaron (Mrs.)	Plat & Survey of Dower Allotment	2/21/1872	Fauquier Co.	Chancery	1878-022
Drummond	James	Admr. Bond	1766	Fauquier Co.	Probate, Box 44	1766-004
Drummond	Mary	Guardian Bond	1784	Fauquier Co.	Probate, Box 48	1784-001
Drummond	Molly	Guardian Bond	1779	Fauquier Co.	Probate, Box 48	1779-004
Drummond	Sally	Guardian Bond	1779	Fauquier Co.	Probate, Box 48	1779-004
Drummond	Sarah	Guardian Bond	1784	Fauquier Co.	Probate, Box 48	1784-001
Drummond	William	Admtrx. Bond	1776	Fauquier Co.	Probate, Box 44	1776-004
DUFF						
Duff	George	Will	12/25/1854	Fauquier Co.	Chancery	1885-055

Consolidated Probate Index from the Clerks Loose Papers & the Superior Court/Circuit Court Records 1759-1919

Surname	Given Name	Instrument	Date	County	CLP Record Series	Index #
DUFFEY						
Duffey	Ally	Guardian Bond	1797	Fauquier Co.	Probate, Box 48	1808-012
Duffey	Ann	Guardian Bond	1808	Fauquier Co.	Probate, Box 48	1808-004
Duffey	Bernard	Guardian Bond	1808	Fauquier Co.	Probate, Box 48	1808-004
Duffey	Polley	Guardian Bond	1797	Fauquier Co.	Probate, Box 48	1808-012
DUGARD						
Dugard	John	Admrs. Bond	1777	Fauquier Co.	Probate, Box 44	1777-012
DULANEY (See also Dulany)						
Dulaney	Bladen	Will	1/27/1857	Fauquier Co.	Chancery	1861-017
Dulaney	Bladen	Will	1/27/1857	Fauquier Co.	Chancery	1894-072
Dulaney	Bladen	Exor. Acct.	6/1/1867	Fauquier Co.	Chancery	1894-072
Dulaney	Bladen	Plat & Survey of Division of "Cloverland"	8/6/1870	Fauquier Co.	Chancery	1894-072
Dulaney	Bladen	Plat & Survey of Division of "Saint's Hill"	12/21/1878	Fauquier Co.	Chancery	1894-072
DULANY (See also Dulaney)						
Dulany	Bladen	Will	1/27/1857	Fauquier Co.	Chancery	1875-007
Dulany	French	Report of Division	10/8/1874	Fauquier Co.	Chancery	1886-033
Dulany	French	Plat & Survey Of Division	10/1/1874	Fauquier Co.	Chancery	1886-033
Dulany	John B.	Will	12/9/1878	Fauquier Co.	Chancery	1908-046
Dulany	William S.	Plat & Survey Of Division	11/1866	Fauquier Co.	Chancery	1866-068
Dulany	William S.	Admr. Appt.	6/22/1874	Fauquier Co.	Chancery	1875-020
DULIN						
Dulin	William	Court order to Appraise Estate	7/1801	Fauquier Co.	Probate, Box 39	1801-003
DUNBAR						
Dunbar	John A.	Admr. Acct.	11/27/1880	Fauquier Co.	Chancery	1896-016
Dunbar	Thomas S.	Will	7/31/1908	Fauquier Co.	Chancery	1909-028

Consolidated Probate Index from the Clerks Loose Papers & the Superior Court/Circuit Court Records 1759-1919

Surname	Given Name	Instrument	Date	County	CLP Record Series	Index #
DUNCAN						
Duncan	Charles	Appraisement	3/23/1819	Fauquier Co.	Probate, Box 50	1818-002
Duncan	Charles	Sales	2/20/1820	Fauquier Co.	Probate, Box 39	1818-005
Duncan	Charles	Report of Division with Plat & Survey	9/18/1857	Fauquier Co.	Chancery	1857-036
Duncan	Charles	Will	2/23/1857	Fauquier Co.	Chancery	1876-003
Duncan	Charles	Exor. Acct.	6/15/1858	Fauquier Co.	Chancery	1876-003
Duncan	Charles	Exor. Acct.	7/7/1859	Fauquier Co.	Chancery	1876-003
Duncan	Charles	Report of Division	6/1889	Fauquier Co.	Chancery	1889-052
Duncan	Charles	Plat & Survey Of Division	6/1889	Fauquier Co.	Chancery	1889-052
Duncan	Charles P.	Guardian Appt.	2/2/1857	Henry Co. MO.	Chancery	1876-003
Duncan	Edwin C.	Guardian Appt.	2/2/1857	Henry Co. MO.	Chancery	1876-003
Duncan	Elzy B.	Guardian Appt.	2/2/1857	Henry Co. MO.	Chancery	1876-003
Duncan	Harriett	Guardian Appt.	2/2/1857	Henry Co. Mo.	Chancery	1876-003
Duncan	Joseph	Will	9/23/1793	Fauquier Co.	Chancery	1798-010
Duncan	Juliet E.	Guardian Appt.	2/2/1857	Henry Co. MO.	Chancery	1876-003
Duncan	Lucinda	Will	9/27/1869	Fauquier Co.	Chancery	1876-003
Duncan	Lucinda	Will	9/27/1869	Fauquier Co.	Chancery	1890-051
Duncan	Lydia	Exor. Bond	1797	Fauquier Co.	Probate, Box 46	1797-012
Duncan	Sarah E.	Guardian Appt.	2/2/1857	Henry Co. MO.	Chancery	1876-00

Consolidated Probate Index from the Clerks Loose Papers & the Superior Court/Circuit Court Records 1759-1919

Surname	Given Name	Instrument	Date	County	CLP Record Series	Index #
EATON						
Eaton	John	Admr. Bond	1782	Fauquier Co.	Probate, Box 45	1782-002
EDMONDS						
Edmonds	Alexander	Guardian Bon	1811	Fauquier Co.	Probate, Box 49	1811-005
Edmonds	Courtney Ann	Will	8/15/1839	Alexandria Co. VA.	Chancery	1849-016
Edmonds	Elias	Exor. Bond	1784	Fauquier Co.	Probate, Box 45	1784-010
Edmonds	Elias	Guardian Bond	1800	Fauquier Co.	Probate, Box 48	1800-003
Edmonds	Elias	Admr. Bond	5/27/1811	Fauquier Co.	Probate, Box 50	1811-001
Edmonds	Elias	Admrs. Bond	1811	Fauquier Co.	Probate, Box 47	1811-008
Edmonds	Elias	Plat & Survey	9/4/18--	Fauquier Co.	Chancery	1824-034
Edmonds	Elias Jr.	Guardian Bond	1806	Fauquier Co.	Probate, Box 49	1806-010
Edmonds	Elizabeth	Guardian Bond	1806	Fauquier Co.	Probate, Box 49	1806-009
Edmonds	Elizabeth	Guardian Bond	1814	Fauquier Co.	Probate, Box 49	1814-005
Edmonds	Elizabeth E.	Guardian Chosen	3/29/1832	Fauquier Co.	Probate, Box 40	1832-003
Edmonds	Helen	Guardian Bond	1811	Fauquier Co.	Probate, Box 49	1811-005
Edmonds	John	Will (Nuncupative)	3/4/1799	Fauquier Co.	Probate, Box 39	1799-003
Edmonds	John	Appraisement	8/27/1829	Fauquier Co.	Probate, Box 50	1828-003
Edmonds	John	Inventory + Appraisement	8/27/1829	Fauquier Co.	Chancery	1855-013
Edmonds	John William	Guardian Bond	1811	Fauquier Co.	Probate, Box 49	1811-005
Edmonds	Josephine	Guardian Bond	12/8/1884	Fauquier Co.	Probate, Box 54 Superior/Circuit Ct	1884-005
Edmonds	Judith S.	Guardian Bond	1811	Fauquier Co.	Probate, Box 49	1811-005
Edmonds	Lewis	Admr. Bond	9/12/1857	Fauquier Co.	Probate, Box 52 Superior/Circuit Ct	1857-004
Edmonds	Lewis	Appraisement	11/23/1857	Fauquier Co.	Probate, Box 52 Superior/Circuit Ct.	1857-007
Edmonds	Lewis	Sales	1/11/1858	Fauquier Co.	Probate, Box 52 Superior/Circuit Ct.	1858-006
Edmonds	Margaret B.	Will	10/24/1871	Fauquier Co.	Chancery	1897-012
Edmonds	Octavia	Guardian Bond	1804	Fauquier Co.	Probate, Box 49	1804-008

Consolidated Probate Index from the Clerks Loose Papers & the Superior Court/Circuit Court Records 1759-1919

Surname	Given Name	Instrument	Date	County	CLP Record Series	Index #
EDMONDS (Cont.)						
Edmonds	Richard C.	Guardian Bond	1811	Fauquier Co.	Probate, Box 49	1811-005
Edmonds	Sarah Ann	Guardian Bond	1814	Fauquier Co.	Probate, Box 49	1814-005
Edmonds	Sydnor	Admr. Bond	10/9/1943	Fauquier Co.	Probate, Box 51	1843-001
Edmonds	William F.	Exor. Bond	11/22/1822	Fauquier Co.	Superior/Circuit Ct. Chancery	1855-053
EDRINGTON						
Edrington	Margaret A.	Guardian Bond	1820	Fauquier Co.	Probate, Box 49	1820-001
EDWARDS						
Edwards	Benjamin	Admr. Appt.	9/4/1866	Baltimore, MD.	Chancery	1874-060
Edwards	John	Admr. Bond	1771	Fauquier Co.	Probate, Box 44	1771-004
Edwards	John	Admrs. Bond	1814	Fauquier Co.	Probate, Box 47	1814-020
Edwards	John	Guardian Bond	1814	Fauquier Co.	Probate, Box 49	1814-001
Edwards	William	Admrs. Bond	1815	Fauquier Co.	Probate, Box 47	1815-004
ELDRED						
Eldred	E. B.	Appraisement	8/12/1877	Fauquier Co.	Chancery	1908-052
Eldred	E. B.	Admr. Bond	2/23/1897	Fauquier Co.	Chancery	1900-002
Eldred	Eppa A.	Guardian Bond	2/23/1897	Fauquier Co.	Chancery	1900-002
ELKINS						
Elkins	David	Will	1/21/1828	Culpeper Co. VA.	Chancery	1835-023
Elkins	David	Will	1/21/1828	Culpeper Co. VA.	Chancery	1835-043
ELLIOTT						
Elliott	Elizabeth	Guardian Bond	1783	Fauquier Co.	Probate, Box 48	1783-001
Elliott	John	Admr. Acct. Settled	12/1802	Fauquier Co.	Chancery	1803-068
Elliott	John	Inventory	Undated	Fauquier Co.	Chancery	1803-068
Elliott	John	Division	8/15/1803	Fauquier Co.	Chancery	1803-068
Elliott	Milly	Guardian Bond	1783	Fauquier Co.	Probate, Box 48	1783-001
Elliott	Mima	Guardian Bond	1783	Fauquier Co.	Probate, Box 48	1783-001
Elliott	Molly	Guardian Bond	1783	Fauquier Co.	Probate, Box 48	1783-001

Consolidated Probate Index from the Clerks Loose Papers & the Superior Court/Circuit Court Records 1759-1919

Surname	Given Name	Instrument	Date	County	CLP Record Series	Index #
ELLIOTT (Cont.)						
Elliott	Reuben	Exor. Bond	1780	Fauquier Co.	Probate, Box 45	1780-005
Elliott	Reuben	Guardian Bond	1783	Fauquier Co.	Probate, Box 48	1783-001
Elliott	Thomas	Guardian Bond	1783	Fauquier Co.	Probate, Box 48	1783-001
ELLIS						
Ellis	James	Exor. Bond	1815	Fauquier Co.	Probate, Box 47	1815-019
Ellis	John	Exor. Bond	1779	Fauquier Co.	Probate, Box 45	1779-009
Ellis	Nellie B.	Guardian Appt.	9/25/1905	Fauquier Co.	Probate, Box 55 Superior/Circuit Ct.	1905-013
Ellis	Owen	Admr. Bond	1809	Fauquier Co.	Probate, Box 47	1809-014
EMBREY (See also Embry)						
Embrey	Elizabeth	Relinquishment	1818	Fauquier Co.	Probate, Box 39	1818-009
Embrey	Fanny	Committee Appt.	4/7/1857	Fauquier Co.	Chancery	1867-002
Embrey	Jeptha	Plat & Survey of Dower Allotment	4/9/1877	Fauquier Co.	Chancery	1899-003
Embrey	Jeptha	Division	5/25/1881	Fauquier Co.	Chancery	1899-003
Embrey	Lucy	Plat & Survey of Dower Allotment	11/29/1884	Fauquier Co.	Chancery	1903-007
Embrey	Robert	Will	12/28/1857	Fauquier Co.	Chancery	1877-031
Embrey	Robert	Exor. Acct.	2/13/1859	Fauquier Co.	Chancery	1877-031
Embrey	Sarah	Heirs	Undated	Fauquier Co.	Chancery	1844-009
Embrey	William	Will	5/25/1856	Fauquier Co.	Chancery	1903-004
Embrey	William	Will	5/25/1857	Fauquier Co.	Chancery	1870-044
Embrey	William	Report of Division	3/1881	Fauquier Co.	Chancery	1903-007
Embrey	William	Report of Division Of Slaves	4/16/1860	Fauquier Co.	Chancery	1903-007
Embrey	William Sr.	Report of Division Of Slaves	6/24/1829	Fauquier Co.	Chancery	1868-209
EMBRY (See also Embrey)						
Embry	George	Court order for Sales	12/1798	Fauquier Co.	Probate, Box 39	1798-001
Embry	George	Guardian Chosen	1804	Fauquier Co.	Probate, Box 39	1804-003
Embry	George	Guardian Bond	1804	Fauquier Co.	Probate, Box 49	1804-003

Consolidated Probate Index from the Clerks Loose Papers & the Superior Court/Circuit Court Records 1759-1919

Surname	Given Name	Instrument	Date	County	CLP Record Series	Index #
EMBRY (Cont.)						
Embry	Lewis	Guardian Chosen	1804	Fauquier Co.	Probate, Box 39	1804-003
Embry	Lewis	Guardian Bond	1804	Fauquier Co.	Probate, Box 49	1804-003
Embry	Robert	Guardian Bond	1791	Fauquier Co.	Probate, Box 48	1791-002
Embry	Robert	Exor. Bond	1815	Fauquier Co.	Probate, Box 47	1815-004
EMMONS						
Emmons	James	Will (Extract)	1839	Fauquier Co.	Chancery	1846-057
Emmons	James	Will	11/25/1839	Fauquier Co.	Chancery	1853-002
Emmons	James	Will	11/25/1839	Fauquier Co.	Chancery	1853-006
Emmons	James	Will	11/25/1839	Fauquier Co.	Chancery	1854-006
Emmons	James	Will	11/25/1839	Fauquier Co.	Chancery	1859-050
Emmons	Joseph	Admr. Bond	1767	Fauquier Co.	Probate, Box 44	1767-006
EMORY						
Emory	Robert (Rev.)	Will	5/25/1848	Baltimore, MD.	Chancery	1892-038
ENGLISH						
English	[Illegible]	Guardian Bond	1807	Fauquier Co.	Probate, Box 49	1807-010
English	Betsy	Guardian Bond	1808	Fauquier Co.	Probate, Box 49	1808-007
English	Frosty	Guardian Bond	1807	Fauquier Co.	Probate, Box 49	1807-010
English	James	Guardian Bond	1807	Fauquier Co.	Probate, Box 49	1807-011
English	Joseph	Admr. Bond	1807	Fauquier Co.	Probate, Box 47	1807-009
English	Polley	Guardian Bond	1807	Fauquier Co.	Probate, Box 49	1807-005
English	Zeph	Admr. Appt.	6/15/1887	Alexandria, VA.	Chancery	1899-016
ENGS						
Engs	Philip W.	Will	6/10/1875	New Yor, City, NY	Chancery	1880-002
ENSOR						
Ensor	George	Guardian Bond	1810	Fauquier Co.	Probate, Box 49	1810-015
Ensor	George	Admr. Bond	1810	Fauquier Co.	Probate, Box 47	1810-009
Ensor	James	Guardian Bond	1810	Fauquier Co.	Probate, Box 49	1810-015
Ensor	Jemima	Dower Allotment In Slaves	Undated	Fauquier Co.	Chancery	1848-034
Ensor	Nelly	Guardian Bond	1810	Fauquier Co.	Probate, Box 49	1810-015
Ensor	Polly	Guardian Bond	1810	Fauquier Co.	Probate, Box 49	1810-015

Consolidated Probate Index from the Clerks Loose Papers & the Superior Court/Circuit Court Records 1759-1919

Surname	Given Name	Instrument	Date	County	CLP Record Series	Index #
ENSOR (Cont.)						
Ensor	Stephen	Guardian Bond	1810	Fauquier Co.	Probate, Box 49	1810-015
Ensor	Thomas	Guardian Bond	1810	Fauquier Co.	Probate, Box 49	1810-015
ESKRIDGE						
Eskridge	Alexander W.	Guardian Bond	9/19/1855	Fauquier Co.	Chancery	1855-044
Eskridge	Andrew J.	Will	5/22/1854	Fauquier Co.	Chancery	1871-073
Eskridge	Emily	Guardian Bond	6/26/1837	Fauquier Co.	Chancery	1844-045
Eskridge	Harriet	Guardian Bond	6/26/1837	Fauquier Co.	Chancery	1844-045
Eskridge	Meredith (Mrs.)	Dower Allotment	10/15/1874	Fauquier Co.	Chancery	1875-009
Eskridge	Mildred	Guardian Bond	6/26/1837	Fauquier Co.	Chancery	1844-045
Eskridge	Samuel L.	Will	4/10/1856	Fauquier Co.	Chancery	1871-073
Eskridge	Samuel	Will	4/10/1856	Fauquier Co.	Probate, Box 52 Superior/Circuit Ct.	1856-001
Eskridge	Samuel L.	Exor. Acct.	9/5/1860	Fauquier Co.	Probate, Box 52 Superior/Circuit Ct.	1860-005
ETHERINGTON						
Etherington	Elizabeth	Admr. Bond	1778	Fauquier Co.	Probate, Box 45	1778-015
Etherington	John Sr.	Admr. Bond	1769	Fauquier Co.	Probate, Box 44	1769-002
EUSTACE						
Eustace	Elizabeth	Guardian Bond	11/12/1819	Fauquier Co.	Chancery	1858-018
Eustace	Jessie Lee	Guardian Appt.	4/20/1907	Fauquier Co.	Chancery	1911-033
Eustace	Lillian Alice	Guardian Appt.	4/20/1907	Fauquier Co.	Chancery	1911-033
Eustace	Sarah M.	Dower Allotment	12/21/1839	Fauquier Co.	Chancery	1841-002
Eustace	William	Admr. Bond	1826	Fauquier Co.	Probate, Box 47	1826-001
Eustace	William	Admtrx. Appt.	9/26/1826	Fauquier Co.	Chancery	1841-002
Eustace	William	Admtrx. Bond	9/26/1826	Fauquier Co.	Chancery	1841-002
Eustace	William	Admr. Acct.	11/28/1827	Fauquier Co.	Chancery	1841-002
Eustace	William	Sales	8/27/1828	Fauquier Co.	Chancery	1841-002
EVAN (See also Evans)						
Evan	Thomas A. H.	Estate Administration Granted by Court	1845	Fairfax Co. VA.	Chancery	1860-030

Consolidated Probate Index from the Clerks Loose Papers & the Superior Court/Circuit Court Records 1759-1919

Surname	Given Name	Instrument	Date	County	CLP Record Series	Index #
EVANS (See also Evan)						
Evans	Cadwalader	Guardian Appt.	6/13/1891	Philadelphia, PA.	Chancery	1894-063
Evans	Elisha B.	Will	5/22/1843	Fauquier Co.	Chancery	1854-049
Evans	Llewellan W.	Guardian Appt.	6/13/1891	Philadelphia, PA.	Chancery	1894-063
Evans	Richard	Inventory + Appraisement	5/27/1811	Fauquier Co.	Chancery	1837-023
Evans	Richard	Sales	4/23/1816	Fauquier Co.	Chancery	1837-023
Evans	Susannah	Will	11/17/1890	Philadelphia, PA.	Chancery	1894-063
Evans	Susannah E.	Guardian Appt.	6/13/1891	Philadelphia, PA.	Chancery	1894-063
Evans	William	Admr. Bond	1829	Fauquier Co.	Probate, Box 47	1829-001
Evans	William	Inventory +	5/1826	Fauquier Co.	Probate, Box 40	1826-001
EWELL						
Ewell	Charlotte	Will	7/7/1823	Pr. Wm. Co. VA.	Chancery	1879-002
Ewell	Jesse	Will	5/5/1805	Pr. Wm. Co. VA.	Chancery	1879-002

Consolidated Probate Index from the Clerks Loose Papers & the Superior Court/Circuit Court Records 1759-1919

Surname	Given Name	Instrument	Date	County	CLP Record Series	Index #
FAIRFAX						
Fairfax	Denny	Will	6/12/1802	Richmond Co. VA.	Chancery	1839-019
Fairfax	Denny	Certificate of Probate Granted	6/11/1805	Fauquier Co. VA.	Land Records & Disputes	1839-019
Fairfax	George William	Will	11/18/1790	Richmond Co. VA.	Land Records & Disputes	1824-011 OS Land
Fairfax	Lord Thomas	Will	3/5/1782	Frederick Co. VA.	Chancery	1839-019
FARRELL						
Farrell	William F.	Estate committed to Sheriff	1904	Fauquier Co.	Probate, Box 55 Superior/Circuit Ct.	1904-010
FARROW						
Farrow	Maria	Guardian Bond	1808	Fauquier Co.	Probate, Box 49	1808-009
Farrow	Susannah	Will	3/16/1852	Fauquier Co.	Chancery	1859-002
Farrow	Susannah	Exor. Acct.	5/1/1853	Fauquier Co.	Chancery	1859-002
FEAGAN (See also Feagans, Feagin)						
Feagan	Benjamin	Will	5/23/1870	Fauquier Co.	Chancery	1872-037
Feagan	John Sr.	Will	3/26/1849	Fauquier Co.	Chancery	1899-005
Feagan	William	Guardian Bond	1781	Fauquier Co.	Probate, Box 48	1781-002
FEAGANS (See also Feagan, Feagin)						
Feagans	Hannah	Division of Slaves	2/1/1858	Fauquier Co.	Chancery	1899-005
Feagans	John	Will	3/26/1849	Fauquier Co.	Chancery	1873-030
Feagans	John	Exor. Bond	3/26/1949	Fauquier Co.	Chancery	1873-030
FEAGIN (See also Feagan, Feagans)						
Feagin	Edward	Exor. Bond	1780	Fauquier Co.	Probate, Box 45	1780-013
FELLOWS						
Fellows	Louis P.	Will	9/25/1866	New York City, NY.	Chancery	1880-002
FERGUSON						
Ferguson	Bessie	Guardian Appt.	8/10/1908	Fauquier Co.	Probate, Box 56 Superior/Circuit Ct.	1908-013
Ferguson	Harriett	Will	8/27/1866	Fauquier Co.	Chancery	1870-030
Ferguson	William	Guardian Appt.	8/10/1908	Fauquier Co.	Probate, Box 56 Superior/Circuit Ct.	1908-013

Consolidated Probate Index from the Clerks Loose Papers & the Superior Court/Circuit Court Records 1759-1919

Surname	Given Name	Instrument	Date	County	CLP Record Series	Index #
FICKLIN						
Ficklin	Charles	Will	6/25/1816	Fauquier Co.	Chancery	1832-073
Ficklin	Frances M.	Will	12/27/1843	Stafford Co. VA.	Chancery	1871-077
Ficklin	Harriet	Guardian Bond	1816	Fauquier Co.	Probate, Box 49	1816-010
Ficklin	Strother	Will	11/6/1827	Stafford Co. VA.	Chancery	1871-077
Ficklin	William P.	Admr. Appt.	1/26/1874	Fauquier Co.	Chancery	1875-020
FIELD (See also Fields)						
Field	Betsy	Admr. Bond	1806	Fauquier Co.	Probate, Box 46	1806-022
Field	Daniel	Exor. Bond	1783	Fauquier Co.	Probate, Box 46	1783-019
FIELDING						
Fielding	Edwin	Exor. Bond	1783	Fauquier Co.	Probate, Box 45	1783-015
FIELDS (See also Field)						
Field	Daniel	Will	3/24/1783	Fauquier Co.	Probate, Box 50	1783-001
FINNIE						
Finnie	John	Exors. Bond	1760	Fauquier Co.	Probate, Box 44	1760-005
FISHBACK						
Fishback	Amanda	Guardian Bond	1/24/1831	Fauquier Co.	Probate, Box 50	1831-004
Fishback	Amanda	Guardian Bond	1/24/1831	Fauquier Co.	Chancery	1836-003
Fishback	Amanda	Guardian Bond	1/24/1831	Fauquier Co.	Chancery	1846-022
Fishback	Amanda	Guardian Acct.	Undated	Fauquier Co.	Chancery	1846-022
Fishback	Amanda	Guardian Acct. (Extract)	Undated	Fauquier Co.	Chancery	1846-022
Fishback	Amanda	Guardian Acct.	10/24/1832	Fauquier Co.	Chancery	1846-022
Fishback	Amanda	Guardian Acct.	6/23/1835	Fauquier Co.	Chancery	1846-022
Fishback	Ann	Guardian Bond	11/26/1827	Fauquier Co.	Chancery	1836-014
Fishback	Ann	Guardian Acct.	10/24/1832	Fauquier Co.	Chancery	1836-003
Fishback	Ann J.	Guardian Bond	1/24/1831	Fauquier Co.	Chancery	1846-018
Fishback	Ann J.	Guardian Bond	1/24/1831	Fauquier Co.	Probate, Box 50 Addendum Folder	1831-004
Fishback	Elvira	Guardian Acct.	1/24/1831	Fauquier Co.	Chancery	1836-003
Fishback	Enoch	Admrs. Bond	1815	Fauquier Co.	Probate, Box 47	1815-062

Consolidated Probate Index from the Clerks Loose Papers & the Superior Court/Circuit Court Records 1759-1919

Surname	Given Name	Instrument	Date	County	CLP Record Series	Index #
FISHBACK (Cont.)						
Fishback	James	Guardian Bond	11/26/1827	Fauquier Co.	Chancery	1836-014
Fishback	James	Guardian Acct.	7/30/1835	Fauquier Co.	Chancery	1863-052
Fishback	John	Guardian Bond	1799	Fauquier Co.	Probate, Box 48	1799-003
Fishback	John	Will	3/17/1828	Culpeper Co. VA.	Chancery	1882-014
Fishback	Josiah	Guardian Bond	1799	Fauquier Co.	Probate, Box 48	1799-003
Fishback	Josiah	Admr. Acct.	11/24/1851	Fauquier Co.	Chancery	1853-036
Fishback	Margaret	Guardian Acct.	1/24/1831	Fauquier Co.	Probate, Box 50 Addendum Folder	1831-004
Fishback	Margaret	Guardian Acct.	1/24/1831	Fauquier Co.	Chancery	1836-003
Fishback	Margaret	Guardian Acct.	10/24/1832	Fauquier Co.	Chancery	1836-003
Fishback	Margaret	Guardian Acct.	1/24/1831	Fauquier Co.	Chancery	1846-022
Fishback	Margaret	Guardian Acct. (Extract)	Undated	Fauquier Co.	Chancery	1846-022
Fishback	Mary	Guardian Bond	1/24/1831	Fauquier Co.	Probate, Box 50 Addendum Folder	1831-004
Fishback	Mary	Guardian Acct.	1/24/1831	Fauquier Co.	Chancery	1836-003
Fishback	Mary	Guardian Bond	11/26/1827	Fauquier Co.	Chancery	1836-006
Fishback	Mary	Guardian Bond	1/24/1831	Fauquier Co.	Chancery	1846-018
Fishback	Mary	Guardian Acct. (Extract)	Undated	Fauquier Co.	Chancery	1846-018
Fishback	Mary	Guardian Acct.	11/12/1833	Fauquier Co.	Chancery	1846-018
Fishback	Nelson	Guardian Bond	1805	Fauquier Co.	Probate, Box 49	1805-003
Fishback	Nelson	Report of Division	5/1840	Fauquier Co.	Chancery	1840-034
Fishback	Nelson	Plat & Survey Of Division	5/1840	Fauquier Co.	Chancery	1840-034
Fishback	Nelson N.	Admr. Appt.	10/23/1843	Fauquier Co.	Chancery	1868-008
Fishback	Philip	Relinquishment	1815	Fauquier Co.	Probate, Box 39	1815-062
Fishback	Philip	Estate Acct.	1/13/1828	Fauquier Co.	Chancery	1833-045
Fishback	Philip	Admr. Acct.	3/8/1830	Fauquier Co.	Chancery	1833-045
Fishback	Philip	Admr. Bond	9/24/1827	Fauquier Co.	Chancery	1859-014

Consolidated Probate Index from the Clerks Loose Papers & the Superior Court/Circuit Court Records 1759-1919

Surname	Given Name	Instrument	Date	County	CLP Record Series	Index #
FISHER						
Fisher	Harry	Committee Appt.	9/29/1909	Fauquier Co.	Probate, Box 56 Superior/Circuit Ct.	1909-017
Fisher	Harry C.	Committee Resigned	10/16/1909	Fauquier Co.	Probate, Box 56 Superior/Circuit Ct.	1909-017
Fisher	Harry C.	Committee Appt.	10/16/1909	Fauquier Co.	Probate, Box 56 Superior/Circuit Ct.	1909-017
Fisher	Samuel	Will	11/25/1841	Fauquier Co.	Chancery	1844-017
Fisher	Samuel	Will	11/25/1841	Fauquier Co.	Chancery	1855-055
Fisher	Samuel	Division of Slaves	10/1842	Fauquier Co.	Chancery	1855-055
Fisher	Samuel	Plat & Survey Of "Pine Grove"	8/23/1845	Fauquier Co.	Chancery	1855-055
Fisher	Samuel	Inventory + Appraisement of Slaves	3/20/1850	Fauquier Co.	Chancery	1855-055
Fisher	Samuel	Will	11/25/1841	Fauquier Co.	Chancery	1881-003
Fisher	Thomas	Will	5/22/1854	Fauquier Co.	Chancery	1892-074
FITZGERALD						
Fitzgerald	Elizabeth Ann	Will	2/21/1881	Fredericksburg, VA.	Chancery	1887-002
Fitzgerald	James	Will	6/7/1852	Spotsylvania Co. VA.	Chancery	1873-051
Fitzgerald	James H.	Plat & Survey Of Division	Undated	Fauquier Co.	Chancery	1873-051
Fitzgerald	Thomas	Plat & Survey	Undated	Fauquier Co.	Chancery	1873-051
FITZHUGH						
Fitzhugh	Frances T. B.	Guardian Appt.	1/24/1841	Fauquier Co.	Chancery	1846-049
Fitzhugh	Frances T. B.	Guardian Bond	1/24/1841	Fauquier Co.	Chancery	1846-049
Fitzhugh	George	Will	4/29/1823	Fauquier Co.	Chancery	1823-001
Fitzhugh	George	Will	4/29/1823	Fauquier Co.	Chancery	1835-053
Fitzhugh	George	Will	4/29/1823	Fauquier Co.	Chancery	1839-011
Fitzhugh	George	Will	4/29/1823	Fauquier Co.	Chancery	1877-053
Fitzhugh	George W's Heirs	Plat & Survey Of Division	9/16/1875	Fauquier Co.	Chancery	1875-061
Fitzhugh	George W. T.	Guardian Appt.	1/24/1841	Fauquier Co.	Chancery	1846-049
Fitzhugh	George W. T.	Guardian Bond	1/24/1841	Fauquier Co.	Chancery	1846-049

Consolidated Probate Index from the Clerks Loose Papers & the Superior Court/Circuit Court Records 1759-1919

Surname	Given Name	Instrument	Date	County	CLP Record Series	Index #
FITZHUGH (Cont.)						
Fitzhugh	Giles	Will	2/28/1853	Fauquier Co.	Chancery	1854-045
Fitzhugh	Giles	Will	2/28/1853	Fauquier Co.	Chancery	1859-010
Fitzhugh	Lucy B.	Will	3/3/1853	Fauquier Co.	Chancery	1868-018
Fitzhugh	Lucy B.	Exor. Acct.	2/1858	Fauquier Co.	Chancery	1868-018
Fitzhugh	Lucy B.	Will	2/27/1860	Fauquier Co.	Chancery	1878-028
Fitzhugh	Richard	Will	8/16/1821	Fairfax Co. VA.	Chancery	1872-041
Fitzhugh	Susannah	Will	8/18/1856	Fairfax Co. Va.	Chancery	1872-041
Fitzhugh	Thomas	Exor. Bond	12/25/1843	Fauquier Co.	Probate, Box 50	1843-001
Fitzhugh	Thomas L.	Guardian Appt.	1/24/1841	Fauquier Co.	Chancery	1846-049
Fitzhugh	Thomas L.	Guardian Bond	1/24/1841	Fauquier Co.	Chancery	1846-049
Fitzhugh	Thomas Ludwell	Guardian Bond	1817	Fauquier Co.	Probate, Box 49	1817-007
Fitzhugh	William D. (Dr.)	Report of Division	6/15/1839	Fauquier Co.	Chancery	1839-057
Fitzhugh	William D. (Dr.)	Plat & Survey Of Division	2/1/1839	Fauquier Co.	Chancery	1839-057
Fitzhugh	William D. (Dr.)	Division of Slaves	6/11/1839	Fauquier Co.	Chancery	1839-057
Fitzhugh	William D. (Dr.)	Report of Division Of Land + Slaves	6/11/1839	Fauquier Co.	Chancery	1839-057
Fitzhugh	William D. (Dr.)	Plat & Survey Of Division	2/1/1839	Fauquier Co.	Chancery	1855-086
Fitzhugh	William T.	Guardian Appt.	1/24/1841	Fauquier Co.	Chancery	1846-049
Fitzhugh	William T.	Guardian Bond	1/24/1841	Fauquier Co.	Chancery	1846-049
Fitzhugh	William T.	Court order to Settle Guardian Acct.	8/1843	Fauquier Co.	Probate, Box 40	1845-002
FLETCHER						
Fletcher	Aaron	Guardian Bond	1811	Fauquier Co.	Probate, Box 49	1811-007
Fletcher	Benjamin	Admr. Appt.	10/1821	Fauquier Co.	Chancery	1868-105
Fletcher	Benjamin	Court order to Appraise Estate	10/1821	Fauquier Co.	Chancery	1868-105
Fletcher	Eliza V.	Will	12/12/1887	Fauquier Co.	Probate, Box 54 Superior/Circuit Ct.	1887-003

Consolidated Probate Index from the Clerks Loose Papers & the Superior Court/Circuit Court Records 1759-1919

Surname	Given Name	Instrument	Date	County	CLP Record Series	Index #
FLETCHER (Cont.)						
Fletcher	Eliza V.	Exor. Acct.	4/6/1889	Fauquier Co.	Probate, Box 54	1889-004
Fletcher	John	Will	3/21/1827	Culpeper Co. VA.	Chancery	1848-006
Fletcher	John	Sales	4/18/1827	Culpeper Co. VA.	Chancery	1848-006
Fletcher	John G.	Plat & Survey Of Division	3/12/1877	Fauquier Co.	Chancery	1877-007
Fletcher	John G.	Plat & Survey Of Division	3/1882	Fauquier Co.	Chancery	1888-049
Fletcher	Joshua Jr.	Admr. Bond	8/15/1865	Fauquier Co.	Chancery	1892-061
Fletcher	Moses	Admr. Bond	1815	Fauquier Co.	Probate, Box 47	1815-046
Fletcher	Robert	Will	8/25/1845	Fauquier Co.	Chancery	1887-014
Fletcher	Sarah	Exors. Bond	1815	Fauquier Co.	Probate, Box 47	1815-014
Fletcher	William	Will	8/25/1856	Fauquier Co.	Chancery	1873-001
Fletcher	William	Will	8/25/1856	Fauquier Co.	Chancery	1881-056
Fletcher	William	Will	10/25/1886	Fauquier Co.	Chancery	1894-026
FLINN						
Flinn	Nancy	Plat & Survey of Dower Allotment	1/19/1861	Fauquier Co.	Chancery	1861-014
FLOWEREE (See also Flowerree)						
Floweree	Daniel	Guardian Bond	1815	Fauquier Co.	Probate, Box 49	1815-028
Floweree	Daniel	Division	2/1815	Fauquier Co.	Probate, Box 50	1815-004
Floweree	Joseph S.	Guardian Bond	1815	Fauquier Co.	Probate, Box 49	1815-028
Floweree	Kemp	Exor. Bond	1809	Fauquier Co.	Probate, Box 47	1809-022
Floweree	Kitty A.	Guardian Bond	1815	Fauquier Co.	Probate, Box 49	1815-028
Floweree	Susanna W.	Guardian Bond	1815	Fauquier Co.	Probate, Box 49	1815-028
Floweree	William K.	Guardian Bond	1815	Fauquier Co.	Probate, Box 49	1815-028
FLOWERREE (See also Floweree)						
Flowerree	Abner	Will	11/24/1854	Fauquier Co.	Chancery	1859-065
Flowerree	Abner	Will	11/27/1854	Fauquier Co.	Chancery	1871-026
Flowerree	Abner	Division	11/27/1854	Fauquier Co.	Chancery	1871-026
Floweree	Catharine L.	Will	7/24/1837	Fauquier Co.	Chancery	1842-019
Flowerree	Catharine L.	Will	7/24/1837	Fauquier Co.	Chancery	1860-029

Consolidated Probate Index from the Clerks Loose Papers & the Superior Court/Circuit Court Records 1759-1919

Surname	Given Name	Instrument	Date	County	CLP Record Series	Index #
FLOWERREE (Cont.)						
Flowerree	Catharine L.	Will	7/24/1837	Fauquier Co.	Chancery	1870-028
Flowerree	Daniel	Admrs. Bond	1815	Fauquier Co.	Probate, Box 47	1815-049
Flowerree	Daniel	Sales	2/1815	Fauquier Co.	Chancery	1839-006
Flowerree	Daniel	Report of Division	3/14/1815	Fauquier Co.	Chancery	1839-006
Flowerree	Daniel	Plat & Survey Of Division	3/14/1815	Fauquier Co.	Chancery	1839-006
Flowerree	Daniel	Report of Division Of Slaves	10/22/1816	Fauquier Co.	Chancery	1839-006
Flowerree	Daniel	Memo of Sales	Undated	Fauquier Co.	Chancery	1839-006
Flowerree	Edith Maria	Will	11/25/1840	Fauquier Co.	Chancery	1860-016
Flowerree	Edith Maria	Will	11/25/1840	Fauquier Co.	Chancery	1870-028
Flowerree	John	Division of Slaves	5/1822	Fauquier Co.	Chancery	1835-048
Flowerree	Kemp	Will	3/27/1809	Fauquier Co.	Chancery	1877-003
Flowerree	Kemp	Exor. Bond	3/27/1809	Fauquier Co.	Chancery	1877-003
Flowerree	Kemp	Exor. Acct.	8/22/1835	Fauquier Co.	Chancery	1877-003
Flowerree	Susan W.	Will	9/26/1836	Fauquier Co.	Chancery	1846-005
Flowerree	Susan W.	Exor. Acct.	Undated	Fauquier Co.	Chancery	1846-005
Flowerree	Susan W.	Exor. Acct.	11/28/1836	Fauquier Co.	Chancery	1846-005
Flowerree	Susan W.	Exor. Acct.	8/19/1841	Fauquier Co.	Chancery	1846-005
Flowerree	Susan W.	Exor. Acct.	9/6/1841	Fauquier Co.	Chancery	1846-005
Flowerree	Trennace	Letters of Gdnship	2/5/1908	Mason Co. IL.	Chancery	1908-038
Flowerree	Trennace	Gdn. Qualification	4/27/1905	Fauquier Co.	Chancery	1909-021
Flowerree	William	Admr. Bond	1813	Fauquier Co.	Probate, Box 47	1813-017
Flowerree	William	Division	5/27/1823	Fauquier Co.	Chancery	1823-023
FOLEY						
Foley	Andrew	Will	1/23/1832	Fauquier Co.	Chancery	1855-088
Foley	Andrew	Sale of Slaves	1855	Fauquier Co.	Chancery	1855-088
Foley	Bryant	Exor. Bond	1811	Fauquier Co.	Probate, Box 47	1811-014

Consolidated Probate Index from the Clerks Loose Papers & the Superior Court/Circuit Court Records 1759-1919

Surname	Given Name	Instrument	Date	County	CLP Record Series	Index #
FOLEY (Cont.)						
Foley	Elizabeth	Plat & Survey Of Division	10/23/1809	Fauquier Co.	Chancery	1813-012
Foley	Elizabeth	Admr. Appt.	5/14/1838	Rapphk. Co. VA.	Chancery	1859-008
Foley	James	Exor. Bond	1797	Fauquier Co.	Probate, Box 46	1797-011
Foley	James	Will	10/14/1793	Fauquier Co.	Chancery	1815-030
Foley	James	Appraisement	6/ 1797	Fauquier Co.	Chancery	1815-030
Foley	James	Will	8/28/1826	Fauquier Co.	Chancery	1836-026
Foley	James	Exor. Bond	8/28/1826	Fauquier Co.	Chancery	1836-026
Foley	James	Will	8/28/1826	Fauquier Co.	Chancery	1847-021
Foley	Leah	Guardian Bond	1801	Fauquier Co.	Probate, Box 48	1801-011
Foley	Leah	Guardian Bond	1803	Fauquier Co.	Probate, Box 49	1803-001
Foley	Mary	Guardian Bond	1817	Fauquier Co.	Probate, Box 49	1817-012
Foley	Thomas	Will	5/26/1828	Fauquier Co.	Chancery	1859-008
Foley	Thomas	Exor. Bond	5/26/1828	Fauquier Co.	Chancery	1859-008
Foley	Thomas	Exor. Acct.	9/29/1829	Fauquier Co.	Chancery	1859-008
Foley	Thomas	Exor. Acct.	5/24/1830	Fauquier Co.	Chancery	1859-008
Foley	Thomas Sr.	Exor. Acct.	7/26/1830	Fauquier Co.	Probate, Box 50	1830-001
Foley	William	Will	2/27/1837	Fauquier Co.	Chancery	1845-003
FOOTE						
Foote	George	Exor. Bond	1759	Fauquier Co.	Probate, Box 44	1759-006
Foote	George	Extrx. Bond	1763	Fauquier Co.	Probate, Box 44	1763-001
Foote	George	Extrx. Bond	1775	Fauquier Co.	Probate, Box 44	1775-010
Foote	George William	Deed of Partition, R. H. Helm Estate	4/3/1825	Fauquier Co.	Chancery	1848-009
Foote	Gilson	Admtrx. Bond	1769	Fauquier Co.	Probate, Box 44	1769-005
Foote	Henry S.	Deed of Partition, R. H. Helm	4/3/1825	Fauquier Co.	Chancery	1848-009
Foote	Hester	Guardian Bond	1794	Fauquier Co.	Probate, Box 48	1794-001

Consolidated Probate Index from the Clerks Loose Papers & the Superior Court/Circuit Court Records 1759-1919

Surname	Given Name	Instrument	Date	County	CLP Record Series	Index #
FOOTE (Cont.)						
Foote	Richard	Guardian Bond	1760	Fauquier Co.	Probate, Box 48	1760-002
Foote	Richard	Guardian Bond	1766	Fauquier Co.	Probate, Box 48	1766-001
Foote	Richard	Guardian Bond	1769	Fauquier Co.	Probate, Box 48	1769-002
Foote	Richard	Exor. Bond	1780	Fauquier Co.	Probate, Box 45	1780-012
Foote	Richard	Inventory + Appraisement	9/15/1819	Fauquier Co.	Chancery	1836-017
Foote	Richard	Exor. Bond	8/28/1822	Fauquier Co.	Chancery	1836-017
Foote	Richard	Admr. Appt.	7/8/1834	Fauquier Co.	Chancery	1836-017
Foote	Richard Helm	Will	1/20/1812	Fauquier Co.	Probate, Box 39	1819-005
Foote	Richard Helm	Will	7/1817	Fauquier Co.	Probate, Box 39	1819-005
Foote	Richard Helm	Will	4/13/1819	Fauquier Co.	Probate, Box 40	1822-001
Foote	Richard Helm	Will	4/13/1819	Fauquier Co.	Chancery	1836-017
Foote	Richard Helm	Will	4/13/1819	Fauquier Co.	Chancery	1845-015
Foote	Richard Helm	Extrx. Bond	1819	Fauquier Co.	Probate, Box 47	1819-002
Foote	Richard Helm	Deed of Partition Among Heirs	4/5/1825	Fauquier Co.	Chancery	1845-015
Foote	Richard Helm	Inventory	9/15/1829	Fauquier Co.	Probate, Box 39	1819-001
Foote	Richard H.	Will	4/17/1818	Fauquier Co.	Chancery	1848-008
Foote	Richard H.	Will	4/13/1819	Fauquier Co.	Chancery	1848-009
Foote	Richard H.	Report of Division	4/8/1869	Fauquier Co.	Chancery	1869-032
Foote	Richard H.	Plat & Survey Of Division	4/8/1869	Fauquier Co.	Chancery	1869-032
Foote	Richard H.	Will	3/28/1864	Baltimore, MD.	Chancery	1874-058
Foote	William	Guardian Bond	1760	Fauquier Co.	Probate, Box 48	1760-002
Foote	William	Guardian Bond	1766	Fauquier Co.	Probate, Box 48	1766-001
Foote	William	Guardian Bond	1769	Fauquier Co.	Probate, Box 48	1769-002
Foote	William	Admtrx. Bond	1772	Fauquier Co.	Probate, Box 44	1772-002
Foote	William	Will	4/23/1833	Fauquier Co.	Chancery	1842-015

Consolidated Probate Index from the Clerks Loose Papers & the Superior Court/Circuit Court Records 1759-1919

Surname	Given Name	Instrument	Date	County	CLP Record Series	Index #
FORBES						
Forbes	Alfred F.	Resolution of Respect at Death	9/6/1895	Fauquier Co.	Probate, Box 55 Superior/Circuit Ct.	1895-020
Forbes	Alfred T.	Will	7/22/1895	Fauquier Co.	Chancery	1896-020
Forbes	John Murray	Resolution for Memorial of Life	4/9/1893	Fauquier Co.	Probate, Box 55 Superior/Circuit Ct.	1893-003
FORD						
Ford	Hezekiah	Will	11/24/1874	Fauquier Co.	Chancery	1881-066
Ford	Lillie	Guardian Appt.	11/3/1906	Fauquier Co.	Probate, Box 56	1906-009
FORDYCE						
Fordyce	Wesley	Guardian Appt.	12/12/1877	Fauquier Co.	Chancery Superior/Circuit Ct.	1877-047
FOSTER						
Foster	James W.	Will	5/28/1866	Fauquier Co.	Chancery	1867-022
Foster	Leonard	Guardian Bond	4/25/1892	Fauquier Co.	Chancery	1898-061
Foster	Mary E.	Will (Draft)	6/26/1886	Fauquier Co.	Chancery	1892-074
Foster	Mary E.	Will	7/28/1890	Fauquier Co.	Chancery	1892-074
Foster	Mary E.	Heirs	Undated	Fauquier Co.	Chancery	1892-074
Foster	Quincy	Guardian Bond	4/25/1892	Fauquier Co.	Chancery	1898-061
FOWKE						
Fowke	Ada	Guardian Bond	7/26/1858	Fauquier Co.	Chancery	1869-082
Fowke	Elizabeth	Admrs. Bond	1781	Fauquier Co.	Probate, Box 45	1781-010
Fowke	Ella	Guardian Bond	7/26/1858	Fauquier Co.	Chancery	1869-082
Fowke	Frederick	Guardian Bond	7/26/1858	Fauquier Co.	Chancery	1869-082
Fowke	George	Guardian Bond	1781	Fauquier Co.	Probate, Box 45	1781-001
Fowke	Mary	Guardian Bond	7/26/1858	Fauquier Co.	Chancery	1869-082
Fowke	Sallie	Guardian Bond	7/26/1858	Fauquier Co.	Chancery	1869-082
FOWLER						
Fowler	Charles	Guardian Bond	1801	Fauquier Co.	Probate, Box 48	1801-009
Fowler	Elizabeth M.	Guardian Bond	1801	Fauquier Co.	Probate, Box 48	1801-003
Fowler	John A.	Guardian Bond	1801	Fauquier Co.	Probate, Box 48	1801-003
Fowler	William	Inventory	12/19/1807	Fauquier Co.	Chancery	1830-110

Consolidated Probate Index from the Clerks Loose Papers & the Superior Court/Circuit Court Records 1759-1919

Surname	Given Name	Instrument	Date	County	CLP Record Series	Index #
FOWLER (Cont.)						
Fowler	William	Admr. Acct. Settled	6/1809	Fauquier Co.	Chancery	1830-110
Fowler	William	Guardian Bond	1801	Fauquier Co.	Probate, Box 48	1801-003
FOX						
Fox	Billy	Admr. Acct.	7/25/1866	Fauquier Co.	Chancery	1875-020
Fox	Elizabeth	Exor. Bond	2/27/1809	Fauquier Co.	Probate, Box 47	1809-003
Fox	Elizabeth	Division of Dower Slaves	2/27/1809	Fauquier Co.	Chancery	1867-001
Fox	John	Will	4/5/1859	Fauquier Co.	Probate, Box 52 Superior/Circuit Ct.	1859-005
Fox	John	Inventory + Appraisement	8/13/1859	Fauquier Co.	Probate, Box 52 Superior/Circuit Ct.	1859-006
Fox	John	Admr. Bond	9/23/1869	Fauquier Co.	Probate, Box 53 Superior/Circuit Ct.	1869-006
Fox	John	Admr. Bond	9/8/1872	Fauquier Co.	Probate, Box 53 Superior/Circuit Ct.	1872-003
Fox	John	Admr. Bond	9/3/1873	Fauquier Co.	Probate, Box 53 Superior/Circuit Ct.	1873-002
Fox	John	Admr. Bond	12/15/1874	Fauquier Co.	Probate, Box 53 Superior/Circuit Ct.	1874-009
Fox	John	Admr. Acct.	9/6/1876	Fauquier Co.	Probate, Box 54 Superior/Circuit Ct.	1876-006
Fox	John	Will	4/5/1859	Fauquier Co.	Chancery	1867-001
Fox	John	Will	4/5/1859	Fauquier Co.	Chancery	1876-065
Fox	John	Will	4/5/1859	Fauquier Co.	Chancery	1902-001
Fox	John	Inventory + Appraisement	7/7/1859	Fauquier Co.	Chancery	1902-001
Fox	John	Admr. Acct.	8/15/1867	Fauquier Co.	Chancery	1902-001
Fox	John	Plat & Survey of Home Tract	11/1867	Fauquier Co.	Chancery	1902-001
Fox	John	Plat & Survey of Great Run Farm	7/1868	Fauquier Co.	Chancery	1902-001
Fox	John	Plat & Survey of Division, Lot # 1 Marsh Farm	2/1875	Fauquier Co.	Chancery	1902-001

Consolidated Probate Index from the Clerks Loose Papers & the Superior Court/Circuit Court Records 1759-1919

Surname	Given Name	Instrument	Date	County	CLP Record Series	Index #
FOX (Cont.)						
Fox	John	Plat & Survey of Subdivision of Marsh Tract	8/1875	Fauquier Co.	Chancery	1902-001
Fox	John	Plat & Survey of Subdivision of Great Run Tract	9/1875	Fauquier Co.	Chancery	1902-001
Fox	John	Plat & Survey of Division of Harris Holder Tract	9/1875	Fauquier Co.	Chancery	1902-001
Fox	John	Admr. Acct.	9/6/1876	Fauquier Co.	Chancery	1902-001
Fox	John	Estate Memo Book	Undated	Fauquier Co.	Chancery	1902-001
Fox	John	Will	4/5/1859	Fauquier Co.	Chancery	1902-002
Fox	John	Inventory + Appraisement	5/21/1859	Fauquier Co.	Chancery	1902-002
Fox	John	Plat & Survey Of Division of Harris Tract	4/1874	Fauquier Co.	Chancery	1902-002
Fox	John	Admr. Acct.	7/7/1860	Fauquier Co.	Chancery	1902-004
Fox	John	Estate Papers	1860-1877	Fauquier Co.	Probate, Box 42 Fox Estate &c Papers	1860-001 to 1877-001
Fox	John	Estate Papers	1870	Fauquier Co.	Probate, Box 42 Fox Estate &c Papers	1872-001
Fox	Matthias	Admr. Bond	1809	Fauquier Co.	Probate, Box 47	1809-017
Fox	Samuel	Admr. Appt.	7/25/1859	Fauquier Co.	Chancery	1866-032
Fox	Samuel	Will	10/22/1804	Fauquier Co.	Chancery	1867-001
Fox	Samuel	Division of Slaves	7/12/1805	Fauquier Co.	Chancery	1867-001
Fox	Samuel	Inventory + Appraisement	11/13/1804	Fauquier Co.	Chancery	1867-001
Fox	Samuel	Admr. Acct.	9/1806	Fauquier Co.	Chancery	1867-001
Fox	Samuel	Will	10/22/1804	Fauquier Co.	Chancery	1867-006

Consolidated Probate Index from the Clerks Loose Papers & the Superior Court/Circuit Court Records 1759-1919

Surname	Given Name	Instrument	Date	County	CLP Record Series	Index #
FOX (Cont.)						
Fox	William	Will	3/5/1867	Fauquier Co.	Chancery	1889-075
Fox	William	Admr. Bond	10/26/1860	Fauquier Co.	Chancery	1875-020
Fox	William	Inventory + Appraisement	7/11/1860	Fauquier Co.	Chancery	1875-020
FRANEY						
Franey	John	Admr. Report	12/21/1886	Fauquier Co.	Chancery	1908-021
FRAZIER						
Frazier	Daniel	Admtrx. Bond	1765	Fauquier Co.	Probate, Box 44	1765-001
FREEMAN						
Freeman	Harris	Guardian Bond	1817	Fauquier Co.	Probate, Box 49	1817-001
Freeman	Harris	Admr. Acct.	11/16/1824	Culpeper Co. VA.	Probate, Box 40	1831-004
Freeman	Harris	Admr. Acct.	11/20/1826	Culpeper Co. VA.	Probate, Box 40	1831-004
Freeman	Harris	Admr. Acct.	7/21/1828	Culpeper Co. VA.	Probate, Box 40	1831-004
Freeman	Harris	Admr. Acct.	3/22/1828	Culpeper Co. VA.	Probate, Box 40	1831-004
Freeman	James	Will	4/22/1751	Fauquier Co.	Chancery	1762-001
Freeman	James	Appraisement	1751	Fauquier Co.	Chancery	1762-001
Freeman	James	Will	6/27/1792	Fauquier Co.	Chancery	1850-063
Freeman	James	Guardian Bond	1797	Fauquier Co.	Probate, Box 48	1797-004
Freeman	James	Admr. Bond	1814	Fauquier Co.	Probate, Box 47	1814-010
Freeman	James	Admr. Bond	1814	Fauquier Co.	Probate, Box 47	1814-023
Freeman	James	Will	1/22/1877	Fauquier Co.	Chancery	1894-004
Freeman	James	Will	1/22/1877	Fauquier Co.	Chancery	1894-004
Freeman	James	Will	1/22/1877	Fauquier Co.	Chancery	1899-029
Freeman	Martin	Report of Division	11/1897	Fauquier Co.	Chancery	1899-029
Freeman	Martin	Plat & Survey Of Division	11/1897	Fauquier Co.	Chancery	1899-029
Freeman	William C.	Will	6/27/1827	Fauquier Co.	Chancery	1848-035
Freeman	William C.	Sales	9/13/1827	Fauquier Co.	Chancery	1848-035
Freeman	William C.	Sales	12/5/1827	Fauquier Co.	Chancery	1848-035
Freeman	William C.	Admr. Acct.	6/1829	Fauquier Co.	Chancery	1848-035

Consolidated Probate Index from the Clerks Loose Papers & the Superior Court/Circuit Court Records 1759-1919

Surname	**Given Name**	**Instrument**	**Date**	**County**	**CLP Record Series**	**Index #**
FREEMAN (Cont.)						
Freeman	William C.	Admr. Acct.	6/1831	Fauquier Co.	Chancery	1848-035
Freeman	William C.	Admr. Acct.	1833	Fauquier Co.	Chancery	1848-035
Freeman	William C.	Estate Acct.	9/28/1835	Fauquier Co.	Chancery	1848-035
Freeman	William C.	Admr. Acct.	1836	Fauquier Co.	Chancery	1848-035
Freeman	William C.	Admr. Acct.	3/1837	Fauquier Co.	Chancery	1848-035
Freeman	William C.	Admr. Acct.	10/7/1837	Fauquier Co.	Chancery	1848-035
Freeman	William C.	Admr. Acct.	Undated	Fauquier Co.	Chancery	1848-035
Freeman	William C.	Will	6/27/1827	Fauquier Co.	Chancery	1850-021
Freeman	William C.	Will	3/26/1827	Fauquier Co.	Chancery	1868-207
FRENCH						
French	Elizabeth	Admr. Bond	1808	Fauquier Co.	Probate, Box 47	1808-008
French	George	Admr. Bond	9/22/1834	Fauquier Co.	Chancery	1851-001
French	J. B.	Will	6/9/1843	Mecklinburg Co. NC.	Chancery	1869-049
French	John	Exors. Bond	1806	Fauquier Co.	Probate, Box 47	1806-017
French	Reuben	Admr. Bond	1/23/1826	Fauquier Co.	Chancery	1851-001
French	Reuben	Inventory + Appraisement	2/27/1826	Fauquier Co.	Chancery	1851-001
FROUGHTON						
Froughton,	E.	Admr. Appt.	1908	Fauquier Co.	Probate, Box 56	1908-003
FULLER						
Fuller	Thomas J. D.	Guardian Appt.	12/17/1878	Washington, DC	Chancery	1880-007
Fuller	Thomas J. D.	Guardian Bond	12/19/1879	Fauquier Co.	Chancery	1879-037
Fuller	Thomas J. D.	Guardian Appt.	12/17/1878	Fauquier Co.	Chancery	1880-038
FULTON						
Fulton	Mary	Guardian Bond	8/25/1830	Fauquier Co.	Chancery	1846-006
Fulton	Mary	Guardian Bond	5/27/1835	Fauquier Co.	Chancery	1848-028
Fulton	Mary	Gdnship Revoked	5/1841	Fauquier Co.	Chancery	1848-028
Fulton	Mary	Court order to Settle Guardian Acct.	3/27/1843	Fauquier Co.	Probate, Box 40	1845-002

Consolidated Probate Index from the Clerks Loose Papers & the Superior Court/Circuit Court Records 1759-1919

Surname	**Given Name**	**Instrument**	**Date**	**County**	**CLP Record Series**	**Index #**
FULTON (Cont.)						
Fulton	Mary	Guardian Acct.	4/5/1845	Fauquier Co.	Chancery	1848-028
Fulton	William Henry	Guardian Bond	8/25/1830	Fauquier Co.	Chancery	1846-006
Fulton	William Henry	Guardian Bond	5/27/1835	Fauquier Co.	Chancery	1848-028
Fulton	William Henry	Guardian Acct.	4/5/1845	Fauquier Co.	Chancery	1848-028
FURCROM						
Furcrom	Henry W.	Will	2/4/1904	Manchester, VA.	Chancery	1904-034
Furcrom	Henry W.	Appraisement	Undated	Fauquier Co.	Chancery	1904-034
FURR						
Furr	Charles	Admtrx. Bond	1807	Fauquier Co.	Probate, Box 47	1807-029
Furr	Thomas	Exors. Bond	1783	Fauquier Co.	Probate, Box 45	1783-004
Furr	Thomas	Heirs	1785	Fauquier Co.	Probate, Box 39	1785-004

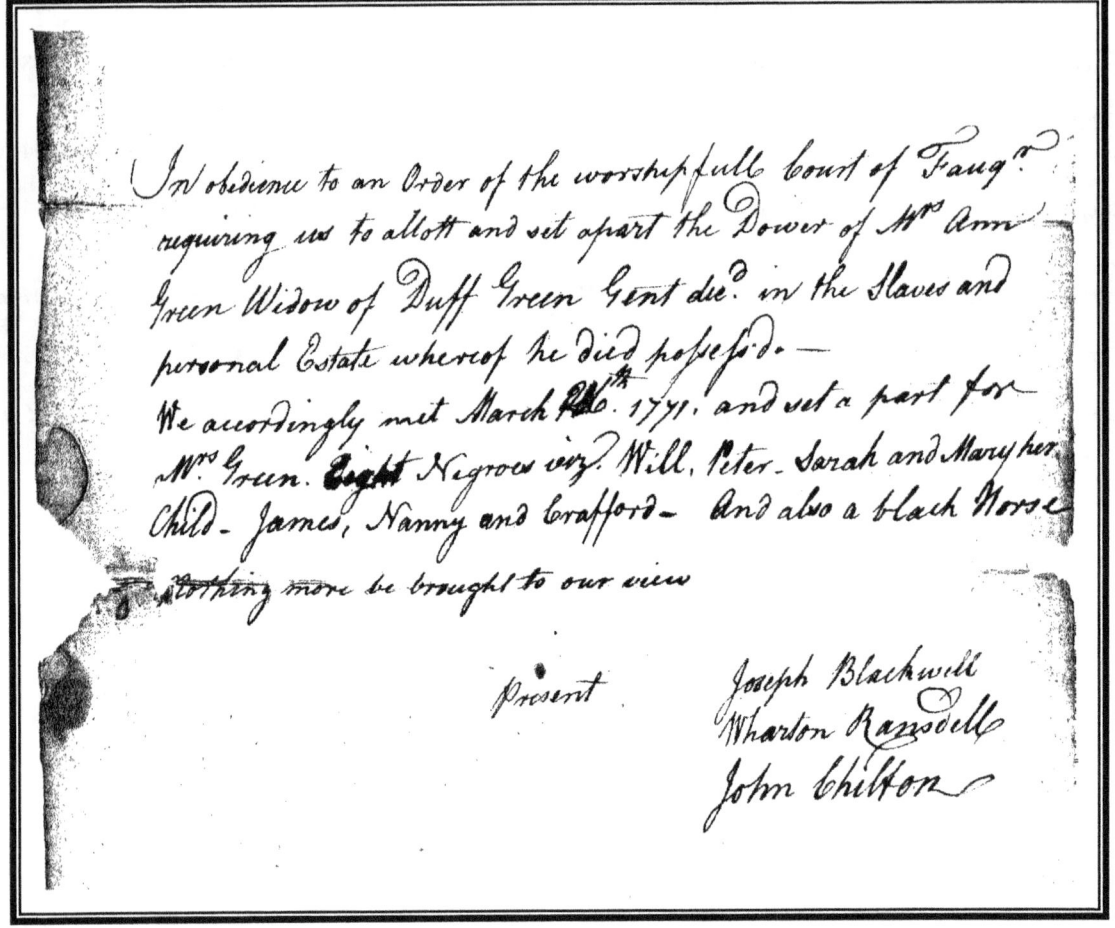

Plate 1. Probate. Scanned Image from Box 39. Wills, &c. 1771-001. Dower Allotment to Mrs. Ann Green

Consolidated Probate Index from the Clerks Loose Papers & the Superior Court/Circuit Court Records 1759-1919

Surname	Given Name	Instrument	Date	County	CLP Record Series	Index #
GABBY						
Gabby	William	Will	9/14/1841	Loudoun Co. VA.	Chancery	1843-027
Gabby	William	Will	9/23/1841	Washington Co. MD.	Chancery	1844-002
GAINES						
Gaines	William	Will	6/22/1818	Stafford Co. VA.	Chancery	1837-014
Gaines	William	Will	8/10/1818	Stafford Co. VA.	Chancery	1838-008
Gaines	William	Inventory + Appraisement	8/18/1818	Stafford Co. VA.	Chancery	1838-008
Gaines	William	Inventory	5/19/1819	Stafford Co. VA.	Chancery	1838-008
Gaines	William	Exor. Acct.	6/1824	Stafford Co. VA.	Chancery	1838-008
Gaines	William	Sales	1/5/1825	Stafford Co. VA.	Chancery	1838-008
Gaines	William	Exor. Acct.	7/11/1825	Stafford Co. VA.	Chancery	1838-008
Gaines	William	Exor. Acct.	1829	Fauquier Co.	Chancery	1838-008
Gaines	William	Heirs	12/19/1836	Fauquier Co.	Chancery	1838-008
Gaines	William H.	Will	1/27/1885	Fauquier Co.	Chancery	1886-008
Gaines	William H.	Admr. Appt.	1/28/1909	Fauquier Co.	Probate, Box 56 Superior/Circuit Ct.	1909-003
GALLAGHER						
Gallagher	Charles S.	Will	1/23/1893	Moniteau Co. MO.	Chancery	1903-072
Gallagher	Margaret S.	Will	6/7/1886	Pr. Wm. Co. VA.	Chancery	1903-072
GALLOWAY						
Galloway	Fanny L.	Committee Appt.	6/30/1906	Fauquier Co.	Probate, Box 56 Superior/Circuit Ct.	1906-004
GARDNER						
Gardner	Charles	Will	2/26/1798	Fauquier Co.	Probate, Box 50	1796-001
GARNER						
Garner	Daniel	Admr. Bond	1783	Fauquier Co.	Probate, Box 45	1783-011
Garner	James	Extrx. Bond	1807	Fauquier Co.	Probate, Box 47	1807-018
Garner	John	Admtrx. Bond	1762	Fauquier Co.	Probate, Box 44	1762-003
Garner	John	Court order to Appraise estate	7/1762	Fauquier Co.	Probate, Box 39	1762-001
Garner	John	Will	6/27/1842	Fauquier Co.	Chancery	1869-026
Garner	Newton L.	Admr. Bond	1815	Fauquier Co.	Probate, Box 47	1815-047

Consolidated Probate Index from the Clerks Loose Papers & the Superior Court/Circuit Court Records 1759-1919

Surname	**Given Name**	**Instrument**	**Date**	**County**	**CLP Record Series**	**Index #**
GARNER (Cont.)						
Garner	Samuel	List of Property At Death	1802	Fauquier Co.	Probate, Box 39	1803-003
Garner	Smith	Admtrx. Bond	1797	Fauquier Co.	Probate, Box 46	1797-001
Garner	Smith	Guardian Bond	1807	Fauquier Co.	Probate, Box 49	1807-012
Garner	Thomas	Will	6/8/1726	Stafford Co. VA.	Chanacery	1793-012
Garner	Thomas	Exor. Bond	1776	Fauquier Co.	Probate, Box 44	1776-006
GARRISON						
Garrison	Nehemiah	Admr. Bond	1814	Fauquier Co.	Probate, Box 47	1814-017
Garrison	Washington	Will	12/27/1886	Fauquier Co.	Chancery	1899-015
GASKINS						
Gaskins	Ann E.	Guardian Bond	1798	Fauquier Co.	Probate, Box 48	1798-001
Gaskins	Fannie	Report of Division	3/17/1898	Fauquier Co.	Chancery	1903-043
Gaskins	Fannie	Plat & Survey Of Division	3/17/1898	Fauquier Co.	Chancery	1903-043
Gaskins	Jesse	Admr. Appt.	2/6/1909	Fauquier Co.	Probate, Box 56 Superior/Circuit Ct.	1909-004
Gaskins	John	Guardian Bond	1800	Fauquier Co.	Probate, Box 48	1800-002
Gaskins	John	Will	5/30/1867	Fauquier Co.	Chancery	1879-022
Gaskins	John	Will	5/30/1867	Fauquier Co.	Chancery	1887-001
Gaskins	John	Admr. Appt.	3/4/1871	Fauquier Co.	Chancery	1887-001
Gaskins	John	Report of Division	3/1875	Fauquier Co.	Chancery	1887-001
Gaskins	John	Plat & Survey Of Division	3/1875	Fauquier Co.	Chancery	1887-001
Gaskins	John H.	Admr. Bond	10/10/1851	Fauquier Co.	Probate, Box 52 Superior/Circuit Ct.	1851-003
Gaskins	John H.	Division of Slaves	5/12/1852	Fauquier Co.	Chancery	1879-023
Gaskins	John H.	Sales	5/27/1852	Fauquier Co.	Probate, Box 52 Superior/Circuit Ct.	1852-005
Gaskins	John H.	Inventory + Appraisement	11/26/1852	Fauquier Co.	Probate, Box 52	1852-004
Gaskins	Thomas	Admr. Appt.	11/5/1910	Fauquier Co.	Probate, Box 56 Superior/Circuit Ct.	1910-006

Consolidated Probate Index from the Clerks Loose Papers & the Superior Court/Circuit Court Records 1759-1919

Surname	Given Name	Instrument	Date	County	CLP Record Series	Index #
GAUNT						
Gaunt	John	Admr. Bond	1815	Fauquier Co.	Probate, Box 47	1851-039
Gaunt	Mary	Admr. Bond	1/27/18334	Fauquier Co.	Chancery	1840-003
Gaunt	Mary	Admr. Acct.	8/1834	Fauquier Co.	Chancery	1868-170
Gaunt	Mary	Report of Division Of Slaves	8/30/1834	Fauquier Co.	Chancery	1868-170
GENT						
Gent	Mary	Admr. Bond	1770	Fauquier Co.	Probate, Box 44	1770-008
GEORGE						
George	Addison J.	Will	8/17/1861	Fauquier Co.	Chancery	1871-119
George	Annie S.	Renunciation	8/18/1863	Culpeper Co. VA.	Chancery	1872-002
George	Catharine	Report of Division	6/1873	Fauquier Co.	Chancery	1876-041
George	Catharine	Plat & Survey Of Division	6/1873	Fauquier Co.	Chancery	1876-041
George	Cumberland	Will	10/19/1863	Culpeper Co. VA.	Chancery	1872-002
George	Fanny	Guardian Bond	1791	Fauquier Co.	Probate, Box 48	1797-001
George	Jane	Guardian Bond	1817	Fauquier Co.	Probate, Box 48	1817-019
George	Joseph	Extrx. Bond	1815	Fauquier Co.	Probate, Box 47	1815-010
George	Joseph S.	Will	8/6/1858	Fauquier Co.	Chancery	1871-119
George	Lydia	Petition to divide Estate of Joseph George	11/23/1830	Fauquier Co.	Probate, Box 40	1830-004
George	Lydia	Petition to Allot Dower	11/23/1830	Fauquier Co.	Probate, Box 40	1830-004
George	Margaret	Admr. Bond	1808	Fauquier Co.	Probate, Box 46	1808-021
George	Nicholas	Extrx. Bond	1779	Fauquier Co.	Probate, Box 45	1779-003
George	Nicholas	Exor. Bond	1796	Fauquier Co.	Probate, Box 46	1796-005
George	Parnach	Admrs. Bond	1797	Fauquier Co.	Probate, Box 46	1797-005
George	Peyton	Guardian Bond	1791	Fauquier Co.	Probate, Box 48	1791-004
George	Peyton	Guardian Bond	1817	Fauquier Co.	Probate, Box 49	1817-019
George	Peyton	Will	9/25/1848	Baltimore, MD.	Chancery	1875-001

Consolidated Probate Index from the Clerks Loose Papers & the Superior Court/Circuit Court Records 1759-1919

Surname	**Given Name**	**Instrument**	**Date**	**County**	**CLP Record Series**	**Index #**
GIBB (See also Gibbs)						
Gibb	Cornelia Walton	Guardian Appt.	7/9/1906	Fauquier Co.	Probate, Box 56 Superior/Circuit Ct.	1908-012
Gibb	Elizabeth H.	Guardian Appt.	7/9/1906	Fauquier Co.	Probate, Box 56 Superior/Circuit Ct.	1908-012
Gibb	John W.	Guardian Appt.	7/9/1906	Fauquier Co.	Probate, Box 56 Superior/Circuit Ct.	1908-012
GIBBS (See also Gibb)						
Gibbs	John	Will	5/4/1904	New York City, NY.	Chancery	1912-002
GIBERNE						
Giberne	Mary	Will	6/5/1820	Richmond Co. VA.	Chancery	1847-011
GIBSON						
Gibson	Charles M.	Will	1/27/1873	Fauquier Co.	Chancery	1900-043
Gibson	Charity	Guardian Bond	1807	Fauquier Co.	Probate, Box 49	1807-006
Gibson	Eliza	Guardian Bond	1809	Fauquier Co.	Probate, Box 49	1809-006
Gibson	Esther	Will	8/24/1825	Loudoun Co. VA.	Chancery	1851-020
Gibson	George	Admr. Bond	1807	Fauquier Co.	Probate, Box 46	1807-006
Gibson	Jonathan (Capt.)	Inventory + Appraisement	1790	Fauquier Co.	Chancery	1801-027
Gibson	Jonathan	Summons to settle His Admr. Acct.	1/1793	Fauquier Co.	Probate, Box 39	1793-005
Gibson	Jonathan	Admr. Bond	1809	Fauquier Co.	Probate, Box 47	1809-002
Gibson	Jonathan Catlett	Guardian Bond	1789	Fauquier Co.	Probate, Box 48	1789-001
Gibson	Judy	Guardian Bond	1807	Fauquier Co.	Probate, Box 48	1807-006
Gibson	Mary	Guardian Bond	1807	Fauquier Co.	Probate, Box 48	1807-006
Gibson	Sarah	Real + Personal Property Rec'd in Lieu of Dower	Undated	Fauquier Co.	Chancery	1840-058
Gibson	Sarah A.	Guardian Chosen	9/1826	Fauquier Co.	Probate, Box 40	1826-002
Gibson	Thomas	Guardian Bond	1809	Fauquier Co.	Probate, Box 48	1809-006
Gibson	William	Exor. Bond	1813	Fauquier Co.	Probate, Box 47	1813-003
Gibson	William	Admtrx. Bond	10/19/1835	Fauquier Co.	Probate, Box 51 Superior/Circuit Ct.	1836-001

Consolidated Probate Index from the Clerks Loose Papers & the Superior Court/Circuit Court Records 1759-1919

Surname	Given Name	Instrument	Date	County	CLP Record Series	Index #
GIBSON (Cont.)						
Gibson	William	Report of Division Of Slaves	11/27/1835	Fauquier Co.	Chancery	1879-045
Gibson	William	Division of Slaves	12/26/1835	Fauquier Co.	Chancery	1840-058
Gibson	William	Inventory + Appraisement	5/3/1836	Fauquier Co.	Probate, Box 51 Superior/Circuit Ct.	1836-001
GLANVILLE						
Glanville	Thomas	Admr. Bond	1812	Fauquier Co.	Probate, Box 47	1812-007
GLASCOCK						
Glascock	Alfred	Admr. Bond	9/13/1872	Fauquier Co.	Probate, Box 53 Superior/Circuit Ct.	1872-010
Glascock	Alvin D.	Guardian Appt.	6/25/1860	Fauquier Co.	Chancery	1860-066
Glascock	Bushrod H.	Will	6/13/1853	Loudoun Co. VA.	Chancery	1879-040
Glascock	Charles	Will	5/28/1849	Fauquier Co.	Chancery	1856-048
Glascock	Daniel	Report of Division	2/28/1837	Fauquier Co.	Chancery	1837-042
Glascock	Daniel	Plat & Survey	2/28/1837	Fauquier Co.	Chancery	1837-042
Glascock	Daniel	Report of Division Of Slaves	2/28/1837	Fauquier Co.	Chancery	1837-042
Glascock	Edwin C.	Guardian Appt.	6/25/1860	Fauquier Co.	Chancery	1860-066
Glascock	Francis	Inventory + Appraisement	5/20/1820	Fauquier Co.	Probate, Box 40	1824-001
Glascock	Frederick N.	Guardian Appt.	6/25/18160	Fauquier Co.	Chancery	1860-066
Glascock	George	Will	4/25/1826	Fauquier Co.	Chancery	1832-004
Glascock	George	Plat & Survey Of Division	10/1867	Fauquier Co.	Chancery	1869-054
Glascock	Jesse	Plat & Survey Of Division	9/17/1830	Fauquier Co.	Chancery	1831-001
Glascock	Jesse	Plat & Survey	9/17/1830	Fauquier Co.	Chancery	1831-025
Glascock	John	Exor. Bond	1765	Fauquier Co.	Probate, Box 44	1765-002
Glascock	John	Exor. Bond	1784	Fauquier Co.	Probate, Box 45	1784-002
Glascock	Lucy B.	Guardian Appt.	6/25/1860	Fauquier Co.	Chancery	1860-066
Glascock	Nancy	Relinquishment	5/1829	Fauquier Co.	Probate, Box 40	1829-002
Glascock	Nancy	Dower Allotment In Slaves	3/31/1831	Fauquier Co.	Chancery	1868-119

Consolidated Probate Index from the Clerks Loose Papers & the Superior Court/Circuit Court Records 1759-1919

Surname	Given Name	Instrument	Date	County	CLP Record Series	Index #
GLASCOCK (Cont.)						
Glascock	Peter	Plat & Survey Of Division	9/1830	Fauquier Co.	Chancery	1830-142 OS Chy
Glascock	Rebecca Edith	Guardian Appt.	6/25/1860	Fauquier Co.	Chancery	1860-066
Glascock	Thomas	Will	9/23/1793	Fauquier Co.	Chancery	1837-047
Glascock	Thomas	Admr. Acct.	7/1/1837	Fauquier Co.	Chancery	1838-014
Glascock	Thomas	Report of Sale Of Slaves in Estate	12/3/1830	Fauquier Co.	Chancery	1837-047
Glascock	Travers	Admr. Bond	1784	Fauquier Co.	Probate, Box 45	1784-013
Glascock	William	Will	2/23/1857	Fauquier Co.	Chancery	1876-056
Glascock	William	Plat & Survey Of Division	7/1857	Fauquier Co.	Chancery	1871-080
GLASSELL						
Glassell	John	Will	11/18/1850	Culpeper Co. VA.	Chancery	1884-020
Glassell	John	Appraisement	11/1850	Culpeper Co. VA.	Chancery	1884-020
GLENDENNING						
Glendenning	Eli	Guardian Bond	1801	Fauquier Co.	Probate, Box 48	1801-005
Glendenning	Elizabeth	Guardian Bond	1800	Fauquier Co.	Probate, Box 48	1800-005
Glendenning	George's Children	Court Order	1809	Fauquier Co.	Probate, Box 39	1809-002
Glendenning	Molly	Guardian Bond	1801	Fauquier Co.	Probate, Box 48	1801-005
Glendenning	Peter	Guardian Bond	1801	Fauquier Co.	Probate, Box 48	1801-005
Glendenning	Rozy	Guardian Bond	1801	Fauquier Co.	Probate, Box 48	1801-005
Glendenning	Sydney	Guardian Bond	1801	Fauquier Co.	Probate, Box 48	1801-005
GOODWIN						
Goodwin	William L. B.	Will	11/20/1859	Fauquier Co.	Chancery	1894-028
GORDON						
Gordon	Ann E.	Report of Division Of Dower	3/29/1883	Fauquier Co.	Chancery	1900-042
Gordon	Ann E.	Plat & Survey Of Division of Dower	3/29/1883	Fauquier Co.	Chancery	1900-042
Gordon	Elizabeth C.	Guardian Chosen	7/30/1834	Fauquier Co.	Chancery	1834-038
Gordon	Francis	Guardian Bond	1810	Fauquier Co.	Probate, Box 48	1810-007
Gordon	Lucy Ann Harrison	Guardian Chosen	7/30/1834	Fauquier Co.	Chancery	1834-008

Consolidated Probate Index from the Clerks Loose Papers & the Superior Court/Circuit Court Records 1759-1919

Surname	Given Name	Instrument	Date	County	CLP Record Series	Index #
GORDON (Cont.)						
Gordon	Maria F.	Guardian Chosen	7/30/1834	Fauquier Co.	Chancery	1834-008
Gordon	Thomas	Admr. Bond	1808	Fauquier Co.	Probate, Box 46	1808-010
GORE						
Gore	Thomas	Court Order to Appraise Estate	9/1804	Fauquier Co.	Probate, Box 39	1804-001
GOTT						
Gott	Elizabeth	Guardian Bond	1776	Fauquier Co.	Probate, Box 48	1776-002
GRAHAM						
Graham	George	Report of Division	9/13/1834	Fauquier Co.	Chancery	1837-015
Graham	George	Plat & Survey Of Division	9/13/1834	Fauquier Co.	Chancery	1837-015
Graham	John	Admr. Bond	1767	Fauquier Co.	Probate, Box 44	1767-002
Graham	Nancy	Guardian Bond	1797	Fauquier Co.	Probate, Box 48	1797-007
GRANGER						
Granger	Robert S.	Heirs	1894	Fauquier Co.	Chancery	1895-020
GRANT						
Grant	John	Guardian Bond	1797	Fauquier Co.	Probate, Box 48	1797-005
Grant	Obed	Will	4/12/1904	Fauquier Co.	Probate, Box 50 Addendum Folder	1904-001
Grant	Peter	Admr. Bond	1815	Fauquier Co.	Probate, Box 47	1815-043
Grant	Peter	Will	3/29/1818	Fauquier Co.	Probate, Box 50	1818-004
GRAY						
Gray	Henry	Guardian Bond	1810	Fauquier Co.	Probate, Box 49	1810-009
Gray	Nancy	Guardian Bond	1815	Fauquier Co.	Probate, Box 49	1815-018
GRAYSON						
Grayson	Frances Edmonds	Guardian Bond	1808	Fauquier Co.	Probate, Box 49	1808-001
Grayson	Frances Edmonds	Guardian Bond	1808	Fauquier Co.	Probate, Box 49	1808-013
Grayson	T. M.	Will	4/5/1899	Fauquier Co.	Probate, Box 55 Superior/Circuit Ct.	1899-003
Grayson	William	Will	12/7/1790	Fauquier Co.	Probate, Box 39	1790-001
GREEN						
Green	Ann	Relinquishment	1766	Fauquier Co.	Probate, Box 39	1766-002
Green	Ann (Mrs.)	Dower Allotment In Slaves	3/26/1771	Fauquier Co.	Probate, Box 39	1771-001

Consolidated Probate Index from the Clerks Loose Papers & the Superior Court/Circuit Court Records 1759-1919

Surname	Given Name	Instrument	Date	County	CLP Record Series	Index #
GREEN (Cont.)						
Green	Charles	Report of Division	3/1/1820	Fauquier Co.	Chancery	1838-001
Green	Charles	Plat & Survey Of Division	3/1/1820	Fauquier Co.	Chancery	1838-001
Green	Charles T.	Resolution for Memorial of Life	12/16/1898	Fauquier Co.	Probate, Box 55 Superior/Circuit Ct.	1898-002
Green	Duff	Admrs. Bond	1766	Fauquier Co.	Probate, Box 44	1766-002
Green	Duff	Guardian Bond	1771	Fauquier Co.	Probate, Box 48	1771-006
Green	Elinor	Guardian Bond	1771	Fauquier Co.	Probate, Box 48	1771-006
Green	Elisa	Guardian Bond	1797	Fauquier Co.	Probate, Box 48	1797-010
Green	Elizaabeth	Guardian Bond	1771	Fauquier Co.	Probate, Box 48	1771-006
Green	Elizabeth	Will	4/1821	Fauquier Co.	Probate, Box 50	1821-001
Green	Florence	Guardian Appt.	8/20/1907	Fauquier Co.	Probate, Box 56 Superior/Circuit Ct.	1907-014
Green	Frank Newton	Guardian Appt.	8/20/1907	Fauquier Co.	Probate, Box 56 Superior/Circuit Ct.	1907-014
Green	George	Exors. Bond	1807	Fauquier Co.	Probate, Box 46	1807-026
Green	Henry	Guardian Bond	1771	Fauquier Co.	Probate, Box 48	1771-006
Green	Hugh R.	Admr. Bond	9/26/1842	Fauquier Co.	Chancery	1860-034
Green	Hugh R.	Admr. Bond	9/26/1842	Fauquier Co.	Chancery	1870-013
Green	Iris	Guardian Appt.	9/20/1907	Fauquier Co.	Probate, Box 56 Superior/Circuit Ct.	1907-014
Green	James	Estate Papers	1838	Fauquier Co.	Probate, Box 40	1838-001
Green	John	Guardian Bond	1771	Fauquier Co.	Probate, Box 48	1771-005
Green	John G.	Guardian Bond	9/26/1871	Fauquier Co.	Chancery	1881-028
Green	Joseph	Will	2/27/1815	Fauquier Co.	Probate, Box 50	1815-003
Green	Joseph	Will	2/27/1815	Fauquier Co.	Chancery	1857-002
Green	Joseph	Exors. Bond	1814	Fauquier Co.	Probate, Box 47	1815-021
Green	Lucy	Relinquishment	6/1823	Fauquier Co.	Probate, Box 40	1823-003
Green	Mabel	Guardian Appt.	8/20/1907	Fauquier Co.	Probate, Box 56 Superior/Circuit Ct.	1907-014

Consolidated Probate Index from the Clerks Loose Papers & the Superior Court/Circuit Court Records 1759-1919

Surname	Given Name	Instrument	Date	County	CLP Record Series	Index #
GREEN (Cont.)						
Green	Mary E.	Admr. Bond	4/8/1869	Fauquier Co.	Probate, Box 56 Superior/Circuit Ct.	1869-004
Green	Robert	Guardian Bond	1797	Fauquier Co.	Probate, Box 48	1797-010
Green	Robert	Sales	3/1820	Fauquier Co.	Chancery	1834-009
Green	Susanna	Guardian Bond	1797	Fauquier Co.	Probate, Box 48	1797-010
Green	Whitson	Inventory + Appraisement	4/30/1821	Frederick Co. VA.	Chancery	1859-012
Green	Whitson	Report of Division Of Slaves	9/24/1858	Fauquier Co.	Chancery	1859-012
Green	William	Guardian Bond	1771	Fauquier Co.	Probate, Box 48	1771-006
Green	Willis	Guardian Bond	1771	Fauquier Co.	Probate, Box 48	1771-006
GREGG						
Gregg	James W.	Will	10/22/1900	Fauquier Co.	Chancery	1903-082
GRIFFITH						
Griffith	Elijah	Will	9/25/1843	Fauquier Co.	Chancery	1854-056
Griffith	Elijah	Will	9/25/1843	Fauquier Co.	Chancery	1857-015
Griffith	Elijah	Will	9/25/1843	Fauquier Co.	Chancery	1866-005
Griffith	Elijah	Division of Slaves	9/1843	Fauquier Co.	Chancery	1866-005
Griffith	Elijah	Will	9/25/1843	Fauquier Co.	Chancery	1866-043
Griffith	Elijah	Will	9/25/1843	Fauquier Co.	Chancery	1867-012
Griffith	Elijah	Will	9/25/1843	Fauquier Co.	Chancery	1871-016
Griffith	Elijah	Will	9/25/1843	Fauquier Co.	Chancery	1871-022
Griffith	Harriett	Plat & Survey Dower Allotment	Undated	Fauquier Co.	Chancery	1871-079
Griffith	Harriett	Division of Slaves	Undated	Fauquier Co.	Chancery	1871-079
GRIGSBY						
Grigsby	Ely	Guardian Bond	1793	Fauquier Co.	Probate, Box 48	1793-005
Grigsby	Helen	Guardian Bond	1793	Fauquier Co.	Probate, Box 48	1793-004
Grigsby	John	Admtrx. Bond	1771	Fauquier Co.	Probate, Box 44	1771-012
Grigsby	John	Guardian Bond	1812	Fauquier Co.	Probate, Box 49	1812-006
Grigsby	Kemp B.	Will	5/27/1878	Fauquier Co.	Chancery	1903-035

Consolidated Probate Index from the Clerks Loose Papers & the Superior Court/Circuit Court Records 1759-1919

Surname	**Given Name**	**Instrument**	**Date**	**County**	**CLP Record Series**	**Index #**
GRIGSBY (Cont.)						
Grigsby	Nathaniel	Guardian Bond	1812	Fauquier Co.	Probate, Box 49	1812-006
Grigsby	Nathaniel	Will	8/29/1846	Fauquier Co.	Chancery	1860-002
Grigsby	Nathaniel	Will	8/29/1846	Fauquier Co.	Chancery	1903-034
Grigsby	Sally	Guardian Bond	1812	Fauquier Co.	Probate, Box 49	1812-006
Grigsby	Sally	Sales	6/15/1844	Fauquier Co.	Chancery	1866-007
Grigsby	Samuel	Exor. Bond	1781	Fauquier Co.	Probate, Box 45	1781-006
Grigsby	Samuel	Will	10/22/1785	Fauquier Co.	Chancery	1810-015
Grigsby	Thornton	Admr. Bond	10/6/1837	Fauquier Co.	Probate, Box 51 Superior/Circuit Ct.	1837-002
Grigsby	William	Inventory + Appraisement	5/3/1782	Fauquier Co.	Chancery	1798-025
Grigsby	William	Admtrx. Bond	1783	Fauquier Co.	Probate, Box 45	1782-013
Grigsby	William	Appraisement Of Slaves	4/24/1843	Fauquier Co.	Chancery	1854-012
Grigsby	William	Exor. Acct.	4/5/1853	Fauquier Co.	Chancery	1854-012
GRIMES						
Grimes	Ambrose	Guardian Appt.	11/3/1904	Fauquier Co.	Probate, Box 55 Superior/Circuit Ct.	1904-012
Grimes	Myrtle	Guardian Appt.	11/3/1904	Fauquier Co.	Probate, Box 55 Superior/Circuit Ct.	1904-012
Grimes	Polly	Guardian Bond	1809	Fauquier Co.	Probate, Box 49	1809-005
GRIMSLEY						
Grimsley	Sarah	Relinquishment	11/1819	Fauquier Co.	Probate, Box 39	1818-007
GROOME						
Groome	Susan Townsen	Guardian Appt.	12/2/1905	Fauquier Co.	Probate, Box 55 Superior/Circuit Ct.	1905-009
GRUBBS						
Grubbs	William	Admtrx. Bond	1774	Fauquier Co.	Probate, Box 44	1774-012
GUNNELL						
Gunnell	James	Admr. Bond	5/22/1822	Fauquier Co.	Probate, Box 50	1822-001
GUTRIDGE						
Gutridge	John	Admr. Bond	1815	Fauquier Co.	Probate, Box 50	1815-052
Gutridge	John F.	Guardian Acct.	1828	Fauquier Co.	Probate, Box 40	1828-001
Gutridge	Reuben	Admtrx. Bond	1815	Fauquier Co.	Probate, Box 47	1815-066

Consolidated Probate Index from the Clerks Loose Papers & the Superior Court/Circuit Court Records 1759-1919

Surname	Given Name	Instrument	Date	County	CLP Record Series	Index #
HADDUX						
Haddux	Ezekiel	Court order to Appraise Estate	10/1795	Fauquier Co.	Probate, Box 39	1796-001
HAGAN						
Hagan	John	Guardian Curator Appt.	9/17/1877	Monroe Co. MO.	Chancery	1902-006
HAILEY						
Hailey	Polly	Guardian Bond	1794	Fauquier Co.	Probate, Box 48	1794-003
Hailey	Polly	Guardian Bond	1806	Fauquier Co.	Probate, Box 49	1806-004
HAINES (See also Hains, Haynes)						
Haines	Daniel	Will	6/27/1864	Fauquier Co.	Chancery	1885-019
Haines	Joseph	Guardian Bond	1803	Fauquier Co.	Probate, Box 49	1803-009
Haines	Simon	Admr. Bond	1813	Fauquier Co.	Probate, Box 47	1813-024
HAINS (See also Haines, Haynes)						
Hains	Daniel	Will	1853	Fauquier Co.	Probate, Box 50 Addendum Folder	1863-001
Hains	Daniel	Will	2/19/1853	Fauquier Co.	Probate, Box 50 Addendum Folder	1863-001
Hains	Daniel	Will	2/20/1863	Fauquier Co.	Probate, Box 50 Addendum Folder	1863-001
Hains	Daniel	Will	6/27/1864	Fauquier Co.	Chancery	1866-017
Hains	Daniel	Plat & Survey Of Division	9/17/1866	Fauquier Co.	Chancery	1866-017
HALE						
Hale	George	Exor. Bond	1806	Fauquier Co.	Probate, Box 46	1806-028
Hale	John	Admr. Bond	1807	Fauquier Co.	Probate, Box 46	1807-015
Hale	Smith	Will	4/17/1817	Woodford Co. KY.	Chancery	1832-061
Hale	Smith	Will	4/1817	Woodford Co. KY.	Chancery	1833-026
Hale	William	Will	2/7/1811	Fauquier Co.	Chancery	1837-048
Hale	William	Will	3/28/1818	Fauquier Co.	Chancery	1847-018
Hale	William	Report of Division	3/28/1818	Fauquier Co.	Chancery	1847-018
Hale	William	Plat & Survey	3/28/1818	Fauquier Co.	Chancery	1847-018
HALEY						
Haley	Margaret	Sales	11/1822	Fauquier Co.	Probate, Box 40	1821-001

Consolidated Probate Index from the Clerks Loose Papers & the Superior Court/Circuit Court Records 1759-1919

Surname	**Given Name**	**Instrument**	**Date**	**County**	**CLP Record Series**	**Index #**
HALL						
Hall	Elisha	Will	3/25/1751	Fairfax Co. VA.	Chancery	1792-011
Hall	Richard Lingan	Exors. Bond	1774	Fauquier Co.	Probate, Box 44	1774-013
Hall	Richard Lingan	Extrx. Bond	1774	Fauquier Co.	Probate, Box 44	1774-014
Hall	Richard Lingan	Exor. Bond	1778	Fauquier Co.	Probate, Box 45	1778-022
HALLEY						
Halley	Amanda V.	Committee Resignation	10/5/1906	Fauquier Co.	Probate, Box 56 Superior/Circuit Ct.	1906-007
Halley	Amanda V.	Committee Appt.	10/5/1906	Fauquier Co.	Probate, Box 56 Superior/Circuit Ct.	1906-007
Halley	Samuel H. (Dr.)	Will	3/23/1885	Fauquier Co.	Chancery	1890-002
Halley	Samuel H. (Dr.)	Appraisement	12/14/1885	Fauquier Co.	Chancery	1890-002
Halley	Samuel H. (Dr.)	Report of Division	6/1/1886	Fauquier Co.	Chancery	1890-002
HAMILTON						
Hamilton	Hugh	Will	11/29/1876	Fauquier Co.	Chancery	1889-062
Hamilton	Hugh	Report of Division	11/1883	Fauquier Co.	Chancery	1889-062
Hamilton	Hugh	Plat & Survey Of Division	11/1883	Fauquier Co.	Chancery	1889-062
HAMPTON						
Hampton	Alfred	Guardian Bond	1813	Fauquier Co.	Probate, Box 49	1813-004
Hampton	Catharine	Guardian Appt.	1/25/1828	Fauquier Co.	Probate, Box 40	1828-005
Hampton	Edward	Guardian Appt.	1/25/1828	Fauquier Co.	Probate, Box 40	1828-005
Hampton	Eliza B.	Admr. Acct.	9/1840	Fauquier Co.	Probate, Box 40	1843-003
Hampton	Eliza B.	Admr. Acct.	1843	Fauquier Co.	Probate, Box 40	1843-003
Hampton	Eliza B.	Estate Accts.	1843	Fauquier Co.	Probate, Box 40	1843-003
Hampton	Henry	Guardian Bond	1817	Fauquier Co.	Probate, Box 49	1817-009
Hampton	Jeremiah	Guardian Bond	1813	Fauquier Co.	Probate, Box 49	1813-004
Hampton	John (Mrs.)	Dower Allotment	11/30/1829	Fauquier Co.	Chancery	1868-120
Hampton	John	Plat & Survey Of Division	11/30/1829	Fauquier Co.	Chancery	1868-120
Hampton	Joseph	Guardian Bond	1813	Fauquier Co.	Probate, Box 49	1813-004
Hampton	Joseph	Plat & Survey	1813	Fauquier Co.	Chancery	1818-026

Consolidated Probate Index from the Clerks Loose Papers & the Superior Court/Circuit Court Records 1759-1919

Surname	Given Name	Instrument	Date	County	CLP Record Series	Index #
HAMPTON (Cont.)						
Hampton	Margaret	Guardian Appt.	1/25/1828	Fauquier Co.	Probate, Box 40	1828-005
Hampton	Mary	Relinquishment	10/22/1821	Fauquier Co.	Probate, Box 40	1821-002
Hampton	Richard	Will	12/22/1766	Fauquier Co.	Chancery	1792-011
Hampton	Richard	Extrx. Bond	1766	Fauquier Co.	Probate, Box 44	1766-011
Hampton	Richard	Exor. Bond	1767	Fauquier Co.	Probate, Box 44	1767-003
Hampton	Richard	Appraisement	6/27/1767	Fauquier Co.	Chancery	1792-011
Hampton	Robert	Guardian Appt.	1/25/1828	Fauquier Co.	Probate, Box 40	1828-005
Hampton	Silas	Heirs	1832	Fauquier Co.	Probate, Box 40	1845-003
Hampton	Silas	Guardian Accts.	1832	Fauquier Co.	Probate, Box 40	1845-003
Hampton	Silas H.	Admr. Acct.	1837-1845	Fauquier Co.	Probate, Box 40	1844-001
Hampton	Silas H.	Admr. Acct.	1837-1845	Fauquier Co.	Probate, Box 40	1844-001
Hampton	Silas H.	Admr. Acct.	1873-1845	Fauquier Co.	Probate, Box 40	1844-001
Hampton	Silas H.	Division	Undated	Fauquier Co.	Probate, Box 40	1845-001
Hampton	Wade	Guardian Appt.	1/25/1828	Fauquier Co.	Probate, Box 40	1828-001
Hampton	William C.	Admr. Bond	10/23/1821	Fauquier Co.	Chancery	1868-120
HAMRICK						
Hamrick	James	Admtrx. Bond	1778	Fauquier Co.	Probate, Box 45	1778-020
HAND						
Hand	William	Admr. Bond	1760	Fauquier Co.	Probate, Box 45	1760-006
HANSBROUGH						
Hansbrough	Elijah	Will	8/27/1849	Fauquier Co.	Chancery	1872-006
Hansbrough	Gabriel	Court Order for Sheriff To Administer Estate	8/1802	Fauquier Co.	Probate, Box 39	1802-001
Hansbrough	Jonathan	Division of Slaves	12/28/1861	Fauquier Co.	Chancery	1869-070
Hansbrough	Peter	Will	10/21/1822	Culpeper Co. VA.	Chancery	1866-002
Hansbrough	William	Will	12/18/1837	Culpeper Co. VA.	Chancery	1840-005

Consolidated Probate Index from the Clerks Loose Papers & the Superior Court/Circuit Court Records 1759-1919

Surname	Given Name	Instrument	Date	County	CLP Record Series	Index #
HARDING						
Harding	John	Curator Bond	9/12/1871	Fauquier Co.	Probate, Box 53 Superior/Circuit Ct.	1871-004
Harding	John	Curator Acct.	4/7/1874	Fauquier Co.	Probate, Box 53 Superior/Circuit Ct.	1874-002
Harding	John	Admr. Bond	9/7/1875	Fauquier Co.	Probate, Box 53 Superior/Circuit Ct.	1875-012
Harding	Philip	Guardian Bond	1815	Fauquier Co.	Probate, Box 49	1815-008
HARDY						
Hardy	Joshua	Inventory + Appraisement	5/2/1837	Fauquier Co.	Probate, Box 51 Superior/Circuit Ct.	1837-001
HARPER						
Harper	Robert	Will	10/15/1782	Berkeley Co. WV.	Chancery	1848-011
Harper	Robert	Inventory + Appraisement	10/20/1782	Berkeley Co. WV.	Chancery	1848-011
Harper	Robert	Exor. Acct.	1/21/1807	Berkeley Co. WV.	Chancery	1848-011
Harper	Robert	Exor. Acct.	1/261807	Berkeley Co. WV.	Chancery	1848-011
HARREL (See also Harrell)						
Harrel	James	Admr. Bond	1763	Fauquier Co.	Probate, Box 44	1763-002
HARRELL (See also Harrel)						
Harrell	A. G.	Report of Division	5/14/1903	Fauquier Co.	Chancery	1903-039
Harrell	A. G.	Survey of Division	5/14/1903	Fauquier Co.	Chancery	1903-039
HARRIS						
Harris	Sarah	Admr. Acct.	8/25/1845	Fauquier Co.	Probate, Box 40	1845-003
Harris	Sarah	Death 10/23/1839 (in Admr. Acct.)	8/25/1845	Fauquier Co.	Probate, Box 40	1845-003
Harris	Thomas	Will	6/27/1815	Fauquier Co.	Probate, Box 50	1825-001
Harris	Thomas	Will	5/23/1825	Fauquier Co.	Chancery	1868-128
HARRISON						
Harrison	Benjamin	Summons, to settle Jonathan Gibson's Admr. Acct.	10/1793	Fauquier Co.	Probate, Box 39	1793-005
Harrison	Burr	Guardian Bond	1775	Fauquier Co.	Probate, Box 48	1775-001
Harrison	Burr	Guardian Bond	1784	Fauquier Co.	Probate, Box 48	1784-007
Harrison	Burr (a Lunatic)	Act of Relief For his children	3/5/1832	Richmond, VA.	Chancery	1835-007

Consolidated Probate Index from the Clerks Loose Papers & the Superior Court/Circuit Court Records 1759-1919

Surname	Given Name	Instrument	Date	County	CLP Record Series	Index #
HARRISON (Cont.)						
Harrison	Charles	Guardian Bond	1802	Fauquier Co.	Probate, Box 49	1802-007
Harrison	Eleanor	Guardian Bond	1804	Fauquier Co.	Probate, Box 49	1804-010
Harrison	Frederick	Guardian Bond	1804	Fauquier Co.	Probate, Box 49	1804-010
Harrison	George	Plat & Survey Of Estate	9/3/1839	Fauquier Co.	Chancery	1839-058
Harrison	George	Report of Division	9/14/1839	Fauquier Co.	Chancery	1839-058
Harrison	George	Division of Slaves	9/14/1839	Fauquier Co.	Chancery	1839-058
Harrison	George	Plat & Survey	11/29/1839	Fauquier Co.	Chancery	1839-058
Harrison	George	Report of Division	3/1847	Fauquier Co.	Chancery	1839-058
Harrison	George	Plat & Survey Of Division	3/1847	Fauquier Co.	Chancery	1839-058
Harrison	George	Division of Slaves	5/3/1847	Fauquier Co.	Chancery	1847-038
Harrison	Gustavus	Guardian Bond	1804	Fauquier Co.	Probate, Box 49	1804-010
Harrison	Howard H.	Guardian Appt.	2/2/1878	Fauquier Co.	Chancery	1878-004
Harrison	Laura	Guardian Appt.	2/2/1878	Fauquier Co.	Chancery	1878-004
Harrison	Lucy	Guardian Bond	1775	Fauquier Co.	Probate, Box 48	1775-001
Harrison	Nancy	Guardian Bond	1804	Fauquier Co.	Probate, Box 48	1804-010
Harrison	Susan	Guardian Appt.	2/2/1878	Fauquier Co.	Chancery	1878-004
Harrison	Thomas	Exors. Bond	1774	Fauquier Co.	Probate, Box 44	1774-008
Harrison	William	Guardian Bond	1775	Fauquier Co.	Probate, Box 48	1775-001
Harrison	William	Admtrx. Bond	1775	Fauquier Co.	Probate, Box 44	1775-005
Harrison	William	Guardian Bond	1783	Fauquier Co.	Probate, Box 45	1783-003
Harrison	William	Guardian Acct.	4/16/1791	Fauquier Co.	Chancery	1801-029
Harrison	William	Guardian Bond	1804	Fauquier Co.	Probate, Box 49	1804-010
Harrison	William H.	Guardian Appt.	2/2/1878	Fauquier Co.	Chancery	1878-004
HART						
Hart	Catharine	Will	5/25/1868	Fauquier Co.	Chancery	1880-068
Hart	Catharine	Report of Division	11/1/1868	Fauquier Co.	Chancery	1880-068
Hart	Catharine	Plat & Survey Of Division	11/1/1868	Fauquier Co.	Chancery	1880-068

Consolidated Probate Index from the Clerks Loose Papers & the Superior Court/Circuit Court Records 1759-1919

Surname	Given Name	Instrument	Date	County	CLP Record Series	Index #
HART (Cont.)						
Hart	Catharine R.	Will	5/28/1868	Fauquier Co.	Chancery	1887-021
Hart	Catharine R.	Report of Division	1/8/1876	Fauquier Co.	Chancery	1883-064
Hart	Catharine R.	Plat & Survey Of Division	1/8/1876	Fauquier Co.	Chancery	1883-064
Hart	John R.	Report of Division	12/1896	Fauquier Co.	Chancery	1897-047
Hart	John R.	Plat & Survey Of Division	12/1896	Fauquier Co.	Chancery	1897-047
HARTMAN						
Hartman	Jacob	Admr. Bond	1/26/1881	York Co. PA.	Chancery	1894-074
Hartman	Laura	Report of Dower Allotment	8/21/1880	Fauquier Co.	Chancery	1894-074
Hartman	Peter	Appraisement	7/19/1880	Fauquier Co.	Probate, Box 54 Superior/Circuit Ct.	1880-004
Hartman	Peter	Sales Account	7/19/1880	Fauquier Co.	Probate, Box 54 Superior/Circuit Ct.	1880-004
Hartman	Peter	Heirs	7/28/1880	Fauquier Co.	Chancery	1894-074
Hartman	Peter	Appraisement of Real Estate	9/21/1880	Fauquier Co.	Chancery	1894-074
Hartman	Peter (Mrs.)	Dower Allotment	11/11/1880	Fauquier Co.	Chancery	1894-074
HATCHER						
Hatcher	Hattie E.	Admr. Appt.	6/3/1909	Fauquier Co.	Probate, Box 56 Superior/Circuit Ct.	1909-000
HATHAWAY						
Hathaway	Elizabeth	Will	1/23/1893	Fauquier Co.	Chancery	1906-020
Hathaway	Elizabeth	Plat & Survey Of Division	2/1893	Fauquier Co.	Chancery	1906-020
Hathaway	Elizabeth	Report of Partition	4/7/1894	Fauquier Co.	Chancery	1906-020
Hathaway	James H.	Will	7/25/1892	Fauquier Co.	Chancery	1906-020
Hathaway	James H.	Plat & Survey Of Division	12/1893	Fauquier Co.	Chancery	1906-020
Hathaway	James H.	Report of Partition	4/7/1894	Fauquier Co.	Chancery	1906-020
Hathaway	John	Exors. Bond	1786	Fauquier Co.	Probate, Box 45	1786-007
Hathaway	Sewell	Heirs	Undated	Fauquier Co.	Chancery	1902-051

Consolidated Probate Index from the Clerks Loose Papers & the Superior Court/Circuit Court Records 1759-1919

Surname	Given Name	Instrument	Date	County	CLP Record Series	Index #
HAWKING (See also Hawkins)						
Hawking	Adelaid	Guardian Bond	1815	Fauquier Co.	Probate, Box 49	1815-010
HAWKINS (See also Hawking)						
Hawkins	Alice C.	Will	7/28/1817	Fauquier Co.	Probate, Box 50	1817-002
HAYNES (See also Haines, Hain)						
Haynes	Daniel	Guardian Bond	1803	Fauquier Co.	Probate, Box 49	1803-005
HAYNIE						
Haynie	Martha	Will	8/23/1847	Fauquier Co.	Chancery	1854-003
Haynie	Martha	List of Property	Undated	Fauquier Co.	Chancery	1854-003
HEADLEY						
Headley	Thomas	Guardian Bond	1791	Fauquier Co.	Probate, Box 48	1791-001
HEARLEY						
Hearley	William	Will	12/13/1880	Fauquier Co.	Probate, Box 54 Superior/Circuit Ct.	1880-009
Hearley	William	Exor. Bond	12/13/1880	Fauquier Co.	Probate, Box 54 Superior/Circuit Ct.	1880-009
HEDGMAN						
Hedgman	Peter	Will	8/9/1815	Stafford Co. VA.	Land Records & Disputes	1830-019
HEFLIN						
Heflin	Anna	Guardian Bond	1805	Fauquier Co.	Probate, Box 49	1805-009
Heflin	Dorcas	Guardian Bond	1804	Fauquier Co.	Probate, Box 49	1804-012
Heflin	George A.	Guardian Bond	9/19/1879	Fauquier Co.	Chancery	1879-029
Heflin	J. T.	Heirs	Undated	Fauquier Co.	Chancery	1910-031
Heflin	Polly	Guardian Bond	1805	Fauquier Co.	Probate, Box 49	1805-013
Heflin	W. B.	Appraisement	2/19/1914	Fauquier Co.	Probate, Box 50 Addendum Folder	1919-001
Heflin	William	Will	4/19/1858	Fauquier Co.	Probate, Box 52 Superior/Circuit Ct.	1858-004
Heflin	William	Inventory + Appraisement	5/5/1858	Fauquier Co.	Probate, Box 52 Superior/Circuit Ct.	1858-005
Heflin	William	Sales	1/5/1858	Fauquier Co.	Probate, Box 52 Superior/Circuit Ct.	1858-011
Heflin	William	Sales	1/8/1859	Fauquier Co.	Probate, Box 52 Superior/Circuit Ct.	1859-010
Heflin	William	Exor. Acct.	4/3/1860	Fauquier Co.	Probate, Box 52 Superior/Circuit Ct.	1860-001

Consolidated Probate Index from the Clerks Loose Papers & the Superior Court/Circuit Court Records 1759-1919

Surname	Given Name	Instrument	Date	County	CLP Record Series	Index #
HEFLIN (Cont.)						
Heflin	William	Exor. Acct.	4/2/1861	Fauquier Co.	Probate, Box 52 Superior/Circuit Ct.	1861-004
Heflin	William	Exor. Acct.	4/7/1868	Fauquier Co.	Probate, Box 53 Superior/Circuit Ct.	1868-002
Heflin	William	Exor. Acct.	4/6/1870	Fauquier Co.	Probate, Box 53 Superior/Circuit Ct.	1870-002
Heflin	William	Will	4/19/1858	Fauquier Co.	Chancery	1859-063
Heflin	William	Will	4/19/1858	Fauquier Co.	Chancery	1871-020
Heflin	William	Will	4/19/1858	Fauquier Co.	Chancery	1880-059
Heflin	William	Sales	9/13/1858	Fauquier Co.	Chancery	1880-059
Heflin	William	Sale of Slaves Belonging to Estate	1/1/1859	Fauquier Co.	Chancery	1880-059
Heflin	William	Exor.Acct.	2/19/1861	Fauquier Co.	Chancery	1880-059
HELM						
Helm	Erasmus	Guardian Bond	1815	Fauquier Co.	Probate, Box 49	1815-005
Helm	Mary A.	Will	7/24/1882	Fauquier Co.	Chancery	1883-064
Helm	Mary A.	Renunciation	11/18/1880	Fauquier Co.	Chancery	1883-043
HENDERSON						
Henderson	Janet	Will	5/3/1848	Fauquier Co.	Chancery	1869-009
Henderson	Janet	Exor. Bond	5/3/1848	Fauquier Co.	Probate, Box 51 Superior/Circuit Ct.	1848-006
Henderson	Janet	Exor.Acct.	5/7/1850	Fauquier Co.	Probate, Box 52 Superior/Circuit Ct.	1850-001
Henderson	Janet	Inventory + Appraisement	5/7/1850	Fauquier Co.	Probate, Box 52 Superior/Circuit Ct.	1850-002
Henderson	Thomas	Will	9/4/1900	Fauquier Co.	Probate, Box 55 Superior/Circuit Ct.	1898-006
Henderson	Thomas	Appraisement	10/20/1899	Fauquier Co.	Probate, Box 55 Superior/Circuit Ct.	1899-001
Henderson	Thomas	Sales	2/1/1900	Fauquier Co.	Probate, Box 55 Superior/Circuit Ct.	1900-001
Henderson	Thomas	Collateral Inheritance Tax	1/24/1900	Fauquier Co.	Probate, Box 55 Superior/Circuit Ct.	1900-002
Henderson	Thomas	Exor. Acct.	9/4/1900	Fauquier Co.	Probate, Box 55 Superior/Circuit Ct.	1900-005

Consolidated Probate Index from the Clerks Loose Papers & the Superior Court/Circuit Court Records 1759-1919

Surname	**Given Name**	**Instrument**	**Date**	**County**	**CLP Record Series**	**Index #**
HENRY						
Henry	Joanna	Guardian Bond	9/13/1883	Fauquier Co.	Chancery	1883-071
Henry	Patrick	Guardian Bond	9/13/1883	Fauquier Co.	Chancery	1883-070
Henry	Patrick	Guardian Bond	6/25/1889	Fauquier Co.	Chancery	1900-049
Henry	Richard	Will	4/28/1854	Fauquier Co.	Probate, Box 50 Addendum Folder	1854-001
HENSLEE						
Henslee	Jack Pierce	Guardian Bond	1805	Fauquier Co.	Probate, Box 49	1805-012
HERNDON						
Herndon	A. W.	Admr. Appt.	7/3/1910	Fauquier Co.	Probate, Box 56 Superior/Circuit Ct.	1910-009
Herndon	Francis	Guardian Bond	1805	Fauquier Co.	Probate, Box 49	1809-014
Herndon	John C.	Admr. Bond	1815	Fauquier Co.	Probate, Box 48	1815-051
Herndon	Traverse	Will	9/25/1854	Fauquier Co.	Chancery	1872-026
HERRIFORD						
Herriford	Margaret	Admr. Bond	1811	Fauquier Co.	Probate, Box 48	1811-010
HICKERSON						
Hickerson	Absalom	Guardian Bond	1815	Fauquier Co.	Probate, Box 49	1815-020
Hickerson	Betsey	Relinquishment	2/28/1831	Fauquier Co.	Probate, Box 40	1831-006
Hickerson	Elizabeth	Dower Allotment	1/1816	Fauquier Co.	Chancery	1866-027
Hickerson	Harriet	Guardian Bond	1815	Fauquier Co.	Probate, Box 49	1815-006
Hickerson	Harriott	Guardian Bond	1817	Fauquier Co.	Probate, Box 49	1817-026
Hickerson	Hiram	Guardian Bond	1816	Fauquier Co.	Probate, Box 49	1816-011
Hickerson	Jinsy	Guardian Bond	1815	Fauquier Co.	Probate, Box 49	1815-030
Hickerson	Joseph	Exor. Bond	1815	Fauquier Co.	Probate, Box 47	1815-009
Hickerson	Joseph	Will	4/24/1815	Fauquier Co.	Chancery	1860-020
Hickerson	Joseph	Appraisement	11/9/1815	Fauquier Co.	Chancery	1860-020
Hickerson	Joseph	Sales	11/9-10/1815	Fauquier Co.	Chancery	1860-020
Hickerson	Joseph	Sales	12/25/1815	Fauquier Co.	Chancery	1860-020
Hickerson	Joseph	Sales of Slaves	12/25/1815	Fauquier Co.	Chancery	1860-020
Hickerson	Joseph	Report of Division	1/28/1818	Fauquier Co.	Chancery	1822-024
Hickerson	Joseph	Guardian Chosen	10/20/1832	Fauquier Co.	Probate, Box 40	1832-001

Consolidated Probate Index from the Clerks Loose Papers & the Superior Court/Circuit Court Records 1759-1919

Surname	Given Name	Instrument	Date	County	CLP Record Series	Index #
HICKERSON (Cont.)						
Hickerson	Joseph	Will	4/24/1815	Fauquier Co.	Chancery	1866-027
Hickerson	Marshall	Admr. Bond	8/27/1821	Fauquier Co.	Chancery	1860-020
Hickerson	Marshall	Appraisement	Undated	Fauquier Co.	Chancery	1860-020
Hickerson	Maryan	Guardian Bond	1815	Fauquier Co.	Probate, Box 49	1815-030
Hickerson	Nathaniel	Will	11/28/1814	Fauquier Co.	Chancery	1843-061
Hickerson	Nathaniel	Report of Division	10/3/1835	Fauquier Co.	Chancery	1843-061
Hickerson	Nathaniel	Plat & Survey Of Division	10/3/1835	Fauquier Co.	Chancery	1843-061
Hickerson	Nathaniel	Heirs	Undated	Fauquier Co.	Chancery	1843-061
Hickerson	Sandford	Guardian Bond	1815	Fauquier Co.	Probate, Box 49	1815-006
Hickerson	Sanford	Guardian Bond	1817	Fauquier Co.	Probate, Box 49	1817-026
HILL						
Hill	Elizabeth	Exor. Acct.	2/11/1826	Stafford Co. VA.	Probate, Box 40	1826-003
Hill	Henry	Admr. Appt.	3/17/1868	Culpeper Co. VA.	Chancery	1866-076
HILLARY (See also Hilliary)						
Hillary	H. A.	Power of Attorney	9/9/1890	Staunton, VA.	Probate, Box 54 Superior/Circuit Ct.	1890-003
HILLIARY (See also Hillary)						
Hilliary	William P.	Will	9/13/1890	Fauquier Co.	Probate, Box 54 Superior/Circuit Ct.	1890-003
HITCH						
Hitch	Aquilla	Guardian Bond	1807	Fauquier Co.	Probate, Box 49	1807-009
Hitch	Aria	Guardian Bond	1805	Fauquier Co.	Probate, Box 49	1805-015
Hitch	Cassandra	Will	8/27/1827	Fauquier Co.	Chancery	1841-003
Hitch	Cassandra	Will	8/27/1827	Fauquier Co.	Chancery	1842-018
Hitch	Cassandra	Admr. Appt.	8/28/1828	Fauquier Co.	Chancery	1842-018
Hitch	Clement	Inventory + Sales	6/27/1805	Fauquier Co.	Probate, Box 50	1805-001
Hitch	Dorcas	Guardian Bond	1805	Fauquier Co.	Probate, Box 49	1805-004
Hitch	Elias	Guardian Bond	1805	Fauquier Co.	Probate, Box 49	1805-002

Consolidated Probate Index from the Clerks Loose Papers & the Superior Court/Circuit Court Records 1759-1919

Surname	Given Name	Instrument	Date	County	CLP Record Series	Index #
HITCH (Cont.)						
Hitch	Freeman	Division of Slaves (In Comr. Report)	1832	Fauquier Co.	Chancery	1832-070
Hitch	Freeman	Admr. Acct. (In Comr. Report)	1832	Fauquier Co.	Chancery	1832-070
Hitch	John	Will	5/25/1802	Fauquier Co.	Probate, Box 50	1802-004
Hitch	John	Admr. Bond	5/25/1802	Fauquier Co.	Probate, Box 50	1803-004
Hitch	John	Will	5/22/1848	Fauquier Co.	Chancery	1859-052
Hitch	Lloyd	Guardian Bond	1805	Fauquier Co.	Probate, Box 49	1805-016
Hitch	Maria	Guardian Bond	1811	Fauquier Co.	Probate, Box 49	1811-002
Hitch	Nancy	Inventory + Appraisement	Undated	Fauquier Co.	Chancery	1841-081
Hitch	Nancy	Sales	3/18/1840	Fauquier Co.	Chancery	1841-081
Hitch	Nancy	Admr. Bond	2/24/1840	Fauquier Co.	Chancery	1861-003
Hitch	Nathan	Admtrx. Bond	1811	Fauquier Co.	Probate, Box 47	1811-012
Hitch	Nathan	Division	6/15/1818	Fauquier Co.	Chancery	1861-003
Hitch	Tilman	Will	3/25/1822	Fauquier Co.	Chancery	1832-070
Hitch	Tilman	Appraisement	4/22/1822	Fauquier Co.	Chancery	1832-009
Hitch	Truman	Appraisement	11/28/1814	Fauquier Co.	Probate, Box 50	1814-002
Hitch	Truman	Sales	2/26/1816	Fauquier Co.	Probate, Box 50	1816-002
Hitch	Truman	Admr. Acct. (in Comr. Report)	1/24/1826	Fauquier Co.	Chancery	1832-070
Hitch	Truman	Division of Slaves	1/24/1826	Fauquier Co.	Chancery	1832-070
Hitch	William M.	Will	8/26/1833	Fauquier Co.	Probate, Box 50 Addendum Folder	1833-005
HITT						
Hitt	Aldredge	Guardian Bond	1810	Fauquier Co.	Probate, Box 49	1810-005
Hitt	Benjamin	Will	11/28/1844	Fauquier Co.	Chancery	1871-026
Hitt	Benjamin	Division	2/1851	Fauquier Co.	Probaate, Box 50	1851-001
Hitt	Daniel	Heirs	10/17/1825	Fauquier Co.	Chancery	1852-053

Consolidated Probate Index from the Clerks Loose Papers & the Superior Court/Circuit Court Records 1759-1919

Surname	Given Name	Instrument	Date	County	CLP Record Series	Index #
HITT (Cont.)						
Hitt	Elizabeth	Guardian Bond	1806	Fauquier Co.	Probate, Box 49	1806-017
Hitt	Elizabeth	Guardian Bond	1810	Fauquier Co.	Probate, Box 49	1810-005
Hitt	Hannah	Will	8/27/1846	Fauquier Co.	Chancery	1855-008
Hitt	Hannah	Admr. Bond	9/30/1846	Fauquier Co.	Chancery	1856-031
Hitt	John	Admr. Bond	1782	Fauquier Co.	Probate, Box 45	1782-006
Hitt	Lucinda	Guardian Bond	1810	Fauquier Co.	Probate, Box 49	1810-005
Hitt	Nimrod	Guardian Bond	1810	Fauquier Co.	Probate, Box 49	1810-005
Hitt	Peter	Exors. Bond	1772	Fauquier Co.	Probate, Box 44	1772-004
Hitt	Peter	Admtrx. Bond	1785	Fauquier Co.	Probate, Box 45	1785-014 OS Probate
Hitt	Peter	Admtrx. Bond	1786	Fauquier Co.	Probate, Box 45	1786-016
Hitt	Peter	Will	10/25/1802	Fauquier Co.	Chancery	1855-008
Hitt	Peter	Inventory	12/21/1803	Fauquier Co.	Chancery	1855-008
Hitt	Peter	Admr. Bond	1810	Fauquier Co.	Probate, Box 47	1810-007
Hitt	Peter	Sales of Slaves	Undated	Fauquier Co.	Chancery	1822-019
Hitt	Peter Jr.	Admr. Bond	1810	Fauquier Co.	Probate, Box 47	1810-008
Hitt	Polly	Guardian Bond	1810	Fauquier Co.	Probate, Box 47	1810-005
Hitt	Reuben	Will	9/25/1865	Fauquier Co.	Chancery	1894-013
Hitt	Stephen	Guardian Bond	1806	Fauquier Co.	Probate, Box 49	1806-003
Hitt	Stephen	Plat & Survey Of Division	8/31/1841	Fauquier Co.	Chancery	1842-062
Hitt	Susan	Guardian Bond	1806	Fauquier Co.	Probate, Box 49	1806-008
HIXSON						
Hixson	Benjamin	Admr. Appt.	9/14/1858	Loudoun Co. VA.	Chancery	1880-047
HOFFMAN						
Hoffman	Alice W.	Guardian Acct.	9/7/1892	Fauquier Co.	Probate, Box 55 Superior/Circuit Ct.	1892-007
Hoffman	Alice W.	Guardian Acct.	4/3/1894	Fauquier Co.	Probate, Box 55 Superior/Circuit Ct.	1894-003
Hoffman	Alice W.	Guardian Acct.	4/6/1898	Fauquier Co.	Probate, Box 55 Superior/Circuit Ct.	1894-003

Consolidated Probate Index from the Clerks Loose Papers & the Superior Court/Circuit Court Records 1759-1919

Surname	Given Name	Instrument	Date	County	CLP Record Series	Index #
HOFFMAN (Cont.)						
Hoffman	Annie B.	Guardian Appt.	12/5/1890	Alexandria, VA.	Chancery	1898-022
Hoffman	C. W.	Report of Division	1/13/1894	Fauquier Co.	Chancery	1894-023
Hoffman	C. W.	Plat & Survey Of Division	1/13/1894	Fauquier Co.	Chancery	1894-023
Hoffman	Ora L.	Guardian Appt.	10/9/1890	Fauquier Co.	Chancery	1890-059
Hoffman	Ora L.	Guardian Appt.	12/5/1890	Alexandria, VA.	Chancery	1898-022
Hoffman	Ora L.	Guardian Acct.	9/7/1892	Fauquier Co.	Chancery	1898-022
HOGAIN						
Hogain	John	Admtrx. Bond	1770	Fauquier Co.	Probate, Box 44	1770-001
Hogain	Margaret	Admr. Bond	1767	Fauquier Co.	Probate, Box 44	1767-001
HOLDER						
Holder	Davis	Admr. Bond	1813	Fauquier Co.	Probate, Box 47	1813-026
HOLLODAY						
Holloday	Elizabeth	Admr. Appt.	1854	Orange Co. VA.	Chancery	1859-006
HOLMAN						
Holman	George F.	Will	9/16/1885	Fauquier Co.	Probate, Box 54 Superior/Circuit Ct.	1885-005
Homan	George F.	Admr. Bond	9/16/1885	Fauquier Co.	Probate, Box 54 Superior/Circuit Ct.	1885-005
HOLMES (See also Homes, Hoomes, Hooms)						
Holmes	James	Will	7/15/1907	Fauquier Co.	Probate, Box 50	1907-001
Holmes	James S.	Will	8/24/1857	Fauquier Co.	Chancery	1870-039
Holmes	James S.	Appraisement	11/25/1857	Fauquier Co.	Chancery	1894-012
Homes	James S.	Sales	12/14/1857	Fauquier Co.	Chancery	1894-012
HOLTON						
Holton	Alexander	Exor. Bond	1782	Fauquier Co.	Probate, Box 45	1782-021
HOLTZCLAW						
Holtzclaw	Aga	Guardian Bond	1786	Fauquier Co.	Probate, Box 45	1786-001
Holtzclaw	Archibald	Guardian Bond	1786	Fauquier Co.	Probate, Box 45	1786-001
Holtzclaw	Betsy	Guardian Bond	1786	Fauquier Co.	Probate, Box 45	1786-001
Holtzclaw	Eli	Will	11/27/1848	Fauquier Co.	Chancery	1850-062
Holtzclaw	Eli	Will	11/27/1848	Fauquier Co.	Chancery	1859-022

Consolidated Probate Index from the Clerks Loose Papers & the Superior Court/Circuit Court Records 1759-1919

Surname	Given Name	Instrument	Date	County	CLP Record Series	Index #
HOLTZCLAW (Cont.)						
Holtzclaw	Eli	Will	11/27/1848	Fauquier Co.	Chancery	1869-036
Holtzclaw	Eli	Will	11/27/1848	Fauquier Co.	Chancery	1877-019
Holtzclaw	Frances	Relinquishment	10/23/1849	Fauquier Co.	Probate, Box 51 Superior/Circuit Ct.	1849-002
Holtzclaw	Harmon	Admr. Bond	1772	Fauquier Co.	Probate, Box 44	1772-001
Holtzclaw	Jacob	Exor. Bond	1760	Fauquier Co.	Probate, Box 44	1760-003
Holtzclaw	Joseph	Admtrx. Bond	1786	Fauquier Co.	Probate, Box 44	1786-015 OS Probate
Holtzclaw	Sally	Guardian Bond	1786	Fauquier Co.	Probate, Box 48	1786-001
Holtzclaw	Sally	Guardian Bond	1794	Fauquier Co.	Probate, Box 48	1794-004
Holtzclaw	Stephen	Guardian Bond	1786	Fauquier Co.	Probate, Box 48	1786-001
Holtzclaw	Stephen	Guardian Bond	1789	Fauquier Co.	Probate, Box 48	1789-002
Holtzclaw	William	Will (Extract)	3/17/1893	Fauquier Co.	Chancery	1903-003
HOMES (See also Holmes, Hoomes, Hooms)						
Homes	James	Inventory + Appraisement	2/8/1803	Fauquier Co.	Chancery	1833-046
HONEY						
Honey	Mary (Ramey)	Dower Allotment	12/12/1897	Fauquier Co.	Chancery	1899-039
Honey	William	Admtrx. Bond	1808	Fauquier Co.	Probate, Box 47	1808-014
HOOE						
Hooe	Fanny	Estate Acct.	11/21/1818	Fauquier Co.	Probate, Box 39	1818-010
Hooe	Henry Dade	Will	2/1/1807	Fauquier Co.	Land Records & Disputes	1832-004
Hooe	Howson	Relinquishment	10/1819	Fauquier Co.	Probate, Box 39	1819-002
Hooe	Jane	Guardian Bond	1816	Fauquier Co.	Probate, Box 49	1816-003
Hooe	John	Heirs	10/1819	Fauquier Co.	Probate, Box 39	1819-002
Hooe	John	Exor. Acct.	11/18/1824	Fauquier Co.	Chancery	1858-018
Hooe	Mary	Admr. Bond	4/6/1877	Fauquier Co.	Probate, Box 54 Superior/Circuit Ct.	1887-001
Hooe	R. H.	Relinquishment	10/1819	Fauquier Co.	Probate, Box 39	1819-002

Consolidated Probate Index from the Clerks Loose Papers & the Superior Court/Circuit Court Records 1759-1919

Surname	Given Name	Instrument	Date	County	CLP Record Series	Index #
HOOMES (See also Holmes, Homes, Hooms)						
Hoomes	Sarah Ann	Petition for Relinquishment	10/1805	Fauquier Co.	Probate, Box 39	1805-003
Hoomes	Sarah Ann	Petition for Division	10/18105	Fauquier Co.	Probate, Box 39	1805-003
HOOMS (See also Holmes, Homes, Hoomes)						
Hooms	Diademe	Guardian Chosen	1810	Fauquier Co.	Probate, Box 39	1810-002
HOON						
Hoon	Nancy Ida	Will	10/27/1908	Fauquier Co.	Chancery	1916-002
HOPPER						
Hopper	Joseph	Exors. Bond	1811	Fauquier Co.	Probate, Box 47	1811-002
Hopper	Lucy	Guardian Chosen	1/26/1823	Fauquier Co.	Probate, Box 40	1823-001
Hopper	Lucy	Guardian Bond	1/26/1823	Fauquier Co.	Probate, Box 40	1823-001
Hopper	Mary	Will	5/23/1842	Fauquier Co.	Chancery	1844-045
HORD						
Hord	Ambrose	Will	9/15/1869	Fauquier Co.	Chancery	1876-065
Hord	Ambrose	Appraisement	5/17/1872	Fauquier Co.	Probate, Box 53 Superior/Circuit Ct.	1872-004
Hord	Ambrose	Sales	5/17/1872	Fauquier Co.	Probate, Box 53 Superior/Circuit Ct.	1872-004
Hord	Charity	Will	10/25/1870	Fauquier Co.	Chancery	1902-026
Hord	Enos	Will	4/26/1815	Fauquier Co.	Chancery	1883-004
Hord	Enos	Will	4/23/1869	Fauquier Co.	Chancery	1880-042
Hord	Enos	Will	4/26/1869	Fauquier Co.	Chancery	1886-012
Hord	Enos	Will	4/26/1869	Fauquier Co.	Chancery	1892-056
Hord	Enos	Plat & Survey Of Division	8/1876	Fauquier Co.	Chancery	1900-037
Hord	Enos	Plat & Survey Of Division	7/1879	Fauquier Co.	Chancery	1900-037
Hord	Enos	Admr. Acct.	12/4/1877	Fauquier Co.	Chancery	1900-037
Hord	Enos	Admr. Acct.	12/6/1878	Fauquier Co.	Chancery	1900-037
Hord	James	Will	7/22/1822	Fauquier Co.	Chancery	1850-008
Hord	James	Will	7/22/1822	Fauquier Co.	Chancery	1902-026

Consolidated Probate Index from the Clerks Loose Papers & the Superior Court/Circuit Court Records 1759-1919

Surname	Given Name	Instrument	Date	County	CLP Record Series	Index #
HORD (Cont.)						
Hord	James	Plat & Survey Of Division of "Elk Marsh" Tract	4/22/1874	Fauquier Co.	Chancery	1902-026
Hord	Richard	Exor. Acct.	11/27/1827	Fauquier Co.	Chancery	1852-017
Hord	Thomas	Will	5/9/1855	St. Mary's Parish, LA.	Chancery	1876-046
Hord	William	Will	5/26/1855	Fauquier Co.	Chancery	1900-037
Hord	William	Will	5/26/1855	Fauquier Co.	Chancery	1902-026
HORNER						
Horner	Barbara L.	Will	9/7/1853	Fauquier Co.	Chancery	1869-009
Horner	Frederick	Guardian Bond	1817	Fauquier Co.	Probate, Box 49	1817-006
Horner	Gustavus	Will	2/28/1813	Fauquier Co.	Chancery	1841-012
Horner	Gustavus	Will	2/28/1815	Fauquier Co.	Chancery	1849-007
Horner	Gustavus	Will	2/28/1815	Fauquier Co.	Chancery	1851-018
Horner	Gustavus	Will	2/28/1815	Fauquier Co.	Chancery	1851-018
Horner	Gustavus	Inventory + Appraisement	9/27/1847	Fauquier Co.	Chancery	1851-019
Horner	Gustavus	Sales	9/27/1847	Fauquier Co.	Chancery	1851-019
Horner	Gustavus	Exors. Bond	1815	Fauquier Co.	Probate, Box 47	1815-006
Horner	Gustavus Richard B.	Will	8/22/1892	Warrenton, VA.	Chancery	1896-043
Horner	Gustavus Richard B.	Report of Division	9/9/1895	Fauquier Co.	Chancery	1896-043
Horner	Gustavus Richard B.	Plat & Survey	9/9/1895	Fauquier Co.	Chancery	1896-043
Horner	Inman	Will	7/23/1860	Fauquier Co.	Chancery	1872-074
Horner	Inman	Will	7/23/1860	Fauquier Co.	Chancery	1885-014
Horner	Inman	Report of Division	9/1869	Fauquier Co.	Chancery	1885-014
Horner	Inman	Plat & Survey Of Division	9/1869	Fauquier Co.	Chancery	1885-014
Horner	Inman	Will	7/23/1860	Fauquier Co.	Chancery	1889-006
Horner	Inman	Will	7/23/1860	Fauquier Co.	Chancery	1892-030
Horner	Inman	Will	7/23/1860	Fauquier Co.	Chancery	1893-018

Consolidated Probate Index from the Clerks Loose Papers & the Superior Court/Circuit Court Records 1759-1919

Surname	Given Name	Instrument	Date	County	CLP Record Series	Index #
HORNER (Cont.)						
Horner	John B.	Guardian Bond	1817	Fauquier Co.	Probate, Box 49	1817-006
Horner	Joseph	Report of Division	6/15/1871	Fauquier Co.	Chancery	1882-002
Horner	Joseph	Plat & Survey	6/15/1871	Fauquier Co.	Chancery	1882-002
Horner	Marianna	Guardian Bond	1817	Fauquier Co.	Probate, Box 49	1817-006
Horner	Richard B.	Guardian Bond	1817	Fauquier Co.	Probate, Box 49	1817-006
Horner	Robert	Sales	1832	Fauquier Co.	Chancery	1838-003
Horner	Robert	Admr. Acct.	7/15/1833	Fauquier Co.	Chancery	1838-003
Horner	Robert	Admr. Acct.	1837	Fauquier Co.	Chancery	1838-003
Horner	William	Exor. Acct.	10/18/1844	Fauquier Co.	Probate, Box 51 Superior/Circuit Ct.	1844-005
Horner	William E.	Will	9/14/1857	Fauquier Co.	Probate, Box 52 Superior/Circuit Ct.	1857-003
Horner	William Edmonds	Will	3/23/1853	Philadelphia, PA.	Chancery	1872-065
HOTCHKISS						
Hotchkiss	W. P.	Report of Partition	5/17/1910	Fauquier Co.	Chancery	1910-030
HOWARD						
Howard	Elizabeth	Guardian Bond	1811	Fauquier Co.	Probate, Box 49	1811-004
HOWDERSHELL						
Howdershell	Elizabeth	Admr. Acct.	6/1860	Fauquier Co.	Chancery	1893-042
Howdershell	Jacob	Will	5/24/1875	Fauquier Co.	Chancery	1888-022
Howdershell	John	Will	12/24/1866	Fauquier Co.	Chancery	1893-042
HOWE (See also Howell)						
Howe	Clarence C.	Guardian Appt.	10/27/1906	Fauquier Co.	Probate, Box 56 Superior/Circuit Ct.	1906-008
HOWELL (See also Howe)						
Howell	George	Admtrx. Bond	1786	Fauquier Co.	Probate, Box 45	1786-011 OS Probate
HUBBELL						
Hubbell	Marion Eugene	Guardian Appt.	10/3/1909	Fauquier Co.	Probate, Box 56 Superior/Circuit Ct.	1909-020

Consolidated Probate Index from the Clerks Loose Papers & the Superior Court/Circuit Court Records 1759-1919

Surname	Given Name	Instrument	Date	County	CLP Record Series	Index #
HUDNALL						
Hudnall	Albert	Will	8/26/1851	Fauquier Co.	Chancery	1886-021
Hudnall	Albert	Admr. Bond	8//1851	Fauquier Co.	Chancery	1886-021
Hudnall	Albert	Appraisement	9/22/1851	Fauquier Co.	Chancery	1886-021
Hudnall	Albert	Sales	Undated	Fauquier Co.	Chancery	1886-021
Hudnall	Albert	Exor. Acct.	9/25/1859	Fauquier Co.	Chancery	1886-021
Hudnall	Albert	Admr. Appt.	1/24/1866	Fauquier Co.	Chancery	1886-021
Hudnall	Fanny	Guardian Bond	5/2/6/1834	Fauquier Co.	Chancery	1848-023
Hudnall	Elizabeth (alias Elizabeth Mann)	Grantee, Deed Of Partition	10/12/1867	Fauquier Co.	Probate, Box 50	1867-001
Hudnall	Francis	Will	5/29/1829	Fauquier Co.	Chancery	1842-018
Hudnall	James	Will	1/26/1852	Fauquier Co.	Chancery	1886-014
Hudnall	John	Grantor, Deed Of Partition	10/12/1867	Fauquier Co.	Probate, Box 50	1867-001
Hudnall	John F.	Admr. Bond	1813	Fauquier Co.	Probate, Box 47	1813-019
Hudnall	Ludwell	Admr. Acct.	Undated	Fauquier Co.	Chancery	1902-029
Hudnall	Rush	Grantor, Deed Of Partition	10/12/1867	Fauquier Co.	Probate, Box 50	1867-001
Hudnall	Thomas	Grantor, Deed Of Partition	10/27/1867	Fauquier Co.	Probate, Box 50	1867-001
Hudnall	Westwood	Grantor, Deed Of Partition	10/27/1867	Fauquier Co.	Probate, Box 50	1867-001
Hudnall	William	Will	4/7/1858	Fauquier Co.	Probate, Box 52 Superior/Circuit Ct.	1858-002
Hudnall	William	Summons for Exor. Re Probate of Will	4/7/1858	Fauquier Co.	Probate, Box 52 Superior/Circuit Ct.	1858-003
Hudnall	William	Appraisement	12/12/1858	Fauquier Co.	Probate, Box 52	1858-007
Hudnall	William	Exor. Acct.	9/6/1859	Fauquier Co.	Probate, Box 52 Superior/Circuit Ct.	1859-008
Hudnall	William	Exor. Acct.	9/5/1860	Fauquier Co.	Probate, Box 52 Superior/Circuit Ct.	1860-003
Hudnall	William	Admr. Bond	12/12/1865	Fauquier Co.	Probate, Box 52 Superior/Circuit Ct	1865-003

Consolidated Probate Index from the Clerks Loose Papers & the Superior Court/Circuit Court Records 1759-1919

Surname	Given Name	Instrument	Date	County	CLP Record Series	Index #
HUDNALL (Cont.)						
Hudnall	William	Will	4/7/1858	Fauquier Co.	Chancery	1875-053
Hudnall	William	Will	4/6/1858	Fauquier Co.	Chancery	1886-021
Hudnall	William	Exor. Qualified	4/9/1858	Fauquier Co.	Chancery	1886-021
Hudnall	William	Exor. Acct.	9/6/1859	Fauquier Co.	Chancery	1886-021
Hudnall	William	Exor. Acct.	4/15/1860	Fauquier Co.	Chancery	1886-021
Hudnall	William	Admr. Appt.	12/12/1865	Fauquier Co.	Chancery	1866-021
HUGER						
Huger	Benjamin	Will	12/24/1877	Fauquier Co.	Chancery	1882-008
HULETT						
Hulett	Leroy	Admrs. Bond	1782	Fauquier Co.	Probate, Box 45	1782-004
HUME						
Hume	Asa	Admr. Acct.	Undated	Fauquier Co.	Chancery	1835-042
Hume	Asa	Will	9/27/1831	Fauquier Co.	Chancery	1850-005
Hume	George	Guardian Bond	1791	Fauquier Co.	Probate, Box 48	1791-005
Hume	Hannah	Guardian Bond	1791	Fauquier Co.	Probate, Box 48	1791-005
Hume	Jane	Guardian Bond	1810	Fauquier Co.	Probate, Box 49	1810-008
Hume	Peggy	Guardian Bond	1810	Fauquier Co.	Probate, Box 49	1819-012
Hume	Robert	Admrs. Bond	1809	Fauquier Co.	Probate, Box 47	1809-010
Hume	Susan H.	Plat & Survey Of Division	2/3/1906	Fauquier Co.	Chancery	1906-045
Hume	William M.	Admr. Appt.	12/4/1873	Fauquier Co.	Chancery	1903-057
HUMPHREY (See also Humphreys)						
Humphrey	Alonzo	Guardian Appt.	4/19/1909	Fauquier Co.	Probate, Box 56 Superior/Circuit Ct.	1909-007
Humphrey	Rebecca	Guardian Appt.	4/19/1909	Fauquier Co.	Probate, Box 56 Superior/Circuit Ct.	1909-007
Humphrey	Scott C.	Guardian Appat.	4/19/1909	Fauquier Co.	Probate, Box 56 Superior/Circuit Ct.	1909-007
HUMPHREYS (See also Humphrey)						
Humphreys	William	Will	9/1804	Fauquier Co.	Probate, Box 50	1804-001
HUMSTON						
Humston	Edward	Will	6/22/1795	Fauquier Co.	Probate, Box 50	1793-001

Consolidated Probate Index from the Clerks Loose Papers & the Superior Court/Circuit Court Records 1759-1919

Surname	Given Name	Instrument	Date	County	CLP Record Series	Index #
HUNTON						
Hunton	Ann	Relinquishment	1/1829	Fauquier Co.	Probate, Box 40	1829-003
Hunton	Catharine R.	Admr. Bond	1815	Fauquier Co.	Probate, Box 47	1815-050
Hunton	Eppa	Will	1/1834	Fauquier Co.	Chancery	1841-055
Hunton	Eppa	Plat & Survey Of Division	10/27/1834	Fauquier Co.	Chancery	1841-055
Hunton	Eppa's Heirs	Plat & Survey Of Division	8/25/1841	Fauquier Co.	Chancery	1841-055
Hunton	Eppa	Exor. Acct.	1837	Fauquier Co.	Chancery	1841-055
Hunton	Eppa	Resolution for Memorial of Life	12/9/1908	Fauquier Co.	Probate, Box 56 Superior/Circuit Ct.	1908-019
Hunton	George	Guardian Bond	1795	Fauquier Co.	Probate, Box 48	1795-001
Hunton	J. G.	Will	1/25/1906	Fauquier Co.	Chancery	1907-032
Hunton	James	Plat & Survey	12/1/1827	Fauquier Co.	Chancery	1868-130
Hunton	James	Report of Division Of Slaves	12/27/1824	Fauquier Co.	Chancery	1868-130
Hunton	James	Admr. Bond	4/23/1875	Fauquier Co.	Probate, Box 53 Superior/Circuit Ct.	1875-004
Hunton	James	Admr. Acct.	4/6/1878	Fauquier Co.	Probate, Box 53 Superior/Circuit Ct.	1878-003
Hunton	John	Admrs. Bond	1809	Fauquier Co.	Probate, Box 47	1809-011
Hunton	John B.	Guardian Bond	7/28/1828	Fauquier Co.	Chancery	1843-030
Hunton	Robert	Guardian Bond	10/26/1830	Fauquier Co.	Chancery	1843-030
Hunton	Robert	Guardian Bond	8/21/1831	Fauquier Co.	Chancery	1843-030
Hunton	Robert	Guardian Acct.	9/25/1832	Fauquier Co.	Chancery	1843-030
Hunton	Robert	Guardian Acct.	9/24/1833	Fauquier Co.	Chancery	1843-030
Hunton	Robert	Guardian Acct.	1/27/1835	Fauquier Co.	Chancery	1843-030
Hunton	Robert	Guardian Acct.	11/24/1835	Fauquier Co.	Chancery	1843-030
Hunton	Robert	Guardian Acct.	10/25/1836	Fauquier Co.	Chancery	1843-030
Hunton	Robert	Guardian Acct	8/1837	Fauquier Co.	Chancery	1843-030
Hunton	Robert	Guardian Acct.	10/22/1838	Fauquier Co.	Chancery	1843-030

Consolidated Probate Index from the Clerks Loose Papers & the Superior Court/Circuit Court Records 1759-1919

Surname	Given Name	Instrument	Date	County	CLP Record Series	Index #
HUNTON (Cont.)						
Hunton	Robert	Guardian Acct.	9/23/1839	Fauquier Co.	Chancery	1843-030
Hunton	Robert	Guardian Acct.	9/28/1840	Fauquier Co.	Chancery	1843-030
Hunton	Robert	Guardian Acct.	10/26/1841	Fauquier Co.	Chancery	1843-030
Hunton	William	Exors. Bond	1809	Fauquier Co.	Probate, Box 47	1809-019
Hunton	William	Estate Accounts	1838	Fauquier Co.	Probate, Box 40	1839-001
Hunton	William	Exor. Acct.	1838	Fauquier Co.	Probate, Box 40	1839-001
Hunton	William	Will	8/27/1838	Fauquier Co.	Chancery	1840-011
Hunton	William	Report of Division Of Slaves	8/10/1840	Fauquier Co.	Chancery	1840-011
Hunton	William	Will	8/27/1838	Fauquier Co.	Chancery	1896-006
Hunton	William E.	Inventory	9/14/1832	Fauquier Co.	Land Records & Disputes	1835-013
Hunton	William E.	Sales	9/15/1832	Fauquier Co.	Land Records & Disputes	1835-013
Hunton	William S.	Admr. Appt.	10/27/1906	Fauquier Co.	Probate, Box 56 Superior/Circuit Ct.	1906-006
HURMANS						
Hurmans	John	Exors. Bond	1775	Fauquier Co.	Probate, Box 44	1775-006
HURST						
Hurst	Albert P.	Guardian Appt.	3/24/1908	Fauquier Co.	Probate, Box 56 Superior/Circuit Ct.	1908-008
Hurst	Frank M.	Guardian Appt.	3/24/1908	Fauquier Co.	Probate, Box 56 Superior/Circuit Ct.	1908-008
Hurst	Minnie Mary	Guardian Appt.	3/24/1908	Fauquier Co.	Probate, Box 56 Superior/Circuit Ct.	1908-008
Hurst	William H.	Guardian Appt.	3/24/1908	Fauquier Co.	Probate, Box 56 Superior/Circuit Ct.	1908-008
HURXTHAL						
Hurxthal	W. E.	Will	11/23/1896	Fauquier Co.	Chancery	1897-017
HUTCHISON						
Hutchison	Ann	Plat & Survey Of Dower Allotment	9/1877	Fauquier Co.	Chancery	1878-020
Hutchison	Lemuel	Admr. Bond	9/8/1873	Fauquier Co.	Probate, Box 53 Superior/Circuit Ct.	1873-004

Consolidated Probate Index from the Clerks Loose Papers & the Superior Court/Circuit Court Records 1759-1919

Surname	Given Name	Instrument	Date	County	CLP Record Series	Index #
HUTTON						
Hutton	Isaac G.	Admr. Appt.	6/28/1858	Fairfax Co. VA.	Chancery	1891-046
HYDE						
Hyde	Reginald	Admtrx. Appt.	6/21/1907	Fauquier Co.	Probate, Box 56 Superior/Circuit Ct.	1907-007
IDEN						
Iden	George	Admr. Bond	9/5/1860	Fauquier Co.	Probate, Box 52 Superior/Circuit Ct.	1860-004
INGLE (See also Ingles)						
Ingle	Joseph W.	Appraisement	10/22/1875	Fauquier Co.	Probate, Box 53 Superior/Circuit Ct.	1875-010
Ingle	Joseph W.	Sales	10/22/1875	Fauquier Co.	Probate, Box 53 Superior/Circuit Ct.	1875-010
Ingle	Joseph W.	Admr. Acct.	9/6/1876	Fauquier Co.	Probate, Box 54	1876-007
INGLES (See also Ingle)						
Ingles	John	Admr. Bond	9/9/1874	Fauquier Co.	Probate, Box 53 Superior/Circuit Ct.	1874-006
INGRAM						
Ingram	Nancy	Guardian Bond	1815	Fauquier Co.	Probate, Box 49	1815-025
IVEY						
Ivey	John K.	Will	9/6/1892	Fauquier Co.	Probate, Box 55 Superior/Circuit Ct.	1892-003
Ivey	John K.	Admr. Appt.	9/17/1892	Fauquier Co.	Probate, Box 55 Superior/Circuit Ct.	1892-003
Ivey	John K.	Sales	2/3/1894	Fauquier Co.	Probate, Box 55 Superior/Circuit Ct.	1894-001

Consolidated Probate Index from the Clerks Loose Papers & the Superior Court/Circuit Court Records 1759-1919

Surname	Given Name	Instrument	Date	County	CLP Record Series	Index #
JACKMAN						
Jackman	Thomas	Exor. Bond	1782	Fauquier Co.	Probate, Box 45	1782-011
JACKSON						
Jackson	A. M.	Motion for Stock Transfer	1/8/1889	Fauquier Co.	Probate, Box 54 Superior/Circuit Ct.	1889-003
Jackson	Billey	Admrs. Bond	1815	Fauquier Co.	Probate, Box 47	1815-038
Jackson	Elizabeth E.	Will	5/7/1851	Fauquier Co.	Probate, Box 52	1851-002
Jackson	Elizabeth L.	Will	5/5/1851	Fauquier Co.	Chancery	1875-048
Jackson	Hilda	Guardian Appt.	7/27/1907	Fauquier Co.	Probate, Box 56 Superior/Circuit Ct.	1907-011
Jackson	J. E.	Will	4/3/1895	Fauquier Co.	Probate, Box 55 Superior/Circuit Ct.	1895-002
Jackson	John F.	Will	3/24/1856	Fauquier Co.	Chancery	1873-036
Jackson	Joseph Morris	Guardian Appt.	7/27/1907	Fauquier Co.	Probate, Box 56 Superior/Circuit Ct.	1907-011
Jackson	Lindsey O'Neal	Guardian Appt.	7/27/1907	Fauquier Co.	Probate, Box 56 Superior/Circuit Ct.	1907-011
Jackson	Lucy Ann	Guardian Appt.	7/27/1907	Fauquier Co.	Probate, Box 56 Superior/Circuit Ct.	1907-011
JACOB						
Jacob	John	Chosen as Guardian For nephews George And Lewis Embrey	1804	Fauquier Co.	Probate, Box 39	1804-003
JAMES						
James	Aldridge (Mrs.)	Dower Allotment	6/23/1849	Fauquier Co.	Chancery	1852-006
James	Aldridge (Mrs.)	Plat & Survey Of Dower Allotment	6/23/1849	Fauquier Co.	Chancery	1852-006
James	Benjamin	Will	1/23/1804	Fauquier Co.	Chancery	1840-030
James	Benjamin	Will	1/23/1804	Fauquier Co.	Chancery	1866-027
James	Benjamin	Plat & Survey Of Division	2/1860	Fauquier Co.	Chancery	1866-030
James	Benjamin	Will	1/23/1804	Baltimore, MD.	Chancery	1875-005
James	Dr's Widow	Plat & Survey Of Dower Allotment	1/26/1872	Fauquier Co.	Chancery	1877-056

Consolidated Probate Index from the Clerks Loose Papers & the Superior Court/Circuit Court Records 1759-1919

Surname	Given Name	Instrument	Date	County	CLP Record Series	Index #
JAMES (Cont.)						
James	Elizabeth	Will	10/27/1834	Fauquier Co.	Chancery	1852-006
James	Elizabeth	Will	10/27/1834	Fauquier Co.	Chancery	1859-006
James	George	Guardian Bond	1776	Fauquier Co.	Probate, Box 48	1776-003
James	John	Exors. Bond	1779	Fauquier Co.	Probate, Box 45	1779-001
James	John	Guardian Bond	1817	Fauquier Co.	Probate, Box 49	1817-027
James	John W.	Plat & Survey Of Division	4/23/1858	Fauquier Co.	Chancery	1866-030
James	Julia C.	Will	5/27/1901	Fauquier Co.	Chancery	1905-041
James	Mary	Guardian Bond	1817	Fauquier Co.	Probate, Box 49	1817-027
James	Sarah E.	Will	5/28/1860	Fauquier Co.	Chancery	1873-025
James	Sarah E.	Will	5/28/1860	Fauquier Co.	Chancery	1877-056
James	Sarah E.	Admr. Acct.	1861	Fauquier Co.	Chancery	1877-056
James	Sarah E.	Admr. Acct.	12/1/1869	Fauquier Co.	Chancery	1877-056
James	Susan	Plat & Survey Of Division	6/24/1868	Fauquier Co.	Chancery	1870-053
James	Susan	Plat & Survey	7/1868	Fauquier Co.	Chancery	1910-008
James	Thomas	Guardian Bond	1776	Fauquier Co.	Probate, Box 48	1776-003
James	Thomas	Guardian Bond	1817	Fauquier Co.	Probate, Box 49	1817-027
James	William	Guardian Bond	1871	Fauquier Co.	Probate, Box 49	1817-027
JEFFRIES (See also Jeffris)						
Jeffries	Alexander	Will	7/22/1867	Fauquier Co.	Chancery	1890-024
Jeffries	Alexander Sr.	Admr. Bond	1806	Fauquier Co.	Probate, Box 47	1806-013
Jeffries	Enoch	Will	2/25/1834	Fauquier Co.	Chancery	1850-020
Jeffries	Enoch	Will	2/25/1834	Fauquier Co.	Chancery	1868-134
Jeffries	George	Admtrs. Bond	1815	Fauquier Co.	Probate, Box 47	1815-054
Jeffries	James E.	Report of Division	11/18/1850	Fauquier Co.	Chancery	1850-074
Jeffries	James E.	Plat & Survey Of Division	11/18/1850	Fauquier Co.	Chancery	1850-074
Jeffries	James Payne	Resolution for Memorial of Life	12/9/1908	Fauquier Co.	Probate, Box 56 Superior/Circuit Ct.	1808-020

Consolidated Probate Index from the Clerks Loose Papers & the Superior Court/Circuit Court Records 1759-1919

Surname	**Given Name**	**Instrument**	**Date**	**County**	**CLP Record Series**	**Index #**
JEFFRIES (Cont.)						
Jeffries	James R.	Guardian Appt.	4/8/1889	Fauquier Co.	Chancery	1889-036
Jeffries	Joseph	Will	6/28/1897	Fauquier Co.	Chancery	1903-009
Jeffries	Moses	Heirs	1859	Fauquier Co.	Chancery	1859-011
JEFFRIS (See also Jeffries)						
Jeffris	John	Admr. Bond	1808	Fauquier Co.	Probate, Box 46	1808-002
Jeffris	John	Admr. Bond	1809	Fauquier Co.	Probate, Box 47	1809-007
Jeffris	Joseph	Exors. Bond	1808	Fauquier Co.	Probate, Box 47	1808-025
JENIFER						
Jenifer	Walter Hanson	Will	2/4/1786	Charles Co. MD.	Chancery	1851-002
JENKINS						
Jenkins	Joshua	Heirs	3/27/1780	Fauquier Co.	Military Records	1809-001
JENNINGS						
Jennings	Augustin	Exors. Bond	1778	Fauquier Co.	Probate, Box 45	1778-006
Jennings	Augustine	Will	8/28/1815	Fauquier Co.	Chancery	1868-159
Jennings	Augustine	Exor. Bond	1815	Fauquier Co.	Probate, Box 47	1815-008
Jennings	Benjamin	Guardian Bond	1785	Fauquier Co.	Probate, Box 48	1785-002
Jennings	Berryman	Admtrx. Bond	1782	Fauquier Co.	Probate, Box 45	1782-012
Jennings	Berryman	Guardian Bond	1794	Fauquier Co.	Probate, Box 48	1794-005
Jennings	Carola A.	Division of Real Estate	9/18/1844	Fauquier Co.	Chancery	1852-005
Jennings	Carola G. A.	Estate Acct.	8/7/1835	Fauquier Co.	Chancery	1852-005
Jennings	Hannah	Exor. Bond	1809	Fauquier Co.	Probate, Box 47	1809-004
Jennings	J. C.	Admr. Bond	4/16/1884	Fauquier Co.	Probate, Box 54 Superior/Circuit Ct.	1884-001
Jennings	John C.	Appraisement	38/30/1884	Fauquier Co.	Probate, Box 54 Superior/Circuit Ct.	1884-004
Jennings	Lewis	Plat & Survey Of Division	3/24/1834	Fauquier Co.	Chancery	1832-016
Jennings	Lewis	Will	5/24/1831	Fauquier Co.	Chancery	1866-029
Jennings	Lewis	Inventory + Appraisement	5/24/1831	Fauquier Co.	Chancery	1866-029
Jennings	Lewis	Admr. Bond	1/26/1842	Fauquier Co.	Chancery	1866-029

Consolidated Probate Index from the Clerks Loose Papers & the Superior Court/Circuit Court Records 1759-1919

Surname	Given Name	Instrument	Date	County	CLP Record Series	Index #
JENNINGS (Cont.)						
Jennings	Lewis	Admr. Acct.	6/24/1845	Fauquier Co.	Chancery	1866-029
Jennings	Lewis	Division of Slaves	12/29/1845	Fauquier Co.	Chancery	1866-029
Jennings	Lewis	Admr. Acct.	1/24/1848	Fauquier Co.	Chancery	1866-029
Jennings	Lewis T. S.	Will	5/6/1854	Davidson Co. TN.	Chancery	1855-035
Jennings	Lucy	Guardian Acct.	10/10/1848	Fauquier Co.	Chancery	1852-005
Jennings	Margaret	Admr. Bond	12/26/1842	Fauquier Co.	Chancery	1866-029
Jennings	Margaret	Inventory + Appraisement	12/26/1842	Fauquier Co.	Chancery	1866-029
Jennings	Margaret	Sales	1/17/1843	Fauquier Co.	Chancery	1866-029
Jennings	Margaret	Admr. Acct.	6/24/1845	Fauquier Co.	Chancery	1866-029
Jennings	Margaret	Admr. Acct.	1/24/1848	Fauquier Co.	Chancery	1866-029
Jennings	Mary E.	Dower Allotment	4/23/1873	Fauquier Co.	Chancery	1900-026
Jennings	Mary E.	Plat & Survey Of Dower Allotment	4/23/1873	Fauquier Co.	Chancery	1900-026
Jennings	Mary E.	Plat & Survey Of Dower Allotment	1/19/1904	Fauquier Co.	Chancery	1906-007
Jennings	Sally	Guardian Bond	1784	Fauquier Co.	Probate, Box 48	1784-005
JETT						
Jett	Francis	Estate Sales	10/21/1801	Fauquier Co.	Chancery	1824-032
Jett	Francis	Admr. Bond	1814	Fauquier Co.	Probate, Box 47	1814-004
Jett	Francis	Estate Accts.	1837	Fauquier Co.	Probate, Box 40	1873-001
Jett	Francis M.	Will	7/25/1859	Fauquier Co.	Chancery	1875-075
Jett	Francis M.	Appraisement	7/25/1859	Fauquier Co.	Chancery	1889-060
Jett	Maria	Guardian Bond	1804	Fauquier Co.	Probate, Box 49	1804-001
Jett	Polly	Guardian Bond	1805	Fauquier Co.	Probate, Box 49	1805-010
Jett	Sally	Guardian Bond	1804	Fauquier Co.	Probate, Box 49	1804-001
Jett	Susan	Will	6/10/1850	Rapphk. Co. VA.	Chancery	1886-022
Jett	Susan	Exor. Acct.	9/9/1851	Fauquier Co.	Chancery	1886-022
Jett	Susan	Exor. Acct.	8/5/1856	Fauquier Co.	Chancery	1886-022

Consolidated Probate Index from the Clerks Loose Papers & the Superior Court/Circuit Court Records 1759-1919

Surname	Given Name	Instrument	Date	County	CLP Record Series	Index #
JETT (Cont.)						
Jett	Susan	Exor. Acct.	11/23/1857	Fauquier Co.	Chancery	1886-022
Jett	Susan	Exor. Acct.	6/30/1858	Fauquier Co.	Chancery	1886-022
Jett	William H.	Will	12/22/1856	Fauquier Co.	Chancery	1875-075
Jett	William H.	Admr. Appt.	8/25/1858	Fauquier Co.	Chancery	1886-040
Jett	William H.	Admr. Bond	8/25/1858	Fauquier Co.	Chancery	1886-040
Jett	William H.	Admr. Bond	1/28/1871	Fauquier Co.	Chancery	1886-040
Jett	William H.	Will	12/22/1856	Fauquier Co.	Chancery	1893-001
Jett	William H.	Admr. Appt.	8/25/1858	Fauquier Co.	Chancery	1893-001
Jett	William Sr.	Curator Bond	5/15/1851	Fauquier Co.	Probate, Box 52 Superior/Circuit Ct.	1851-008
JEWELL						
Jewell	Ellen	Guardian Appt.	5/14/1838	Fauquier Co.	Chancery	1841-009
Jewell	Frances Ann	Guardian Appt.	5/14/1838	Fauquier Co.	Chancery	1841-009
Jewell	Mary Elizabeth	Guardian Appt.	5/14/1838	Fauquier Co.	Chancery	1841-009
Jewell	Sarah	Guardian Appt.	5/14/1838	Fauquier Co.	Chancery	1841-009
JOHNSON (See also Johnston)						
Johnson	Ann R.	Admrs. Appt.	9/25/1905	Fauquier Co.	Probate, Box 55 Superior/Circuit Ct.	1905-012
Johnson	Daniel	Guardian Bond	1806	Fauquier Co.	Probate, Box 49	1806-002
Johnson	George	Admr. Bond	1780	Fauquier Co.	Probate, Box 45	1780-002
Johnson	Jeffrey	Exor. Bond	1783	Fauquier Co.	Probate, Box 45	1783-016
Johnson	Moses	Court order to Settle Estate	1/1805	Fauquier Co.	Probate, Box 39	1805-001
Johnson	Moses	Will	3/29/1843	Fauquier Co.	Chancery	1866-069
Johnson	Moses	Will	3/29/1843	Fauquier Co.	Chancery	1871-086
Johnson	Moses	Inventory + Appraisement	12/23/1845	Fauquier Co.	Chancery	1871-086
Johnson	Moses	Will	8/25/1868	Fauquier Co.	Chancery	1908-039
Johnson	Moses	Plat & Survey Of Division	1/27/1908	Fauquier Co.	Chancery	1908-039
Johnson	Moses	Report of Partition	4/2/1908	Fauquier Co.	Chancery	1908-039

Consolidated Probate Index from the Clerks Loose Papers & the Superior Court/Circuit Court Records 1759-1919

Surname	Given Name	Instrument	Date	County	CLP Record Series	Index #
JOHNSON (Cont.)						
Johnson	Polly	Guardian Bond	1806	Fauquier Co.	Probate, Box 49	1806-002
Johnson	Samuel	Will	8/10/1842	Fauquier Co.	Chancery	1847-052
Johnson	Samuel	Inventory + Appraisement	2/28/1843	Fauquier Co.	Chancery	1847-052
Johnson	Susan	Guardian Bond	1797	Fauquier Co.	Probate, Box 48	1797-002
Johnson	Tunis	Will	5/23/1808	Fauquier Co.	Chancery	1817-018
Johnson	Tunis	Inventory + Appraisement	7/25/1808	Fauquier Co.	Chancery	1871-018
Johnson	William	Guardian Bond	1804	Fauquier Co.	Probate, Box 49	1804-004
Johnson	Younger	Guardian Bond	1780	Fauquier Co.	Probate, Box 48	1780-003
JOHNSTON (See also Johnson)						
Johnston	Aaron	Guardian Bond	1780	Fauquier Co.	Probate, Box 48	1762-001
Johnston	Bailey	Admr. Bond	1811	Fauquier Co.	Probate, Box 47	1811-005
Johnston	Baldwin	Admr. Bond	1809	Fauquier Co.	Probate, Box 47	1809-016
Johnston	Charlotte	Guardian Bond	1803	Fauquier Co.	Probate, Box 49	1803-004
Johnston	Daniel	Guardian Bond	1803	Fauquier Co.	Probate, Box 49	1803-004
Johnston	Dennis	Guardian Bond	1815	Fauquier Co.	Probate, Box 49	1815-021
Johnston	Francis	Guardian Bond	1762	Fauquier Co.	Probate, Box 48	1762-001
Johnston	Harvey	Guardian Bond	1811	Fauquier Co.	Probate, Box 49	1811-006
Johnston	John	Admr. Bond	1797	Fauquier Co.	Probate, Box 46	1797-003
Johnston	Lucy	Will	5/28/1860	Fauquier Co.	Probate, Box 50	1860-002
Johnston	Malinda	Guardian Bond	1811	Fauquier Co.	Probate, Box 49	1811-006
Johnston	Mary	Guardian Bond	1803	Fauquier Co.	Probate, Box 49	1803-004
Johnston	Moses	Division	9/20/1806	Fauquier Co.	Chancery	1806-015
Johnston	Smith	Admtrx. Bond	1797	Fauquier Co.	Probate, Box 46	1797-006
Johnston	Tunis	Exors. Bond	1808	Fauquier Co.	Probate, Box 46	1808-003
Johnston	Whitfield	Guardian Bond	1811	Fauquier Co.	Probate, Box 49	1811 006

Consolidated Probate Index from the Clerks Loose Papers & the Superior Court/Circuit Court Records 1759-1919

Surname	**Given Name**	**Instrument**	**Date**	**County**	**CLP Record Series**	**Index #**
JONES						
Jones	A. B.	Admr. Bond	9/15/1871	Fauquier Co.	Chancery	1871-005
Jones	A. B.	Appraisement	5/4/1872	Fauquier Co.	Chancery	1872-005
Jones	A. B.	Sales	5/4/1872	Fauquier Co.	Chancery	1872-005
Jones	A. B.	Admr. Acct.	7/7/1874	Fauquier Co.	Chancery	1874-003
Jones	Charles	Admr. Bond	1775	Fauquier Co.	Probate, Box 44	1775-011
Jones	Diadema	Plat & Survey Of Dower Allotment	10/14/1859	Fauquier Co.	Chancery	1894-073
Jones	Diadema	Report of Dower In Slaves	11/29/1859	Fauquier Co.	Chancery	1894-073
Jones	Elijah	Guardian Bond	1790	Fauquier Co.	Probate, Box 48	1790-001
Jones	James	Admtrx. Bond	1806	Fauquier Co.	Probate, Box 46	1806-015
Jones	James F.	Inventory + Appraisement	10/25/1866	Fauquier Co.	Chancery	1887-002
Jones	John	Admr. Bond	1783	Fauquier Co.	Probate, Box 45	1783-001
Jones	William	Exor. Bond	1815	Fauquier Co.	Probate, Box 47	1815-007
Jones	William	Appraisement	10/24/1835	Fauquier Co.	Chancery	1850-069
Jones	William	Will	8/26/1847	Fauquier Co.	Chancery	1871-053
Jones	William	Will	8/26/1851	Fauquier Co.	Chancery	1894-073
Jones	William R.	Will	4/25/1859	Fauquier Co.	Chancery	1890-053
Jones	William R.	Will	4/25/1859	Fauquier Co.	Chancery	1893-035
Jones	William R.	Exor. Bond	4/25/1859	Fauquier Co.	Chancery	1893-035
Jones	William R.	Exor. Acct.	8/9/1866	Fauquier Co.	Chancery	1893-035
Jones	William R.	Estate Settlement	1/6/1870	Fauquier Co.	Chancery	1893-035
Jones	William R.	Exor. Acct.	4/8/1874	Fauquier Co.	Chancery	1893-035
JOYCE						
Joyce	Susan C.	Will	4/29/1830	Fauquier Co.	Probate, Box 50	1830-002
JULIUS						
Julius	Henry	Will	9/28/1896	Fauquier Co.	Chancery	1907-009

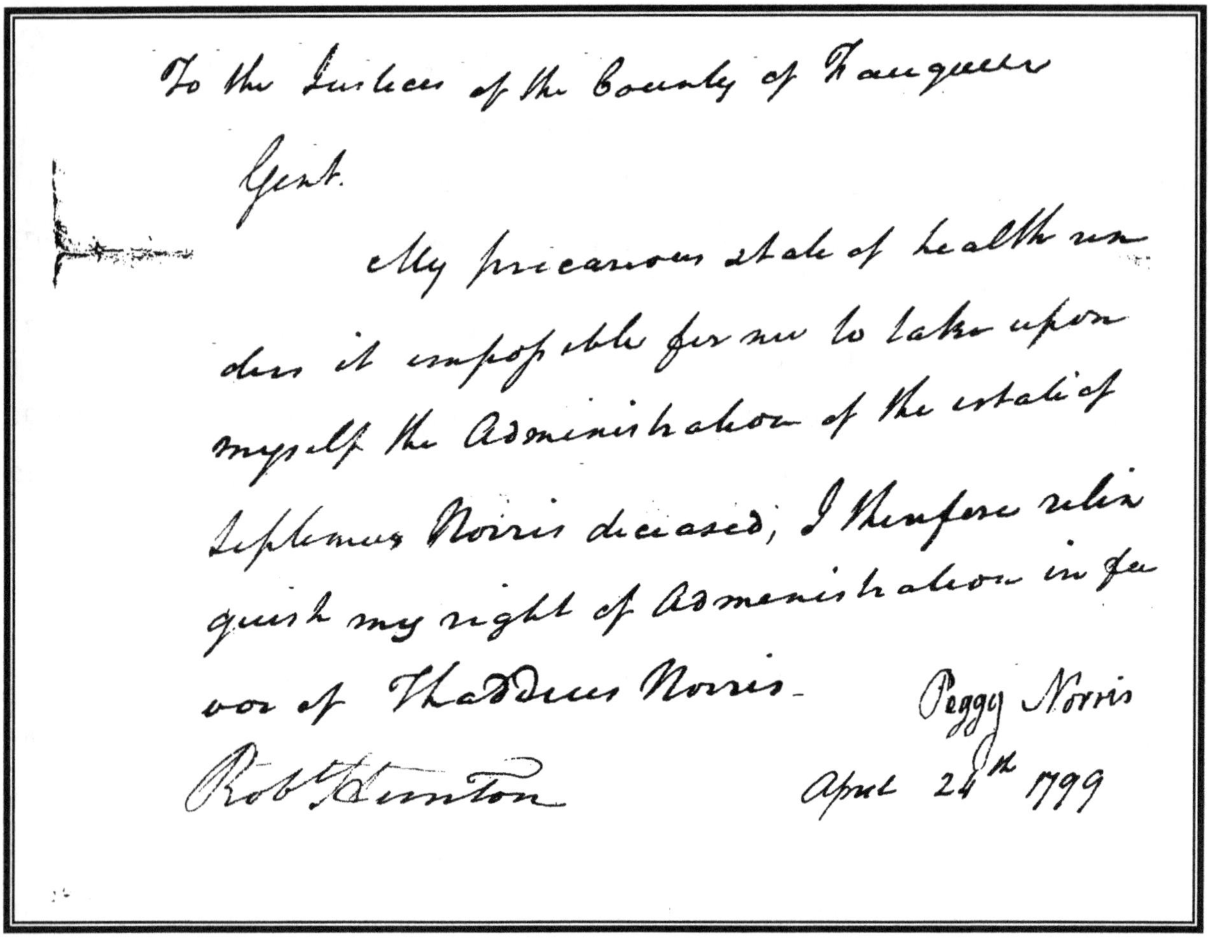

Consolidated Probate Index from the Clerks Loose Papers & the Superior Court/Circuit Court Records 1759-1919

> To the Justices of the County of Fauquier
> Gent.
>
> My precarious state of health renders it impossible for me to take upon myself the Administration of the estate of Septimus Norris deceased; I therefore relinquish my right of Administration in favor of Thaddeus Norris.
>
> Peggy Norris
> Rob Hinton
> April 24th 1799

Plate 2. Probate. Scanned Image from Box 39. Wills &c. 1799-002. Peggy Norris' Relinquishment of Administration of Estate of Septimus Norris, decd. to her son Thaddeus Norris.

Consolidated Probate Index from the Clerks Loose Papers & the Superior Court/Circuit Court Records 1759-1919

Surname	Given Name	Instrument	Date	County	CLP Record Series	Index #
KAMPER (See also Kemper)						
Kamper	Agatha	Guardian Bond	1785	Fauquier Co.	Probate, Box 48	1785-001
Kamper	Herman	Admr. Bond	1774	Fauquier Co.	Probate, Box 44	1774-015
Kamper	Morris	Admr. Bond	1782	Fauquier Co.	Probate, Box 45	1782-017
Kamper	Sarah	Guardian Bond	1785	Fauquier Co.	Probate, Box 48	1785-001
Kamper	Sukey	Guardian Bond	1785	Fauquier Co.	Probate, Box 48	1785-001
Kamper	Susanna	Guardian Bond	1785	Fauquier Co.	Probate, Box 48	1785-001
Kamper	William	Guardian Bond	1785	Fauquier Co.	Probate, Box 48	1785-001
KANE						
Kane	Ambrose	Admr. Appt.	9/29/1909	Fauquier Co.	Probate, Box 56 Superior/Circuit Ct.	1909-016
KEARNS (See also Kerns)						
Kearns	Elizabeth	Will	4/2/1878	Fauquier Co.	Probate, Box 54 Superior/Circuit Ct.	1878-001
KEEBLE						
Keeble	Anderson	Admr. Acct. Settled	10/26/1832	Fauquier Co.	Chancery	1868-148
Keeble	Anderson	Report of Division Of Slaves	12/17/132	Fauquier Co.	Chancery	1868-148
Keeble	Fanny Watson	Guardian Bond	1817	Fauquier Co.	Probate, Box 49	1817-005
Keeble	Grace	Will	4/24/1797	Fauquier Co.	Probate, Box 50	1796-002
Keeble	Harriett	Guardian Bond	1813	Fauquier Co.	Probate, Box 49	1813-007
Keeble	Harriett	Will	11/21/1816	Fauquier Co.	Chancery	1840-068
Keeble	Richard	Will	4/28/1812	Fauquier Co.	Chancery	1840-068
Keeble	Richard	Admr. Bond	1812	Fauquier Co.	Probate, Box 47	1812-009
KEITH						
Keith	Alexander D.	Report of Division	12/1853	Fauquier Co.	Chancery	1857-009
Keith	Elizabeth	Guardian Bond	1789	Fauquier Co.	Probate, Box 48	1789-006
Keith	George	Guardian Bond	1809	Fauquier Co.	Probate, Box 49	1809-007
Keith	Isham	Division of Slaves	1803	Fauquier Co.	Probate, Box 50	1803-002
Keith	James (Judge)	Resolution on Appt. To Supreme Ct. of Appeals	4/2/1895	Fauquier Co.	Probate, Box 55 Superior/Circuit Ct.	1895-006
Keith	John	Admr. Bond	1808	Fauquier Co.	Probate, Box 46	1808-008

Consolidated Probate Index from the Clerks Loose Papers & the Superior Court/Circuit Court Records 1759-1919

Surname	Given Name	Instrument	Date	County	CLP Record Series	Index #
KEITH (Cont.)						
Keith	Marshall	Will	1/3/1842	Columbia Co. GA.	Chancery	1854-067
Keith	Marshall	Appraisement	8/30/1849	Fauquier Co.	Chancery	1871-061
Keith	Marshall	Admr. Acct.	5/21/1851	Fauquier Co.	Chancery	1871-061
Keith	Marshall	Plat & Survey	7/1871	Fauquier Co.	Chancery	1871-061
Keith	Marshall	Will	1/12/1866	Columbia Co. GA.	Chancery	1882-027
Keith	Mary V. P.	Guardian Appt.	11/25/1854	Fauquier Co.	Chancery	1871-061
Keith	Mary V. P.	Guardian Bond	11/27/1854	Fauquier Co.	Chancery	1875-016
Keith	Susan G.	Guardian Chosen	3/1818	Fauquier Co.	Probate, Box 39	1818-011
Keith	Susan G.	Guardian Appt.	10/22/1849	Fauquier Co.	Probate, Box 51 Superior/Circuit Ct.	1849-001
Keith	Susan G.	Guardian Appt.	11/25/1854	Fauquier Co.	Chancery	1871-061
Keith	Thomas	Admtrx. Bond	1806	Fauquier Co.	Probate, Box 46	1806-004
Keith	Thomas	Sales	12/14/1810	Fauquier Co.	Chancery	1824-049
Keith	Thomas	Plat & Survey Of Division	10/25/1811	Fauquier Co.	Chancery	1824-049
Keith	Thomas	Appraisement + Division of Slaves	Undated	Fauquier Co.	Chancery	1824-049
Keith	Thomas	Will	6/21/1844	Mason Co. KY	Chancery	1866-031
KELLOGG						
Kellogg	William A.	Admr. Acct.	9/1/1893	Fauquier Co.	Chancery	1900-007
KELLY						
Kelly	Alexander	Exor. Accts.	1829-1833	Fauquier Co.	Chancery	1858-018
Kelly	Alexander	Sale of Slaves	6/20/1834	Fauquier Co.	Chancery	1858-018
Kelly	Alexander	Sale of Real Estate	9/6/1834	Fauquier Co.	Chancery	1858-018
Kelly	Alexander D.	Will	1/26/1829	Fauquier Co.	Chancery	1847-017
Kelly	Alexander D.	Exor. Bond	1829	Fauquier Co.	Probate, Box 47	1829-002
Kelly	George P.	Guardian Bond	1810	Fauquier Co.	Probate, Box 49	1810-006
Kelly	James W.	Guardian Bond	1810	Fauquier Co.	Probate, Box 49	1810-006
Kelly	John	Admr. Bond	1783	Fauquier Co.	Probate, Box 45	1783-008
Kelly	John	Will	8/25/1820	Fauquier Co.	Chancery	1849-045

Consolidated Probate Index from the Clerks Loose Papers & the Superior Court/Circuit Court Records 1759-1919

Surname	Given Name	Instrument	Date	County	CLP Record Series	Index #
KELLY (Cont.)						
Kelly	John	Sale of Slaves	9/19/1848	Fauquier Co.	Chancery	1849-045
Kelly	John	Will	8/25/1820	Fauquier Co.	Chancery	1851-038
Kelly	John P.	Guardian Bond	1810	Fauquier Co.	Probate, Box 49	1810-006
Kelly	John P.	Will	5/1871	Culpeper Co. VA.	Chancery	1899-011
Kelly	John P.	Will	5/1871	Culpeper Co. VA.	Chancery	1903-006
Kelly	John P.	Will	5/1871	Culpeper Co. VA.	Chancery	1906-006
Kelly	Mary L.	Guardian Acct.	12/18/1903	Fauquier Co.	Probate, Box 55 Superior/Circuit Ct.	1903-003
Kelly	Richard P.	Guardian Bond	1810	Fauquier Co.	Probate, Box 49	1810-006
Kelly	Susanna	Guardian Bond	1810	Fauquier Co.	Probate, Box 49	1810-006
KEMP						
Kemp	Peter	Relinquishment	11/15/1815	Fauquier Co.	Probate, Box 39	1815-002
KEMPER (See also Kamper)						
Kemper	Charles	Will	2/25/1875	Fauquier Co.	Chancery	1886-023
Kemper	Frederick	Admr. Bond	1784	Fauquier Co.	Probate, Box 45	1784-006
Kemper	George	Will	8/25/1856	Fauquier Co.	Chancery	1892-021
Kemper	George (Capt.)	Heirs	Undated	Fauquier Co.	Military Records	1866-001
Kemper	H. F.	Plat & Survey Of Division	3/1/1894	Fauquier Co.	Chancery	1900-007
Kemper	H. F.	Report of Division	8/1/1894	Fauquier Co.	Chancery	1900-007
Kemper	Henry F.	Admr. Appt.	9/22/1856	Fauquier Co.	Chancery	1893-004
Kemper	Jacob	Exors. Bond	1806	Fauquier Co.	Probate, Box 46	1806-002
Kemper	John	Admr. Acct.	8/7/1836	Fauquier Co.	Chancery	1868-147
Kemper	Susan M.	Will	11/25/1878	Fauquier Co.	Chancery	1880-012
Kemper	Susan M.	Will	11/25/1878	Fauquier Co.	Chancery	1886-023
KENARD (See also Kennard, Kenneard)						
Kenard	Elizabeth	Guardian Appt.	11/27/1826	Fauquier Co.	Chancery	1833-024
Kenard	Elizabeth	Guardian Appt.	8/28/1827	Fauquier Co.	Chancery	1833-024
Kenard	Elizabeth	Guardian Appt.	10/1827	Fauquier Co.	Chancery	1833-024
Kenard	Elizabeth	Guardian Accts.	Undated	Fauquier Co.	Chancery	1833-024

Consolidated Probate Index from the Clerks Loose Papers & the Superior Court/Circuit Court Records 1759-1919

Surname	Given Name	Instrument	Date	County	CLP Record Series	Index #
KENARD (Cont.)						
Kenard	Elizabeth	List of Slaves	Undated	Fauquier Co.	Chancery	1833-024
Kenard	Joshua	Sales	4/25/1823	Fauquier Co.	Chancery	1833-024
KENDALL						
Kendall	F. M.	Exor. Appt.	5/27/1907	Fauquier Co.	Probate, Box 56 Superior/Circuit Ct.	1907-004
KENNARD (See also Kenard, Kenneard)						
Kennard	Elizabeth	Guardian Acct.	2/27/1821	Fauquier Co.	Chancery	1833-024
Kennard	Elizabeth	Inventory as Ward	4/22/1823	Fauquier Co.	Chancery	1833-024
Kennard	Elizabeth	Guardian Acct.	6/23/1823	Fauquier Co.	Chancery	1833-024
Kennard	Elizabeth	Guardian Acct. Settled	3/25/1824	Fauquier Co.	Chancery	1833-024
Kennard	Elizabeth	Guardian Acct. Settled	4/26/1825	Fauquier Co.	Chancery	1833-024
Kennard	Elizabeth	Guardian Acct.	6/24/1825	Fauquier Co.	Chancery	1833-024
Kennard	Elizabeth	Guardian Acct.	3/25/1826	Fauquier Co.	Chancery	1833-024
Kennard	Elizabeth	Guardian Acct.	5/12/1826	Fauquier Co.	Chancery	1833-024
Kennard	Elizabeth	Guardian Acct.	6/26/1826	Fauquier Co.	Chancery	1833-024
Kennard	Elizabeth	Guardian Acct.	6/25/1827	Fauquier Co.	Chancery	1833-024
Kennard	Elizabeth	Guardian Acct.	Undated	Fauquier Co.	Chancery	1833-024
Kennard	Elizabeth	Guardian Acct. Settled	6/25/1827	Fauquier Co.	Chancery	1833-024
Kennard	Elizabeth	Guardian Acct.	6/23/1823	Fauquier Co.	Chancery	1840-004
Kennard	Elizabeth	Guardian Acct.	3/29/1825	Fauquier Co.	Chancery	1840-004
Kennard	Elizabeth	Guardian Acct.	3/26/1829	Fauquier Co.	Chancery	1840-004
Kennard	Elizabeth	Guardian Acct.	Undated	Fauquier Co.	Chancery	1840-004
Kennard	Joshua	Sales	3/25/1823	Fauquier Co.	Chancery	1833-024
Kennard	Joshua	Will	3/25/1817	Fauquier Co.	Chancery	1840-026
Kennard	Joshua	Estate Acct.	Undated	Fauquier Co.	Chancery	1840-026
KENNEARD (See also Kenard, Kennard)						
Kenneard	Harrison	Guardian Bond	1817	Fauquier Co.	Probate, Box 49	1817-020

Consolidated Probate Index from the Clerks Loose Papers & the Superior Court/Circuit Court Records 1759-1919

Surname	Given Name	Instrument	Date	County	CLP Record Series	Index #
KENNER						
Kenner	Howson	Exors. Bond	1778	Fauquier Co.	Probate, Box 45	1778-010
Kenner	Rodham	Will	1//23/1793	Fauquier Co.	Chancery	1846-008
KENT						
Kent	Stella	Will	2/19/1885	Fauquier Co.	Chancery	1889-025
KERCHIVAL						
Kerchival	Elijah	Will	9/27/1847	Fauquier Co.	Chancery	1871-087
Kerchival	Elijah	Will	9/27/1847	Fauquier Co.	Chancery	1889-001
Kerchival	Matilda	Committee Bond	9/8/1857	Fauquier Co.	Probate, Box 52 Superior/Circuit Ct.	1857-002
KERNS (See also Kearns)						
Kerns	Marshall	Admr. Appt.	7/26/1889	Fauquier Co.	Chancery	1891-017
KERRICK						
Kerrick	Hugh	Will	4/23/1894	Fauquier Co.	Chancery	1897-042
KERTON						
Kerton	Anthony	Will	10/24/1803	Fauquier Co.	Chancery	1869-040
Kerton	Anthony	Inventory + Appraisement	11/2/1803	Fauquier Co.	Chancery	1869-040
Kerton	Frances	Will	1/27/1846	Fauquier Co.	Chancery	1869-040
KEY						
Key	James	Admr. Bond	Undated	Fauquier Co.	Probate, Box 46	Undated-001
Key	John A.	Court Order to Settle Admr. Acct.	12/23/1825	Fauquier Co.	Probate, Box 40	1846-001
KIDWELL						
Kidwell	Dorcas	Guardian Bond	1796	Fauquier Co.	Probate, Box 48	1796-004
Kidwell	William	Guardian Bond	1796	Fauquier Co.	Probate, Box 48	1796-004
KINCHELOE						
Kincheloe	Elizabeth	Will	4/22/1844	Fauquier Co.	Chancery	1855-033
Kincheloe	Elizabeth	Will	4/22/1844	Fauquier Co.	Chancery	1872-024
Kincheloe	Garland B.	Guardian Appt.	5/6/1905	Fauquier Co.	Probate, Box 55 Superior/Circuit Ct.	1905-007
Kincheloe	Gordon W.	Guardian Appt.	5/6/1905	Fauquier Co.	Probate, Box 55 Superior/Circuit Ct.	1905-007
Kincheloe	Hardwick	Will	12/28/1846	Fauquier Co.	Chancery	1878-020

Consolidated Probate Index from the Clerks Loose Papers & the Superior Court/Circuit Court Records 1759-1919

Surname	Given Name	Instrument	Date	County	CLP Record Series	Index #
KINCHELOE (Cont.)						
Kincheloe	James	Will	8/22/1836	Fauquier Co.	Chancery	1839-022
Kincheloe	James	Will	8/22/1836	Fauquier Co.	Chancery	1853-008
Kincheloe	James	Inventory + Appraisement	10/24/1836	Fauquier Co.	Chancery	1853-008
Kincheloe	James	Exor. Acct.	3/20/1839	Fauquier Co.	Chancery	1853-008
Kincheloe	James	Exor. Acct.	9/28/1840	Fauquier Co.	Chancery	1853-008
Kincheloe	James	Exor. Acct.	2/23/1843	Fauquier Co.	Chancery	1853-008
Kincheloe	James	Appraisement	10/24/1834	Fauquier Co.	Chancery	1855-033
Kincheloe	James	Exor. Acct.	3/26/1839	Fauquier Co.	Chancery	1855-033
Kincheloe	James	Exor. Acct.	2/28/1848	Fauquier Co.	Chancery	1869-024
Kincheloe	James	Will	8/22/1836	Fauquier Co.	Chancery	1872-024
Kincheloe	James	Inventory + Appraisement	10/24/1836	Fauquier Co.	Chancery	1872-024
Kincheloe	James G.	Guardian Appt.	6/29/1907	Fauquier Co.	Probate, Box 56 Superior/Circuit Ct.	1907-009
Kincheloe	John	Will	9/4/1826	Loudoun Co. VA.	Chancery	1838-021
Kincheloe	John	Exor. Bond	10/9/1826	Loudoun Co. VA.	Chancery	1838-021
Kincheloe	John	Inventory + Appraisement	11/13/1826	Loudoun Co. VA.	Chancery	1838-021
Kincheloe	Julius R.	Guardian Appt.	5/6/1905	Fauquier Co.	Probate, Box 55 Superior/Circuit Ct.	1905-007
Kincheloe	Mary Virginia	Guardian Appt.	5/6/1905	Fauquier Co.	Probate, Box 55 Superior/Circuit Ct.	1905-007
Kincheloe	Robert D.	Guardian Appt.	5/6/1905	Fauquier Co.	Probate, Box 55 Superior/Circuit Ct.	1905-007
Kincheloe	William P.	Guardian Appt.	5/6/1905	Fauquier Co.	Probate, Box 55 Superior/Circuit Ct.	1905-007
KING						
King	Isaac	Admr. Bond	1779	Fauquier Co.	Probate, Box 45	1779-006
King	W. W.	Will	12/20/1907	Fauquier Co.	Chancery	1910-019
KINZER						
Kinzer	H. E.	Will	12/9/1904	Fauquier Co.	Chancery	1910-028

Consolidated Probate Index from the Clerks Loose Papers & the Superior Court/Circuit Court Records 1759-1919

Surname	Given Name	Instrument	Date	County	CLP Record Series	Index #
KIRK						
Kirk	William	Exors. Bond	1780	Fauquier Co.	Probate, Box 45	1780-010
Kirk	William	Exor. Bond	1783	Fauquier Co.	Probate, Box 45	1783-002
KIRKPATRICK						
Kirkpatrick	Mary	Renunciation	1/1828	Fauquier Co.	Probate, Box 40	1828-006
Kirkpatrick	Mary	Dower Allotment	1/27/1829	Fauquier Co.	Chancery	1835-044
Kirkpatrick	William	Report of Division	2/11/1829	Fauquier Co.	Chancery	1835-044
Kirkpatrick	William	Plat & Survey Of Division	2/11/1829	Fauquier Co.	Chancery	1853-044
Kirkpatrick	William	Will	3/24/1824	Fauquier Co.	Chancery	1879-013
KLIPSTEIN (See also Klipstine)						
Klipstein	Florence C.	Guardian Bond	3/24/1876	Fauquier Co.	Chancery	1876-022
Klipstein	Florence C.	Guardian Acct.	9/8/1887	Fauquier Co.	Probate, Box 54 Superior/Circuit Ct.	1887-005
Klipstein	Florence C.	Guardian Acct.	9/7/1892	Fauquier Co.	Probate, Box 55 Superior/Circuit Ct.	1892-005
Klipstein	Florence C.	Guardian Acct.	9/4/1895	Fauquier Co.	Probate, Box 55 Superior/Circuit Ct.	1895-003
Klipstein	Florence C.	Guardian Acct.	9/6/1896	Fauquier Co.	Probate, Box 55 Superior/Circuit Ct.	1896-003
Klipstein	Philip J.	Guardian Bond	3/24/1876	Fauquier Co.	Chancery	1876-022
Klipstein	Thomas	Plat & Survey Of Division	9/1875	Fauquier Co.	Chancery	1875-030
KLIPSTINE (See also Klipstein)						
Klipstine	Florence C.	Guardian Acct.	4/6/1878	Fauquier Co.	Probate, Box 54 Superior/Circuit Ct.	1878-005
KNOX						
Knox	Alexander	Will	4/12/1784	Stafford Co. VA.	Land Records & Disputes	1830-019
Knox	Betsy	Relinquishment	7/23/1796	Fauquier Co.	Probate, Box 39	1796-002
Knox	Robert	Exor. Bond	1785	Fauquier Co.	Probate, Box 45	1785-005
Knox	Susannah	Will	11/1823	Stafford Co. VA.	Land Records & Disputes	1830-019

In pursuance of an order of Court for the appraisement of personal Estate of Wm Smith deceased we whose names are undersigned have proceeded to appraise and Inventory the said Estate as follows at the dwelling house of the said William Smith . . . .

	£				£		
Negro Nace	100	"	"	One young Bay	20	"	"
Tom	90	"	"	One Waggon & gear	24	"	"
Joseph	100	"	"	Five Sets of plow gear	2	"	"
Jacob	90	"	"	415 feet of Plank	1	7	"
Patience	70	"	"	Four flax Brakes	"	10	"
Cumboo	40	"	"	Sixteen Sheep & 10p	8	"	"
Judah	60	"	"	8 Cows with their Calves	40	"	"
Frank	60	"	"	One Bull	6	"	"
Sampson	50	"	"	Two Steers	15	"	"
Manuel	45	"	"	Two Small Steers	3	12	"
Lewis	125	"	"	Three Heifers	6	"	"
Lydia	45	"	"	One Cow	4	10	"
David	90	"	"	One wheat fan	2	8	"
Rose	36	"	"	Seven Tubs & one half bushel	"	18	"
Jenny	36	"	"	7½ Bushels of flax Seed	1	"	"
Kitty	30	"	"	Four Stacks of hay	60	"	"
Scipio	36	"	"	48 hogs and 12 Pigs	60	"	"
Charles	36	"	"	Blacksmiths Tools & Bellows	12	"	"
Hanison	25	"	"	9 Shovel plows & four Stocks	3	"	"
Kingston	20	"	"	Eight hoes	"	12	"
Clary	60	"	"	Three Scythes and Cradles	1	10	"
Hannah	60	"	"	Seven Axes Hooks	"	14	"
Phillis & Chila	70	"	"	Twenty two tubs & Casks	3	"	"
Ben	20	"	"	Three plow plates	"	18	"
One Black horse	15	"	"	Three Jugs & one Butter pot	"	15	"
One white Do	15	"	"	Three Spades & three augers	"	18	"
One Black riding Do	20	"	"	One lock Chain	"	12	"
One Bay Do	15	"	"	Four Axes	1	10	"

Plate 3. Probate. Scanned Image from Box 39. Wills &c. 1810-002. Page 1 of William Smith's Inventory and Appraisement.

Consolidated Probate Index from the Clerks Loose Papers & the Superior Court/Circuit Court Records 1759-1919

Surname	Given Name	Instrument	Date	County	CLP Record Series	Index #
LACEY						
Lacey	James	Admtrx. Bond	1815	Fauquier Co.	Probate, Box 47	1815-005
LAKE						
Lake	George	Estate Papers	7/25/1843	Fauquier Co.	Probate, Box 50 Addendum Folder	1843-006
Lake	Helen E.	Relinquishment	9/16/1889	Fauquier Co.	Chancery	1894-042
Lake	Isaac	Will	4/28/1851	Fauquier Co.	Chancery	1883-001
Lake	Isaac	Appraisement	6/23/1851	Fauquier Co.	Chancery	1883-001
Lake	Isaac	Sales	1851	Fauquier Co.	Chancery	1883-001
Lake	Isaac	Exor. Acct.	6/20/1852	Fauquier Co.	Chancery	1883-001
Lake	Isaac	Exor. Acct.	10/23/1853	Fauquier Co.	Chancery	1883-001
Lake	John	Exor. Bond	1807	Fauquier Co.	Probate, Box 46	1807-027
Lake	Marshall	Will	12/15/1888	Fauquier Co.	Chancery	1894-042
Lake	Sophia	Admr. Bond	1/11/1869	Fauquier Co.	Probate, Box 53 Superior/Circuit Ct.	1869-001
Lake	Susanna	Relinquishment	4/24/1819	Fauquier Co.	Probate, Box 39	1819-004
LAKINAN						
Lakinan	------	Admr. Bond	1806	Fauquier Co.	Probate, Box 46	1806-031
LAMKIN (See also Lampkin)						
Lamkin	John C.	Admr. Bond	9/13/1834	Fauquier Co.	Probate, Box 51 Superior/Circuit Ct.	1834-001
Lamkin	John C.	Estate Acct.	10/4/1836	Fauquier Co.	Probate, Box 51 Superior/Circuit Ct.	1836-002
LAMPKIN (See also Lamkin)						
Lampkin	Peter	Will	6/23/1823	Fauquier Co.	Chancery	1837-011
LANGFITT						
Langfitt	John	Will	10/12/1813	Stafford Co. VA.	Chancery	1846-076
LARRANCE (See also Laurence, Lawrence)						
Larrance	Edward	Exor. Bond	1786	Fauquier Co.	Probate, Box 45	1786-002
Larrance	Spencer	Admr. Bond	1808	Fauquier Co.	Probate, Box 47	1808-026
LATHAM						
Latham	Jere D.	Admr. Bond	9/18/1885	Fauquier Co.	Probate, Box 54 Superior/Circuit Ct.	1885-006
Latham	Jesse	Sale of Slaves	1/29/1832	Fauquier Co.	Chancery	1835-068

Consolidated Probate Index from the Clerks Loose Papers & the Superior Court/Circuit Court Records 1759-1919

Surname	Given Name	Instrument	Date	County	CLP Record Series	Index #
LATHAM (Cont.)						
Latham	Jesse	Admr. Acct.	11/29/1832	Fauquier Co.	Chancery	1835-068
Latham	R. W.	Admr. Appt.	4/5/1876	Fauquier Co.	Probate, Box 54 Superior/Circuit Ct.	1876-002
Latham	Susan	Guardian Appt.	8/21/1855	Fauquier Co.	Chancery	1858-036
LATIMORE						
Latimore	John	Will	8/25/1761	Pr. Wm. Co. VA.	Chancery	1868-190
LAURA						
Laura	George W.	Guardian Appt.	4/23/1860	Fauquier Co.	Chancery	1861-012
LAURENCE (See also Larrance, Lawrence)						
Laurence	William M.	Admr. Acct.	9/26/1836	Fauquier Co.	Chancery	1860-025
LAWLER						
Lawler	Mary	Admtrx. Appt.	9/4/1895	Fauquier Co.	Probate, Box 55 Superior/Circuit Ct.	1895-008
Lawler	Mary	Admtrx. Acct.	4/6/1897	Fauquier Co.	Probate, Box 55 Superior/Circuit Ct.	1897-001
Lawler	William	Admr. Appt.	3/23/1908	Fauquier Co.	Probate, Box 56 Superior/Circuit Ct.	1908-007
LAWRENCE (See also Larrance, Laurence)						
Lawrence	John C.	Guardian Bond	11/23/1842	Culpeper Co. VA.	Chancery	1844-002
Lawrence	Mason	Admr. Bond	1836	Fauquier Co.	Probate, Box 47	1836-001
Lawrence	W. Harvey	Committee Appt.	9/24/1909	Fauquier Co.	Probate, Box 56 Superior/Circuit Ct.	1909-008
Lawrence	William (Mrs.)	Dower Allotment	9/14/1857	Fauquier Co.	Chancery	1871-030
LAWS						
Laws	E. T. (Mrs.)	Division of Dower	6/21/1902	San Francisco, CA.	Chancery	1902-043
Laws	John	Admrs. Bond	1771	Fauquier Co.	Probate, Box 44	1771-009
LAWSON						
Lawson	Anna Steptoe	Exor. Bond	1784	Fauquier Co.	Probate, Box 45	1771-009
Lawson	James	Report of Division	8/25/1825	Fauquier Co.	Chancery	1835-055
Lawson	James	Plat & Survey Of Division	8/25/1825	Fauquier Co.	Chancery	1835-055
Lawson	James	Plat & Survey Of Division	10/28/1835	Fauquier Co.	Chancery	1835-055
Lawson	James	Will	4/22/1872	Fauquier Co.	Chancery	1873-084

Consolidated Probate Index from the Clerks Loose Papers & the Superior Court/Circuit Court Records 1759-1919

Surname	Given Name	Instrument	Date	County	CLP Record Series	Index #
LEACHMAN						
Leachman	John	Admtrx. Bond	1805	Fauquier Co.	Probate, Box 46	1805-001
LEATH						
Leath	William B.	Guardian Appt.	12/27/1889	Fauquier Co.	Chancery	1884-001
LEAVIL						
Leavil	Joseph	Admtrx. Bond	1775	Fauquier Co.	Probate, Box 44	1775-003
LEE						
Lee	Alice	Renunciation	3/3/1899	Fauquier Co.	Probate, Box 55 Superior/Circuit Ct.	1899-003
Lee	Fanny	Division of "Greenview"	5/17/1867	Fauquier Co.	Probate, Box 50 Addendum Folder	1833-006
Lee	Fanny	Plat & Survey Of Division	5/17/1867	Fauquier Co.	Chancery	1869-001
Lee	Hancock	Plat & Survey Of Division	4/14/1856	Fauquier Co.	Chancery	1867-007
Lee	Henry	Guardian Bond	1763	Fauquier Co.	Probate, Box 48	1763-001
Lee	John	Renunciation	1766	Fauquier Co.	Probate, Box 39	1766-010
Lee	John	Guardian Bond	1813	Fauquier Co.	Probate, Box 49	1813-002
Lee	John A.	Will	2/28/1858	Fauquier Co.	Chancery	1876-001
Lee	John A.	Division of "Greenview"	2/4/1834	Fauquier Co.	Probate, Box 50 Addendum Folder	1833-006
Lee	Mary	Guardian Bond	1763	Fauquier Co.	Probate, Box 48	1763-001
Lee	Mary	Admr. Bond	1767	Fauquier Co.	Probate, Box 44	1767-007
Lee	Mary	Guardian Bond	1813	Fauquier Co.	Probate, Box 49	1813-002
Lee	Mary W.	Division of "Greenview"	2/4/1834	Fauquier Co.	Probate, Box 50 Addendum Folder	1833-006
Lee	Richard	Guardian Bond	1763	Fauquier Co.	Probate, Box 48	1763-001
Lee	Sarah	Guardian Bond	1763	Fauquier Co.	Probate, Box 48	1763-001
Lee	Willis	Guardian Bond	1763	Fauquier Co.	Probate, Box 48	1763-001
Lee	Willis	Admrs. Bond	1813	Fauquier Co.	Probate, Box 47	1813-023
LEONARD						
Leonard	Thomas	Guardian Bond	1805	Fauquier Co.	Probate, Box 49	1805-018

Consolidated Probate Index from the Clerks Loose Papers & the Superior Court/Circuit Court Records 1759-1919

Surname	Given Name	Instrument	Date	County	CLP Record Series	Index #
LEWIS						
Lewis	Ann	Guardian Bond	1803	Fauquier Co.	Probate, Box 49	1803-010
Lewis	Britain	Will	7/25/1822	Fauquier Co.	Chancery	1846-038
Lewis	Britain	Exor. Bond	2/23/1824	Fauquier Co.	Chancery	1846-038
Lewis	Britain	Admr. Appt.	9/23/1837	Fauquier Co.	Chancery	1846-038
Lewis	Edward	Exor. Acct.	7/1812	Jefferson Co. WV	Chancery	1848-011
Lewis	Eliza	Dower Allotment	4/19/1860	Fauquier Co.	Chancery	1880-047
Lewis	Elizabeth	Guardian Bond	1798	Fauquier Co.	Probate, Box 48	1798-003
Lewis	Harriet	Guardian Bond	1815	Fauquier Co.	Probate, Box 49	1815-031
Lewis	Henry	Guardian Bond	1815	Fauquier Co.	Probate, Box 49	1815-031
Lewis	Henry M.	Report of Division with Plat & Survey	1/27/1855	Fauquier Co.	Chancery	1855-060
Lewis	Jackson	Will	7/20/1881	Fauquier Co.	Probate, Box 50 Addendum Folder	1881-001
Lewis	James	Will	1/26/1802	Fauquier Co.	Probate, Box 50	1802-002
Lewis	James	Admr. Bond	1814	Fauquier Co.	Probate, Box 47	1814-007
Lewis	Louisa	Guardian Bond	1815	Fauquier Co.	Probate, Box 49	1815-031
Lewis	Lydia	Will	7/22/1844	Fauquier Co.	Chancery	1846-038
Lewis	Malinda	Will	4/24/1841	Fauquier Co.	Chancery	1846-038
Lewis	Sarah	Exor. Bond	1778	Fauquier Co.	Probate, Box 45	1778-021
LINDSAY						
Lindsay	Huldah	Admr. Bond	12/16/1881	Fauquier Co.	Probate, Box 54 Superior/Circuit Ct.	1881-003
LOFLAND						
Lofland	H. M.	Admr. Appt.	5/23/1904	Fauquier Co.	Probate, Box 55 Superior/Circuit Ct.	1904-004
Lofland	Margaret	Admr. Appt.	2/28/1908	Fauquier Co.	Probate, Box 55 Superior/Circuit Ct.	1908-006
LOGAN						
Logan	Alice	Will	6/27/1859	Fauquier Co.	Chancery	1899-006
Logan	Alice	Appraisement	9/26/1859	Fauquier Co.	Chancery	1899-006
LOGIA						
Logia	Alexander	Will	1/22/1816	Fauquier Co.	Probate, Box 50	1816-001

Consolidated Probate Index from the Clerks Loose Papers & the Superior Court/Circuit Court Records 1759-1919

Surname	Given Name	Instrument	Date	County	CLP Record Series	Index #
LOMAX						
Lomax	Edward	Admr. Bond	1/5/1887	Fauquier Co.	Probate, Box 54 Superior/Circuit Ct.	1887-007
Lomax	Edward	Appraisement	6/10/1887	Fauquier Co.	Probate, Box 54 Superior/Circuit Ct.	1887-008
Lomax	Edward	Sales	6/10/1887	Fauquier Co.	Probate, Box 54 Superior/Circuit Ct.	1887-008
Lomax	John	Will	6/25/1832	Fauquier Co.	Chancery	1854-002
Lomax	John	Inventory + Appraisement	9/24/1833	Fauquier Co.	Chancery	1854-002
Lomax	John	Inventory + Division of Slaves	10/29/1844	Fauquier Co.	Chancery	1854-002
Lomax	John	Sales	10/29/1844	Fauquier Co.	Chancery	1854-002
Lomax	John	Will	6/25/1832	Fauquier Co.	Chancery	1894-014
LOVE						
Love	George	Will	9/26/1853	Fauquier Co.	Chancery	1872-026
LOVING						
Loving	James	Will	5/4/1861	Fauquier Co.	Probate, Box 50 Addendum Folder	1861-001
LOW (See also Lowe)						
Low	Elizabeth	Bond for Legacy	1817	Fauquier Co.	Probate, Box 47	1817-014
LOWE (See also Low)						
Lowe	John	Admr. Bond	1809	Fauquier Co.	Probate, Box 47	1809-018
LOWRY						
Lowry	George	Extrx. Bond	1813	Fauquier Co.	Probate, Box 47	1813-004
LUCKETT						
Luckett	Narcissa Jane	Admr. Appt.	3/30/1904	Fauquier Co.	Probate, Box 55 Superior/Circuit Ct.	1904-001
Luckett	Richard	Will	6/24/1850	Fauquier Co.	Chancery	1891-041
LUKE						
Luke	John	Admr. Bond	1811	Fauquier Co.	Probate, Box 47	1811-006
LUNCEFORD (See also Lunsford)						
Lunceford	Baldwin	Will	10/10/1850	Fauquier Co.	Probate, Box 52 Superior/Circuit Ct.	1850-005
Lunceford	Baldwin	Exor. Bond	10/10/1850	Fauquier Co.	Probate, Box 52 Superior/Circuit Ct.	1850-005

Consolidated Probate Index from the Clerks Loose Papers & the Superior Court/Circuit Court Records 1759-1919

Surname	Given Name	Instrument	Date	County	CLP Record Series	Index #
LUNCEFORD (Cont.)						
Lunceford	Baldwin	Will	10/8/1850	Fauquier Co.	Chancery	1854-010
Lunceford	Baldwin	Appraisement	10/8/1850	Fauquier Co.	Chancery	1854-010
Lunceford	Baldwin	Sales	11/2/1851	Fauquier Co.	Chancery	1854-010
Lunceford	Benjamin	Admr. Appt.	8/23/1869	Fauquier Co.	Chancery	1903-069
LUNSFORD (See also Lunceford)						
Lunsford	Amos	Admr. Bond	1784	Fauquier Co.	Probate, Box 45	1784-003
Lunsford	Benjamin	Guardian Bond	1807	Fauquier Co.	Probate, Box 49	1807-008
Lunsford	George	Admr. Bond	1787	Fauquier Co.	Probate, Box 45	1787-002
LUTRELL (See also Luttrell)						
Lutrell	Lott	Guardian Bond	1787	Fauquier Co.	Probate, Box 45	1787-001
LUTTRELL (See also Lutrell)						
Luttrell	Michael	Exors. Bond	1778	Fauquier Co.	Probate, Box 45	1778-005
Luttrell	Richard	Exors. Bond	1766	Fauquier Co.	Probate, Box 44	1766-008

Consolidated Probate Index from the Clerks Loose Papers & the Superior Court/Circuit Court Records 1759-1919

Surname	Given Name	Instrument	Date	County	CLP Record Series	Index #
MacNEIL						
MacNeil	John	Will	7/22/1801	Fauquier Co.	Chancery	1868-176
MACRAE						
Macrae	Amanda (Carr)	Report of Division	1/25/1832	Fauquier Co.	Chancery	1833-051
Macrae	Amanda	Plat & Survey Of Division	4/1832	Fauquier Co.	Chancery	1833-051
Macrae	Amanda (Carr)	Plat & Survey Of Division	6/1832	Fauquier Co.	Chancery	1833-051
MADDOX (See also Maddux)						
Maddox	Alexander	Guardian Bond	1804	Fauquier Co.	Probate, Box 49	1804-013
Maddox	Jeremiah	Guardian Bond	1804	Fauquier Co.	Probate, Box 49	1804-013
MADDUX (See also Maddox)						
Maddux	Alexander	Admtrx. Bon	1785	Fauquier Co.	Probate, Box 45	1785-011 OS Probate
Maddux	Alferina	Guardian Bond	1810	Fauquier Co.	Probate, Box 49	1810-011
Maddux	Dorcas	Guardian Bond	1810	Fauquier Co.	Probate, Box 49	1810-010
Maddux	Dorcas	Will	11/28/1853	Fauquier Co.	Chancery	1854-061
Maddux	Dorcas	Will	11/28/1853	Fauquier Co.	Chancery	1873-031
Maddux	Dorcas	Appraisement	12/15/1853	Fauquier Co.	Chancery	1873-031
Maddux	Dorcas	Sales	12/15/1853	Fauquier Co.	Chancery	1873-031
Maddux	Elizabeth	Relinquishment	6/1801	Fauquier Co.	Probate, Box 39	1801-002
Maddux	Elizabeth	Dower Allotment	1803	Fauquier Co.	Chancery	1824-026
Maddux	Evalina	Guardian Bond	1810	Fauquier Co.	Probate, Box 49	1810-011
Maddux	Frances	Guardian Bond	1810	Fauquier Co.	Probate, Box 49	1810-010
Maddux	Mahaley	Guardian Bond	1810	Fauquier Co.	Probate, Box 49	1810-011
Maddux	Maria	Guardian Bond	1810	Fauquier Co.	Probate, Box 49	1810-011
Maddux	Matilda	Guardian Bond	1810	Fauquier Co.	Probate, Box 49	1810-011
Maddux	Thomas	Admtrx. Bond	1780	Fauquier Co.	Probate, Box 45	1780-011
Maddux	Thomas	Extrx. Bond	1783	Fauquier Co.	Probate, Box 45	1783-005
Maddux	Thomas	Sales	11/19/1801	Fauquier Co.	Chancery	1824-026
Maddux	Thomas	Inventory	1/24/1803	Fauquier Co.	Chancery	1824-026

Consolidated Probate Index from the Clerks Loose Papers & the Superior Court/Circuit Court Records 1759-1919

Surname	Given Name	Instrument	Date	County	CLP Record Series	Index #
MADDUX (Cont.)						
Maddux	Thomas	Admr. Bond	1806	Fauquier Co.	Probate, Box 46	1806-009
Maddux	Thomas L.	Will	9/20/1839	Fauquier Co.	Chancery	1854-061
Maddux	Thomas L.	Inventory + Appraisement	9/20/1839	Fauquier Co.	Chancery	1854-061
Maddux	Thomas L.	Will	8/26/1833	Fauquier Co.	Chancery	1856-003
Maddux	Thomas L.	Will	8/26/1839	Fauquier Co.	Chancery	1873-031
Maddux	Thomas L.	Inventory + Appraisement	8/26/1839	Fauquier Co.	Chancery	1873-031
Maddux	William	Guardian Bond	1810	Fauquier Co.	Probate, Box 49	1810-010
Maddux	William	Will	5/28/1810	Fauquier Co.	Probate, Box 50	1810-001
Maddux	William	Admr. Bond	8/27/1810	Fauquier Co.	Probate, Box 47	1810-001
Maddux	William	Admtrx. Bond	1810	Fauquier Co.	Probate, box 47	1810-004
Maddux	William	Will	5/28/1810	Fauquier Co.	Chancery	1847-037
Maddux	William	Will	3/2/1810	Fauquier Co.	Chancery	1848-038
Maddux	William	Report of Sale Of Slaves	5/5/1847	Fauquier Co.	Chancery	1848-038
MADISON						
Madison	C. D.	Appraisement	12/22/1897	Fauquier Co.	Probate, Box 55 Superior/Circuit Ct.	1897-007
Madison	Carrie	Guardian Appt.	6/10/1909	Fauquier Co.	Probate, Box 56 Superior/Circuit Ct.	1909-010
Madison	Charles D.	Will	9/7/1897	Fauquier Co.	Chancery	1897-006
Madison	Charles D.	Will	9/7/1897	Fauquier Co.	Chancery	1898-046
MAHORNEY						
Mahorney	Henry	Admtrx. Bond	1762	Fauquier Co.	Probate, Box 44	1762-001
MAINEMARROW						
Mainemarrow	John	Will	5/2/1760	Fauquier Co.	Probate, Box 50	1760-001
MALLARD						
Mallard	William	Exors. Bond	1782	Fauquier Co.	Probate, Box 45	1782-008
MALLORY						
Mallory	Philip Sr.	Will	10/28/1811	Fauquier Co.	Probate, Box 50	1808-001

Consolidated Probate Index from the Clerks Loose Papers & the Superior Court/Circuit Court Records 1759-1919

Surname	Given Name	Instrument	Date	County	CLP Record Series	Index #
MALVIN						
Malvin	Horace	Appraisement	12/18/1892	Fauquier Co.	Chancery	1894-044
Malvin	Horace	Estate Acct.	4/1893	Fauquier Co.	Chancery	1894-045
Malvin	John	Will	1/25/1876	Fauquier Co.	Chancery	1888-055
Malvin	Judy	Estate Acct.	4/1893	Fauquier Co.	Chancery	1894-045
Malvin	Thomas	Grantee, Deed Of Partition	10/12/1867	Fauquier Co.	Probate, Box 50 Addendum Folder	1867-001
Malvin	Elizabeth (alias Elizabeth Hudnall)	Grantee, Deed Of Partition	10/12/1867	Fauquier Co.	Probate, Box 50 Addendum Folder	1867-001
MAN (See also Mann)						
Man	Mary	Admr. Bond	1778	Fauquier Co.	Probate, Box 45	1778-017
MANN (See also Man)						
Mann	Barnett	Will	2/25/1833	Fauquier Co.	Chancery	1890-010
Mann	John (alias John Hudnall)	Grantor, Deed Of Partition	10/12/1867	Fauquier Co.	Probate, Box 50 Addendum Folder	1867-001
Mann	Mildred (alias Mildred Hudnall)	Grantor, Deed Of Partition	10/12/1867	Fauquier Co.	Probate, Box 50 Addendum Folder	1867-001
Mann	Rush (alias Rush Hudnall)	Grantor, Deed Of Partition	10/27/1867	Fauquier Co.	Probate, Box 50 Addendum Folder	1867-001
Mann	Thomas (alias Thos. Hudnall)	Grantor, Deed Of Partition	10/27/1867	Fauquier Co.	Probate, Box 50 Addendum Folder	1867-001
Mann	Wilfred (alias Wilfred Hudnall)	Grantor, Deed Of Partition	10/27/1867	Fauquier Co.	Probate, Box 50 Addendum Folder	1867-001
MANYETT						
Manyett	C. C.	Admr. Appt.	9/15/1896	Fauquier Co.	Probate, Box 55 Superior/Circuit Ct.	1896-002
MARKHAM						
Markham	James	Admr. Acct.	6/18/1830	Fauquier Co.	Chancery	1839-016
Markham	James	Admr. Acct.	7/2/1832	Fauquier Co.	Chancery	1839-016
Markham	James	Admr. Acct.	12/4/1832	Fauquier Co.	Chancery	1839-016
MARKS						
Marks	Nimrod	Will	4/7/1871	Fauquier Co.	Probate, Box 53 Superior/Circuit Ct.	1871-003

Consolidated Probate Index from the Clerks Loose Papers & the Superior Court/Circuit Court Records 1759-1919

Surname	Given Name	Instrument	Date	County	CLP Record Series	Index #
MARR						
Marr	Daniel	Guardian Bond	1772	Fauquier Co.	Probate, Box 48	1772-003
Marr	Daniel	Will	11/27/1826	Fauquier Co.	Chancery	1834-026
Marr	Daniel	Exor. Bond	11/27/1826	Fauquier Co.	Chancery	1834-026
Marr	Daniel	Inventory + Appraisement	11/27/1826	Fauquier Co.	Chancery	1834-026
Marr	Daniel	Admr. Appt.	7/24/1832	Fauquier Co.	Chancery	1834-026
Marr	Daniel	Will	11/27/1826	Fauquier Co.	Chancery	1854-041
Marr	Daniel	Inventory + Appraisement	12/20/1826	Fauquier Co.	Chancery	1854-041
Marr	Daniel	Sales	1/5/1829	Fauquier Co.	Chancery	1854-041
Marr	Daniel	Exor. Acct.	11/29/1833	Fauquier Co.	Chancery	1854-041
Marr	Daniel	Will	11/27/1826	Fauquier Co.	Chancery	1859-034
Marr	Daniel	Exor. Bond	12/27/1826	Fauquier Co.	Chancery	1859-034
Marr	John Q.	Admr. Appt.	1/27/1873	Fauquier Co.	Chancery	1886-040
Marr	John Q.	Admr. Appt.	11/28/1865	Fauquier Co.	Chancery	1893-004
Marr	John Q.	Plat & Survey Of his Estate	6/4/1868	Fauquier Co.	Chancery	1893-011
Marr	Thomas	Guardian Bond	1772	Fauquier Co.	Probate, Box 48	1772-003
MARSHALL						
Marshall	Alexander	Guardian Bond	1807	Fauquier Co.	Probate, Box 49	1807-003
Marshall	Alice	Guardian Appt.	1/25/1887	Fauquier Co.	Chancery	1891-036
Marshall	Ashton A.	Guardian Bond	4/8/1873	Fauquier Co.	Chancery	1873-008
Marshall	C. Lewis	Guardian Bond	4/8/1873	Fauquier Co.	Chancery	1873-008
Marshall	Cary Ambler	Guardian Appt.	1/25/1887	Fauquier Co.	Chancery	1891-036
Marshall	Charles	Admtrx. Bond	1806	Fauquier Co.	Probate, Box 46	1806-005
Marshall	Charles	Guardian Bond	1807	Fauquier Co.	Probate, Box 49	1807-003
Marshall	Eliza L. S.	Will	8/24/1868	Fauquier Co.	Chancery	1883-061
Marshall	Eliza L. S.	Extrx. Qualification	9/29/1852	Fauquier Co.	Chancery	1900-047
Marshall	Eliza L. S.	Will	8/24/1868	Fauquier Co.	Chancery	1900-047

Consolidated Probate Index from the Clerks Loose Papers & the Superior Court/Circuit Court Records 1759-1919

Surname	Given Name	Instrument	Date	County	CLP Record Series	Index #
MARSHALL (Cont.)						
Marshall	Elizabeth	Plat & Survey Of Dower Allotment In Mt. Blanc	7/1849	Fauquier Co.	Chancery	1850-002
Marshall	Elizabeth	Plat & Survey	8/1849	Fauquier Co.	Chancery	1850-002
Marshall	Elizabeth	Guardian Bond	4/8/1873	Fauquier Co.	Chancery	1873-008
Marshall	F. Lewis	Report of Division	11/21/1870	Fauquier Co.	Chancery	1897-037
Marshall	F. Lewis	Plat & Survey Of Division	11/21/1870	Fauquier Co.	Chancery	1897-037
Marshall	J. A. (Dr.)	Admr. Appt.	8/24/1868	Fauquier Co.	Chancery	1900-045
Marshall	James Edward	Guardian Bond	4/8/1873	Fauquier Co.	Chancery	1890-038
Marshall	James Edward	Plat & Survey Of Division (Mt. Blanc)	12/1877	Fauquier Co.	Chancery	1890-038
Marshall	James K.	Plat & Survey Of Division	Undated	Fauquier Co.	Chancery	1835-052 OS
Marshall	James K.	Will	10/23/1865	Fauquier Co.	Chancery	1866-075
Marshall	James K.	Will	10/23/1865	Fauquier Co.	Chancery	1880-034
Marshall	James K.	Will	10/23/1865	Fauquier Co.	Chancery	1885-047
Marshall	James K.	Report of Division	12/1873	Fauquier Co.	Chancery	1885-047
Marshall	James K.	Plat & Survey Of Division	12/1873	Fauquier Co.	Chancery	1885-047
Marshall	James M.	Will	8/9/1848	Fauquier Co.	Chancery	1849-003
Marshall	James M.	Report of Division	5/12/1849	Fauquier Co.	Chancery	1849-003
Marshall	James M.	Plat & Survey Of Division	5/12/1849	Fauquier Co.	Chancery	1849-003
Marshall	James M.	Plats & Surveys Of Division	1/1/1856	Fauquier Co.	Chancery	1855-061
Marshall	Jane	Guardian Bond	1807	Fauquier Co.	Probate, Box 49	1807-003
Marshall	Jaquelin A.	Will	9/27/1852	Fauquier Co.	Chancery	1883-061
Marshall	Jaqueline (Dr.)	Will	9/27/1852	Fauquier Co.	Chancery	1900-047
Marshall	Jaqueline (Dr.)	Report of Division	9/1868	Fauquier Co.	Chancery	1900-047

Consolidated Probate Index from the Clerks Loose Papers & the Superior Court/Circuit Court Records 1759-1919

Surname	Given Name	Instrument	Date	County	CLP Record Series	Index #
MARSHALL (Cont.)						
Marshall	Jaqueline (Dr.)	Plat & Survey Of Division	9/1868	Fauquier Co.	Chancery	1900-047
Marshall	John	Will (Revoked)	9/24/1832	Fauquier Co.	Chancery	1838-006
Marshall	John	Codicil to Will	1/5/1832	Fauquier Co.	Chancery	1838-006
Marshall	John	Will	7/10/1835	Fauquier Co.	Chancery	1838-006
Marshall	John	Sales	5/4/18--	Fauquier Co.	Chancery	1838-006
Marshall	John	Plat & Survey Of Division	1836	Fauquier Co.	Chancery	1838-006
Marshall	John	Plat & Survey Of Division of lands In Hampshire Co.	10/3/1840	Fauquier Co.	Chancery	1841-019
Marshall	John	Report of Division	5/20/1845	Fauquier Co.	Chancery	1845-006
Marshall	John	Plat & Survey Of Division	5/20/1845	Fauquier Co.	Chancery	1845-006
Marshall	John	Report of Partition	6/29/1842	Fauquier Co.	Chancery	1848-012
Marshall	John	Plat & Survey Of Division #1	9/6/1844	Fauquier Co.	Chancery	1847-012
Marshall	John	Plat & Survey Of Division #2	9/6/1844	Fauquier Co.	Chancery	1847-012
Marshall	John	Plat & Survey Of Division #3	9/6/1844	Fauquier Co.	Chancery	1847-012
Marshall	John	Survey of Division Of Land in Fauquier + Warren Co. VA.	10/1/1844	Fauquier Co.	Chancery	1848-016
Marshall	John	Will	7/10/1835	Richmond, VA.	Chancery	1848-033
Marshall	John	Will	7/10/1835	Richmond, VA.	Chancery	1850-002
Marshall	John (of Mt. Blanc)	Will	7/22/1872	Fauquier Co.	Chancery	1890-038
Marshall	John	Guardian Bond	4/8/1873	Fauquier Co.	Chancery	1873-008
Marshall	John	Plat & Survey Of Division (Mt. Blanc)	12/1877	Fauquier Co.	Chancery	1890-038

Consolidated Probate Index from the Clerks Loose Papers & the Superior Court/Circuit Court Records 1759-1919

Surname	Given Name	Instrument	Date	County	CLP Record Series	Index #
MARSHALL (Cont.)						
Marshall	Lucy	Guardian Bond	1807	Fauquier Co.	Probate, Box 49	1807-003
Marshall	Martin	Guardian Bond	1807	Fauquier Co.	Probate, Box 49	1807-003
Marshall	Mary	Guardian Appt.	9/8/1891	Fairfax Co. VA.	Chancery	1891-057
Marshall	Mary M.	Guardian Bond	4/8/1873	Fauquier Co.	Chancery	1873-008
Marshall	Mary Morris	Appraisement	7/28/1892	Fauquier Co.	Probate, Box 55 Superior/Circuit Ct.	1892-002
Marshall	Mildred P.	Will	4/24/1882	Fauquier Co.	Chancery	1911-030
Marshall	Mumford	Will	7/25/1842	Fauquier Co.	Chancery	1869-008
Marshall	Mumford	Exor. Acct.	5/24/1854	Fauquier Co.	Chancery	1869-008
Marshall	Mumford	Inventory + Appraisement	12/25/1854	Fauquier Co.	Chancery	1869-008
Marshall	Mumford	Sales	1/18/1855	Fauquier Co.	Chancery	1869-008
Marshall	Philip	Guardian Bond	7/8/1873	Fauquier Co.	Chancery	1873-008
Marshall	Susanna	Guardian Bond	1807	Fauquier Co.	Probate, Box 49	1807-003
Marshall	Thomas	Guardian Bond	1808	Fauquier Co.	Probate, Box 49	1808-011
Marshall	Thomas	Report of Division	9/25/1843	Fauquier Co.	Chancery	1843-034
Marshall	Thomas	Guardian Appt.	1/25/1887	Fauquier Co.	Chancery	1891-036
Marshall	William	Report of Division	12/6/1825	Fauquier Co.	Chancery	1834-031
Marshall	William	Plat & Survey Of Division	12/6/1825	Fauquier Co.	Chancery	1834-031
MARTIN						
Martin	Alfred P.	Admr. Bond	2/25/1850	Fauquier Co.	Chancery	1872-023
Martin	Charles	Exors. Bond	1786	Fauquier Co.	Probate, Box 45	1786-001
Martin	Charles	Sales	9/10/1816	Fauquier Co.	Probate, Box 39	1816-001
Martin	Charles	Admr. Bond	8/17/1829	Fauquier Co.	Probate, Box 39	1815-003
Martin	Charles	Appraisement	4/1822	Fauquier Co.	Probate, Box 40	1822-003
Martin	Charles	Will	1/23/1806	Fauquier Co.	Chancery	1815-003
Martin	Charles	Will	7/21/1815	Fauquier Co.	Chancery	1815-003
Martin	Charles	Admr. Bond	7/21/1815	Fauquier Co.	Chancery	1815-003

Consolidated Probate Index from the Clerks Loose Papers & the Superior Court/Circuit Court Records 1759-1919

Surname	Given Name	Instrument	Date	County	CLP Record Series	Index #
MARTIN (Cont.)						
Martin	Charles	Curator Acct.	7/21/1815	Fauquier Co.	Chancery	1815-003
Martin	Charles	Admr. Bond	4/12/1834	Fauquier Co.	Chancery	1815-003
Martin	Charles	Will	1/13/1814	Fauquier Co.	Chancery	1833-007
Martin	Eliza Ann	Guardian Bond	2/25/1850	Fauquier Co.	Chancery	1872-023
Martin	Elizabeth	Estate Accts.	12/1842	Fauquier Co.	Probate, Box 50	1842-001
Martin	Elizabeth	Request to settle Exor. Acct.	12/11/1843	Fauquier Co.	Probate, Box 50	1843-001
Martin	Francis	Estate Accts.	Undated	Fauquier Co.	Chancery	1832-060
Martin	Francis	Division of Slaves (Extract)	9/10/1825	Fauquier Co.	Chancery	1847-022
Martin	Francis	Heirs	Undated	Fauquier Co.	Chancery	1847-022
Martin	Francis	Admr. Bond	11/22/1824	Fauquier Co.	Chancery	1866-036
Martin	Mary Ann	Heirs (in Distribution Of money from sale Of Real Estate)	12/18/1882	Fauquier Co.	Chancery	1890-010
Martin	Tilman	Extrx. Bond	1779	Fauquier Co.	Probate, Box 45	1779-005
MASON						
Mason	Catharine	Guardian Bond	1805	Fauquier Co.	Probate, Box 49	1805-017
Mason	Daniel	Guardian Bond	1805	Fauquier Co.	Probate, Box 49	1805-017
Mason	Edgar	Exor. Bond	12/4/1908	Fauquier Co.	Probate, Box 56 Superior/Circuit Ct.	1908-018
MASSEY (See also Massie)						
Massey	Asa	Admrs. Bond	1815	Fauquier Co.	Probate, Box 47	1815-037
Massey	Dolley	Admr. Bond	1815	Fauquier Co.	Probate, Box 47	1815-058
MASSIE (See also Massey)						
Massie	Benjamin	Guardian Bond	1802	Fauquier Co.	Probate, Box 49	1802-009
Massie	Dolly	Guardian Bond	1802	Fauquier Co.	Probate, Box 49	1802-003
Massie	Dolly	Guardian Bond	1815	Fauquier Co.	Probate, Box 49	1815-012
Massie	Joseph	Guardian Bond	1802	Fauquier Co.	Probate, Box 49	1802-009
Massie	Nimrod	Guardian Bond	1802	Fauquier Co.	Probate, Box 49	1802-003
Massie	Nimrod	Guardian Bond	1815	Fauquier Co.	Probate, Box 49	1815-012

Consolidated Probate Index from the Clerks Loose Papers & the Superior Court/Circuit Court Records 1759-1919

Surname	Given Name	Instrument	Date	County	CLP Record Series	Index #
MASSIE (Cont.)						
Massie	Robert	Guardian Bond	1802	Fauquier Co.	Probate, Box 49	1802-003
Massie	Robert	Guardian Bond	1815	Fauquier Co.	Probate, Box 49	1815-012
Massie	Samuel	Guardian Bond	1802	Fauquier Co.	Probate, Box 49	1802-003
Massie	Samuel	Guardian Bond	1802	Fauquier Co.	Probate, Box 49	1802-009
Massie	Thomas	Will	10/20/1801	Fauquier Co.	Chancery	1824-002
MATTHEW (See also Matthews)						
Matthew	Robert	Exor. Bond	1767	Fauquier Co.	Probate, Box 44	1767-004
MATTHEWS (See also Matthew)						
Matthews	Chichester	Guardian Bond	1770	Fauquier Co.	Probate, Box 48	1770-004
Matthews	Dudley	Guardian Bond	1771	Fauquier Co.	Probate, Box 48	1771-003
Matthews	Lucetta	Dower (with Plat)	6/30/1875	Fauquier Co.	Probate, Box 53 Superior/Circuit Ct.	1875-002
MATHIS						
Mathis	Chichester	Guardian Bond	1770	Fauquier Co.	Probate, Box 48	1770-003
MAUZEY (See also Mauzy)						
Mauzey	John	Will	8/17/1803	Fauquier Co.	Chancery	1809-039
Mauzey	John	Will	8/1803	Fauquier Co.	Land Records & Disputes	1811-015
Mauzey	Mary	Will	3/14/1758	Stafford Co. VA.	Land Records & Disputes	1811-015
Mauzey	Mary	Exor. Bond	1769	Fauquier Co.	Probate, Box 44	1769-004
Mauzey	Peter	Will	6/11/1751	Stafford Co. VA.	Land Records & Disputes	1769-001
MAUZY (See also Mauzey)						
Mauzy	Eliza	Guardian Bond	1807	Fauquier Co.	Probate, Box 49	1807-002
Mauzy	John	Exors. Bond	1764	Fauquier Co.	Probate, Box 44	1764-002
Mauzy	Margaret	Guardian Bond	1804	Fauquier Co.	Probate, Box 49	1804-007
Mauzy	Margaret	Guardian Bond	1807	Fauquier Co.	Probate, Box 49	1807-002
McABOY						
McAboy	Murphey	Division of Real Estate	12/30/1802	Fauquier Co.	Land Records	1802-006
McBEE						
McBee	Benjamin	Admtrx. Bond	1808	Fauquier Co.	Probate, Box 46	1808-006

Consolidated Probate Index from the Clerks Loose Papers & the Superior Court/Circuit Court Records 1759-1919

Surname	Given Name	Instrument	Date	County	CLP Record Series	Index #
McCLANAHAM (See also McClanahan)						
McClanaham	Benjamin	Guardian Bond	1815	Fauquier Co.	Probate, Box 49	1815-011
McClanaham	Fleet	Guardian Bond	1815	Fauquier Co.	Probate, Box 49	1815-011
McClanaham	Jared	Admr. Bond	1813	Fauquier Co.	Probate, Box 47	1813-022
McClanaham	John	Guardian Bond	1815	Fauquier Co.	Probate, Box 49	1815-011
McClanaham	William	Guardian Bond	1815	Fauquier Co.	Probate, Box 49	1815-011
McCLANAHAN (See also McClanaham)						
McClanahan	George	Guardian Bond	1801	Fauquier Co.	Probate, Box 48	1801-008
McClanahan	George M.	Guardian Appt.	8/1825	Fauquier Co.	Chancery	1841-067
McCLEAN (See also McLean)						
McClean	Catharine	Guardian Acct.	10/11/1836	Fauquier Co.	Chancery	1866-006
McClean	Daniel	Will	2/1/1823	Alexandria, VA.	Chancery	1866-006
McClean	Daniel	Exor. Acct. (4 filed)	10/11/1836	Fauquier Co.	Chancery	1866-006
McClean	Daniel H.	Guardian Acct.	10/11/1836	Fauquier Co.	Chancery	1866-006
McClean	Hannah	Guardian Acct.	10/11/1836	Fauquier Co.	Chancery	1866-006
McClean	Wilmer	Guardian Acct.	5/9/1857	Fauquier Co.	Chancery	1866-006
McCONCHIE (See also McConkie, McConkey, McKonkey)						
McConchie	Alexander	Report of Division	12/10/1812	Fauquier Co.	Chancery	1834-022
McConchie	Alexander	Plat & Survey Of Division	12/10/1812	Fauquier Co.	Chancery	1834-022
McConchie	Ann	Exor. Bond	1813	Fauquier Co.	Probate, Box 47	1813-010
McConchie	Elizabeth	Admr. Appt.	8/25/1857	Fauquier Co.	Chancery	1867-002
McConchie	L. A.	Admtrx. Qualification	11/30/1908	Fauquier Co.	Probate, Box 56 Superior/Circuit Ct.	1908-017
McCONKEY (See also McConchie, McConkie, McKonkey)						
McConkey	Robert	Guardian Bond	1811	Fauquier Co.	Probate, Box 49	1811-001
McConkey	William	Guardian Bond	1811	Fauquier Co.	Probate, Box 49	1811-001
McCONKIE (See also McConchie, McConkey, McKonkey)						
McConkie	Vanessa	Guardian Appt.	4/1/1907	Fauquier Co.	Probate, Box 56 Superior/Circuit Ct.	1907-002
McCORMAC (See also McCormack, McCormick)						
McCormac	Stephen	Exor. Bond	1786	Fauquier Co.	Probate, Box 45	1786-003

Consolidated Probate Index from the Clerks Loose Papers & the Superior Court/Circuit Court Records 1759-1919

Surname	Given Name	Instrument	Date	County	CLP Record Series	Index #
McCORMACK (See also McCormac, McCormick)						
McCormack	Ann	Petition for Adm. of Estate of James McCormick	Undated	Fauquier Co.	Probate, Box 39	Undated-001
McCORMICK (See also McCormac, McCormack)						
McCormick	Charles N.	Will	12/23/1839	Fauquier Co.	Chancery	1843-027
McCormick	Charles N.	Will	12/23/1839	Fauquier Co.	Chancery	1844-017
McCormick	Eleanor	Admr. Appt.	3/22/1841	Fauquier Co.	Chancery	1866-024
McCormick	James	Extrx. Bond	1759	Fauquier Co.	Probate, Box 44	1759-004
McCOY						
McCoy	Hezekiah	Report of Division	11/26/1847	Fauquier Co.	Chancery	1848-071
McCoy	Hezekiah	Plat & Survey	11/26/1847	Fauquier Co.	Chancery	1848-071
McCoy	Leonard	Appraisement	10/26/1857	Fauquier Co.	Chancery	1860-009
McCoy	Leonard	Report of Division Of Slaves	12/27/1859	Fauquier Co.	Chancery	1860-009
McDONALD						
McDonald	Helen	Guardian Bond	1772	Fauquier Co.	Probate, Box 48	1772-001
McGEORGE						
McGeorge	John	Report of Division Of Slaves	3/24/1832	Fauquier Co.	Chancery	1868-151
McGREGOR						
McGregor	Malcomb	Admr. Bond	1785	Fauquier Co.	Probate, Box 45	1785-009 OS
McKENNY (See also McKinney, McKinny)						
McKenny	Matthew	Admtrx. Bond	1812	Fauquier Co.	Probate, Box 47	1812-017
McKINNEY (See also McKenny, McKinny)						
McKinney	Anne	Guardian Bond	1816	Fauquier Co.	Probate, Box 49	1816-001
McKINNY (See also McKenny, McKinney)						
McKinny	Mary	Will	10/28/1867	Fauquier Co.	Chancery	1889-017
McKINSTER						
McKinster	Elizabeth H.	Admr. Appt.	9/7/1880	Fauquier Co.	Probate, Box 54 Superior/Circuit Ct.	1880-005
McKONKEY (See also McConchie, McConkey, McConkie)						
McKonkey	Robert	Admtrx. Bond	1807	Fauquier Co.	Probate, Box 46	1807-034
McLEAN (See also McClean)						
McLean	John	Admr. Bond	1777	Fauquier Co.	Probate, Box 44	1777-017

Consolidated Probate Index from the Clerks Loose Papers & the Superior Court/Circuit Court Records 1759-1919

Surname	Given Name	Instrument	Date	County	CLP Record Series	Index #
McLEAREN						
McLearen	Algernon S.	Will	9/6/1906	Fauquier Co.	Chancery	1910-009
McMULLIN						
McMullin	Archibald	Admr. Bond	1815	Fauquier Co.	Probate, Box 47	1815-061
McNAMARA						
McNamara	John	Admr. Bond	1761	Fauquier Co.	Probate, Box 44	1761-002
McNeill (See also McNeal)						
McNeill	Catharine	Admr. Bond	1808	Fauquier Co.	Probate, Box 46	1808-012
McNISH						
McNish	David	Plat & Survey Of Division	12/4/1805	Fauquier Co.	Chancery	1812-013
McNish	David	Division of Slaves	12/4/1805	Fauquier Co.	Chancery	1812-013
McNish	Horatio	Guardian Bond	1802	Fauquier Co.	Probate, Box 49	1802-004
McNish	Horatio	Guardian Bond	1806	Fauquier Co.	Probate, Box 49	1806-012
McNish	Horatio	Guardian Bond	1817	Fauquier Co.	Probate, Box 49	1817-015
McNish	Polly	Guardian Bond	1802	Fauquier Co.	Probate, Box 49	1802-004
McNish	Polly	Guardian Bond	1806	Fauquier Co.	Probate, Box 49	1806-015
McNish	William	Guardian Bond	1802	Fauquier Co.	Probate, Box 49	1802-004
McPHELIN						
McPhelin	Ann	Will	2/21/1862	Fauquier Co.	Chancery	1869-007
MEEKS						
Meeks	John	Admr. Appt.	5/24/1906	Fauquier Co.	Probate, Box 56 Superior/Circuit Ct.	1906-001
Meeks	John	Admr. Acct.	12/26/1907	Fauquier Co.	Chancery	1908-028
Meeks	Mary	Report of Division	9/3/1896	Fauquier Co.	Chancery	1896-050
Meeks	Mary	Plat & Survey Of Division	9/3/1896	Fauquier Co.	Chancery	1896-050
Meeks	Mary J.	Appraisement	8/19/1896	Fauquier Co.	Chancery	1896-001
MEGEATH						
Megeath	Jennie	Guardian Appt.	9/21/1878	Fauquier Co.	Chancery	1878-042
Megeath	Minnie E.	Guardian Appt.	9/21/1878	Fauquier Co.	Chancery	1878-042
MENEFEE						
Menefee	Banks S.	Will	6/27/1859	Fauquier Co.	Chancery	1909-034

Consolidated Probate Index from the Clerks Loose Papers & the Superior Court/Circuit Court Records 1759-1919

Surname	Given Name	Instrument	Date	County	CLP Record Series	Index #
METCALF (See also Metcalfe)						
Metcalf	Christopher	Admrs. Bond	1777	Fauquier Co.	Probate, Box 44	1777-005
Metcalf	James	Admrs. Bond	1776	Fauquier Co.	Probate, Box 44	1776-008
METCALFE (See also Metcalf)						
Metcalfe	Elizabeth Judith	Guardian Bond	1809	Fauquier Co.	Probate, Box 49	1809-008
Metcalfe	James	Guardian Bond	1809	Fauquier Co.	Probate, Box 49	1809-008
Metcalfe	Kitty	Guardian Bond	1809	Fauquier Co.	Probate, Box 49	1809-008
METEER						
Meteer	Mary A.	Will	5/4/1877	New Orleans, LA.	Chancery	1880-036
MICHAEL						
Michael	Daniel	Admr. Bond	1815	Fauquier Co.	Probate, box 47	1815-036
MILLER						
Miller	Sarah	Court Order for Appraisement	12/9/1833	Fauquier Co.	Chancery	1834-010
Miller	Simon	Exor. Bond	1770	Fauquier Co.	Probate, box 44	1770-002
Miller	William	Admr. Bond	1808	Fauquier Co.	Probatte, Box 46	1808-005
Miller	William	Will	1/25/1820	Fauquier Co.	Chancery	1834-010
Miller	William	Sales	11/20/1833	Fauquier Co.	Chancery	1834-010
Miller	William	Appraisement	12/20/1833	Fauquier Co.	Chancery	1834-010
MILLHOLLEN						
Millhollen	Patrick	Plat & Survey Of Division	7/1832	Fauquier Co.	Chancery	1859-082
MILLON						
Millon	Washington	Sales	10/22/1875	Fauquier Co.	Probate, Box 53 Superior/Circuit Ct.	1875-007
MING						
Ming	Victoria	Will	4/5/1869	Pr. Wm. Co. VA.	Chancery	1881-032
MINOR						
Minor	Robert	Extrx. Qualification	12/9/1871	Fauquier Co.	Chancery	1904-002
MINTER						
Minter	Jacob	Exor. Bond	1773	Fauquier Co.	Probate, Box 44	1773-006
Minter	Jacob	Admr. Acct.	7/25/1791	Fauquier Co.	Chancery	1807-037
Minter	Joseph	Extrx. Bond	1774	Fauquier Co.	Probate, Box 44	1774-003
Minter	Joseph	Will	5/26/1817	Fauquier Co.	Probate, Box 50	1817-003

Consolidated Probate Index from the Clerks Loose Papers & the Superior Court/Circuit Court Records 1759-1919

Surname	Given Name	Instrument	Date	County	CLP Record Series	Index #
MITCHELL						
Mitchell	Benjamin	Admr. Bond	1/23/1826	Fauquier Co.	Chancery	1854-057
Mitchell	Benjamin	Inventory + Appraisement	2/27/1826	Fauquier Co.	Chancery	1854-057
Mitchell	Benjamin	Report of Division	3/25/1847	Fauquier Co.	Chancery	1847-045
Mitchell	Benjamin	Plat & Survey Of Division	3/25/1847	Fauquier Co.	Chancery	1847-045
Mitchell	Charlotte M.	Report of Division	12/21/1889	Fauquier Co.	Chancery	1896-010
Mitchell	Charlotte M.	Plat & Survey Of Division	12/21/1889	Fauquier Co.	Chancery	1896-010
Mitchell	James	Guardian Acct.	2/26/1842	Fauquier Co.	Chancery	1854-057
Mitchell	John	Admr. Bond	1784	Fauquier Co.	Probate, Box 45	1784-007
Mitchell	John	Will	12/23/1851	Fauquier Co.	Chancery	1857-057
Mitchell	John	Will	12/23/1851	Fauquier Co.	Chancery	1870-002
Mitchell	John	Exor. Acct.	12/3/1866	Fauquier Co.	Chancery	1870-002
Mitchell	John	Exor. Acct.	5/8/1870	Fauquier Co.	Chancery	1870-002
Mitchell	John	Exor. Acct	3/4/1873	Fauquier Co.	Chancery	1870-002
MOFFETT						
Moffett	John A.	Heirs	1892	Fauquier Co.	Chancery	1892-075
Moffett	John H.	Extrx. Bond	1814	Fauquier Co.	Probate, Box 47	1814-003
Moffett	M. R. (Mrs.)	Admr. Appt.	3/28/1904	Fauquier Co.	Probate, Box 55 Superior/Circuit Ct.	1904-002
MONROE (See also Munroe)						
Monroe	Richard S.	Admtrx. Appt.	8/31/1906	Fauquier Co.	Probate, Box 56 Superior/Circuit Ct.	1906-005
MONTGOMERY						
Montgomery	Francis	Will	11/27/1814	Pr. Wm. Co. VA.	Chancery	1866-007
Montgomery	William	Will	10/1804	Pr. Wm. Co. VA.	Chancery	1866-007
MOONEY						
Mooney	Nicholas	Will	11/28/1831	Fauquier Co.	Chancery	1866-037
Mooney	Nicholas	Will	12/28/1837	Fauquier Co.	Chancery	1873-012

Consolidated Probate Index from the Clerks Loose Papers & the Superior Court/Circuit Court Records 1759-1919

Surname	Given Name	Instrument	Date	County	CLP Record Series	Index #
MOONEY (Cont)						
Mooney	Nicholas	Report of Division Of Slaves	12/27/1860	Fauquier Co.	Chancery	1873-012
Mooney	Nicholas C.	Will	11/28/1831	Fauquier Co.	Probate, Box 50	1831-003
Mooney	Nicholas	Will	11/28/1831	Fauquier Co.	Chancery	1856-030
Mooney	Nicholas C.	Will	11/28/1831	Fauquier Co.	Chancery	1869-026
MOORE						
Moore	Catharine	Relinquishment	1828	Fauquier Co.	Probate, Box 40	1828-002
Moore	Frances E.	Appraisement	1/1/1897	Fauquier Co.	Probate, Box 55 Superior/Circuit Ct.	1897-003
Moore	Frances E.	Sales	1/21/1897	Fauquier Co.	Probate, Box 55 Superior/Circuit Ct.	1897-004
Moore	George	Admr. Acct.	3/24/1838	Snow Co. FL.	Chancery	1847-040
Moore	Samuel	Guardian Bond	1795	Fauquier Co.	Probate, Box 48	1795-003
Moore	Sarah	Trustee Acct.	9/15/1837	Fauquier Co.	Chancery	1837-022
MORAN						
Moran	Sylvanus	Plat & Survey Of Division	7/26/1854	Fauquier Co.	Chancery	1877-004
Moran	William	Plat & Survey Of Division	1843	Fauquier Co.	Chancery	1870-015
Moran	William	Will	10/22/1849	Fauquier Co.	Chancery	1870-015
Moran	William	Will	7/23/1850	Fauquier Co.	Chancery	1904-003
Moran	William	Report of Division	1879	Fauquier Co.	Chancery	1904-003
MOREHEAD						
Morehead	Beverly Nelson	Guardian Bond	1811	Fauquier Co.	Probate, Box 49	1811-011
Morehead	James (Capt.)	Will	2/22/1847	Fauquier Co.	Chancery	1848-039
Morehead	James (Capt.)	Report of Division	10/13/1848	Fauquier Co.	Chancery	1848-039
Morehead	James (Capt.)	Plat & Survey Of Division	10/13/1848	Fauquier Co.	Chancery	1848-039
Morehead	James	Will	2/22/1847	Fauquier Co.	Chancery	1900-008
Morehead	James	Report of Division	3/15/1892	Fauquier Co.	Chancery	1900-008
Morehead	James	Plat & Survey Of Division	3/15/1892	Fauquier Co.	Chancery	1900-008

Consolidated Probate Index from the Clerks Loose Papers & the Superior Court/Circuit Court Records 1759-1919

Surname	Given Name	Instrument	Date	County	CLP Record Series	Index #
MOREHEAD (Cont.)						
Morehead	John	Exors. Bond	1768	Fauquier Co.	Probate, Box 44	1768-007
Morehead	Lucy	Guardian Bond	1811	Fauquier Co.	Probate, Box 49	1811-011
Morehead	Margaret	Guardian Bond	1803	Fauquier Co.	Probate, Box 49	1803-003
Morehead	Presley	Guardian Bond	1769	Fauquier Co.	Probate, Box 48	1769-001
Morehead	Samuel	Extrx. Bond	1797	Fauquier Co.	Probate, Box 46	1797-010
Morehead	Samuel	Guardian Bond	1803	Fauquier Co.	Probate, Box 49	1803-003
Morehead	William	Admr. Bond	1809	Fauquier Co.	Probate, Box 47	1809-009
MORGAN						
Morgan	Abel	Exors. Bond	1814	Fauquier Co.	Probate, Box 47	1814-004
Morgan	Caroline W.	Dower Allotment	5/14/1816	Fauquier Co.	Chancery	1824-027
Morgan	Charles	Exor. Bond	1766	Fauquier Co.	Probate, Box 44	1766-005
Morgan	Charles	Admr. Bond	1770	Fauquier Co.	Probate, Box 44	1770-005
Morgan	Charles	Exor. Bond	1809	Fauquier Co.	Probate, Box 47	1809-025
Morgan	Charles	Admr. Bond	1809	Fauquier Co.	Probate, Box 47	1809-026
Morgan	Charles	Will	8/28/1854	Fauquier Co.	Chancery	1871-043
Morgan	Daniel	Admr. Bond	1806	Fauquier Co.	Probate, Box 46	1806-016
Morgan	Daniel	Guardian Bond	1816	Fauquier Co.	Probate, Box 49	1816-009
Morgan	George A.	Will	6/30/1859	Fauquier Co.	Chancery	1888-029
Morgan	George A.	Exor. Bond	8/22/1859	Fauquier Co.	Chancery	1888-029
Morgan	James	Admr. Bond	1765	Fauquier Co.	Probate, Box 44	1765-004
Morgan	James	Admr. Bond	1814	Fauquier Co.	Probate, Box 47	1814-021
Morgan	John	Will	7/24/1821	Fauquier Co.	Chancery	1839-002
Morgan	John	Admr. Bond	8/27/1821	Fauquier Co.	Chancery	1839-002
Morgan	John	Sales	1821	Fauquier Co.	Chancery	1839-002
Morgan	John	Admr. Acct.	11/22/1824	Fauquier Co.	Chancery	1839-002
Morgan	Joseph	Admr. Bond	1785	Fauquier Co.	Probate, Box 45	1785-010 OS Probate
Morgan	Joseph	Plat & Survey Of Division	10/1853	Fauquier Co.	Chancery	1869-057

Consolidated Probate Index from the Clerks Loose Papers & the Superior Court/Circuit Court Records 1759-1919

Surname	Given Name	Instrument	Date	County	CLP Record Series	Index #
MORGAN (Cont.)						
Morgan	Joseph	Admr. Acct.	1854	Fauquier Co.	Chancery	1871-043
Morgan	Joseph	Division of Slaves	12/25/1854	Fauquier Co.	Chancery	1871-043
Morgan	Joseph	Admr. Acct.	1856	Fauquier Co.	Chancery	1871-043
Morgan	Josephine M. E.	Will	10/25/1852	Fauquier Co.	Chancery	1859-062
Morgan	Josephine M. E.	Will	10/26/1852	Fauquier co.	Chancery	1880-024
Morgan	Mildred	Relinquishment	1806	Fauquier Co.	Probate, Box 39	1806-016
Morgan	Randle	Exors. Bond	1773	Fauquier Co.	Probate, Box 44	1773-010
Morgan	Randle	Guardian Bond	1773	Fauquier Co.	Probate, Box 48	1773-004
Morgan	Simon	Will	2/25/1793	Fauquier Co.	Probate, Box 39	1793-004
Morgan	Simon	Exor. Bond	1810	Fauquier Co.	Probate, Box 47	1810-012
Morgan	Thornton Jones	Guardian Bond	1791	Fauquier Co.	Probate, Box 48	1791-003
Morgan	William	will	4/13/1764	Middlesex Co. VA.	Chancery	1784-012
Morgan	William	Guardian Bond	1816	Fauquier Co.	Probate, Box 49	1816-009
Morgan	William J.	Division of Slaves	5/14/1816	Fauquier Co.	Chancery	1824-027
Morgan	William J.	Admr. Bond	9/10/1870	Fauquier Co.	Probate, Box 53 Superior/Circuit Ct.	1870-006
Morgan	William J.	Inventory + Appraisement	1/23/1871	Fauquier Co.	Probate, Box 53 Superior/Circuit Ct.	1871-001
Morgan	William J.	Sales	1/23/1871	Fauquier Co.	Probate, Box 53 Superior/Circuit Ct.	1871-002
MORRIS						
Morris	Alexander	Guardian Bond	1810	Fauquier Co.	Probate, Box 49	1810-001
Morris	Alexander	Guardian Bond	1810	Fauquier Co.	Probate, Box 49	1810-016
Morris	Alexander	Guardian Bond	1813	Fauquier Co.	Probate, Box 49	1813-003
Morris	Catharine	Relinquishment	8/1818	Fauquier Co.	Probate, Box 39	1818-008
Morris	Fanny P.	Guardian Bond	1810	Fauquier Co.	Probate, Box 49	1810-001
Morris	Hannah R.	Guardian Bond	1810	Fauquier Co.	Probate, Box 49	1810-001
Morris	Mary	Guardian Bond	1810	Fauquier Co.	Probate, Box 49	1810-016
Morris	Mary	Sale of Dower Land	3/27/1832	Fauquier Co.	Chancery	1868-045

Consolidated Probate Index from the Clerks Loose Papers & the Superior Court/Circuit Court Records 1759-1919

Surname	Given Name	Instrument	Date	County	CLP Record Series	Index #
MORRIS (Cont.)						
Morris	Mary P.	Guardian Bond	1810	Fauquier Co.	Probate, Box 49	1810-001
Morris	Richard	Guardian Bond	1810	Fauquier Co.	Probate, Box 49	1810-016
Morris	Richard P.	Guardian Bond	1810	Fauquier Co.	Probate, Box 49	1810-001
Morris	Richard P.	Report of Division	2/12/1878	Fauquier Co.	Chancery	1903-037
Morris	Richard P.	Plat & Survey of Division of 144 acres On Marsh Road	2/12/1878	Fauquier Co.	Chancery	1903-037
Morris	William	Guardian Bond	1810	Fauquier Co.	Probate, box 49	1810-001
MORRISON						
Morrison	Charles W.F.	Guardian Acct.	1/25/1827	Champagne Co. OH.	Chancery	1839-064
Morrison	Charles W. F.	Guardian Acct.	4/23/1839	Fauquier Co.	Chancery	1839-064
Morrison	Daniel W.	Guardian Acct.	1/25/1827	Champagne Co. OH.	Chancery	1839-064
Morrison	Daniel W.	Guardian Acct.	4/23/1839	Fauquier Co.	Chancery	1839-064
Morrison	Daniel W.	Guardian Bond	11/22/1841	Fauquier Co.	Chancery	1847-034
Morrison	Elizabeth M. R.	Guardian Acct.	4/25/1827	Fauquier Co.	Chancery	1839-064
Morrison	Elizabeth M. R.	Guardian Acct.	4/23/1839	Fauquier Co.	Chancery	1839-064
Morrison	James H. C.	Guardian Acct.	1/25/1827	Champagne Co. OH.	Chancery	1839-064
Morrison	James H. C.	Guardian Acct.	4/23/1839	Fauquier Co.	Chancery	1839-064
Morrison	James H. C.	Guardian Bond	11/22/1841	Fauquier Co.	Chancery	1847-034
MORTON						
Morton	Mary	Guardian Appt.	1/6/1909	Fauquier Co.	Probate, Box 56 Superior/Circuit Ct.	1909-001
MOSS						
Moss	Mildred Jane	Will	10/28/1891	Fauquier Co.	Chancery	1896-006
MOUNT						
Mount	Thomas	Will	9/1/1828	Pr. Wm. Co. VA.	Chancery	1836-013
Mount	William	Will	6/3/1816	Pr. Wm. Co. VA.	Chancery	1836-013
MOUNTJOY						
Mountjoy	Edward	Admtrx. Bond	1777	Fauquier Co.	Probate, Box 44	1777-008
Mountjoy	Edward	Admr. Acct.	10/1777	Stafford Co. VA.	Chancery	1830-148
Mountjoy	Edward	Inventory + Appraisement	9/28/1778	Stafford Co. VA.	Chancery	1830-148

Consolidated Probate Index from the Clerks Loose Papers & the Superior Court/Circuit Court Records 1759-1919

Surname	Given Name	Instrument	Date	County	CLP Record Series	Index #
MOUNTJOY (Cont.)						
Mountjoy	Edward	Admr. Acct.	4/26/1802	Fauquier Co.	Probate, Box 50	1802-001
Mountjoy	William	Will	10/1777	Stafford Co. VA.	Land Records & Disputes	1811-015
Mountjoy	William	Will	10/1777	Stafford Co. VA.	Chancery	1830-148
MOXLEY						
Moxley	Hannah	Guardian Bond	1805	Fauquier Co.	Probate, Box 49	1805-020
Moxley	Jeremiah	Will	2/27/1804	Fauquier Co.	Chancery	1860-038
Moxley	Libby	Guardian Bond	1805	Fauquier Co.	Probate, Box 49	1805-001
Moxley	Lucy	Guardian Bond	1797	Fauquier Co.	Probate, Box 48	1797-003
Moxley	Sibley	Guardian Chosen	1805	Fauquier Co.	Probate, Box 39	1805-021
MUNROE (See also Monroe)						
Munroe	Alexander	Admtrx. Bond	1786	Fauquier Co.	Probate, Box 45	1786-012 OS Probate
MUNRONY						
Munrony	Mary	Admr. Bond	1785	Fauquier Co.	Probate, Box 45	1785-012 OS Probate
MURPHY						
Murphy	Alexander	Guardian Bond	2/14/1842	Fauquier Co.	Chancery	1850-028
MURRAY (See also Murry)						
Murray	Alfred	Will	5/28/1860	Fauquier Co.	Chancery	1876-072
Murray	Alfred	Appraisement	9/11/1860	Fauquier Co.	Chancery	1876-072
Murray	Frances	Guardian Bond	1813	Fauquier Co.	Probate, Box 49	1813-005
Murray	Jane	Plat & Survey Of Dower Allotment	9/19/1876	Fauquier Co.	Chancery	1900-050
Murray	Jane	Report of Division	9/19/1876	Fauquier Co.	Chancery	1900-050
Murray	John	Guardian Bond	1813	Fauquier Co.	Probate, Box 49	1813-005
Murray	John	Will	1/24/1870	Fauquier Co.	Chancery	1893-024
Murray	Mary	Dower Allotment	2/10/1808	Fauquier Co.	Chancery	1824-031
Murray	Ralph	Plat & Survey	2/15/1808	Fauquier Co.	Chancery	1824-031
Murray	Ralph	Exors. Bond	1807	Fauquier Co.	Probate, Box 46	1807-019
Murray	Ralph	Exor. Bond	1807	Fauquier Co.	Probate, Box 46	1807-035
Murray	Ralph	Will	10/26/1807	Fauquier Co.	Chancery	1841-016

Consolidated Probate Index from the Clerks Loose Papers & the Superior Court/Circuit Court Records 1759-1919

Surname	Given Name	Instrument	Date	County	CLP Record Series	Index #
MURRAY (Cont.)						
Murray	Ralph	Will	10/26/1807	Fauquier Co.	Chancery	1841-030
Murray	Ralph	Will	10/26/1807	Fauquier Co.	Chancery	1868-156
Murray	Reuben	Will	6/23/1845	Fauquier Co.	Chancery	1854-042
Murray	Reuben	Will	6/23/1845	Fauquier Co.	Chancery	1900-050
Murray	Sarah	Guardian Bond	1811	Fauquier Co.	Probate, Box 49	1811-008
MURRY (See also Murray)						
Murry	James	Exors. Bond	1783	Fauquier Co.	Probate, Box 45	1783-003

Consolidated Probate Index from the Clerks Loose Papers & the Superior Court/Circuit Court Records 1759-1919

Surname	**Given Name**	**Instrument**	**Date**	**County**	**CLP Record Series**	**Index #**
NALLE (See also Nalley)						
Nalle	Jesse	Admr. Appt.	5/25/1857	Fauquier Co.	Chancery	1889-019
Nalle	Jesse	Division	3/1858	Fauquier Co.	Chancery	1889-019
NALLEY (See also Nalle)						
Nalley	Jesse	Admr. Bond	6/26/1857	Fauquier Co.	Chancery	1889-019
NASH						
Nash	Elijah	Admr. Bond	1777	Fauquier Co.	Probate, Box 44	1777-013
Nash	Lora	Will	3/8/1860	New York Co. NY.	Chancery	1867-036
Nash	Travers	Report of Division with Plat & Survey	3/25/1817	Fauquier Co.	Chancery	1817-020
NEALE						
Neale	Benjamin	Extrx. Bond	1785	Fauquier Co.	Probate, Box 45	1785-006
Neale	Francis	Admr. Bond	4/27/1847	Fauquier Co.	Chancery	1866-036
Neale	John	Exor. Qualification	1/25/1847	Fauquier Co.	Chancery	1866-036
Neale	Joseph	Exors. Bond	1784	Fauquier Co.	Probate, Box 45	1784-005
Neale	Lucy (Mrs.)	Court order to divide Dower Slaves	7/1843	Fauquier Co.	Probate, Box 40	1843-002
Neale	Lucy (Mrs.)	Court order to sell Dower Slaves	7/1843	Fauquier Co.	Probate, Box 40	1843-002
Neale	Matilda	Guardian Bond	1807	Fauquier Co.	Probate, Box 49	1807-004
Neale	William	Admtrx. Bond	1808	Fauquier Co.	Probate, Box 46	1808-006
NEAVILL (See also Nevill)						
Neavill	George	Will	6/27/1774	Fauquier Co.	Chancery	1791-024
Neavill	George	Exor. Acct.	1784	Fauquier Co.	Chancery	1791-024
Neavill	George	Will	6/27/1774	Fauquier Co.	Chancery	1803-067
Neavill	John	Admr. Bond	1768	Fauquier Co.	Probate, Box 44	1768-002
NELSON						
Nelson	Benjamin	Guardian Bond	1778	Fauquier Co.	Probate, Box 48	1778-001
Nelson	Benjamin	Guardian Bond	1785	Fauquier Co.	Probate, Box 48	1785-006
Nelson	Edgar F.	Guardian Appt.	4/10/1880	Fauquier Co.	Chancery	1879-038

Consolidated Probate Index from the Clerks Loose Papers & the Superior Court/Circuit Court Records 1759-1919

Surname	Given Name	Instrument	Date	County	CLP Record Series	Index #
NELSON (Cont.)						
Nelson	George	Will	5/28/1860	Fauquier Co.	Chancery	1873-035
Nelson	George	Will	5/28/1860	Fauquier Co.	Chancery	1889-088
Nelson	George	Report of Division Of Slaves	9/15/1860	Fauquier Co.	Chancery	1889-088
Nelson	George	Report of Division Of Lands	9/20/1873	Fauquier Co.	Chancery	1889-088
Nelson	George	Will	5/28/1860	Fauquier Co.	Chancery	1892-024
Nelson	James	Admtrx. Bond	1771	Fauquier Co.	Probate, Box 44	1771-003
Nelson	James	Admr. Acct. Settled	9/1793	Fauquier Co.	Probate, Box 39	1793-002
Nelson	James	Exor. Bond	1813	Fauquier Co.	Probate, box 47	1813-006
Nelson	John	Inventory + Appraisement	11/1771	Fauquier Co.	Probate, Box 39	1793-002
Nelson	John	Exors. Bond	1784	Fauquier Co.	Probate, Box 45	1784-009
Nelson	Lena S.	Guardian Appt.	4/10/1880	Fauquier Co.	Chancery	1879-038
Nelson	Mary	Admr. Bond	1812	Fauquier Co.	Probate, Box 47	1812-011
Nelson	Mary F.	Appraisement	1/1874	Fauquier Co.	Probate, Box 53 Superior/Circuit Ct.	1874-001
Nelson	Mary F.	Sales	1/1874	Fauquier Co.	Probate, Box 53 Superior/Circuit Ct.	1874-001
Nelson	Minnie L.	Guardian Appt.	4/10/1880	Fauquier Co.	Chancery	1879-038
Nelson	Thomas	Will	1/26/1857	Fauquier Co.	Chancery	1858-008
Nelson	Thomas	Will	1/26/1857	Fauquier Co.	Chancery	1859-055
Nelson	Thomas	Will	1/26/1857	Fauquier Co.	Chancery	1871-115
Nelson	Thomas H.	Plat & Survey Of Division	1/3/1866	Fauquier Co.	Chancery	1866-066
Nelson	Thomas H.	Plat & Survey Of Division	5/24/1866	Fauquier Co.	Chancery	1866-066
Nelson	William	Admr. Bond	1777	Fauquier Co.	Probate, Box 44	1777-004
NEVILL (See also Neavill)						
Nevill	George	Exors. Bond	1774	Fauquier Co.	Probate, Box 44	1774-009

Consolidated Probate Index from the Clerks Loose Papers & the Superior Court/Circuit Court Records 1759-1919

Surname	Given Name	Instrument	Date	County	CLP Record Series	Index #
NEWBY						
Newby	George	Guardian Appt.	7/5/1905	Fauquier Co.	Probate, Box 56 Superior/Circuit Ct.	1907-008
NEWELL						
Newell	Benjamin	Exor. Bond	1782	Fauquier Co.	Probate, Box 45	1782-010
NEWGENT						
Newgent	Ann	Exor. Bond	1785	Fauquier Co.	Probate, Box 45	1785-010
Newgent	Charles	Guardian Bond	1791	Fauquier Co.	Probate, Box 48	1791-006
Newgent	Edward	Guardian Bond	1791	Fauquier Co.	Probate, Box 48	1791-006
Newgent	Jocley	Guardian Bond	1791	Fauquier Co.	Probate, Box 48	1791-006
Newgent	Mary	Guardian Bond	1791	Fauquier Co.	Probate, Box 48	1791-006
NEWHOUSE						
Newhouse	Elizabeth	Guardian Bond	1796	Fauquier Co.	Probate, Box 48	1796-001
NEWMAN						
Newman	Thomas	Will	4/21/1821	Pr. Wm. Co. VA.	Chancery	1840-027
NICHOLS						
Nichols	John	Admr. Bond	1772	Fauquier Co.	Probate, Box 44	1772-007
NICKNESS						
Nickness	Thomas	Court Order to Appraise Estate	7/1801	Fauquier Co.	Probate, Box 39	1801-005
NORRIS						
Norris	Elizabeth	Will	10/26/1840	Fauquier Co.	Chancery	1856-056
Norris	Hannah	Will	12/27/1847	Fauquier Co.	Chancery	1854-013
Norris	Hannah	Exor. Acct.	1/24/1848	Fauquier Co.	Chancery	1854-013
Norris	Hannah	Will	12/27/1847	Fauquier Co.	Chancery	1856-056
Norris	Joseph	Sale of Slaves	12/27/1852	Fauquier Co.	Chancery	1853-041
Norris	Joseph	Admr. Acct.	1/29/1853	Fauquier Co.	Chancery	1853-041
Norris	Joseph	Heirs	Undated	Fauquier Co.	Chancery	1853-041
Norris	Peggy	Relinquishment	4/1799	Fauquier Co.	Probate, Box 39	1799-002
Norris	Richard	Will	10/10/1838	Fauquier Co.	Chancery	1847-017
Norris	Richard	Will	10/10/1838	Fauquier Co.	Chancery	1871-098
Norris	Septimus	Inventory + Appraisement	9/1799	Fauquier Co.	Probate, Box 39	1799-001
Norris	Thaddeus	Exor. Bond	1824	Fauquier Co.	Probate, Box 47	1824-001

Consolidated Probate Index from the Clerks Loose Papers & the Superior Court/Circuit Court Records 1759-1919

Surname	Given Name	Instrument	Date	County	CLP Record Series	Index #
NORRIS (Cont.)						
Norris	Thaddeus	Will	2/24/1824	Fauquier Co.	Chancery	1832-072
Norris	Thaddeus	Will	2/24/1824	Fauquier Co.	Chancery	1847-017
Norris	Thaddeus	Exor. Acct.	3/25/1828	Fauquier Co.	Chancery	1847-017
Norris	Thaddeus	Exor. Acct.	1829	Fauquier Co.	Chancery	1847-017
Norris	Thaddeus	Inventory Certified	9/7/1841	Fauquier Co.	Chancery	1847-017
Norris	Thaddeus	Exor. Acct.	3/23/1828	Fauquier Co.	Chancery	1858-018
Norris	Thaddeus	Will	2/24/1824	Fauquier Co.	Chancery	1871-098
Norris	William	Will	5/24/1802	Fauquier Co.	Chancery	1840-017
Norris	William	Will	5/24/1802	Fauquier Co.	Chancery	1841-008
Norris	William	Will	5/24/1802	Fauquier Co.	Chancery	1854-013
Norris	William	Division of Slaves	1/24/1803	Fauquier Co.	Chancery	1854-013
Norris	William	Division	1854	Fauquier Co.	Chancery	1854-013
Norris	William	Will	4/20/1802	Fauquier Co.	Chancery	1856-066
Norris	William	Plat & Survey	2/26/1856	Fauquier Co.	Chancery	1856-066
Norris	William	Division	1/23/1803	Fauquier Co.	Chancery	1860-022
NORTH						
North	James H.	Admr. Appt.	12/19/1906	Fauquier Co.	Probate, Box 56 Superior/Circuit Ct.	1906-010
NORTON						
Norton	J. H. Heirs	Accts for rents from Effingham Forest tenants	1814-1819	Fauquier Co.	Probate, Box 39	1809-001
NOURSE						
Nourse	Charlotte St. George	Guardian Appt.	7/1/1909	Fauquier Co.	Probate, Box 56 Superior/Circuit Ct.	1909-011
Nourse	Mary Pendleton	Guardian Appt.	7/1/1909	Fauquier Co.	Probate, Box 56 Superior/Circuit Ct.	1909-011
Nourse	Walter Burton	Guardian Appt.	7/1/1909	Fauquier Co.	Probate, Box 56	1909-011
NUGENT (See also Newgent)						
Nugent	Edward	Extrx. Bond	1797	Fauquier Co.	Probate, Box 46	1797-002
NUTT						
Nutt	Anne E.	Will	4/1893	Pr. Wm. Co. VA.	Chancery	1898-063
Nutt	Olivas D.	Guardian Bond	4/9/1858	Fauquier Co.	Chancery	1858-016

Consolidated Probate Index from the Clerks Loose Papers & the Superior Court/Circuit Court Records 1759-1919

Surname	Given Name	Instrument	Date	County	CLP Record Series	Index #
OBANION (See also Obannon, Obanon)						
Obanion	John (Capt.)	Sales	12/11/1775	Fauquier Co.	Probate, Box 39	1793-003
OBANNON (See also Obanion, Obanon)						
Obannon	Bryan	Exors. Bond	1762	Fauquier Co.	Probate, Box 44	1762-004
Obannon	George	Admr. Bond	1777	Fauquier Co.	Probate, Box 44	1777-010
Obannon	James	Guardian Bond	1811	Fauquier Co.	Probate, Box 49	1811-014
Obannon	Jesse	Will	5/28/1844	Fauquier Co.	Probate, Box 50 Addendum Folder	1844-001
Obannon	Jesse	Will	5/28/1844	Fauquier Co.	Chancery	1846-068
Obannon	John	Exors. Bond	1797	Fauquier Co.	Probate, Box 46	1797-013
Obannon	John	Admrs. Bond	1811	Fauquier Co.	Probate, Box 48	1811-013
Obannon	Joseph	Will	2/1824	Fauquier Co.	Chancery	1832-016
Obannon	Joseph	List of Slaves	2/1824	Fauquier Co.	Chancery	1832-016
Obannon	Joseph	Will	6/18/1822	Fauquier Co.	Chancery	1835-067
Obannon	Joseph	Heirs	6/29/1835	Fauquier Co.	Chancery	1835-067
Obannon	Joseph	Admr. Acct.	Undated	Fauquier Co.	Chancery	1835-067
Obannon	Joseph	Will	2/24/1824	Fauquier Co.	Chancery	1837-074
Obannon	Mary S.	Guardian Bond	1814	Fauquier Co.	Probate, Box 49	1814-003
Obannon	Minor	Guardian Bond	1814	Fauquier Co.	Probate, Box 49	1814-003
Obannon	Narcissa G.	Guardian Bond	1814	Fauquier Co.	Probate, Box 49	1814-003
Obannon	Samuel	Sales	Undated	Fauquier Co.	Chancery	1830-132
Obannon	Samuel	Sales of Slaves and Land	Undated	Fauquier Co.	Chancery	1830-132
Obannon	Samuel	Admr. Acct.	Undated	Fauquier Co.	Chancery	1830-132
Obannon	Susanna W.	Guardian Bond	1814	Fauquier Co.	Probate, Box 49	1814-003
Obannon	William	Exor. Bond	1807	Fauquier Co.	Probate, Box 46	1807-021
Obannon	William	Exor. Bond	1808	Fauquier Co.	Probate, Box 46	1808-018
Obannon	William	Court order to Appraise Estate	3/1813	Fauquier Co.	Probate, Box 39	1814-002

Consolidated Probate Index from the Clerks Loose Papers & the Superior Court/Circuit Court Records 1759-1919

Surname	Given Name	Instrument	Date	County	CLP Record Series	Index #
OBANON (See also Obannon, Obanion)						
Obanon	Bryan	Exor. Bond	1762	Fauquier Co.	Probate, Box 44	1762-005
Obanon	Bryant	Guardian Bond	1774	Fauquier Co.	Probate, Box 48	1774-002
Obanon	John	Exor. Bond	1774	Fauquier Co.	Probate, Box 44	1774-004
OLINGER						
Olinger	Elizabeth	Division of Slaves	4/19/1853	Fauquier Co.	Chancery	1891-003
OLIVER						
Oliver	Charles	Admr. Appt.	9/22/1856	Fauquier Co.	Chancery	1893-004
OREAR						
Orear	Peter	Admr. Appt.	10/26/1845	Fauquier Co.	Chancery	1848-037
Orear	Susan	Admr. Bond	4/8/1880	Fauquier Co.	Probate, Box 54 Superior/Circuit Ct.	1880-002
OTTERBACK (See also Utterback)						
Otterback	Philip	Will	6/21/1858	Washington, DC.	Chancery	1883-023
OWENS						
Owens	Anna	Guardian Bond	1816	Fauquier Co.	Probate, Box 49	1816-015
Owens	Anna	Guardian Bond	1816	Fauquier Co.	Probate, Box 49	1816-016
Owens	Asenath	Guardian Bond	1816	Fauquier Co.	Probate, Box 49	1816-015
Owens	Asenath	Guardian Bond	1816	Fauquier Co.	Probate, Box 49	1816-016
Owens	Cuthbert	Will	3/22/1841	Fauquier Co.	Probate, Box 50 Addendum Folder	1840-001
Owens	Cuthbert	Exor. Bond	3/22/1841	Fauquier Co.	Chancery	1851-021
Owens	Cuthbert	Will	3/22/1841	Fauquier Co.	Chancery	1852-006
Owens	Cuthbert	Plats 1 & 2 of Cuthbert Owens Lands	Undated	Fauquier Co.	Chancery	1852-006
Owens	Cuthbert	Will	3/22/1841	Fauquier Co.	Chancery	1894-029
Owens	Cuthbert	Report of Division (Extract)	3/18/1859	Fauquier Co.	Chancery	1894-029
Owens	Cuthbert	Will	3/22/1841	Fauquier Co.	Chancery	1894-030
Owens	Cuthbert	Report of Division (Extract)	3/18/1859	Fauquier Co.	Chancery	1894-030
Owens	Cuthbert	Will	3/22/1841	Fauquier Co.	Chancery	1896-051

Consolidated Probate Index from the Clerks Loose Papers & the Superior Court/Circuit Court Records 1759-1919

Surname	Given Name	Instrument	Date	County	CLP Record Series	Index #
OWENS (Cont.)						
Owens	Elizabeth	Dower Allotment	5/1841	Fauquier Co.	Chancery	1894-029
Owens	Elizabeth	Dower Allotment In Slaves	5/1841	Fauquier Co.	Chancery	1894-030
Owens	Elizabeth	Plat & Survey Of Dower Allotment	5/10/1841	Fauquier Co.	Chancery	1896-048
Owens	Elizabeth	Will	5/28/1860	Fauquier Co.	Chancery	1896-052
Owens	Ephraim	Admr. Bond	1806	Fauquier Co.	Probate, Box 46	1806-014
Owens	Ephraim	Guardian Bond	1816	Fauquier Co.	Probate, Box 49	1816-014
Owens	Esrom	Guardian Bond	1806	Fauquier Co.	Probate, Box 49	1806-001
Owens	Jeremiah	Admr. Bond	1774	Fauquier Co.	Probate, Box 44	1774-007
Owens	Joshua	Guardian Bond	1776	Fauquier Co.	Probate, Box 48	1776-001
Owens	Lucina	Guardian Bond	1816	Fauquier Co.	Probate, Box 49	1816-015
Owens	Lucina	Guardian Bond	1816	Fauquier Co.	Probate, Box 49	1816-016
Owens	Nathaniel	Exors. Bond	1807	Fauquier Co.	Probate, Box 46	1807-023
Owens	Samuel	Guardian Bond	1773	Fauquier Co.	Probate, Box 48	1773-002
Owens	William	Guardian Bond	1816	Fauquier Co.	Probate, Box 48	1816-014
Owens	William M.	Guardian Bond	9/13/1860	Fauquier Co.	Probate, Box 52 Superior/Circuit Ct.	1860-006
Owens	William M.	Guardian Acct.	10/1/1860	Fauquier Co.	Chancery	1894-029

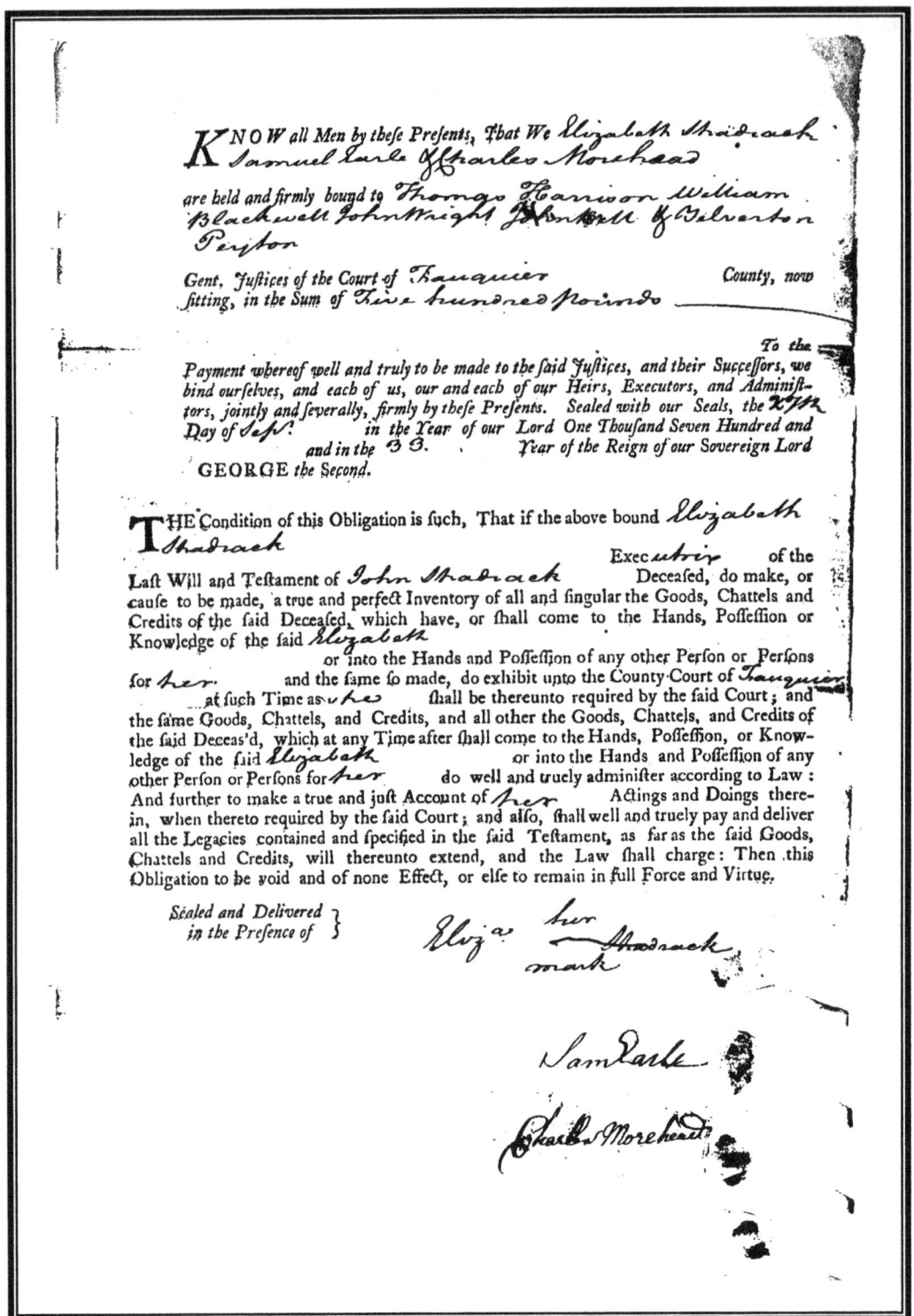

Plate 4. Probate. Scanned Image from Box 44. Administrator & Executor Bonds. 1759-005. John Shadrack's Extrx. Bond.

Consolidated Probate Index from the Clerks Loose Papers & the Superior Court/Circuit Court Records 1759-1919

Surname	Given Name	Instrument	Date	County	CLP Record Series	Index #
PADGETT						
Padgett	Dempsey	Heirs	8/20/1867	Fauquier Co.	Military Records	1867-001
Padgett	Dempsey	Will	11/27/1865	Fauquier Co.	Chancery	1865-010
Padgett	Dempsey	Will	11/27/1865	Fauquier Co.	Chancery	1875-046
Padgett	Dempsey	Will	11/27/1865	Fauquier Co.	Chancery	1886-030
Padgett	Dempsey	Will	11/27/1865	Fauquier Co.	Chancery	1887-030
Padgett	Dempsey	Will	11/27/1865	Fauquier Co.	Chancery	1897-019
PAGE						
Page	Corbin B.	Inventory +	4/30/1846	Fauquier Co.	Chancery	1861-028
Page	Corbin B.	Admr. Bond	8/28/1843	Fauquier Co.	Chancery	1866-051
Page	Corbin B.	Admr. Acct.	11/27/1847	Fauquier Co.	Chancery	1889-020
PALMER						
Palmer	Elizabeth	Guardian Bond	1815	Fauquier Co.	Probate, Box 49	1815-014
Palmer	Joseph	Will	7/26/1852	Fauquier Co.	Chancery	1854-050
Palmer	Joseph	Will	7/26/1852	Richmond Co. VA.	Chancery	1870-007
Palmer	Joseph	Inventory + Appraisement	3/21/1853	Fauquier Co.	Chancery	1870-007
Palmer	Joseph	Admr. Acct.	2/14/1857	Fauquier Co.	Chancery	1870-007
Palmer	Mildred	Will	6/23/1856	Fauquier Co.	Chancery	1870-007
Palmer	Sally	Guardian Bond	1815	Fauquier Co.	Probate, Box 49	1815-014
PARKER						
Parker	Elizabeth	Guardian Bond	1800	Fauquier Co.	Probate, Box 48	1800-004
Parker	Emeline	Will	9/29/1874	FauquierCo.	Chancery	1883-016
Parker	Indy	Guardian Bond	1800	Fauquier Co.	Probate, Box 48	1800-004
Parker	Lucy	Guardian Bond	1800	Fauquier Co.	Probate, Box 48	1800-004
Parker	Vienna	Guardian Bond	8/26/1839	Fauquier Co.	Chancery	1854-012
Parker	Vienna	Guardian Acct.	5/19/1841	Fauquier Co.	Chancery	1854-012
Parker	William	Exors. Bond	1785	Fauquier Co.	Probate, Box 45	1785-007

Consolidated Probate Index from the Clerks Loose Papers & the Superior Court/Circuit Court Records 1759-1919

Surname	Given Name	Instrument	Date	County	CLP Record Series	Index #
PARR						
Parr	James	Will	2/22/1831	Fauquier Co.	Chancery	1836-011
Parr	James	Will	3/26/1832	Fauquier Co.	Chancery	1866-027
Parr	James	Division of Slaves	4/6/1832	Fauquier Co.	Chancery	1866-027
PARSONS						
Parson	Harriet	Renunciation	7/28/1828	Fauquier Co.	Probate, Box 50	1828-002
PATTIE (See also Patty)						
Pattie	Addison L.	Guardian Bond	12/19/1881	Fauquier Co.	Chancery	1881-019
Pattie	Caldwell M.	Guardian Bond	12/19/1881	Fauquier Co.	Chancery	1881-019
Pattie	Mary M.	Guardian Bond	12/19/1881	Fauquier Co.	Chancery	1881-019
Pattie	Meta M. L.	Guardian Bond	12/19/1881	Fauquier Co.	Chancery	1881-019
Pattie	Norville V.	Guardian Bond	12/19/1881	Fauquier Co.	Chancery	1881-019
PATTY (See also Pattie)						
Patty	Dudley	Admr. Bond	1814	Fauquier Co.	Probate, Box 47	1814-009
PAYNE						
Payne	A. D.	Will	3/28/1893	Fauquier Co.	Chancery	1904-017
Payne	Albert Leslie	Guardian Appt.	11/27/1905	Fauquier Co.	Probate, Box 55 Superior/Circuit Ct.	1905-010
Payne	Alexander D. (Capt.)	Resolution in Memory of Life	4/8/1893	Fauquier Co.	Probate, Box 55 Superior/Circuit Ct.	1893-004
Payne	Alice D.	Will	4/28/1900	Fauquier Co.	Chancery	1904-017
Payne	Amos	Will	3/28/1887	Fauquier Co.	Chancery	1888-073
Payne	Arthur M.	Guardian Appt.	8/29/1860	Fauquier Co.	Chancery	1897-002
Payne	C. Bland	Guardian Bond	12/18/1885	Fauquier Co.	Chancery	1885-052
Payne	Daniel	Admr. Bond	1815	Fauquier Co.	Probate, Box 47	1815-048
Payne	Daniel	Admr. Bond	1815	Fauquier Co.	Probate, Box 47	1815-053
Payne	Daniel	Will	10/22/1860	Fauquier Co.	Chancery	1870-006
Payne	Elizabeth	Plat & Survey Of Dower Allotment	12/11/1875	Fauquier Co.	Chancery	1879-005
Payne	Fielding	Admr. Accts.	1845	Fauquier Co.	Chancery	1868-005
Payne	Fielding	Admr. Accts.	1848	Fauquier Co.	Chancery	1868-005
Payne	Francis	Guardian Bond	1785	Fauquier Co.	Probate, Box 48	1785-003

Consolidated Probate Index from the Clerks Loose Papers & the Superior Court/Circuit Court Records 1759-1919

Surname	Given Name	Instrument	Date	County	CLP Record Series	Index #
PAYNE (Cont.)						
Payne	Frank	Will	7/10/1837	Rapphk. Co. VA.	Chancery	1839-038
Payne	Henry F.	Guardian Appt.	8/29/1860	Fauquier Co.	Chancery	1879-002
Payne	J. Scott	Will	1/28/1867	Fauquier Co.	Chancery	1870-006
Payne	J. Scott	Will	1/28/1867	Fauquier Co.	Chancery	1871-111
Payne	J. Scott	Will	1/28/1867	Fauquier Co.	Chancery	1892-043
Payne	James	Guardian Bond	1785	Fauquier Co.	Probate, Box 48	1785-003
Payne	James	Will	9/15/1857	Fauquier Co.	Probate, Box 52 Superior/Circuit Ct.	1857-005
Payne	James	Inventory + Appraisement	8/29/1857	Fauquier Co.	Probate, Box 52 Superior/Circuit Ct.	1857-006
Payne	James	Sales	12/29/1857	Fauquier Co.	Probate, Box 52 Superior/Circuit Ct.	1857-008
Payne	James	Exor. Acct.	4/5/1859	Fauquier Co.	Probate, Box 52 Superior/Circuit Ct.	1859-001
Payne	James	Exor. Acct.	4/3/1860	Fauquier Co.	Probate, Box 52 Superior/Circuit Ct.	1860-002
Payne	James	Exor. Acct.	4/2/1861	Fauquier Co.	Probate, Box 52 Superior/Circuit Ct.	1861-002
Payne	James	Exor. Acct.	4/9/1866	Fauquier Co.	Probate, Box 53 Superior/Circuit Ct.	1866-001
Payne	James	Exor. Bond	4/8/1872	Fauquier Co.	Probate, Box 53 Superior/Circuit Ct.	1872-007
Payne	James	Will	2/28/1848	Fauquier Co.	Chancery	1849-040
Payne	James	Report of Division	12/25/1848	Fauquier Co.	Chancery	1849-040
Payne	James	Plat & Survey Of Division	12/25/1848	Fauquier Co.	Chancery	1849-040
Payne	James	Will	2/28/1848	Fauquier Co.	Chancery	1857-044
Payne	James	Will	2/25/1848	Fauquier Co.	Chancery	1879-001
Payne	James	Report of Division	11/1884	Fauquier Co.	Chancery	1885-028
Payne	James	Plat & Survey Of Division	11/1884	Fauquier Co.	Chancery	1885-028
Payne	James William	Guardian Appt.	11/27/1905	Fauquier Co.	Probate, Box 55 Superior/Circuit Ct.	1905-010

Consolidated Probate Index from the Clerks Loose Papers & the Superior Court/Circuit Court Records 1759-1919

Surname	Given Name	Instrument	Date	County	CLP Record Series	Index #
PAYNE (Cont.)						
Payne	Jesse	Will	1/24/1842	Fauquier Co.	Chancery	1848-088
Payne	Jesse	Will	1/24/1842	Fauquier Co.	Chancery	1868-005
Payne	John	Guardian Bond	1785	Fauquier Co.	Probate, Box 48	1785-003
Payne	John	Report of Division Of Slaves	3/25/1831	Fauquier Co.	Chancery	1832-075
Payne	John	Report of Sale Of Slaves in his Estate	10/22/1835	Fauquier Co.	Chancery	1836-045
Payne	John C.	Will	5/28/1867	Fauquier Co.	Chancery	1889-017
Payne	John J. W.	Guardian Appt.	8/29/1860	Fauquier Co.	Chancery	1897-002
Payne	John Scott	Exor. Acct.	8/8/1868	Fauquier Co.	Probate, Box 50 Addendum Folder	1868-001
Payne	John Scott	Exor. Acct.	7/24/1869	Fauquier Co.	Probate, Box 50 Addendum Folder	1868-001
Payne	John Scott	Exor. Acct.	8/22/1870	Fauquier Co.	Probate, Box 50 Addendum Folder	1868-001
Payne	John Scott	Exor. Acct.	11/27/1871	Fauquier Co.	Probate, Box 50 Addendum Folder	1868-001
Payne	John Scott	Exor. Acct.	12/04/1872	Fauquier Co.	Probate, Box 50 Addendum Folder	1868-001
Payne	John Scott	Exor. Acct.	10/08/1875	Fauquier Co.	Probate, Box 50 Addendum Folder	1868-001
Payne	John Sr.	Admr. Bond	10/25/1830	Fauquier Co.	Chancery	1860-050
Payne	Laura	Guardian Appt.	12/26/1908	Fauquier Co.	Probate, Box 56 Superior/Circuit Ct.	1908-020
Payne	Marshall	Will	12/16/1887	Fauquier Co.	Probate, Box 54 Superior/Circuit Ct.	1887-002
Payne	Marshall	Appraisement	12/16/1887	Fauquier Co.	Probate, Box 54 Superior/Circuit Ct.	1887-002
Payne	Marshall	Will	12/16/1887	Fauquier Co.	Chancery	1899-014
Payne	Minerva	Will	5/22/1882	Fauquier Co.	Chancery	1883-027
Payne	Nancy	Plat & Survey Of Dower Allotment	12/25/1848	Fauquier Co.	Chancery	1879-001
Payne	Richards	Will	11/23/1872	Fauquier Co.	Chancery	1904-017

Consolidated Probate Index from the Clerks Loose Papers & the Superior Court/Circuit Court Records 1759-1919

Surname	Given Name	Instrument	Date	County	CLP Record Series	Index #
PAYNE (Cont.)						
Payne	Sally	Report of Division Of Slaves	1/23/1832	Fauquier Co.	Chancery	1846-077
Payne	Sarah M.	Will	2/23/1907	Fauquier Co.	Chancery	1908-023
Payne	Thomas	Will	1/23/1832	Fauquier Co.	Chancery	1835-020
Payne	Thomas	Will	1/23/1832	Fauquier Co.	Chancery	1846-077
Payne	Thornton	Report of Division	4/5/1876	Fauquier Co.	Chancery	1880-041
Payne	Thornton	Plat & Survey Of Division	4/5/1876	Fauquier Co.	Chancery	1880-041
Payne	W. W.	Exor. Acct.	9/6/1876	Fauquier Co.	Probate, Box 54 Superior/Circuit Ct.	1876-005
Payne	W. W.	Exor. Acct.	12/11/1877	Fauquier Co.	Probate, Box 54 Superior/Circuit Ct.	1877-006
Payne	W. W.	Exor. Acct.	9/3/1878	Fauquier Co.	Probate, Box 54 Superior/Circuit Ct.	1878-008
Payne	W. W.	Exor. Acct	9/7/1880	Fauquier Co.	Probate, Box 54 Superior/Circuit Ct.	1880-006
Payne	W. W.	Exor. Acct.	9/16/1881	Fauquier Co.	Probate, Box 54 Superior/Circuit Ct.	1881-001
Payne	W. W.	Exor. Acct.	9/16/1882	Fauquier Co.	Probate, Box 54	1882-001
Payne	William	Admtrx. Bond	1780	Fauquier Co.	Probate, Box 45	1780-008
Payne	William	Will	9/25/1837	Fauquier Co.	Probate, Box 50	1837-001
Payne	William F.	Will	4/24/1866	Fauquier Co.	Chancery	1877-055
Payne	William W.	Guardian Appt.	8/29/1860	Fauquier Co.	Chancery	1897-002
Payne	William W.	Will	5/12/1874	Fauquier Co.	Chancery	1874-007
Payne	William W.	Exor. Bond	9/18/1874	Fauquier Co.	Probate, Box 53 Superior/Circuit Ct.	1874-007
Payne	William W.	Inventory + Appraisement	10/1875	Fauquier Co.	Probate, Box 53 Superior/Circuit Ct.	1875-003
Payne	William W.	Exor. Acct.	4/5/1876	Fauquier Co.	Probate, Box 53 Superior/Circuit Ct.	1876-003
Payne	William Winter	Will	9/18/1874	Fauquier Co.	Chancery	1883-027
PEAKE						
Peake	John	Extrx. Bond	1780	Fauquier Co.	Probate, Box 45	1780-009

Consolidated Probate Index from the Clerks Loose Papers & the Superior Court/Circuit Court Records 1759-1919

Surname	Given Name	Instrument	Date	County	CLP Record Series	Index #
PEARCE (See also Pierce)						
Pearce	Peter	Exor. Bond	1768	Fauquier Co.	Probate, Box 44	1768-003
Pearce	Rosanna	Guardian Bond	1783	Fauquier Co.	Probate, Box 48	1783-003
Pearce	Susanna	Guardian Bond	1783	Fauquier Co.	Probate, Box 48	1783-003
PEARLE						
Pearle	Ann	Heirs	1/25/1842	Fauquier Co.	Chancery	1858-019
Pearle	Martha	Will	10/19/1795	Fauquier Co.	Probate, Box 50	1795-001
Pearle	Mary Ann	Guardian Appt.	5/2/1850	Brown Co. OH	Chancery	1858-019
Pearle	William	Exors. Bond	1785	Fauquier Co.	Probate, Box 45	1785-004
PENDLETON						
Pendleton	David	Will	3/27/1877	Fauquier Co.	Probate, Box 50	1877-001
Pendleton	George	Admr. Bond	1810	Fauquier Co.	Probate, Box 47	1810-013
Pendleton	Sally	Relinquishment	1810	Fauquier Co.	Probate, Box 47	1810-013
Pendleton	W. W.	Admr. Bond	4/22/1873	Fauquier Co.	Probate, Box 53 Superior/Circuit Ct.	1873-003
PENQUITE						
Penquite	Joseph	Will	5/8/1851	Fauquier Co.	Probate, Box 52 Superior/Circuit Ct.	1851-001
Penquite	Joseph	Inventory + Appraisement	11/4/1851	Fauquier Co.	Probate, Box 52 Superior/Circuit Ct.	1851-010
Penquite	Joseph	Sales	11/4/1851	Fauquier Co.	Probate, Box 52 Superior/Circuit Ct.	1851-011
Penquite	Joseph	Admr. Acct.	3/6/1852	Fauquier Co.	Probate, Box 52 Superior/Circuit Ct.	1852-006
Penquite	Joseph	Will	5/8/1851	Fauquier Co.	Chancery	1890-013
Penquite	William	Will	4/1839	Fauquier Co.	Chancery	1845-017
Penquite	William	Will	4/22/1839	Fauquier Co.	Chancery	1861-010
Penquite	William	Exor. Bond	4/1839	Fauquier Co.	Chancery	1861-010
Penquite	William	Sales	8/30/1839	Fauquier Co.	Chancery	1861-010
Penquite	William	Inventory + Appraisement	3/23/1841	Fauquier Co.	Chancery	1861-010
Penquite	William	Exor. Acct.	3/31/1841	Fauquier Co	Chancery	1861-010
Penquite	William	Exor. Bond	8/23/1841	Fauquier Co.	Chancery	1861-010

Consolidated Probate Index from the Clerks Loose Papers & the Superior Court/Circuit Court Records 1759-1919

Surname	Given Name	Instrument	Date	County	CLP Record Series	Index #
PENQUITE (Cont.)						
Penquite	William	Exor. Acct.	6/30/1842	Fauquier Co.	Chancery	1861-017
Penquite	William	Heirs	1861	Fauquier Co.	Chancery	1861-017
PEPPER						
Pepper	Jeremiah	Admrs. Bond	1812	Fauquier Co.	Probate, Box 47	1812-014
PERRY						
Perry	Pierce	Will	4/21/1856	Culpeper Co. VA.	Chancery	1873-059
PETERKIN						
Peterkin	Emma R.	Will	1/22/1879	Baltimore, MD.	Chancery	1880-036
PETERS						
Peters	Ann Elizabeth	Relinquishment	6/1795	Fauquier Co.	Probate, Box 39	1795-001
Peters	James	Admr. Bond	7/26/1842	Fauquier Co.	Chancery	1855-007
Peters	James	Division	1842	Fauquier Co.	Chancery	1855-007
Peters	James	Report of Division Of Slaves	1842	Fauquier Co.	Chancery	1855-007
Peters	Jesse	Plat & Survey Of Division	12/12/1873	Baltimore, MD.	Chancery	1874-018
Peters	John	Exors. Bond	1781	Fauquier Co.	Probate, Box 45	1781-008
Peters	Obediah	Admrs. Bond	1808	Fauquier Co.	Probate, Box 46	1808-009
PEYTON						
Peyton	C.	List of Dower Slaves	12/1841	Fauquier Co.	Chancery	1843-004
Peyton	Elizabeth	Guardian Bond	1815	Fauquier Co.	Probate, Box 49	1815-004
Peyton	Henry Jr.	Exor. Bond	1815	Fauquier Co.	Probate, Box 47	1815-018
Peyton	John W. B.	Guardian Bond	1815	Fauquier Co.	Probate, Box 49	1815-004
Peyton	Mary D.	Guardian Bond	1815	Fauquier Co.	Probate, Box 49	1815-004
Peyton	Nancy	Guardian Bond	1815	Fauquier Co.	Probate, Box 49	1815-004
Peyton	Peggy	Guardian Bond	1815	Fauquier Co.	Probate, Box 49	1815-004
Peyton	Richard	Admr. Acct.	Undated	Fauquier Co.	Chancery	1843-004
Peyton	Richard H.	Memo of Division Of Slaves	1/4/1842	Fauquier Co.	Chancery	1843-004
Peyton	Richard H.	Plat & Survey Of Division	5/1/1843	Fauquier Co.	Chancery	1843-004

Consolidated Probate Index from the Clerks Loose Papers & the Superior Court/Circuit Court Records 1759-1919

Surname	Given Name	Instrument	Date	County	CLP Record Series	Index #
PEYTON (Cont.)						
Peyton	Richard H. (Capt.)	Heirs	5/26/1840	Fauquier Co.	Chancery	1853-001
Peyton	Susan	Guardian Bond	1811	Fauquier Co.	Probate, Box 49	1811-009
Peyton	Susan Fowke	Guardian Bond	1815	Fauquier Co.	Probate, Box 49	1815-004
PHILIPS (See also Phillips)						
Philips	John P.	Admr. Appt.	2/27/1860	Fauquier Co.	Chancery	1875-003
Philips	William	Guardian Bond	1813	Fauquier Co.	Probate, Box 49	1813-001
PHILLIPS (See also Philips)						
Phillips	J. L.	Will	4/13/1876	Fauquier Co.	Probate, Box 54 Superior/Circuit Ct.	1876-004
Phillips	J. L.	Admr. Bond	4/15/1876	Fauquier Co.	Probate, Box 54 Superior/Circuit Ct.	1876-004
Phillips	J. L.	Appraisement	5/14/1878	Fauquier Co.	Probate, Box 54 Superior/Circuit Ct.	1878-006
Phillips	J. L.	Admr. Acct.	9/3/1878	Fauquier Co.	Probate, Box 54 Superior/Circuit Ct.	1878-007
Phillips	J. L.	Will	4/13/1876	Fauquier Co.	Chancery	1891-052
Phillips	John	Guardian Bond	1810	Fauquier Co.	Probate, Box 49	1810-004
Phillips	Lucy	Guardian Bond	1810	Fauquier Co.	Probate, Box 49	1810-004
Phillips	Richard	Guardian Bond	1810	Fauquier Co.	Probate, Box 49	1810-004
Phillips	Thomas	Inventory +	9/23/1870	Fauquier Co.	Chancery	1875-045
Phillips	W. W.	Report of Division	2/15/1877	Fauquier Co.	Chancery	1879-011
Phillips	W. W.	Plat & Survey Of Division	2/15/1877	Fauquier Co.	Chancery	1879-011
Phillips	W. W.	Report of Division	2/15/1877	Fauquier Co.	Chancery	1893-037
Phillips	W. W.	Plat & Survey Of Division	2/15/1877	Fauquier Co.	Chancery	1893-037
Phillips	William	Admr. Bond	1810	Fauquier Co.	Probate, Box 47	1810-001
Phillips	William W.	Report of Division	2/1877	Fauquier Co.	Chancery	1889-077
Phillips	William Wesley	Will	9/26/1876	Fauquier Co.	Chancery	1888-042
Phillips	William Wesley	Report of Division	2/15/1877	Fauquier Co.	Chancery	1879-042

Consolidated Probate Index from the Clerks Loose Papers & the Superior Court/Circuit Court Records 1759-1919

Surname	Given Name	Instrument	Date	County	CLP Record Series	Index #
PHILLIPS (Cont.)						
Phillips	William Wesley	Plat & Survey Of Division	2/15/1877	Fauquier Co.	Chancery	1879-042
Phillips	William Wesley	Exor. Acct.	8/1883	Fauquier Co.	Chancery	1888-042
PICKETT						
Pickett	Elizabeth	Guardian Chosen	9/1831	Fauquier Co.	Probate, Box 49	1830-001
Pickett	Elizabeth B.	Guardian Bond	1804	Fauquier Co.	Probate, Box 49	1804-002
Pickett	George	Will	3/30/1853	Fauquier Co.	Chancery	1868-011
Pickett	George	Will	3/30/1853	Fauquier Co.	Chancery	1879-044
Pickett	John	Exor. Bond	1803	Fauquier Co.	Chancery	1813-015
Pickett	Martin (Col.)	Will	5/4/1803	Fauquier Co.	Land Records & Disputes	1809-003
Pickett	Steptoe	Guardian Bond	1804	Fauquier Co.	Probate, Box 49	1804-011
Pickett	William	Will	11/24/1766	Fauquier Co.	Land Records & Disputes	1809-003
Pickett	William	Exors. Bond	1766	Fauquier Co.	Probate, Box 44	1766-009
Pickett	William	Exor. Bond	1814	Fauquier Co.	Probate, Box 47	1814-001
Pickett	William (the Elder)	Will	6/27/1814	Fauquier Co.	Chancery	1835-051
Pickett	William	Will	6/23/1817	Fauquier Co.	Chancery	1853-051
Pickett	William	Division of Slaves	1/28/1835	Fauquier Co.	Chancery	1835-051
Pickett	William	Will	6/27/1814	Fauquier Co.	Chancery	1868-011
Pickett	William	Will	6/23/1817	Fauquier Co.	Chancery	1879-044
PIERCE (See also Pearce)						
Pierce	Jane	Admr. Bond	1811	Fauquier Co.	Probate, Box 47	1811-007
Pierce	John	Guardian Bond	1779	Fauquier Co.	Probate Box 48	1779-006
Pierce	John	Will	11/27/1849	Fauquier Co.	Chancery	1853-026
Pierce	John	Exor. Bond	12/24/1849	Fauquier Co.	Chancery	1853-026
Pierce	Josephine	Guardian Bond	5/3/1836	Fauquier Co.	Chancery	1836-034
Pierce	Richard Lewis	Guardian Bond	5/3/1836	Fauquier Co.	Chancery	1836-034
Pierce	Sarah Louisa	Guardian Bond	5/3/1836	Fauquier Co.	Chancery	1836-034

Consolidated Probate Index from the Clerks Loose Papers & the Superior Court/Circuit Court Records 1759-1919

Surname	Given Name	Instrument	Date	County	CLP Record Series	Index #
PINKARD						
Pinkard	Catharine	Admr. Bond	1783	Fauquier Co.	Probate, Box 45	1783-018
POE						
Poe	Samuel	Will	9/10/1819	Culpeper Co. VA.	Probate, Box 39	1819-006
POINDEXTER						
Poindexter	Sophie E.	Will	9/28/1892	Fauquier Co.	Chancery	1907-037
POLLARD						
Pollard	Mildred	Exor. Bond	1813	Fauquier Co.	Probate, Box 47	1813-008
POLLOCK						
Pollock	Elizabeth	Report of Partition	9/1/1899	Fauquier Co.	Chancery	1900-057
Pollock	Elizabeth	Plat & Survey Of Division	9/1/1899	Fauquier Co.	Chancery	1900-057
POOLE						
Poole	Thomas	Will	11/29/1803	Fauquier Co.	Probate, Box 39	1803-001
PORTER						
Porter	Ann	Dower Allotment	12/18/1873	Fauquier Co.	Chancery	1894-003
Porter	John	Will	4/6/1875	Fauquier Co.	Probate, Box 53 Superior/Circuit Ct.	1875-001
Porter	Martin	Will	4/9/1835	Fauquier Co.	Probate, Box 51	1835-001
Porter	Martin	Appraisement	10/6/1835	Fauquier Co.	Probate, Box 51	1835-002
Porter	Martin	Estate Acct.	10/4/1836	Fauquier Co.	Probate, Box 51	1835-003
Porter	Mary	Will	6/21/1882	Fauquier Co.	Chancery	1892-002
Porter	Samuel	Will	12/26/1843	Fauquier Co.	Probate, Box 40	1848-001
Porter	Samuel	Estate Papers	1829-1845	Fauquier Co.	Probate, Box 40	1848-001
Porter	Samuel	Exor. Acct.	1844-1845	Fauquier Co.	Probate, Box 40	1848-001
Porter	Samuel	Exor. Acct.	7/30/1845	Fauquier Co.	Probate, Box 40	1848-001
Porter	Samuel	Exor. Acct.	1846	Fauquier Co.	Probate, Box 40	1848-001
Porter	Samuel Jr.	Exor. Acct.	1807	Fauquier Co.	Probate, Box 46	1807-024
Porter	Susan	Relinquishment	9/27/1824	Fauquier Co.	Probate, Box 40	1824-002
Porter	Thomas	Court Order For Division	1/1800	Fauquier Co.	Probate, Box 39	1800-001
Porter	Thomas	Admr. Appt.	9/27/1824	Fauquier Co.	Chancery	1866-009

Consolidated Probate Index from the Clerks Loose Papers & the Superior Court/Circuit Court Records 1759-1919

Surname	Given Name	Instrument	Date	County	CLP Record Series	Index #
PORTMAN						
Portman	F. A. B.	Admr. Appt.	5/27/1907	Fauquier Co.	Probate, Box 56 Superior/Circuit Ct.	1907-003
Portman	F. A. B.	Court order to Appraise Estate	5/27/1907	Fauquier Co.	Probate, Box 56 Superior/Circuit Ct.	1907-003
PRESTON						
Preston	William	Exor. Bond	1806	Fauquier Co.	Probate, Box 46	1806-011
PRICE						
Price	Ann	Guardian Bond	1780	Fauquier Co.	Probate, Box 48	1780-001
Price	Bennett	Exors. Bond	1774	Fauquier Co.	Probate, Box 44	1774-005
Price	Charlie	Guardian Appt.	6/22/1908	Fauquier Co.	Probate, Box 56 Superior/Circuit Ct.	1908-011
Price	Eleanore	Guardian Appt.	6/22/1908	Fauquier Co.	Probate, Box 56 Superior/Circuit Ct.	1908-011
Price	Elizabeth	Guardian Bond	1780	Fauquier Co.	Probate, Box 48	1780-001
Price	Freda	Guardian Appt.	6/22/1908	Fauquier Co.	Probate, Box 56	1908-011
Price	Judith	Dower Allotment In Land	7/1780	Fauquier Co.	Probate, Box 39	1780-001
Price	Luther R.	Guardian Appt.	6/22/1908	Fauquier Co.	Probate, Box 56 Superior/Circuit Ct.	1908-011
PRIEST						
Priest	Catharine	Guardian Bond	9/5/1855	Fauquier Co.	Chancery	1855-038
Priest	Eliza A.	Guardian Bond	9/5/1855	Fauquier Co.	Chancery	1855-038
Priest	James G.	Admtrx. Acct. Voided	9/9/1897	Fauquier Co.	Probate, Box 55 Superior/Circuit Ct.	1897-005
Priest	James G.	Admtrx. Acct.	4/6/1898	Fauquier Co.	Probate, Box 55 Superior/Circuit Ct.	1898-003
Priest	James G.	Inventory + Appraisement	9/22/1874	Fauquier Co.	Chancery	1906-018
Priest	John	Admr. Bond	1809	Fauquier Co.	Probate, Box 47	1809-006
Priest	Margaret A.	Guardian Bond	9/5/1855	Fauquier Co.	Chancery	1855-038
Priest	Mason	Will	9/25/1848	Fauquier Co.	Chancery	1856-004
Priest	William	Exors. Bond	1781	Fauquier Co.	Probate, Box 45	1781-005

Consolidated Probate Index from the Clerks Loose Papers & the Superior Court/Circuit Court Records 1759-1919

Surname	Given Name	Instrument	Date	County	CLP Record Series	Index #
PRIMM						
Primm	John	Will	2/27/1865	Fauquier Co.	Chancery	1894-067
Primm	John	Report of Division	4/12/1872	Fauquier Co.	Chancery	1894-067
Primm	John	Plat & Survey Of Division	4/12/1872	Fauquier Co.	Chancery	1894-067
Primm	William Sr.	Will	4/26/1829	Fauquier Co.	Probate, Box 50	1818-001
PRINCE						
Prince	Hubbard	Admr. Bond	1778	Fauquier Co.	Probate, Box 45	1778-019
PUTLAND						
Putland	Matilda	Admtrx. Appt.	3/24/1904	Fauquier Co.	Probate, Box 55 Superior/Circuit Ct.	1904-003
PUTNAM						
Putnam	Noah	Admr. Appt.	9/3/1908	Fauquier Co.	Probate, Box 56 Superior/Circuit Ct.	1908-015
QUESENBERRY (See also Quisenberry)						
Quesenberry	Mary	Guardian Bond	1815	Fauquier Co.	Probate, Box 49	1815-009
Quesenberry	Mary	Guardian Bond	1817	Fauquier Co.	Probate, Box 49	1817-017
QUISENBERRY (See also Quesenberry)						
Quisenberry	Edith	Guardian Bond	4/16/1868	Fauquier Co.	Chancery	1875-010
Quisenberry	Elizabeth	Exor. Bond	1815	Fauquier Co.	Probate, Box 47	1815-015
Quisenberry	William P.	Will	7/6/1864	Alexandria Co. VA.	Chancery	1875-010

Consolidated Probate Index from the Clerks Loose Papers & the Superior Court/Circuit Court Records 1759-1919

Surname	Given Name	Instrument	Date	County	CLP Record Series	Index #
RALEY (See also Riley)						
Raley	Thomas	Exor. Bond	1811	Fauquier Co.	Probate, Box 47	1811-003
RAMEY						
Ramey	Alford	Guardian Appt.	11/8/1910	Fauquier Co.	Probate, Box 56 Superior/Circuit Ct.	1910-004
Ramey	Alfred P.	Will	4/10/1905	Fauquier Co.	Probate, Box 50 Addendum Folder	1905-001
Ramey	Ashton	Report of Division	12/12/1897	Fauquier Co.	Chancery	1899-039
Ramey	Edgar	Guardian Appt.	11/8/1910	Fauquier Co.	Probate, Box 56 Superior/Circuit Ct.	1910-004
Ramey	Elizabeth M.	Guardian Appt.	11/8/1910	Fauquier Co.	Probate, Box 56 Superior/Circuit Ct.	1910-004
Ramey	J. Ashton	Guardian Appt.	8/24/1907	Fauquier Co.	Probate, Box 56 Superior/Circuit Ct.	1907-015
Ramey	J. M.	Admr. Appt.	4/1/1907	Fauquier Co.	Probate, Box 56 Superior/Circuit Ct.	1907-001
Ramey	J. M. (Mrs.)	Renunciation	4/19/1907	Fauquier Co.	Probate, Box 56 Superior/Circuit Ct.	1907-001
Ramey	Mary	Plat & Survey Of Dower Allotment	7/14/1892	Fauquier Co.	Chancery	1895-050
RANDELL						
Randell	John	Admtrx. Bond	1812	Fauquier Co.	Probate, Box 47	1812-002
Randell	John C.	Guardian Bond	1806	Fauquier Co.	Probate, Box 49	1808-006
RANDOLPH						
Randolph	Charles C.	Guardian Bond	12/2/1865	Fauquier Co.	Probate, Box 52 Superior/Circuit Ct.	1865-001
Randolph	Charles C.	Admr. Bond	12/12/1865	Fauquier Co.	Probate, Box 52 Superior/Circuit Ct.	1865-002
Randolph	Charles C.	Admr. Bond	9/3/1870	Fauquier Co.	Probate, Box 53 Superior/Circuit Ct.	1870-007
Randolph	Charles C.	Admr. Acct.	1870	Fauquier Co.	Chancery	1904-002
Randolph	Norwood B.	Guardian Bond	12/12/1865	Fauquier Co.	Probate, Box 52 Superior/Circuit Ct.	1865-001
Randolph	Robert	Resolution at Death	9/26/1825	Fauquier Co.	Military Records	1825-001
Randolph	Robert	Report of Division	9/1889	Fauquier Co.	Chancery	1894-062
Randolph	Robert	Plat & Survey of Division	9/1889	Fauquier Co.	Chancery	1894-062

Consolidated Probate Index from the Clerks Loose Papers & the Superior Court/Circuit Court Records 1759-1919

Surname	Given Name	Instrument	Date	County	CLP Record Series	Index #
RANSDELL						
Ransdell	Agnes	Will	6/3/1870	Fauquier Co.	Probate, Box 50 Addendum Folder	1870-001
Ransdell	Charles	Guardian bond	1789	Fauquier Co.	Probate, Box 48	1789-005
Ransdell	Chilton	Extrx. Bond	1808	Fauquier Co.	Probate, Box 46	1808-013
Ransdell	John	Guardian Bond	1796	Fauquier Co.	Probate, Box 48	1796-002
Ransdell	Maria	Guardian Bond	1796	Fauquier Co.	Probate, Box 48	1796-002
Ransdell	Thomas (Capt.)	Heirs	3/1839	Fauquier Co.	Military Records	1839-002
Ransdell	Thornton	Guardian Bond	1789	Fauquier Co.	Probate, Box 48	1789-005
Ransdell	Wharton	Will	6/1786	Fauquier Co.	Probate, Box 39	1786-001
Ransdell	Wharton	Exors. Bond	1786	Fauquier Co.	Probate, Box 45	1796-006
Ransdell	Wharton Jr.	Admtrx. Bond	1785	Fauquier Co.	Probate, Box 45	1785-013 OS Probate
Ransdell	William	Exors. Bond	1776	Fauquier Co.	Probate, Box 44	1776-005
RAWLINGS						
Rawlings	John D.	Will	11/30/1859	Fauquier Co.	Chancery	1873-038
READ (See also Reid)						
Read	James	Guardian Bond	1771	Fauquier Co.	Probate, Box 48	1771-002
REAGER						
Reager	John C.	Guardian Acct.	4/28/1887	Fauquier Co.	Chancery	1892-063
Reager	John C.	Guardian Acct.	11/12/1889	Fauquier Co.	Chancery	1892-063
RECTOR						
Rector	Alfred	Will	11/24/1864	Fauquier Co.	Chancery	1906-001
Rector	Alfred	Sales	10/19/1865	Fauquier Co.	Chancery	1906-001
Rector	Alfred	Report of Division	3/1/1870	Fauquier Co.	Chancery	1906-001
Rector	Alfred	Plat & Survey Of Division	3/1/1870	Fauquier Co.	Chancery	1906-001
Rector	Amanda	Committee Resigned	12/4/1906	Fauquier Co.	Probate, Box 56 Superior/Circuit Ct.	1906-011
Rector	Amanda	Committee, New Appt.	12//4/1906	Fauquier Co.	Probate, Box 56 Superior/Circuit Ct.	1906-011
Rector	Amanda V.	Admr. Qualification	1/26/1909	Fauquier Co.	Probate, Box 56 Superior/Circuit Ct.	1909-002

Consolidated Probate Index from the Clerks Loose Papers & the Superior Court/Circuit Court Records 1759-1919

Surname	Given Name	Instrument	Date	County	CLP Record Series	Index #
RECTOR (Cont.)						
Rector	Benjamin	Will	12/27/1869	Fauquier Co.	Chancery	1884-001
Rector	Braxton	Admr. Appt.	9/26/1826	Fauquier Co.	Chancery	1839-008
Rector	Catherine	Guardian Bond	1782	Fauquier Co.	Probate, Box 48	1782-002
Rector	Charles H.	Admtrx. Appt.	4/7/1903	Fauquier Co.	Probate, Box 55 Superior/Circuit Ct.	1903-001
Rector	Charles H.	Admtrx. Power Of Attorney	4/7/1903	Fauquier Co.	Probate, Box 55 Superior/Circuit Ct.	1903-001
Rector	Elizabeth	Exor. Bond	9/7/1832	Fauquier Co.	Probate, Box 51 Superior/Circuit Ct.	1832-002
Rector	Elizabeth	Will	8/25/1824	Fauquier Co.	Chancery	1855-003
Rector	Enoch	Guardian Bond	1782	Fauquier Co.	Probate, Box 48	1782-002
Rector	Franklin	Admtrx. Appt.	6/10/1907	Fauquier Co.	Probate, Box 56 Superior/Circuit Ct.	1907-005
Rector	Harriet	Will	4/26/1860	Fauquier Co.	Probate, Box 50 Addendum Folder	1860-001
Rector	Henry	Will	6/23/1829	Fauquier Co.	Chancery	1847-055
Rector	Jane	Admr. Bond	5/13/1847	Fauquier Co.	Probate, Box 51 Superior/Circuit Ct.	1847-002
Rector	Jane	Inventory +	5/2/1848	Fauquier Co.	Probate, Box 51 Superior/Circuit Ct.	1847-003
Rector	John	Exors. Bond	1773	Fauquier Co.	Probate, Box 44	1773-002
Rector	John	Admtrx. Bond	1775	Fauquier Co.	Probate, Box 44	1775-009
Rector	John	Guardian Bond	1782	Fauquier Co.	Probate, Box 48	1782-002
Rector	John	Exors. Bond	1815	Fauquier Co.	Probate, Box 47	1815-003
Rector	John Jr.	Admr. Bond	1773	Fauquier Co.	Probate, Box 44	1773-007
Rector	Ludwell	Exor. Acct.	9/21/1855	Fauquier Co.	Probate, Box 52 Superior/Circuit Ct.	1855-012
Rector	Ludwell	Will	10/21/1849	Fauquier Co.	Chancery	1856-023
Rector	Ludwell	Inventory + Appraisement	5/1/1850	Fauquier Co.	Chancery	1856-023
Rector	Ludwell	Division of Slaves	Undated	Fauquier Co.	Chancery	1856-023

Consolidated Probate Index from the Clerks Loose Papers & the Superior Court/Circuit Court Records 1759-1919

Surname	Given Name	Instrument	Date	County	CLP Record Series	Index #
RECTOR (Cont.)						
Rector	Margaret	Will	9/11/1872	Fauquier Co.	Probate, Box 53 Superior/Circuit Ct.	1872-002
Rector	Margaret	Appraisement	11/10/1871	Fauquier Co.	Probate, Box 53 Superior/Circuit Ct.	1871-006
Rector	Nathaniel	Admr. Bond	1806	Fauquier Co.	Probate, Box 46	1806-020
Rector	Peggy	Guardian Bond	1782	Fauquier Co.	Probate, Box 48	1782-002
Rector	Polly	Guardian Bond	1812	Fauquier Co.	Probate, Box 49	1812-008
Rector	R. H.	Will	6/25/1888	Fauquier Co.	Chancery	1888-076
Rector	Sarah	Guardian Bond	1793	Fauquier Co.	Probate, Box 48	1793-001
Rector	Spencer	Committee Bond and Papers	4/17/1884	Fauquier co.	Probate, Box 54 Superior/Circuit Ct.	1884-002
Rector	Thomas	Will	5/21/1850	Fauquier Co.	Chancery	1875-029
Rector	Thomas	Will	6/24/1850	Fauquier Co.	Chancery	1884-037
Rector	Thomas A.	Plat & Survey Of Division	Undated	Fauquier Co.	Chancery	1893-022
Rector	W. F.	Death (in Deposition)	8/2/1900	Butte, MT.	Chancery	1908-009
Rector	W. F.	Heirs (in Deposition)	8/2/1900	Butte, MT.	Chancery	1908-009
Rector	William	Guardian Bond	1782	Fauquier Co.	Probate, Box 48	1782-002
REDD						
Redd	Allen	Extrx. Bond	1808	Fauquier Co.	Probate, Box 46	1808-004
Redd	James	Will	6/6/1853	Culpeper Co. VA.	Chancery	1895-018
Redd	Joseph B.	Admr. Acct.	1/25/1826	Fauquier Co.	Chancery	1868-182
REDDING						
Redding	Timothy	Admr. Bond	1760	Fauquier Co.	Probate, Box 44	1760-009
Redding	William	Guardian Bond	1762	Fauquier Co.	Probate, Box 48	1762-002
REDMAN						
Redman	Richard	Admr. Bond	1759	Fauquier Co.	Probate, Box 44	1759-003
REED (See also Reid)						
Reed	Jael	Admr. Bond	1761	Fauquier Co.	Probate, Box 44	1761-004
Reed	William	Admr. Bond	1815	Fauquier Co.	Probate, Box 47	1815-028

Consolidated Probate Index from the Clerks Loose Papers & the Superior Court/Circuit Court Records 1759-1919

Surname	Given Name	Instrument	Date	County	CLP Record Series	Index #
REID (See also Reed)						
Reid	Adelia	Guardian Bond	10/15/1842	Fauquier Co.	Chancery	1842-029
Reid	America	Guardian Bond	10/15/1842	Fauquier Co.	Chancery	1842-029
Reid	Barilla	Guardian Bond	10/15/1842	Fauquier Co.	Chancery	1842-029
Reid	Clarissa	Guardian Bond	10/15/1842	Fauquier Co.	Chancery	1842-029
Reid	Jane	Guardian Bond	10/15/1842	Fauquier Co.	Chancery	1842-029
Reid	Lavinia	Guardian Bond	10/15/1842	Fauquier Co.	Chancery	1842-029
Reid	Sarah	Plat & Survey Of Dower Allotment	9/1/1900	Fauquier Co.	Chancery	1904-013
REILLY (See also Riley)						
Reilly	Robert L.	Will	8/24/1908	Fauquier Co.	Chancery	1911-013
REITER						
Reiter	Joseph	Admr. Appt.	12/23/1886	Fauquier Co.	Probate, Box 54 Superior/Circuit Ct.	1886-003
RENNOLDS						
Rennolds	John	Admtrx. Bond	1768	Fauquier Co.	Probate, Box 44	1768-001
RHEUAMY						
Rheuamy	Hamilton	Guardian Bond	9/13/1883	Fauquier Co.	Chancery	1883-072
RICE						
Rice	John S.	Will	7/22/1867	Fauquier Co.	Chancery	1867-075
RICH						
Rich	Daniel	Admr. Bond	1783	Fauquier Co.	Probate, Box 45	1783-014
RICHARDS						
Richards	Catharine	Will	4/10/1794	Fauquier Co.	Chancery	1868-098
Richards	Emeline	Will	4/26/1858	Fauquier Co.	Chancery	1876-001
Richards	J. Richards	Application to take State Bar Exam	9/27/1904	Fauquier Co.	Probate, Box 55 Superior/Circuit Ct.	1904-006
Richards	Thomas	Admrs. Bond	1815	Fauquier Co.	Probate, Box 47	1815-059
RICHARDSON						
Richardson	Mary	Admr. Bond	1807	Fauquier Co.	Probate, Box 46	1807-007
Richardson	Richard P.	Will	10/28/1811	Fauquier Co.	Probate, Box 50	1811-003
Richardson	Richard P.	Exors. Bond	1811	Fauquier Co.	Probate, Box 47	1811-004

Consolidated Probate Index from the Clerks Loose Papers & the Superior Court/Circuit Court Records 1759-1919

Surname	Given Name	Instrument	Date	County	CLP Record Series	Index #
RICKETTS						
Ricketts	Hiram A.	Guardian Appt.	11/24/1856	Fauquier Co.	Chancery	1858-022
Ricketts	John	Report of Division Of Slaves	9/21/1857	Fauquier Co.	Chancery	1871-090
Ricketts	Joseph	Admtrx. Bond	1806	Fauquier Co.	Probate, Box 46	1806-026
Ricketts	Mary	Guardian Appt.	11/24/1856	Fauquier Co.	Chancery	1858-022
RILEY (See also Reilly)						
Riley	John	Admr. Bond	1807	Fauquier Co.	Probate, Box 46	1807-013
RIXEY						
Rixey	B. F.	Will (Extract)	9/6/1889	Fauquier Co.	Chancery	1893-031
Rixey	E. B.	Will	12/8/1890	Fauquier Co.	Probate, Box 54 Superior/Circuit Ct.	1890-004
Rixey	Elenora	Will	1/28/1902	Fauquier Co.	Chancery	1905-023
Rixey	John	Appraisement	11/24/1875	Fauquier Co.	Probate, Box 53 Superior/Circuit Ct.	1875-008
Rixey	John	Admr. Acct.	4/10/1877	Fauquier Co.	Probate, Box 54 Superior/Circuit Ct.	1877-003
Rixey	John H.	Will	4/7/1875	Fauquier Co.	Probate, Box 53 Superior/Circuit Ct.	1875-011
Rixey	John H.	Admr. Bond	4/7/1875	Fauquier Co.	Probate, Box 53 Superior/Circuit Ct.	1875-011
Rixey	John H.	Inventory	2/8/1878	Fauquier Co.	Probate, Box 54 Superior/Circuit Ct.	1876-001
Rixey	John H.	Sales	2/8/1878	Fauquier Co.	Probate, Box 54 Superior/Circuit Ct.	1876-001
Rixey	John H.	Admr. Bond	4/18/1885	Fauquier Co.	Probate, Box 54 Superior/Circuit Ct.	1885-002
Rixey	John H.	Admr. Bond	9/9/1893	Fauquier Co.	Probate, Box 55 Superior/Circuit Ct.	1893-002
Rixey	John H.	Will	9/7/1875	Fauquier Co.	Chancery	1902-016
Rixey	Penelope	Division of Slaves	12/28/1861	Fauquier Co.	Chancery	1877-046
Rixey	Richard	Extrx. Bond	6/27/1842	Fauquier Co.	Chancery	1843-030
Rixey	Richard	Will	6/24/1842	Fauquier Co.	Chancery	1873-062

Consolidated Probate Index from the Clerks Loose Papers & the Superior Court/Circuit Court Records 1759-1919

Surname	Given Name	Instrument	Date	County	CLP Record Series	Index #
RIXEY (Cont.)						
Rixey	Richard	Will	6/27/1842	Fauquier Co.	Chancery	1877-046
Rixey	Richard	Report of Division	3/14/1873	Fauquier Co.	Chancery	1900-046
Rixey	Richard	Plat & Survey Of Division	3/14/1873	Fauquier Co.	Chancery	1900-046
Rixey	Samuel	Will	8/1866	Culpeper Co. VA.	Chancery	1890-053
Rixey	William	Will (Extract)	10/18/1879	Fauquier Co.	Chancery	1907-001
ROBERTS						
Roberts	Betsy	Relinquishment	1/1805	Fauquier Co.	Probate, Box 39	1805-005
Roberts	George	Will	4/17/1775	Culpeper Co. VA.	Probate, Box 39	1793-001
ROBINSON						
Robinson	Benjamin	Admtrx. Bond	1781	Fauquier Co.	Probate, Box 45	1781-003
Robinson	Benjamin	Exors. Bond	1785	Fauquier Co.	Probate, Box 45	1785-008
Robinson	Dixon	Will	11/29/822	Fauquier Co.	Probate, Box 50	1816-003
Robinson	Dixon	Admr. Acct.	3/1821	Fauquier Co.	Probate, Box 40	1821-003
Robinson	James	Guardian Bond	1787	Fauquier Co.	Probate, Box 48	1787-002
Robinson	Joseph	Extrx. Bond	1782	Fauquier Co.	Probate, Box 45	1782-019
Robinson	Joseph	Admr. Acct.	1831	Fauquier Co.	Probate, Box 40	1831-007
Robinson	Joseph	Heirs (in Admr. Acct.)	1831	Fauquier Co.	Probate, Box 40	1831-007
Robinson	Malinday N.	Guardian Bond	1815	Fauquier Co.	Probate, Box 49	1815-019
Robinson	Mary	Admr. Bond	1815	Fauquier Co.	Probate, Box 47	1815-027
Robinson	Samuel	Report of Division	1870	Fauquier Co.	Chancery	1876-044
Robinson	Samuel	Plat & Survey Of Division	1870	Fauquier Co.	Chancery	1876-044
Robinson	William	Admr. Bond	1808	Fauquier Co.	Probate, Box 46	1808-017
ROE						
Roe	William	Will	6/28/1848	Fauquier Co.	Chancery	1856-015

Consolidated Probate Index from the Clerks Loose Papers & the Superior Court/Circuit Court Records 1759-1919

Surname	Given Name	Instrument	Date	County	CLP Record Series	Index #
ROGERS						
Rogers	James	Admr. Bond	1815	Fauquier Co.	Probate, Box 47	1815-063
Rogers	Mary E.	Will	9/4/1903	Harford Co. MD.	Chancery	1905-041
Rogers	Robert	Appraisement	9/28/1796	Fauquier Co.	Probate, Box 39	1813-001
Rogers	Robert	Report of Division Of Slaves	9/21/1829	Fredericksburg, VA.	Chancery	1846-029
Rogers	W. W.	Will	9/3/1889	Fauquier Co.	Probate, Box 54 Superior/Circuit Ct.	1889-002
Rogers	W. W.	Appraisement	5/24/1890	Fauquier Co.	Probate, Box 54 Superior/Circuit Ct.	1889-002
Rogers	W. W.	Exor. Acct.	4/7/1891	Fauquier Co.	Probate, Box 55 Superior/Circuit Ct.	1891-001
Rogers	W. W.	Exor. Acct.	9/7/1892	Fauquier Co.	Probate, Box 55 Superior/Circuit Ct.	1892-006
Rogers	W. W.	Exor. Acct.	9/8/1896	Fauquier Co.	Probate, Box 55 Superior/Circuit Ct.	1896-004
Rogers	W. W.	Exor. Acct.	12/15/1898	Fauquier Co.	Probate, Box 55 Superior/Circuit Ct.	1898-001
Rogers	W. W.	Exor. Acct.	9/5/1899	Fauquier Co.	Probate, Box 55 Superior/Circuit Ct.	1899-004
Rogers	W. W.	Exor. Acct.	12/10/1900	Fauquier Co.	Probate, Box 55 Superior/Circuit Ct.	1900-003
Rogers	W. W.	Exor. Acct.	4/9/1902	Fauquier Co.	Probate, Box 55 Superior/Circuit Ct.	1902-001
Rogers	W. W.	Exor. Acct.	12/16/1903	Fauquier Co.	Probate, Box 55 Superior/Circuit Ct.	1903-002
Rogers	Warren W.	Exor. Acct.	2/3/1892	Fauquier Co.	Probate, Box 55 Superior/Circuit Ct.	1894-002
Rogers	Warren W.	Exor. Acct.	4/2/1894	Fauquier Co.	Probate, Box 55 Superior/Circuit Ct.	1895-001
Rogers	Warren W.	Exor. Acct.	9/4/1895	Fauquier Co.	Probate, Box 55 Superior/Circuit Ct.	1895-004
ROLEY						
Roley	Thomas	Guardian Bond	1817	Fauquier Co.	Probate, Box 49	1817-002
ROLLS						
Rolls	Nancy	Petition	1814	Fauquier Co.	Probate, Box 39	1814-016

Consolidated Probate Index from the Clerks Loose Papers & the Superior Court/Circuit Court Records 1759-1919

Surname	Given Name	Instrument	Date	County	CLP Record Series	Index #
ROLLS (Cont.)						
Rolls	Thomas	Admr. Bond	1814	Fauquier Co.	Probate, Box 47	1814-016
ROOKARD						
Rookard	Mary	Guardian Bond	1816	Fauquier Co.	Probate, Box 49	1816-012
ROSE						
Rose	Ann	Guardian Bond	1815	Fauquier Co.	Probate, Box 49	1815-022
Rose	Ann A.	Guardian Bond	1815	Fauquier Co.	Probate, Box 49	1815-015
Rose	Ann A.	Guardian Bond	1821	Fauquier Co.	Probate, Box 49	1821-001
Rose	Cuthbert	Guardian Bond	11/26/1855	Fauquier Co.	Chancery	1894-029
Rose	Cuthbert	Will	5//24/1869	Fauquier Co.	Chancery	1872-057
Rose	Cuthbert	Guardian Appt.	11/26/1855	Fauquier Co.	Chancery	1894-030
Rose	Mary Seymour	Will	9/23/1853	Fauquier Co.	Chancery	1854-018
Rose	Robert R.	Guardian Bond	1815	Fauquier Co.	Probate, Box 49	1815-015
Rose	Sarah Jane	Guardian Appt.	3/1/1859	Fauquier Co.	Chancery	1894-029
Rose	Sarah Jane	Guardian Appt.	3/1/1859	Fauquier Co.	Chancery	1894-030
Rose	William	Guardian Bond	1815	Fauquier Co.	Probate, Box 49	1815-015
ROSSER						
Rosser	John	Admrs. Bond	1783	Fauquier Co.	Probate, Box 45	1783-009
Rosser	John	Will	6/23/1783	Fauquier Co.	Chancery	1785-005
Rosser	Malinda	Guardian Bond	1801	Fauquier Co.	Probate, Box 48	1801-007
ROTHROCK						
Rothrock	Mary R.	Will	10/13/1859	Fredericksburg, VA.	Chancery	1888-052
Rothrock	Mary R.	Inventory + Appraisement	2/9/1860	Fauquier Co.	Chancery	1888-052
Rothrock	Mary R.	Sales	2/9/1860	Fauquier Co.	Chancery	188-052
ROUTT						
Routt	Daniel	Guardian Bond	1806	Fauquier Co.	Probate, Box 49	1806-013
Routt	Elizabeth	Guardian Bond	1802	Fauquier Co.	Probate, Box 48	1802-001
Routt	Gabriel	Guardian Bond	1802	Fauquier Co.	Probate, Box 48	1802-001
Routt	James	Petition to settle Gdnship of 4 children	1806	Fauquier Co.	Probate, Box 39	1806-002
Routt	Kitty	Guardian Bond	1806	Fauquier Co.	Probate, Box 49	1806-013

Consolidated Probate Index from the Clerks Loose Papers & the Superior Court/Circuit Court Records 1759-1919

Surname	Given Name	Instrument	Date	County	CLP Record Series	Index #
ROUTT (Cont.)						
Routt	Peter	Admr. Appt.	1/27/1837	Fauquier Co.	Probate, Box 50	1832-001
Routt	Peter	Admr. Appt.	11/6/1838	Fauquier Co.	Probate, Box 50	1832-001
Routt	Peter	Will	12/26/1836	Fauquier Co.	Chancery	1871-001
Routt	Peter	Plat & Survey Of Division	2/25/1841	Fauquier Co.	Chancery	1871-001
Routt	Peter	Division of Slaves	1/12/1842	Fauquier Co.	Chancery	1871-001
Routt	Peter	Will	12/26/1836	Fauquier Co.	Chancery	1880-019
Routt	Peter	Will	12/26/1832	Fauquier Co.	Chancery	1894-043
Routt	Thomas	Guardian Bond	1802	Fauquier Co.	Probate, Box 49	1802-001
Routt	Thomas	Petition to settle Gdnship	1806	Fauquier Co.	Probate, Box 39	1806-002
ROWELS (See also Rowels)						
Rowels	Thomas	Appraisement	1/24/1815	Fauquier Co.	Chancery	1837-002
Rowels	William	Family Acct. Book	1840-1844	Fauquier Co.	Chancery	1856-014
Rowels	William	Inventory + Appraisement	4/1/1846	Fauquier Co.	Chancery	1856-014
Rowels	William	Sales	4/9/1846	Fauquier Co.	Chancery	1856-014
Rowels	William	Division of Slaves	4/23/1846	Fauquier Co.	Chancery	1856-014
Rowels	William	Will	6/23/1846	Fauquier Co.	Chancery	1856-014
Rowels	William	Exor. Bond	6/23/1846	Fauquier Co.	Chancery	1856-014
ROWLES (See also Rowels)						
Rowles	Thomas	Admr. Bond	11/28/1814	Licking Co. OH.	Chancery	1837-002
ROY						
Roy	Thomas	Admr. Bond	1809	Fauquier Co.	Probate, Box 47	1809-015
RUNNALDS						
Runnalds	James	Extrx. Bond	1776	Fauquier Co.	Probate, Box 44	1776-002
RUSSELL						
Russell	Eliza J.	Will	12/14/1875	Fauquier Co.	Probate, Box 53 Superior/Circuit Ct.	1875-005
Russell	Eliza J.	Exor. Bond	12/14/1875	Fauquier Co.	Probate, Box 53 Superior/Circuit Ct.	1875-005
Russell	Samuel	Will	10/24/1865	Fauquier Co.	Chancery	1881-031

Consolidated Probate Index from the Clerks Loose Papers & the Superior Court/Circuit Court Records 1759-1919

Surname	Given Name	Instrument	Date	County	CLP Record Series	Index #
RUST						
Rust	Benjamin	Plat & Survey Of Division	11/11/1847	Fauquier Co.	Chancery	1860-053
Rust	Benjamin	Plat & Survey	11/13/1850	Fauquier Co.	Chancery	1860-052
Rust	Betty	Guardian Bond	1778	Fauquier Co.	Probate, Box 48	1778-007
Rust	James B.	Will	4/15/1857	Fauquier Co.	Chancery	1857-001
Rust	James B.	Will	4/15/1857	Fauquier Co.	Chancery	1880-029
Rust	Jeremiah	Guardian Bond	1778	Fauquier Co.	Probate, Box 48	1778-006
Rust	John	Admtrx. Bond	1777	Fauquier Co.	Probate, Box 44	1777-006
Rust	John S.	Will	1/8/1834	Fauquier Co.	Chancery	1860-052
Rust	John S.	Will	1/8/1834	Fauquier Co.	Chancery	1866-010
Rust	John S.	Will	2/24/1834	Fauquier Co.	Chancery	1845-018
Rust	John S.	Will	2/24/1855	Fauquier Co.	Chancery	1860-003
Rust	John S.	Exor. Bond	2/24/1834	Fauquier Co.	Chancery	1860-003
Rust	John S.	Will	2/24/1835	Fauquier Co.	Chancery	1866-025
Rust	Nancy	Guardian Bond	1778	Fauquier Co.	Probate, Box 48	1778-004
Rust	Nancy	Guardian Bond	1779	Fauquier Co.	Probate, Box 48	1779-003
Rust	Peter	Guardian Bond	1779	Fauquier Co.	Probate, Box 48	1779-003
Rust	Peter	Will	3/26/1782	Westmoreland Co. VA.	Chancery	1803-016
Rust	Richard	Admr. Bond	1806	Fauquier Co.	Probate, Box 47	1806-021
Rust	Sally	Guardian Bond	1778	Fauquier Co.	Probate, Box 48	1778-004
Rust	Thomas	Guardian Bond	1778	Fauquier Co.	Probate, Box 48	1778-007

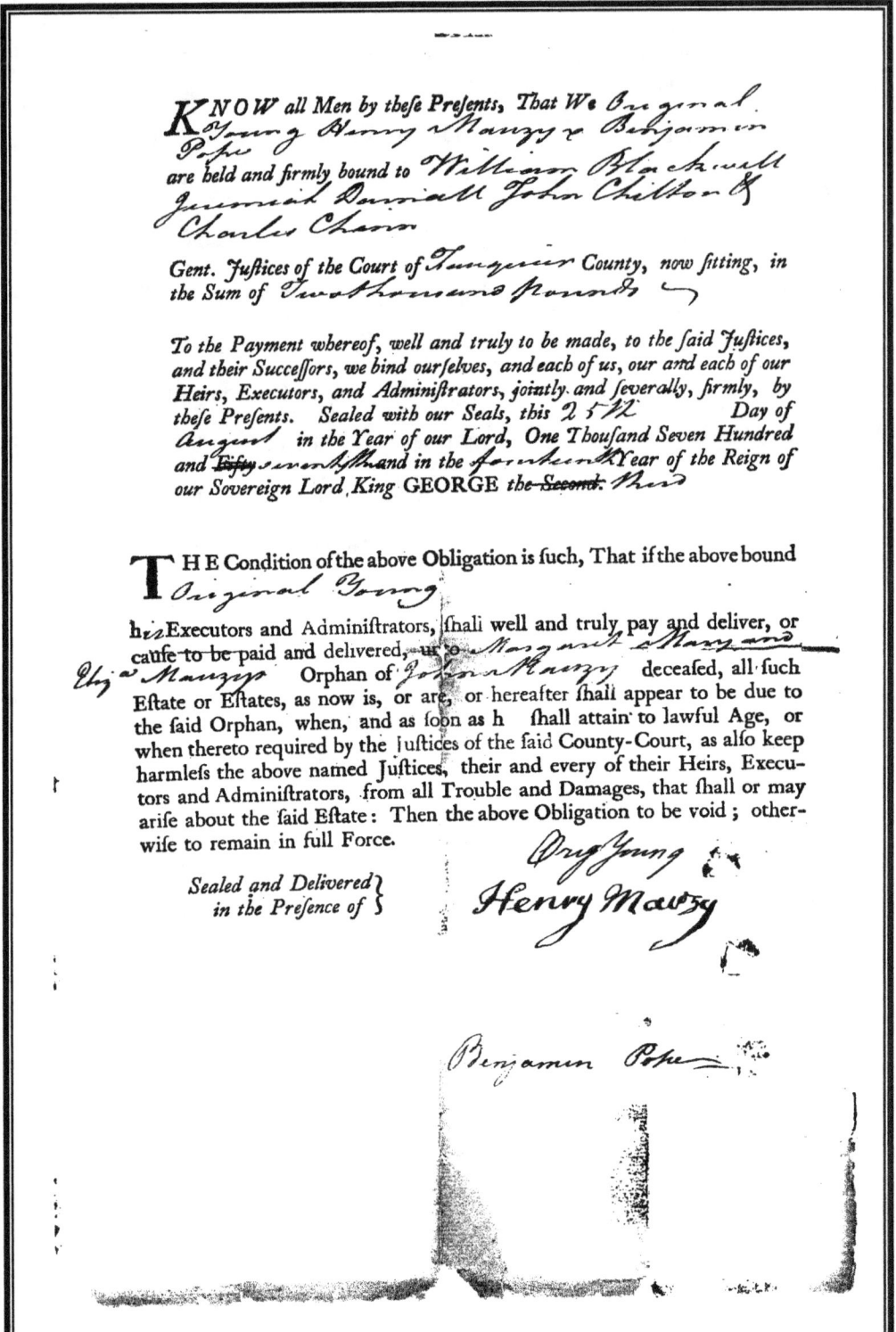

Plate 5. Probate. Scanned Image from Box 49. Guardian Bonds. 1807-002 Margaret and Elizabeth Mauzeys' Guardian Bond.

Consolidated Probate Index from the Clerks Loose Papers & the Superior Court/Circuit Court Records 1759-1919

Surname	Given Name	Instrument	Date	County	CLP Record Series	Index #
SAFFELL						
Saffell	Hattie May	Guardian Bond	10/12/1899	Fleming Co. KY.	Chancery	1900-028
Saffell	James William	Guardian Bond	10/12/1899	Fleming Co. KY.	Chancery	1900-028
Saffell	Mary Edith	Guardian Bond	10/12/1899	Fleming Co. KY.	Chancery	1900-028
Saffell	William	Will	1/20/1893	Fauquier Co.	Chancery	1900-028
Saffell	William	Will	9/28/1895	Fauquier Co.	Chancery	1903-080
SALE						
Sale	Humphrey	Admr. Appt.	3/10/1835	Caroline Co. VA.	Chancery	1835-026
SALLARDS						
Sallards	Rebecca	Guardian Bond	1817	Fauquier Co.	Probate, Box 49	1817-022
SANDERS (See also Saunders)						
Sanders	Briton	Guardian Bond	1793	Fauquier Co.	Probate, Box 48	1793-002
Sanders	Gabriel	Guardian Bond	1793	Fauquier Co.	Probate, Box 48	1793-002
Sanders	James	Guardian Bond	1793	Fauquier Co.	Probate, Box 48	1793-002
Sanders	Larkin	Guardian Bond	1793	Fauquier Co.	Probate, Box 48	1793-002
Sanders	Lewis	Guardian Bond	1793	Fauquier Co.	Probate, Box 48	1793-002
Sanders	Thomas	Guardian Bond	1793	Fauquier Co.	Probate, Box 48	1793-002
SANDS						
Sands	John H.	Admr. Appt.	4/11/1910	Fauquier Co.	Probate, Box 56 Superior/Circuit Ct.	1910-001
SANFORD						
Sanford	James	Admtrx. Bond	1807	Fauquier Co.	Probate, Box 47	1807-011
SANGSTER						
Sangster	Elizabeth	Will	4/12/1869	Fauquier Co.	Chancery	1878-044
SAUFLY						
Saufly	Martha	Will	3/1875	Adair Co. KY.	Chancery	1895-001
Saufly	Martha	Admtrx. Appt.	3/8/1875	Adair Co. KY.	Chancery	1895-001
SAUNDERS (See also Sanders)						
Saunders	Bennett	Admtrx. Bond	9/29/1840	Fauquier Co.	Chancery	1850-006
Saunders	Bennett	Inventory + Appraisement	9/1840	Fauquier Co.	Chancery	1850-006
Saunders	Bennett	Sales	9/1840	Fauquier Co.	Chancery	1850-006
Saunders	Bennett	Admtrx. Acct.	8/26/1842	Fauquier Co.	Chancery	1850-006

Consolidated Probate Index from the Clerks Loose Papers & the Superior Court/Circuit Court Records 1759-1919

Surname	Given Name	Instrument	Date	County	CLP Record Series	Index #
SAUNDERS (Cont.)						
Saunders	Edwin N.	Will	2/28/1866	Fauquier Co.	Chancery	1886-013
Saunders	James	Certification of Bequests of slaves To heirs	11/1/1815	Fauquier Co.	Chancery	1849-014
Saunders	James	Will	5/22/1826	Fauquier Co.	Chancery	1849-014
Saunders	John A.	Will	9/24/1895	Fauquier Co.	Chancery	1901-003
Saunders	John S.	Admtrx. Bond	1815	Fauquier Co.	Probate, Box 47	1815-029
Saunders	Jourdan M.	Heirs	9/12/1892	Fauquier Co.	Chancery	1908-048
Saunders	William	Admr. Acct.	2/26/1832	Fauquier Co.	Probate, Box 50	1833-002
SCOGGIN						
Scoggin	Charles	Admtrx. Bond	1781	Fauquier Co.	Probate, Box 45	1781-002
Scoggin	William	Admtrx. Bond	1782	Fauquier Co.	Probate, Box 45	1782-005
SCOTT						
Scott	Adeline	Will	6/24/1895	Fauquier Co.	Chancery	1908-047
Scott	Alexander	Will	10/25/1819	Fauquier Co.	Chancery	1854-017
Scott	Ann	Guardian Bond	1816	Fauquier Co.	Probate, Box 49	1816-013
Scott	Elizabeth	Will	11/28/1823	Fauquier Co.	Probate, Box 50	1823-002
Scott	Frances B.	Guardian Bond	1816	Fauquier Co.	Probate, Box 49	1816-013
Scott	James	Will	11/22/1779	Fauquier Co.	Probate, Box 50	1779-001
Scott	James	Will	10/7/1782	Fauquier Co.	Chancery	1805-034
Scott	James	Division	5/1807	Fauquier Co.	Probate, Box 50	1807-001
Scott	James C.	Guardian Bond	1816	Fauquier Co.	Probate, Box 49	1816-013
Scott	James Jr.	Exors. Bond	1779	Fauquier Co.	Probate, Box 45	1779-007
Scott	Jane E.	Guardian Bond	1816	Fauquier Co.	Probate, Box 49	1816-013
Scott	John (Clerk)	Extrx. Bond	1785	Fauquier Co.	Probate, Box 45	1785-003
Scott	John	Will	1/3/1850	Fauquier Co.	Chancery	1873-052
Scott	Mary Jane	Will	5/28/1833	Fauquier Co.	Chancery	1833-022
Scott	Mary Jane	Will	5/28/1833	Fauquier Co.	Chancery	1837-066
Scott	Mary Jane	Report of Division Of Land + Slaves	5/10/1850	Fauquier Co.	Chancery	1859-071

Consolidated Probate Index from the Clerks Loose Papers & the Superior Court/Circuit Court Records 1759-1919

Surname	Given Name	Instrument	Date	County	CLP Record Series	Index #
SCOTT (Cont.)						
Scott	Mary M.	Will	11/8/1905	Fauquier Co.	Chancery	1812-015
Scott	Mary S.	Guardian Bond	1816	Fauquier Co.	Probate, Box 49	1816-013
Scott	R. E. Estate	Plat & Survey Of Dower Allotment	2/1886	Fauquier Co.	Chancery	1895-050
Scott	R. E. Estate	Plat & Survey Of Dower Allotment	2/1892	Fauquier Co.	Chancery	1895-050
Scott	Rebecca J.	Admr. Power of Attorney	1/2/1908	Fauquier Co.	Probate, Box 56 Superior/Circuit Ct.	1908-001
Scott	Robert E.	Will	1/28/1850	Fauquier Co.	Chancery	1868-023
Scott	Robert E.	Plat & Survey Of Division	8/29/1867	Fauquier Co.	Chancery	1868-023
Scott	Robert E.	Admr. Appt.	8/30/1865	Fauquier Co.	Chancery	1900-045
Scott	Robert E.	Plat & Survey Of Division of "Gunston"	3/1/1870	Fauquier Co.	Chancery	1908-016
Scott	Sarah	Will	1/28/1799	Fauquier Co.	Chancery	1884-022
Scott	Sarah	Inventory	2/21/1799	Fauquier Co.	Chancery	1884-022
Scott	Sarah	Exor. Acct.	11/29/1810	Fauquier Co.	Chancery	1884-022
Scott	Thomas	Guardian Bond	1816	Fauquier Co.	Probate, Box 49	1816-013
SEALOCK						
Sealock	Daniel M.	Guardian Bond	8/22/1842	Fauquier Co.	Chancery	1843-013
Sealock	Davis Baker	Guardian Bond	8/22/1842	Fauquier Co.	Chancery	1843-013
Sealock	Elizabeth	Guardian Bond	8/22/1842	Fauquier Co.	Chancery	1843-013
Sealock	William	Guardian Bond	8/22/1842	Fauquier Co.	Chancery	1843-013
SEAMAN						
Seaman	Thomas	Admr. Bond	1762	Fauquier Co.	Probate, Box 44	1762-002
SEATON						
Seaton	Hiram	Will	11/24/1849	Fauquier Co.	Chancery	1855-001
Seaton	John	Will	10/24/1803	Fauquier Co.	Chancery	1834-008
Seaton	John	Will	4/21/1898	Alexandria Co. VA.	Chancery	1904-051
Seaton	John A.	Will	4/21/1898	Alexandria Co. VA.	Chancery	1908-002
Seaton	Polly	Guardian Bond	1805	Fauquier Co.	Probate, Box 49	1805-019

Consolidated Probate Index from the Clerks Loose Papers & the Superior Court/Circuit Court Records 1759-1919

Surname	Given Name	Instrument	Date	County	CLP Record Series	Index #
SEATON (Cont.)						
Seaton	Samuel	Guardian Bond	1805	Fauquier Co.	Probate, Box 49	1805-019
Seaton	Viola Virginia	Guardian Appt.	12/1/1915	Westchester Co. NY.	Chancery	1808-002
Seaton	William	Extrx. Bond	1782	Fauquier co.	Probate, Box 45	1782-020
Seaton	William	Guardian Bond	1796	Fauquier Co.	Probate, Box 48	1796-005
SELMAN						
Selman	George	Relinquishment	1812	Fauquier Co.	Probate, Box 38	1812-010
SEMMES (See also Simms)						
Semmes	Matilda	Will	9/12/1881	Fauquier Co.	Probate, Box 54 Superior/Circuit Ct.	1881-004
SETTLE (See also Suttle)						
Settle	A. H.	Estate Papers	1860	Fauquier Co.	Probate, Box 42 Settle &c. Estate Papers	1860-001
Settle	Francis	Admr. Bond	1766	Fauquier Co.	Probate, Box 44	1766-003
Settle	Martin	Admtrx. Bond	1768	Fauquier Co.	Probate, Box 44	1768-004
Settle	Rosanna	Guardian Chosen	3/1805	Fauquier Co.	Probate, Box 39	1805-004
Settle	Samuel	Guardian Chosen	3/1805	Fauquier Co.	Probate, Box 39	1805-004
SHACKELFORD						
Shackleford	Annie Berry	Guardian Bond	9/19/1872	Fauquier Co.	Chancery	1872-063
Shackleford	Annie Berry	Guardian Appt.	9/19/1872	Fauquier Co.	Chancery	1908-010
Shackelford	Benjamin Howard	Will	5/23/1870	Fauquier Co.	Chancery	1894-057
Shackelford	Benjamin Howard	Will	5/23/1870	Fauquier Co.	Chancery	1894-061
Shackelford	Benjamin Howard	Will	5/23/1870	Fauquier Co.	Chancery	1908-010
Shackelford	Benjamin Howard	Will	5/23/1870	Fauquier Co.	Chancery	1908-012
Shackelford	Benjamin Howard	Admr. Appt.	2/21/1871	Fauquier Co.	Chancery	1908-012
Shackelford	George Scott	Guardian Bond	9/19/1872	Fauquier Co.	Chancery	1872-063
Shackelford	George Scott	Guardian Appt.	9/19/1872	Fauquier Co.	Chancery	1908-010
Shackelford	John Howard	Guardian Bond	9/19/1872	Fauquier Co.	Chancery	1872-063
Shackelford	John Howard	Guardian Appt.	9/19/1872	Fauquier Co.	Chancery	1908-010
Shackelford	Jones Green	Guardian Bond	9/19/1872	Fauquier Co.	Chancery	1872-063
Shackelford	Jones Green	Guardian Appt.	9/19/1872	Fauquier Co.	Chancery	1908-010
Shackelford	Lucy	Guardian Bond	9/19/1872	Fauquier Co.	Chancery	1872-063

Consolidated Probate Index from the Clerks Loose Papers & the Superior Court/Circuit Court Records 1759-1919

Surname	Given Name	Instrument	Date	County	CLP Record Series	Index #
SHACKELFORD (Cont)						
Shackelford	Lucy	Guardian Appt.	9/19/1872	Fauquier Co.	Chancery	1908-010
Shackelford	Muscoe	Guardian Bond	9/19/1982	Fauquier Co.	Chancery	1872-063
Shackelford	Muscoe Livingston	Guardian Appt.	9/19/1872	Fauquier Co.	Chancery	1908-010
Shackelford	Robert	Admtrx. Bond	1815	Fauquier Co.	Probate, Box 48	1815-002
SHACKLETT						
Shacklett	Elizabeth	Will	5/6/1848	Fauquier Co.	Probate, Box 51 Superior/Circuit Ct.	1848-005
Shacklett	John	Report of Division	11/22/1824	Fauquier Co.	Chancery	1832-024
Shacklett	Lucy	Guardian Appt.	4/26/1847	Fauquier Co.	Chancery	1849-004
Shacklett	William	Guardian Appt.	4/26/1847	Fauquier Co.	Chancery	1849-004
SHADRACK (See also Shadrick)						
Shadrack	John	Extrx. Bond	1759	Fauquier Co.	Probate, Box 44	1759-005
SHADRICK (See also Shadrack)						
Shadrick	Thomas	Will	4/29/176-	Westmoreland Co. VA.	Land Records & Disputes	1782-001
SHANKS						
Shanks	William	Admrs. Bond	1773	Fauquier Co.	Probate, Box 44	1773-005
SHARP (See also Sharpe)						
Sharp	David	Admtrx. Bond	1782	Fauquier Co.	Probate, Box 45	1782-016
SHARPE (See also Sharp)						
Sharpe	Benjamin	Guardian Bond	1787	Fauquier Co.	Probate, Box 48	1787-003
Sharpe	Linsfield	Exor. Bond	1807	Fauquier Co.	Probate, Box 46	1807-028
Sharpe	William	Guardian Bond	1787	Fauquier Co.	Probate, Box 48	1787-003
SHAW						
Shaw	Aldridge	Guardian Bond	1815	Fauquier Co.	Probate, Box 49	1815-017
Shaw	Archibald	Exor. Bond	1815	Fauquier Co.	Probate, Box 47	1815-020
Shaw	Betsey	Guardian Bond	1815	Fauquier Co.	Probate, Box 49	1815-017
Shaw	William	Guardian Bond	1815	Fauquier Co.	Probate, Box 49	1815-017
SHEARMAN (See also Sherman)						
Shearman	Celia	Admr. Bond	9/11/1854	Fauquier Co.	Probate, Box 52 Superior/Circuit Ct.	1854-001
Shearman	Celia	Will	10/9/1851	Fauquier Co.	Chancery	1851-004

Consolidated Probate Index from the Clerks Loose Papers & the Superior Court/Circuit Court Records 1759-1919

Surname	Given Name	Instrument	Date	County	CLP Record Series	Index #
SHEARMAN (Cont.)						
Shearman	Celia	Will	10/9/1851	Fauquier Co.	Chancery	1857-001
Shearman	Celia	Will	10/9/1851	Fauquier Co.	Chancery	1880-058
Shearman	Thomas	Will	5/22/1854	Fauquier Co.	Chancery	1859-056
SHERMAN						
Sherman	Foxhall	Guardian Bond	1798	Fauquier Co.	Probate, Box 48	1798-002
Sherman	M. C. (Mrs.)	Committee Appt.	4/2/1908	Fauquier Co.	Probate, Box 56 Superior/Circuit Ct.	1908-009
SHINN						
Shinn	Stephen	Admr. Appt.	3/8/1882	Alexandria, VA.	Chancery	1887-015
SHIP						
Ship	Betsey	Guardian Bond	1778	Fauquier Co.	Probate, Box 48	1778-002
Ship	John	Exor. Bond	1778	Fauquier Co.	Probate, Box 45	1778-001
Ship	John	Will	12/25/1848	Fauquier Co.	Chancery	1869-047
Ship	John	Inventory + Appraisement	1/16/1849	Fauquier Co.	Chancery	1869-047
Ship	John	Admr. Appt.	6/26/1853	Fauquier Co.	Chancery	1869-047
Ship	John	Exor. Acct.	6/26/1853	Fauquier Co.	Chancery	1869-047
Ship	Molly	Guardian Bond	1779	Fauquier Co.	Probate, Box 48	1779-001
Ship	Nancy	Guardian Bond	1779	Fauquier Co.	Probate, Box 48	1779-001
SHIPE						
Shipe	J. R.	Estate committed To Sheriff	4/4/1899	Fauquier Co.	Probate, Box 55 Superior/Circuit Ct.	1899-002
Shipe	J. R.	Appraisement	2/22/1900	Fauquier Co.	Probate, Box 55 Superior/Circuit Ct.	1900-007
Shipe	J. R.	Sales	3/16/1900	Fauquier Co.	Probate, Box 55 Superior/Circuit Ct.	1900-004
SHIRLEY						
Shirley	Elizabeth	Guardian Acct.	8/21/1855	Fauquier Co.	Chancery	1858-036
SHIVER						
Shiver	Robert C.	Will	9/9/1886	Fauquier Co.	Probate, Box 54 Superior/Circuit Ct.	1886-001
SHULTS (See also Shultz)						
Shults	Elizabeth	Relinquishment	12/1818	Fauquier Co.	Probate, Box 39	1818-013

Consolidated Probate Index from the Clerks Loose Papers & the Superior Court/Circuit Court Records 1759-1919

Surname	Given Name	Instrument	Date	County	CLP Record Series	Index #
SHULTZ (See also Shults)						
Shultz	Benjamin	Admtrx. Bond	1808	Fauquier Co.	Probate, Box 46	1808-016
SHUMATE						
Shumate	Arthur	Guardian Bond	1817	Fauquier Co.	Probate, Box 49	1817-003
Shumate	Daniel	Admtrx. Bond	1784	Fauquier Co.	Probate, Box 47	1784-016
Shumate	Jane	Guardian Bond	1817	Fauquier Co.	Probate, Box 49	1817-003
Shumate	John	Extrx. Bond	1784	Fauquier Co.	Probate, Box 45	1784-011
Shumate	John	Inventory	8/24/1784	Fauquier Co.	Probate, Box 39	1784-001
Shumate	John	Exor. Bond	1814	Fauquier Co.	Probate, Box 47	1814-006
Shumate	John	Exor. Bond	9/26/1814	Fauquier Co.	Probate, Box 50	1814-003
Shumate	John	Court Order to Appraise Estate	9/1814	Fauquier Co.	Probate, Box 39	1814-001
Shumate	John	Appraisement	11/26/1814	Fauquier Co.	Probate, Box 39	1814-001
Shumate	John	Will	9/26/1814	Fauquier Co.	Chancery	1839-008
Shumate	John	Exor. Bond	9/26/1814	Fauquier Co.	Chancery	1839-008
Shumate	John	Sales	1/12/1820	Fauquier Co.	Chancery	1839-008
Shumate	John Jr.	Admr. Bond	1812	Fauquier Co.	Probate, Box 47	1812-015
Shumate	Joseph	Will	1/27/1846	Fauquier Co.	Chancery	1847-024
Shumate	Lewis (Mrs.)	Dower Allotment	3/17/1879	Fauquier Co.	Chancery	1897-001
Shumate	Taliaferro	Admr. Acct.	12/24/1835	Fauquier Co.	Probate, Box 50	1839-001
Shumate	Thomas	Admr. Acct.	5/23/1836	Fauquier Co.	Probate, Box 50	1836-001
SHUTE						
Shute	John S. F.	Admr. Bond	1815	Fauquier Co.	Probate, Box 47	1815-041
Shute	Samuel M.	Admr. Appt.	6/11/1910	Fauquier Co.	Probate, Box 56 Superior/Circuit Ct.	1910-010
SIAS						
Sias	John	Admtrx. Bond	1775	Fauquier Co.	Probate, Box 44	1775-001
Sias	John	Exor. Bond	1779	Fauquier Co.	Probate, Box 44	1779-002
SIMMS (See also Semmes)						
Simms	Abraham	Guardian Appt.	3/9/1885	Shenandoah Co. VA.	Chancery	1885-023
Simms	John	Admr. Bond	1786	Fauquier Co.	Probate, Box 44	1786-014 OS Probate

Consolidated Probate Index from the Clerks Loose Papers & the Superior Court/Circuit Court Records 1759-1919

Surname	Given Name	Instrument	Date	County	CLP Record Series	Index #
SIMMS (Cont.)						
Simms	Mary	Guardian Appt.	3/9/1885	Shenandoah Co. VA.	Chancery	1885-023
SINCLAIR (See also Sinkler)						
Sinclair	Elizabeth	Will	6/23/1834	Fauquier Co.	Probate, Box 50	1825-002
Sinclair	Gorey	Report of Division	2/1/1883	Fauquier Co.	Chancery	1883-004
Sinclair	Gorey	Plat & Survey Of Division	2/1/1883	Fauquier Co.	Chancery	1883-004
Sinclair	James	Petition for Division Of Estate of Wm. Sinclair	1806	Fauquier Co.	Probate, Box 39	1806-001
Sinclair	James	Will	5/22/1815	Fauquier Co.	Chancery	1883-004
Sinclair	James	Report of Division	4/8/1881	Fauquier Co.	Chancery	1883-004
Sinclair	James	Plat & Survey Of Division	4/8/1881	Fauquier Co.	Chancery	1883-004
Sinclair	Lydia	Petition for Division Of Estate of Wm. Sinclair	1806	Fauquier Co.	Chancery	1883-004
Sinclair	Rosamund	Will	4/27/1856	Fauquier Co.	Chancery	1883-078
Sinclair	Rosamund	Will	2/23/1857	Fauquier Co.	Chancery	1871-025
Sinclair	Rosamund	Will	2/23/1857	Fauquier Co.	Chancery	1876-023
Sinclair	Rosamund	Will	2/23/1857	Fauquier Co.	Chancery	1876-027
Sinclair	Rosamund	Will	2/23/1857	Fauquier Co.	Chancery	1880-042
Sinclair	Rosamund	Will	2/23/1857	Fauquier Co.	Chancery	1900-037
SINGERS						
Singers	Elijah	Admr. Bond	1815	Fauquier Co.	Probate, Box 47	1815-034
SINKLER (See also Sinclair)						
Sinkler	John	Exors. Bond	1771	Fauquier Co.	Probate, Box 44	1771-011
Sinkler	John	Admr. Bond	1776	Fauquier Co.	Probate, Box 44	1776-007
SINSEL						
Sinsel	Elijah	Guardian Bond	1801	Fauquier Co.	Probate, Box 48	1801-001
Sinsel	Harmon	Guardian Bond	1801	Fauquier Co.	Probate, Box 48	1801-001
Sinsel	John	Guardian Bond	1801	Fauquier Co.	Probate, Box 48	1801-001
SISSON						
Sisson	George	Will	10/23/1820	Fauquier Co.	Probate, Box 50	1820-002

Consolidated Probate Index from the Clerks Loose Papers & the Superior Court/Circuit Court Records 1759-1919

Surname	Given Name	Instrument	Date	County	CLP Record Series	Index #
SKINKER						
Skinker	C. B.	Relinquishment	4/5/1900	Fauquier Co.	Probate, Box 55 Superior/Circuit Ct.	1900-006
Skinker	James K.	Will	4/7/1900	Fauquier Co.	Probate, Box 55 Superior/Circuit Ct.	1900-006
Skinker	Peter	Will	8/25/1845	Fauquier Co.	Chancery	1873-040
Skinker	Samuel	Will	2/6/1752	King George Co.	VA. Land Records & Disputes	1809-010
Skinker	William	Will	3/24/1845	Fauquier Co.	Chancery	1873-040
SKINNER						
Skinner	Lucy M.	Admr. Appt.	9/19/1907	Fauquier Co.	Probate, Box 56 Superior/Circuit Ct.	1907-016
Skinner	Lucy M.	Renunciation	9/19/1907	Fauquier Co.	Probate, Box 56 Superior/Circuit Ct.	1907-016
SLAUGHTER						
Slaughter	Martin	Admr. Acct.	3/23/1836	Culpeper Co. VA.	Chancery	1866-076
Slaughter	Martin	Admr. Acct.	5/10/1848	Fauquier Co.	Chancery	1866-076
Slaughter	Mathew	Admtrx. Bond	1807	Fauquier Co.	Probate, Box 46	1807-002
Slaughter	Mathew	Court Order to Appraise Estate	12/1807	Fauquier Co.	Probate, Box 39	1807-001
SMALLWOOD						
Smallwood	George	Will	11/24/1845	Fauquier Co.	Chancery	1853-013
Smallwood	George	Inventory + Appraisement	2/27/1846	Fauquier Co.	Chancery	1853-013
SMARR						
Smarr	Charles	Will	10/28/1865	Fauquier Co.	Chancery	1869-012
Smarr	Charles	Will	3/26/1866	Fauquier Co.	Chancery	1888-033
SMITH						
Smith	----- [Name not found]	Division of Slaves	5/27/1841	Fauquier Co.	Chancery	1839-048
Smith	Abner	Guardian Bond	1777	Fauquier Co.	Probate, Box 48	1777-002
Smith	Abner	Guardian Bond	1789	Fauquier Co.	Probate, Box 48	1789-003
Smith	Agnes E.	Plat & Survey Of Dower Allotment	1873	Fauquier Co.	Chancery	1873-073
Smith	Albert G.	Will	5/23/1892	Fauquier Co.	Chancery	1899-012
Smith	Alexander	Admtrx. Bond	1761	Fauquier Co.	Probate, Box 44	1761-003

Consolidated Probate Index from the Clerks Loose Papers & the Superior Court/Circuit Court Records 1759-1919

Surname	Given Name	Instrument	Date	County	CLP Record Series	Index #
SMITH (Cont.)						
Smith	Ann	Guardian Bond	1789	Fauquier Co.	Probate, Box 48	1789-004
Smith	Ann	Dower Allotment In Slaves	Undated	Fauquier Co.	Chancery	1839-048
Smith	Ann	Dower Allotment In Slaves	8/27/1841	Fauquier Co.	Chancery	1839-048
Smith	Ann E.	Guardian Bond	10/7/1840	Fauquier Co.	Chancery	1840-020
Smith	Augustin	Admr. Bond	1780	Fauquier Co.	Probate, Box 45	1786-006
Smith	Augustine	Will	12/10/1821	Fauquier Co.	Probate, Box 50	1831-001
Smith	Augustine	Admr. Appt.	12/10/1821	Fauquier Co.	Probate, Box 40	1831-001
Smith	Augustine	Admr. Bond	11/2/1824	Fauquier Co.	Chancery	1844-025
Smith	Augustine Sr.	Will	12/10/1821	Fauquier Co.	Chancery	1855-045
Smith	Benjamin F.	Will	3/23/1893	Fauquier Co.	Chancery	1898-063
Smith	Charles	Guardian Bond	1815	Fauquier Co.	Probate, Box 49	1815-032
Smith	Charles B.	Will	7/27/1840	Fauquier Co.	Chancery	1869-028
Smith	Charles B.	Sales	2/15/1841	Fauquier Co.	Chancery	1869-028
Smith	Charles B.	Admr. Acct.	2/13/1844	Fauquier Co.	Chancery	1869-028
Smith	Charlotte	Will	11/28/1854	Fauquier Co.	Probate, Box 50	1853-002
Smith	David	Guardian Appt.	10/27/1910	Fauquier Co.	Probate, Box 56 Superior/Circuit Ct.	1910-005
Smith	Edmonia	Report of Division	4/1882	Fauquier Co.	Chancery	1894-071
Smith	Edward	Sales	11/12/1824	Fauquier Co.	Chancery	1842-013
Smith	Edward	Inventory + Appraisement	5/29/1830	Fauquier Co.	Chancery	1842-013
Smith	Edward	Admr. Acct.	3/31/1832	Fauquier Co.	Chancery	1842-013
Smith	Edward	Admr. Appt.	2/28/1842	Fauquier Co.	Chancery	1843-010
Smith	Eleanor	Admr. Acct.	11/27/1851	Fauquier Co.	Chancery	1860-054
Smith	Elias	Guardian Bond	1809	Fauquier Co.	Probate, Box 49	1809-009
Smith	Elijah	Admr. Bond	1806	Fauquier Co.	Probate, Box 46	1806-023
Smith	Elijah	Appraisement	1/25/1861	Fauquier Co.	Chancery	1878-021

Consolidated Probate Index from the Clerks Loose Papers & the Superior Court/Circuit Court Records 1759-1919

Surname	**Given Name**	**Instrument**	**Date**	**County**	**CLP Record Series**	**Index #**
SMITH (Cont.)						
Smith	Elijah	Admr. Bond	9/21/1861	Fauquier Co.	Chancery	1878-021
Smith	Elijah	Sales	1861	Fauquier Co.	Chancery	1878-021
Smith	Eliza D.	Guardian Bond	1803	Fauquier Co.	Probate, Box 49	1803-007
Smith	Elizabeth	Guardian Bond	1789	Fauquier Co.	Probate, Box 48	1789-004
Smith	Elizabeth	Exor. Bond	1809	Fauquier Co.	Probate, Box 47	1809-001
Smith	Enoch	Guardian Bond	1812	Fauquier Co.	Probate, Box 49	1812-007
Smith	Enoch	Guardian Bond	1816	Fauquier Co.	Probate, Box 49	1816-008
Smith	George W.	Guardian Appt.	1/22/1849	Fauquier Co.	Chancery	1861-015
Smith	George W.	Guardian Acct. Settled	8/10/1860	Fauquier Co.	Chancery	1861-015
Smith	Gloria M.	Guardian Appt.	11/28/1904	Fauquier Co.	Probate, Box 55 Superior/Circuit Ct.	1904-008
Smith	Hannah	Guardian Bond	1766	Fauquier Co.	Probate, Box 48	1766-002
Smith	Harriet B.	Guardian Bond	1806	Fauquier Co.	Probate, Box 49	1806-014
Smith	Hazel D.	Guardian Appt.	11/28/1904	Fauquier Co.	Probate, Box 55 Superior/Circuit Ct.	1904-008
Smith	Hedgman	Will	5/23/1864	Fauquier Co.	Chancery	1873-047
Smith	Hugh	Will	9/22/1817	Fauquier Co.	Chancery	1836-021
Smith	Hugh	Inventory + Appraisement	7/27/1818	Fauquier Co.	Chancery	1836-021
Smith	Hugh	Exor. Acct.	9/24/1821	Fauquier Co.	Chancery	1836-021
Smith	Isaac E.	Report of Division	4/28/1873	Fauquier Co.	Chancery	1873-083
Smith	Isaac E.	Plat & Survey Of Division	4/28/1873	Fauquier Co.	Chancery	1873-083
Smith	Isham	Guardian Bond	1809	Fauquier Co.	Probate, Box 49	1809-004
Smith	James	Guardian Bond	1782	Fauquier Co.	Probate, Box 48	1782-001
Smith	James	Will	7/6/1826	Logan Co. KY.	Chancery	1892-058
Smith	James	Admr. Appt.	8/28/1840	Fauquier Co.	Chancery	1892-058
Smith	James	Division of Slaves	10/12/1844	Fauquier Co.	Chancery	1892-058
Smith	James	Will	9/29/1852	Fauquier Co.	Chancery	1858-004

Consolidated Probate Index from the Clerks Loose Papers & the Superior Court/Circuit Court Records 1759-1919

Surname	Given Name	Instrument	Date	County	CLP Record Series	Index #
SMITH (Cont.)						
Smith	Jane	Guardian Bond	1766	Fauquier Co.	Probate, Box 48	1766-003
Smith	Jane	Will	2/28/1871	Fauquier Co.	Chancery	1908-019
Smith	Janet S.	Guardian Acct.	8/21/1855	Fauquier Co.	Chancery	1858-036
Smith	John	Admrs. Bond	1765	Fauquier Co.	Probate, Box 44	1765-003
Smith	John	Admtrx. Bond	1777	Fauquier Co.	Probate, Box 44	1777-003
Smith	John	Admtrx. Bond	1782	Fauquier Co.	Probate, Box 45	1782-014
Smith	John	Admtrx. Bond	1784	Fauquier Co.	Probate, Box 45	1784-004
Smith	John	Exor. Bond	1811	Fauquier Co.	Probate, Box 47	1811-001
Smith	John	Exor. Bond	1815	Fauquier Co.	Probate, Box 47	1815-011
Smith	John	Admr. Acct.	10/1823	Fauquier Co.	Probate, Box 40	1823-005
Smith	John	Will	9/23/1811	Fauquier Co.	Chancery	1842-001
Smith	John	Will	9/23/1811	Fauquier Co.	Chancery	1846-033
Smith	John	Will (Extract)	9/23/1811	Fauquier Co.	Chancery	1850-004
Smith	John	Will	9/23/1811	Fauquier Co.	Chancery	1855-078
Smith	John	Will	9/23/1811	Baltimore, MD.	Chancery	1874-031
Smith	John	Will	5/22/1813	Fauquier Co.	Chancery	1836-019
Smith	John	Admr. Bond	4/25/1835	Fauquier Co.	Chancery	1859-043
Smith	John	Appraisement	11/29/1831	Fauquier Co.	Chancery	1859-043
Smith	John A. W.	List of Fees for Effingham Forest Tenants	Undated	Fauquier Co.	Probate, Box 39	1809-001
Smith	John A. W.	Inventory + Appraisement	3/26/1833	Fauquier Co.	Chancery	1885-001
Smith	John B.	Sales (Extract)	2/11/1830	Fauquier Co.	Chancery	1868-215
Smith	John Jr.	Admr. Bond	1808	Fauquier Co.	Probate, Box 46	1808-024
Smith	John P.	Admr. Acct.	11/28/1840	Fauquier Co.	Chancery	1855-005
Smith	John P.	Inventory + Appraisement of Slaves	6/9/1841	Fauquier Co.	Chancery	1855-005
Smith	John P.	Will	3/23/1863	Fauquier Co.	Chancery	1868-022

Consolidated Probate Index from the Clerks Loose Papers & the Superior Court/Circuit Court Records 1759-1919

Surname	Given Name	Instrument	Date	County	CLP Record Series	Index #
SMITH (Cont.)						
Smith	John P.	Will	3/25/1863	Fauquier Co.	Chancery	1891-018
Smith	John Thomas	Admr. Acct.	4/10/1877	Fauquier Co.	Probate, Box 54 Superior/Circuit Ct.	1877-004
Smith	Joseph	Admr. Bond	1777	Fauquier Co.	Probate, Box 44	1777-001
Smith	Joseph	Guardian Bond	1782	Fauquier Co.	Probate, Box 48	1782-001
Smith	Joseph	Court Order to Appraise Estate	12/1801	Fauquier Co.	Probate, Box 39 Superior/Circuit Ct.	1801-004
Smith	Joseph	Admr. Accts.	1802	Fauquier Co.	Chancery	1811-046
Smith	Joseph	Admr. Accts.	1809	Fauquier Co.	Chancery	1811-046
Smith	Joseph	Plat & Survey Of Division	7/28/1823	Fauquier Co.	Chancery	1831-026
Smith	Joseph	Report of Division Of Land	8/28/1823	Fauquier Co.	Chancery	1847-003
Smith	Joseph	Survey of Division Of Land	8/28/1823	Fauquier Co.	Chancery	1847-003
Smith	Joseph B.	Report of Division	4/4/1866	Fauquier Co.	Chancery	1891-018
Smith	Joseph B.	Plat & Survey Of Division	4/4/1866	Fauquier Co.	Chancery	1891-018
Smith	Joseph B.	Estate Acct.	1889	Fauquier Co.	Chancery	1891-043
Smith	Kitty A.	Guardian Bond	1803	Fauquier Co.	Probate, Box 49	1803-007
Smith	Leannah	Relinquishment	9/1828	Fauquier Co.	Probate, Box 40	1828-004
Smith	Lewis	Guardian Bond	1784	Fauquier Co.	Probate, Box 48	1784-004
Smith	Livinia	Division	5/19/1909	Fauquier Co.	Chancery	1912-045
Smith	Maria	Guardian Acct.	2/17/1852	Fauquier Co.	Chancery	1867-009
Smith	Marshall	Division of Slaves	Undated	Fauquier Co.	Chancery	1839-048
Smith	Marshall	Admr. Appt.	9/26/1851	Fauquier Co.	Chancery	1892-059
Smith	Mary	Guardian Bond	1772	Fauquier Co.	Probate, Box 48	1772-002
Smith	Mary	Admtrx. Bond	1806	Fauquier Co.	Probate, Box 47	1806-029
Smith	Mary E.	Will	5/12/1852	Fauquier Co.	Probate, Box 52 Superior/Circuit Ct.	1852-001

Consolidated Probate Index from the Clerks Loose Papers & the Superior Court/Circuit Court Records 1759-1919

Surname	Given Name	Instrument	Date	County	CLP Record Series	Index #
SMITH (Cont.)						
Smith	Mary E.	Inventory	6/24/1852	Fauquier Co.	Probate, Box 52 Superior/Circuit Ct.	1852-002
Smith	Mary E.	Admr. Acct.	9/3/1853	Fauquier Co.	Probate, Box 52 Superior/Circuit Ct.	1853-004
Smith	Maryann	Guardian Bond	1815	Fauquier Co.	Probate, Box 49	1815-032
Smith	Matthew	Exor. Bond	1782	Fauquier Co.	Probate, Box 45	1782-003
Smith	Nancy	Relinquishment	1/1831	Fauquier Co.	Probate, Box 40	1831-001
Smith	Naomi	Guardian Appt.	10/27/1910	Fauquier Co.	Probate, Box 56 Superior/Circuit Ct.	1910-005
Smith	P. A. L.	Appraisement	2/2/1880	Fauquier Co.	Probate, Box 54 Superior/Circuit Ct.	1880-001
Smith	P. A. L.	Sales	2/2/1880	Fauquier Co.	Probate, Box 54 Superior/Circuit Ct.	1880-001
Smith	Polly	Heirs	5/1/1911	Fauquier Co.	Chancery	1912-044
Smith	Richard	Guardian Bond	1785	Fauquier Co.	Probate, Box 48	1785-005
Smith	Ruth	Guardian Bond	1777	Fauquier Co.	Probate, Box 48	1777-002
Smith	Ruth	Guardian Bond	1789	Fauquier Co.	Probate, Box 48	1789-004
Smith	Sally	Report of Division Of Slaves	12/27/1839	Baltimore, MD.	Chancery	1874-031
Smith	Samuel	Guardian Bond	1816	Fauquier Co.	Probate, Box 49	1816-002
Smith	Susanna	Admr. Bond	1781	Fauquier Co.	Probate, Box 45	1781-009
Smith	Susanna	Guardian Bond	1789	Fauquier Co.	Probate, Box 48	1789-004
Smith	Thomas A.	Will	3/4/1889	Pr. Wm. Co. VA.	Chancery	1893-028
Smith	Thomas W.	Admr. Appt.	12/2/1907	Fauquier Co.	Probate, Box 56 Superior/Circuit Ct.	1907-018
Smith	Thomas Williamson	Will	8/26/1850	Fauquier Co.	Chancery	1853-040
Smith	Thomas Williamson	Plat & Survey Of Division	1/22/1853	Fauquier Co.	Chancery	1853-040
Smith	Thompson	Will	10/6/1835	Fauquier Co.	Probate, Box 51 Superior/Circuit Ct.	1835-004
Smith	Thompson	Will	10/6/1835	Fauquier Co.	Chancery	1860-023
Smith	Wilhelmina	Guardian Bond	1777	Fauquier Co.	Probate, Box 48	1777-002

Consolidated Probate Index from the Clerks Loose Papers & the Superior Court/Circuit Court Records 1759-1919

Surname	Given Name	Instrument	Date	County	CLP Record Series	Index #
SMITH (Cont.)						
Smith	Willey	Guardian Bond	1789	Fauquier Co.	Probate, Box 48	1789-007
Smith	William	Guardian Bond	1782	Fauquier Co.	Probate, Box 48	1782-001
Smith	William	Inventory + Appraisement	10/24/1803	Fauquier Co.	Probate, Box 39	1810-001
Smith	William	Admtrx. Bond	1813	Fauquier Co.	Probate, Box 47	1813-014
Smith	William	Guardian Bond	1815	Fauquier Co.	Probate, Box 49	1815-032
Smith	William	Admr. Acct.	1/10/1821	Fauquier Co.	Chancery	1835-046
Smith	William	Division of Slaves	1/23/1821	Fauquier Co.	Chancery	1835-046
Smith	William	Report of Division	5/29/1835	Fauquier Co.	Chancery	1835-046
Smith	William	Plat & Survey Of Division	5/29/1835	Fauquier Co.	Chancery	1835-046
Smith	William	Will	2/27/1837	Fauquier Co.	Chancery	1849-050
Smith	William	Report of Division Of Slaves	3/27/1847	Fauquier Co.	Chancery	1849-050
Smith	William	Report of Sales Of Slaves	3//1847	Fauquier Co.	Chancery	1849-050
Smith	William J.	Will	3/25/1871	Fauquier Co.	Chancery	1887-032
Smith	William R.	Will	6/22/1857	Fauquier Co.	Chancery	1898-063
SMOOTE						
Smoote	John	Exor. Bond	1797	Fauquier Co.	Probate, Box 46	1797-008
SNELLING						
Snelling	Benjamin	Extrx. Bond	1774	Fauquier Co.	Probate, Box 44	1774-002
SOUTHARD (See also Suddoth)						
Southard	Francis	Exor. Bond	1779	Fauquier Co.	Probate, Box 45	1779-004
SPICKNELL						
Spicknell	Henry E.	Admr. Bond	8/18/1883	Fauquier Co.	Probate, Box 54 Superior/Circuit Ct.	1883-001
SPILMAN						
Spilman	Baldwin H.	Will	1/5/1893	Fauquier Co.	Chancery	1900-033
Spilman	Jacob	Admr. Bond	1760	Fauquier Co.	Probate, Box 44	1760-011
Spilman	John A.	Appraisement	6/7/1889	Fauquier Co.	Probate, Box 54 Superior/Circuit Ct.	1889-001

Consolidated Probate Index from the Clerks Loose Papers & the Superior Court/Circuit Court Records 1759-1919

Surname	Given Name	Instrument	Date	County	CLP Record Series	Index #
SPILMAN (Cont.)						
Spilman	John A.	Admr. Acct.	4/6/1898	Fauquier Co.	Probate, Box 55 Superior/Circuit Ct.	1898-005
Spilman	Sarah A.	Will	9/26/1893	Fauquier Co.	Chancery	1898-042
SQUIRES						
Squires	John	Admtrx. Bond	1778	Fauquier Co.	Probate, Box 45	1778-004
Squires	Martin	Admtrx. Bond	1814	Fauquier Co.	Probate, Box 47	1814-011
STADLER						
Stadler	Jacob	Extrx. Bond	1813	Fauquier Co.	Probate, Box 47	1813-009
STAMPS						
Stamps	John	Guardian Bond	1817	Fauquier Co.	Probate, Box 49	1817-028
Stamps	Mary	Guardian Bond	1817	Fauquier Co.	Probate, Box 49	1817-028
Stamps	Thomas	Exors. Bond	1763	Fauquier Co.	Probate, Box 44	1763-003
Stamps	William	Exors. Bond	1772	Fauquier Co.	Probate, Box 44	1772-005
Stamps	William	Will	4/25/1772	Fauquier Co.	Chancery	1813-019
Stamps	William	Appraisement	5/22/1772	Fauquier Co.	Chancery	1813-019
Stamps	William	Guardian Bond	1817	Fauquier Co.	Probate, Box 49	1817-028
STANTON						
Stanton	Polly	Relinquishment	6/28/1802	Fauquier Co.	Probate, Box 50	1802-003
Stanton	William Jr.	Admr. Bond	1806	Fauquier Co.	Probate, Box 46	1806-024
STARKE						
Starke	James	Will	9/28/1829	Fauquier Co.	Chancery	1832-062
STEPHENS						
Stephens	Ephraim	Admr. Bond	1814	Fauquier Co.	Probate, Box 47	1814-013
Stephens	Lydia	Will	2/27/1872	Fauquier Co.	Chancery	1892-060
Stephens	Robert	Exors. Bond	1773	Fauquier Co.	Probate, Box 44	1773-008
STEVENSON						
Stevenson	Catherine	Guardian Chosen	1807	Fauquier Co.	Probate, Box 39	1807-001
STEWART (See also Stuart)						
Stewart	Elizabeth	Exors. Bond	1807	Fauquier Co.	Probate, Box 46	1807-016
Stewart	James	Exors. Bond	1781	Fauquier Co.	Probate, Box 45	1781-007
Stewart	Samuel	Admr. Bond	9/6/1870	Fauquier Co.	Probate, Box 53 Superior/Circuit Ct.	1870-003

Consolidated Probate Index from the Clerks Loose Papers & the Superior Court/Circuit Court Records 1759-1919

Surname	Given Name	Instrument	Date	County	CLP Record Series	Index #
STEWART (Cont.)						
Stewart	William	Will	6/23/1835	Fauquier Co.	Chancery	1851-044
Stewart	William	Inventory + Appraisement	1/8/1848	Fauquier Co.	Chancery	1851-044
Stewart	William	Admr. Acct.	2/24/1851	Fauquier Co.	Chancery	1851-044
STIGLER						
Stigler	Alice	Guardian Bond	1816	Fauquier Co.	Probate, Box 49	1816-004
Stigler	Frances	Guardian Bond	1815	Fauquier Co.	Probate, Box 49	1817-018
Stigler	George W.	Guardian Bond	1815	Fauquier Co.	Probate, Box 49	1817-018
STONE						
Stone	George W.	Will	9/17/1877	Culpeper Co. VA.	Chancery	1880-075
Stone	John W.	Plat & Survey Of Division of "Millview"	3/25/1872	Fauquier Co.	Chancery	1879-030
Stone	Joseph	Will	10/27/1818	Fauquier Co.	Probate, Box 50	1818-003
Stone	Richard	Admr. Bond	12/30/1874	Fauquier Co.	Probate, Box 53 Superior/Circuit Ct.	1874-008
Stone	Richard E.	Admr. Acct.	9/6/1876	Fauquier Co.	Probate, Box 54 Superior/Circuit Ct.	1876-008
STONESTREET						
Stonestreet	James	Admtrx. Bond	1807	Fauquier Co.	Probate, Box 46	1807-003
STOVER						
Stover	Catherine	Certificate of Satisfaction of Gdnship	4/23/1832	Bucks Co. PA.	Chancery	1847-006
Stover	Catherine	Guardian Accts.	2/12/1833	Bucks Co. PA.	Chancery	1847-006
Stover	Catherine	Guardian Accts.	3/8/1833	Bucks Co. PA.	Chancery	1847-006
STRIBLING						
Stribling	Caroline M.	Will	11/29/1887	Fauquier Co.	Chancery	1903-071
Stribling	M. C. (Mrs.)	Admtrx. Appt.	12/24/1904	Fauquier Co.	Probate, Box 55 Superior/Circuit Ct.	1904-009
Stribling	Robert M.	Will	9/25/1865	Fauquier Co.	Chancery	1876-007
Stribling	Robert M.	Will	9/25/1865	Fauquier Co.	Chancery	1881-050
Stribling	Robert M.	Report of Division	12/1868	Fauquier Co.	Chancery	1881-050
Stribling	Robert M.	Plat & Survey Of Division	12/1868	Fauquier Co.	Chancery	1881-050

Consolidated Probate Index from the Clerks Loose Papers & the Superior Court/Circuit Court Records 1759-1919

Surname	Given Name	Instrument	Date	County	CLP Record Series	Index #
STRIBLING (Cont.)						
Stribling	William C.	Will	1/27/1868	Fauquier Co.	Chancery	1881-050
STRINGFELLOW						
Stringfellow	Betty B.	Guardian Bond	3/1879	Shelby Co. TN.	Chancery	1881-033
Stringfellow	Brunette Jamison	Guardian Bond	3/1879	Shelby Co. TN.	Chancery	1881-033
Stringfellow	James	Will	5/24/1848	Fauquier Co.	Chancery	1881-033
Stringfellow	Laura H.	Guardian Bond	3/1879	Shelby Co. TN.	Chancery	1881-033
Stringfellow	Lillie Brooks	Guardian Bond	3/1879	Shelby Co. TN.	Chancery	1881-033
Stringfellow	Minnie R.	Guardian Bond	3/1879	Shelby Co. TN.	Chancery	1881-033
Stringfellow	Susan	Will	6/25/1908	Fauquier Co.	Chancery	1912-014
STROTHER						
Strother	Alpheus J.	Admr. Appt.	2/26/1860	Fauquier Co.	Chancery	1892-036
Strother	Elizabeth	Plat & Survey Of Dower Allotment	9/1874	Fauquier Co.	Chancery	1892-036
Strother	Enoch	Admr. Bond	12/26/1842	Fauquier Co.	Chancery	1845-005
Strother	James	Admrs. Bond	1778	Fauquier Co.	Probate, Box 45	1778-011
Strother	James	Will	1/5/1829	Frederick Co. VA.	Chancery	1850-011
Strother	James	Will	3/26/1861	Fauquier Co.	Chancery	1889-019
Strother	John	Admr. Appt.	8/11//1832	Fauquier Co.	Chancery	1836-021
Strother	John	Will	8/24/1864	Fauquier Co.	Chancery	1892-036
Strother	Lewis	Will	5/23/1842	Fauquier Co.	Chancery	1855-021
Strother	Lewis	Will	5/23/1842	Fauquier Co.	Chancery	1871-083
Strother	Lewis	Heirs	Undated	Fauquier Co.	Chancery	1871-083
Strother	Reuben	Admrs. Bond	1815	Fauquier Co.	Probate, Box 47	1815-042
Strother	Susannah	Plat & Survey Of Division	10/1876	Fauquier Co.	Probate, Box 50 Addendum Folder	1876-001
STUART (See also Stewart)						
Stuart	Catharine	Will	9/5/1805	Fauquier Co.	Chancery	1846-001
Stuart	John	Will	1/5/1843	King George Co. VA.	Chancery	1881-027
Stuart	Mary	Will	9/5/1805	King George Co. VA.	Chancery	1846-001
Stuart	Sarah	Will	10/17/1813	King George Co. VA.	Chancery	1846-001

Consolidated Probate Index from the Clerks Loose Papers & the Superior Court/Circuit Court Records 1759-1919

Surname	Given Name	Instrument	Date	County	CLP Record Series	Index #
STUART (Cont.)						
Stuart	William	Admr. Acct.	1832	Fauquier Co.	Probate, Box 40	1832-004
Stuart	William	Will	6/23/1835	Fauquier Co.	Chancery	1846-001
Stuart	William	Will	6/23/1835	Fauquier Co.	Chancery	1872-028
SUDDOTH (See also Southard)						
Suddoth	Asenath	Admr. Bond	3/22/1841	Fauquier Co.	Chancery	1848-036
Suddoth	Bower	Guardian Bond	1801	Fauquier Co.	Probate, Box 48	1801-004
Suddoth	Elizabeth	Guardian Bond	1801	Fauquier Co.	Probate, Box 48	1801-004
Suddoth	Elizabeth	Admrs. Bond	1806	Fauquier Co.	Probate, Box 46	1806-007
Suddoth	Elizabeth	Will	11/25/1867	Fauquier Co.	Chancery	1885-011
Suddoth	Hiram	Guardian Bond	1801	Fauquier Co.	Probate, Box 48	1801-004
Suddoth	James	Report of Division	6/12/1876	Fauquier Co.	Chancery	1890-019
Suddoth	James	Plat & Survey Of Division	6/12/1876	Fauquier Co.	Chancery	1890-019
Suddoth	Margaret	Report of Division	3/25/1860	Fauquier Co.	Chancery	1902-013
Suddoth	Margaret	Appraisement (Extract)	7/21/1860	Fauquier Co.	Chancery	1902-013
Suddoth	Margaret	Report of Division Of Slaves	9/3/1860	Fauquier Co.	Chancery	1902-013
Suddoth	Margaret	Admr. Acct. (in Comr. Report)	9/17/1860	Fauquier Co.	Chancery	1902-013
Suddoth	Margaret	Heirs (in Comr. Report)	9/17/1860	Fauquier Co.	Chancery	1902-013
Suddoth	Margaret	Division of Slaves	9/21/1860	Fauquier Co.	Chancery	1902-013
Suddoth	Margaret	Plat & Survey Of "Lucky Hill" Division	5/1875	Fauquier Co.	Chancery	1902-013
Suddoth	Mary	Guardian Bond	1801	Fauquier Co.	Probate, Box 48	1801-004
Suddoth	Peggy's children	Guardian Bond	1808	Fauquier Co.	Probate, Box 49	1808-010
Suddoth	Sarah	Admr. Bond	1810	Fauquier Co.	Probate, Box 47	1810-014
Suddoth	Susan A.	Court order to Settle Guardian Acct.	5/1845	Fauquier Co.	Probate, Box 40	1845-002
Suddoth	Susanna	Guardian Bond	1801	Fauquier Co.	Probate, Box 48	1801-004

Consolidated Probate Index from the Clerks Loose Papers & the Superior Court/Circuit Court Records 1759-1919

Surname	Given Name	Instrument	Date	County	CLP Record Series	Index #
SULLIVAN						
Sullivan	Ann	Guardian Bond	1793	Fauquier Co.	Probate, Box 47	1793-003
Sullivan	Catharine E.	Guardian Bond	8/26/1833	Fauquier Co.	Chancery	1855-028
Sullivan	Catharine E.	Guardian Acct.	8/26/1833	Fauquier Co.	Chancery	1855-028
Sullivan	Catharine E.	Guardian Bond	12/26/1833	Fauquier Co.	Chancery	1855-024
Sullivan	George	Admtrx. Bond	1778	Fauquier Co.	Probate, Box 45	1778-009
Sullivan	John C.	Admr. Acct.	1847	Fauquier Co.	Chancery	1855-024
Sullivan	John C.	Appraisement Of Slaves	7/7/1847	Fauquier Co.	Chancery	1855-024
Sullivan	John C.	Sales	7/7/1847	Fauquier Co.	Chancery	1855-024
Sullivan	John H.	Guardian Acct.	8/26/1833	Fauquier Co.	Chancery	1855-028
Sullivan	John Holmes	Guardian Bond	12/26/1833	Fauquier Co.	Chancery	1855-024
Sullivan	Mary E.	Guardian Bond	12/26/1833	Fauquier Co.	Chancery	1855-024
Sullivan	Mary E.	Guardian Bond	8/26/1833	Fauquier Co.	Chancery	1855-028
Sullivan	Mary E.	Guardian Acct.	12/26/1833	Fauquier Co.	Chancery	1855-028
SUMMERS						
Summers	George W.	Will	10/23/1893	Fauquier Co.	Chancery	1898-034
Summers	George W.	Admr. Acct.	8/23/1895	Fauquier Co.	Chancery	1898-034
Summers	George W.	Admr. Acct.	2/1/1896	Fauquier Co.	Chancery	1898-034
SUTTLE (See also Settle)						
Suttle	Isaac	Admtrx. Bond	1759	Fauquier Co.	Probate, Box 44	1795-002
SUTTON						
Sutton	Jane	Report of Division	4/2/1894	Fauquier Co.	Chancery	1895-049
Sutton	Jane	Plat & Survey Of Division	4/2/1894	Fauquier Co.	Chancery	1895-049
Sutton	William	Report of Division	4/4/1894	Fauquier Co.	Chancery	1895-049
Sutton	William	Plat & Survey Of Division	4/4/1894	Fauquier Co.	Chancery	1895-049
SWANN						
Swann	John Butler	Will	2/26/1908	Fauquier Co.	Chancery	1911-029

Consolidated Probate Index from the Clerks Loose Papers & the Superior Court/Circuit Court Records 1759-1919

Surname	Given Name	Instrument	Date	County	CLP Record Series	Index #
SWEENY						
Sweeny	Ann	Guardian Bond	1811	Fauquier Co.	Probate, Box 49	1811-015
Sweeny	Hugh	Guardian Bond	1811	Fauquier Co.	Probate, Box 49	1811-015
Sweeny	John Hooe	Guardian Bond	1811	Fauquier Co.	Probate, Box 49	1811-015
Sweeny	Susan	Guardian Bond	1811	Fauquier Co.	Probate, Box 49	1811-015

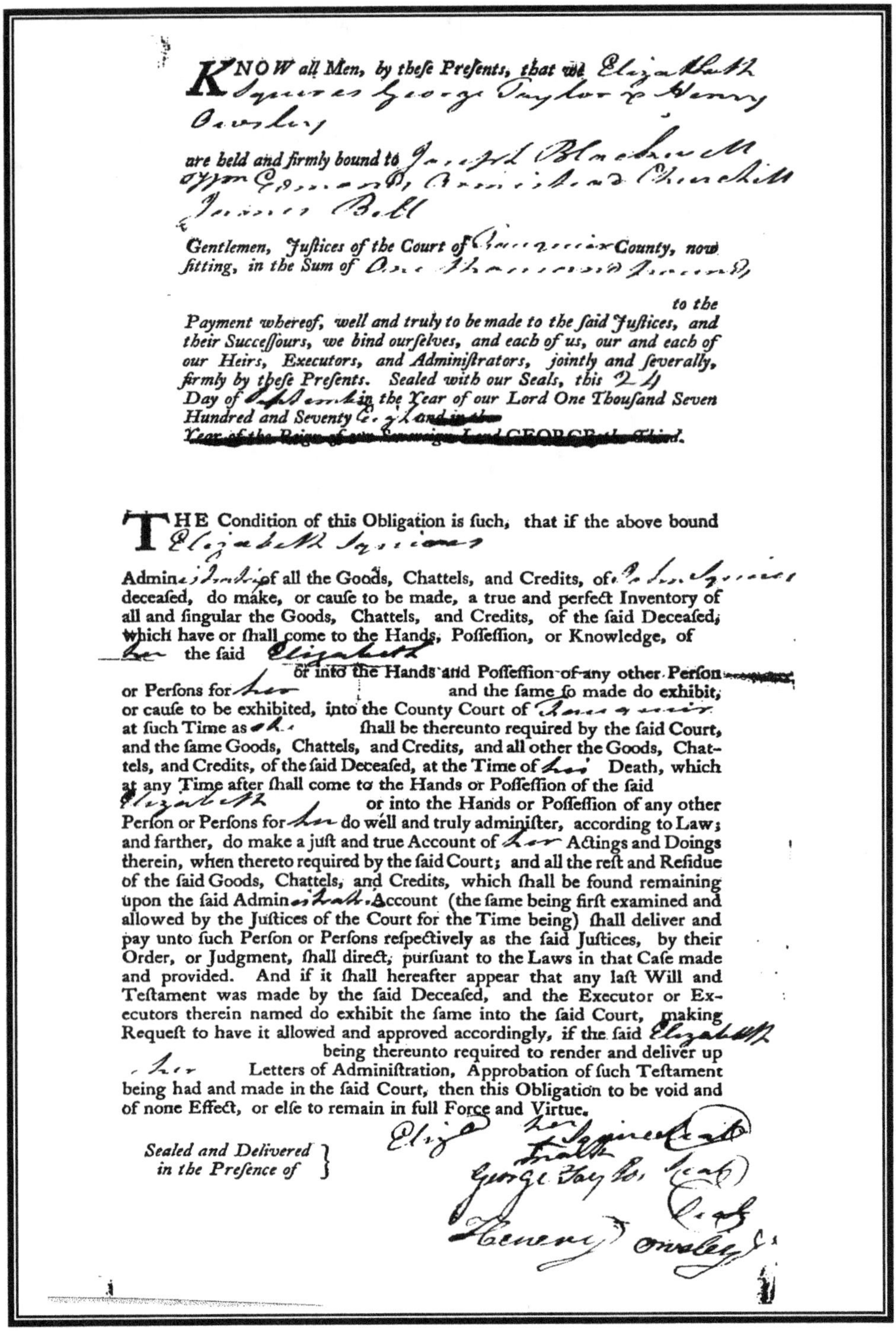

KNOW all Men, by these Presents, that we Elizabeth Squires George Taylor & Henry Owsley

are held and firmly bound to Joseph Blackwell John Edmonds, Armistead Churchill James Bell

Gentlemen, Justices of the Court of Fauquier County, now sitting, in the Sum of One Thousand Pounds

to the Payment whereof, well and truly to be made to the said Justices, and their Successours, we bind ourselves, and each of us, our and each of our Heirs, Executors, and Administrators, jointly and severally, firmly by these Presents. Sealed with our Seals, this 24 Day of September in the Year of our Lord One Thousand Seven Hundred and Seventy Eight ~~and in the Year of the Reign of our Sovereign Lord GEORGE the Third.~~

THE Condition of this Obligation is such, that if the above bound Elizabeth Squires Administratrix of all the Goods, Chattels, and Credits, of John Squires deceased, do make, or cause to be made, a true and perfect Inventory of all and singular the Goods, Chattels, and Credits, of the said Deceased, which have or shall come to the Hands, Possession, or Knowledge, of her the said Elizabeth ~~or into the Hands and Possession of any other Person~~ or Persons for her and the same so made do exhibit, or cause to be exhibited, into the County Court of Fauquier at such Time as she shall be thereunto required by the said Court, and the same Goods, Chattels, and Credits, and all other the Goods, Chattels, and Credits, of the said Deceased, at the Time of his Death, which at any Time after shall come to the Hands or Possession of the said Elizabeth or into the Hands or Possession of any other Person or Persons for her do well and truly administer, according to Law; and farther, do make a just and true Account of her Actings and Doings therein, when thereto required by the said Court; and all the rest and Residue of the said Goods, Chattels, and Credits, which shall be found remaining upon the said Administratrix Account (the same being first examined and allowed by the Justices of the Court for the Time being) shall deliver and pay unto such Person or Persons respectively as the said Justices, by their Order, or Judgment, shall direct, pursuant to the Laws in that Case made and provided. And if it shall hereafter appear that any last Will and Testament was made by the said Deceased, and the Executor or Executors therein named do exhibit the same into the said Court, making Request to have it allowed and approved accordingly, if the said Elizabeth being thereunto required to render and deliver up her Letters of Administration, Approbation of such Testament being had and made in the said Court, then this Obligation to be void and of none Effect, or else to remain in full Force and Virtue.

Sealed and Delivered in the Presence of

Eliza her Squires (Seal)
mark
George Taylor (Seal)
Henery Owsley (Seal)

Plate 6. Probate. Scanned Image from Box 45. Administrator & Executor Bonds. 1778-004. John Squire's Admtrx. Bond.

Consolidated Probate Index from the Clerks Loose Papers & the Superior Court/Circuit Court Records 1759-1919

Surname	Given Name	Instrument	Date	County	CLP Record Series	Index #
TALBERT						
Talbert	Ann	Guardian Bond	1799	Fauquier Co.	Probate, Box 48	1799-001
Talbert	John	Exors. Bond	1796	Fauquier Co.	Probate, Box 46	1796-004
TALIAFERRO						
Taliaferro	Louisa G.	Will	2/12/1844	Caroline Co. VA.	Chancery	1880-045
TAPSCOTT						
Tapscott	Harriet	Guardian Bond	1817	Fauquier Co.	Probate, Box 49	1817-010
Tapscott	Robert	Will	1/8/1896	Fauquier Co.	Chancery	1912-037
Tapscott	Robert	Heirs	1/1/1907	Fauquier Co.	Chancery	1912-037
TATE						
Tate	Thomas M.	Will	8/9/1872	Smythe Co. VA.	Chancery	1894-061
TAYLOR						
Taylor	Amanda	Guardian Bond	8/26/1839	Fauquier Co.	Chancery	1855-035
Taylor	Daniel	Admr. Bond	1815	Fauquier Co.	Probate, Box 47	1815-065
Taylor	Elizabeth	Guardian Bond	1811	Fauquier Co.	Probate, Box 49	1811-010
Taylor	George W.	Guardian Bond	8/26/1839	Fauquier Co.	Chancery	1855-036
Taylor	Henry	Division	7/1802	Fauquier Co.	Chancery	1802-034
Taylor	Ignatius	Guardian Bond	1811	Fauquier Co.	Probate, Box 49	1811-010
Taylor	Joseph	Extrx. Bond	1806	Fauquier Co.	Probate, Box 46	1806-025
Taylor	Joseph	Guardian Bond	1811	Fauquier Co.	Probate, Box 49	1811-010
Taylor	Joseph	Will	4/26/1806	Fauquier Co.	Chancery	1836-023
Taylor	Juniper	Guardian Bond	1811	Fauquier Co.	Probate, Box 49	1811-010
Taylor	Robert I.	Will	10/16/1840	Alexandria Co. DC.	Chancery	1871-096
Taylor	Thoroughgood	Will	9/21/1874	Lancaster Co. VA.	Chancery	1899-011
Taylor	William F.	Admtrx. Bond	1811	Fauquier Co.	Probate, Box 47	1811-011
Taylor	William T.	Sale of Slaves	4/1819	Fauquier Co.	Chancery	1868-223
Taylor	William T.	Division	4/1819	Fauquier Co.	Chancery	1868-223
Taylor	William T.	Admr. Acct.	4/1819	Fauquier Co.	Chancery	1868-223
TEMPLEMAN						
Templeman	Leroy	Admr. Appt.	12/14/1891	Fauquier Co.	Probate, Box 55 Superior/Circuit Ct.	1891-002

Consolidated Probate Index from the Clerks Loose Papers & the Superior Court/Circuit Court Records 1759-1919

Surname	Given Name	Instrument	Date	County	CLP Record Series	Index #
THARPE						
Tharpe	Mary	Will	9/22/1879	Fauquier Co.	Probate, Box 50 Addendum Folder	1879-001
THOMAS						
Thomas	George	Will	1781	Pr. Wm. Co. VA.	Chancery	1815-037
Thomas	George	Inventory + Appraisement	2/27/1781	Pr. Wm. Co. VA.	Chancery	1815-037
Thomas	John	Admtrx. Bond	1777	Fauquier Co.	Probate, Box 44	1777-018
Thomas	John	Plat & Survey Of Division	10/11/1847	Fauquier Co.	Chancery	1872-043
Thomas	John	Plat & Survey Of Division (Extract)	8/10/1879	Fauquier Co.	Chancery	1900-050
Thomas	Nancy	Relinquishment	12/22/1828	Fauquier Co.	Probate, Box 40	1828-007
Thomas	Walker	Admr. Acct.	3/28/1894	Fauquier Co.	Chancery	1895-011
THOMKINS						
Thomkins	Henry	Court Order to Settle Exor. Acct.	1817	Fauquier Co.	Probate, Box 39	1817-004
THOMPSON (See also Thomson)						
Thompson	Alice	Committee Bond	2/29/1820	Fauquier Co.	Chancery	1851-010
Thompson	Daniel	Relinquishment	12/1818	Fauquier Co.	Probate, Box 39	1818-013
Thompson	Eli	Inventory	11/22/1819	Fauquier Co.	Probate, Box 50	1819-002
Thompson	Eli	Admr. Acct. Settled	11/22/1819	Fauquier Co.	Probate, Box 39	1819-002
Thompson	Eli	Appraisement	1/24/1820	Fauquier Co.	Probate, Box 39	1819-002
Thompson	Guy S.	Guardian Appt.	11/27/1905	Fauquier Co.	Probate, Box 55 Superior/Circuit Ct.	1905-011
Thompson	James	Will	2/25/1833	Fauquier Co.	Chancery	1834-021
Thompson	James	Will	2/25/1833	Fauquier Co.	Chancery	1837-020
Thompson	James	Will	2/25/1833	Fauquier Co.	Chancery	1873-011
Thompson	Jane	Guardian Bond	1815	Fauquier Co.	Probate, Box 49	1815-026
Thompson	Jane	Guardian Bond	11/25/1815	Fauquier Co.	Chancery	1855-029
Thompson	Joe F.	Guardian Bond	11/27/1905	Fauquier Co.	Chancery	1905-011
Thompson	John	Guardian Bond	11/24/1857	Fauquier Co.	Chancery	1883-038
Thompson	Joseph	Admr. Appt.	3/25/1851	Fauquier Co.	Chancery	1899-028

Consolidated Probate Index from the Clerks Loose Papers & the Superior Court/Circuit Court Records 1759-1919

Surname	Given Name	Instrument	Date	County	CLP Record Series	Index #
THOMPSON (Cont.)						
Thompson	Joseph	Report of Division Of Slaves	12/23/1851	Fauquier Co.	Chancery	1851-046
Thompson	Joseph	Report of Division Of Real Estate	12/23/1851	Fauquier Co.	Chancery	1851-046
Thompson	Joseph W.	Guardian Bond	11/24/1857	Fauquier Co.	Chancery	1883-038
Thompson	Mary Ann	Admr. Bond	8/24/1854	Fauquier Co.	Chancery	1883-038
Thompson	William	Relinquishment	12/1818	Fauquier Co.	Probate, Box 39	1818-013
Thompson	William	Will	6/24/1823	Fauquier Co.	Land Records & Disputes	1827-007
Thompson	William A.	Admr. Appt.	8/28/1854	Fauquier Co.	Chancery	1899-028
THOMSON (See also Thompson)						
Thomson	J. S.	Plat & Survey Of Division	1/20/1890	Fauquier Co.	Probate, Box 50 Addendum Folder	1890-001
Thomson	James	Admr. Appt.	4/27/1858	Fauquier Co.	Chancery	1882-001
Thomson	James S.	Committee Bond	4/2/1872	Fauquier Co.	Probate, Box 53 Superior/Circuit Ct.	1872-006
Thomson	James S.	Committee Bond	9/14/1872	Fauquier Co.	Probate, Box 53 Superior/Circuit Ct.	1872-011
Thomson	Mary A.	Admr. Appt.	6/9/1871	Rockingham Co. VA.	Chancery	1882-001
THORNBERRY						
Thornberry	Samuel	Will	12/25/1795	Fauquier Co.	Chancery	1830-147
Thornberry	William	Admr. Bond	10/28/1822	Fauquier Co.	Chancery	1837-016
Thornberry	William	Admr. Acct.	5/25/1825	Fauquier Co.	Chancery	1837-016
Thornberry	William	Report of Division	8/1823	Fauquier Co.	Chancery	1842-065
Thornberry	William	Plat & Survey Of Division	8/1823	Fauquier Co.	Chancery	1842-065
THORNHILL						
Thornhill	Bryant	Exors. Bond	1785	Fauquier Co.	Probate, Box 45	1785-001
THORNTON						
Thornton	Fanny H.	Guardian Bond	1817	Fauquier Co.	Probate, Box 49	1817-016
Thornton	Griffin	Guardian Bond	1795	Fauquier Co.	Probate, Box 48	1795-002
Thornton	Lettie	Guardian Bond	1795	Fauquier Co.	Probate, Box 48	1795-004

Consolidated Probate Index from the Clerks Loose Papers & the Superior Court/Circuit Court Records 1759-1919

Surname	Given Name	Instrument	Date	County	CLP Record Series	Index #
TIBBETTS						
Tibbetts	Fanny E.	Admr. Appt.	3/16/1905	Fauquier Co.	Probate, Box 55 Superior/Circuit Ct.	1905-002
Tibbetts	Fanny E.	Admr. Power Of Attorney	3/16/1905	Fauquier Co.	Probate, Box 55 Superior/Circuit Ct.	1905-002
TIDBALL						
Tidball	Josiah	Will	10/23/1848	Fauquier Co.	Chancery	1881-001
Tidball	Josiah	Report of Sale Of Real Estate	4/5/1853	Fauquier Co.	Chancery	1881-001
TILTON						
Tilton	John	Admr. Bond	1767	Fauquier Co.	Probate, Box 44	1767-005
TIMBERLAKE						
Timberlake	Addison	Admr. Bond	9/6/1859	Fauquier Co.	Probate, Box 52 Superior/Circuit Ct.	1859-009
TINSMAN						
Tinsman	Catherine	Guardian Appt.	6/9/1892	Fauquier Co.	Probate, Box 55 Superior/Circuit Ct.	1892-001
TIPPETT						
Tippett	James	Will	1/25/1839	Fauquier Co.	Chancery	1838-019
Tippett	James	Will	1/1/1830	Fauquier Co.	Chancery	1854-068
Tippett	William Estate	Plat & Survey of Dower Allotment	Undated	Fauquier Co.	Chancery	1841-059
TOLER						
Toler	James Henry	Admr. Appt.	6/18/1907	Fauquier Co.	Probate, Box 56 Superior/Circuit Ct.	1907-006
TOLLE						
Tolle	Roger	Extrx. Bond	1780	Fauquier Co.	Probate, Box 45	1780-001
TOMLIN						
Tomlin	John	Admr. Bond	1796	Fauquier Co.	Probate, Box 46	1796-006
Tomlin	John	Will	8/24/1835	Fauquier Co.	Chancery	1856-002
Tomlin	John Jr.	Will	4/26/1830	Fauquier Co.	Chancery	1860-022
Tomlin	John	Sales	11/12/1831	Fauquier Co.	Chancery	1860-022
Tomlin	Stephen	Will	2/26/1850	Fauquier Co.	Chancery	1856-006
Tomlin	Stephen	Will	2/26/1850	Fauquier Co.	Chancery	1870-031
Tomlin	Stephen	Will	2/26/1850	Fauquier Co.	Chancery	1870-036
Tomlin	Stephen	Will	2/26/1850	Fauquier Co.	Chancery	1872-017

Consolidated Probate Index from the Clerks Loose Papers & the Superior Court/Circuit Court Records 1759-1919

Surname	Given Name	Instrument	Date	County	CLP Record Series	Index #
TOMLIN (Cont.)						
Tomlin	William	Admr. Acct.	10/29/1839	Fauquier Co.	Chancery	1840-066
Tomlin	William	Report of Sale Of Slaves	2/26/1828	Fauquier Co.	Chancery	1868-219
TORBERT						
Torbert	John	Will	3/13/1852	Morgan Co. OH.	Chancery	1860-004
Torbert	John	Will	4/9/1860	Ralls Co. MO.	Chancery	1860-004
Torbert	Nancy	Will	4/17/1859	Ralls Co. MO.	Chancery	1903-063
TRIPLETT						
Triplett	Francis	Appraisement	3/1795	Fauquier Co.	Probate, Box 39	1808-001
Triplett	Francis	Sales	5/1795	Fauquier Co.	Probate, Box 39	1808-001
Triplett	Franklin	Admr. Acct.	10/2/1849	Fauquier Co.	Probate, Box 51 Superior/Circuit Ct	1849-004
Triplett	John Jr.	Admr. Bond	1813	Fauquier Co.	Probate, Box 47	1813-021
Triplett	Nancy	Admr. Bond	1/28/1839	Fauquier Co.	Chancery	1842-005
Triplett	Nancy	Sale of Slaves	3/1/1839	Fauquier Co.	Chancery	1842-064
Triplett	Nancy	Inventory of Slaves	8/13/1841	Fauquier Co.	Chancery	1842-064
Triplett	Richard	Will	4/10/1872	Fauquier Co.	Probate, Box 53 Superior/Circuit Ct.	1872-008
Triplett	Richard	Appraisement	6/27/1872	Fauquier Co.	Probate, Box 53 Superior/Circuit Ct.	1872-009
Triplett	Richard	Sales	5/12/1873	Fauquier Co.	Probate, Box 53 Superior/Circuit Ct.	1873-001
TRUMBO						
Trumbo	G. Clyde	Guardian Appt.	9/6/1902	Fauquier Co.	Probate, Box 55 Superior/Circuit Ct.	1902-003
Trumbo	Harry L.	Guardian Appt.	9/6/1902	Fauquier Co.	Probate, Box 55 Superior/Circuit Ct.	1902-003
Trumbo	Jacob Fay	Guardian Appt.	9/6/1902	Fauquier Co.	Probate, Box 55 Superior/Circuit Ct.	1902-003
TUCKER						
Tucker	William A.	Will	3/27/1865	Fauquier Co.	Chancery	1886-021
Tucker	William A.	Exor. Qualification	10/23/1865	Fauquier Co.	Chancery	1886-021
TULLOS (See also Tulloss)						
Tullos	Rodham	Admrs. Bond	1769	Fauquier Co.	Probate, Box 44	1769-003

Consolidated Probate Index from the Clerks Loose Papers & the Superior Court/Circuit Court Records 1759-1919

Surname	Given Name	Instrument	Date	County	CLP Record Series	Index #
TULLOSS (See also Tullos)						
Tulloss	Richard	Admr. Bond	1759	Fauquier Co.	Probate, Box 44	1759-001
Tulloss	William H.	Committee Appt.	8/24/1908	Fauquier Co.	Probate, Box 56 Superior/Circuit Ct.	1908-014
TURLEY						
Turley	Catharine	Relinquishment	4/1819	Fauquier Co.	Probate, Box 39	1819-003
TURNBULL						
Turnbull	Betsey	Guardian Bond	1806	Fauquier Co.	Probate, Box 49	1806-006
Turnbull	James	Guardian Bond	1806	Fauquier Co.	Probate, Box 49	1806-006
Turnbull	John	Guardian Bond	1813	Fauquier Co.	Probate, Box 49	1813-008
Turnbull	Lucy	Guardian Bond	1806	Fauquier Co.	Probate, Box 49	1806-006
Turnbull	Susan	Guardian Bond	1813	Fauquier Co.	Probate, Box 49	1813-008
Turnbull	Susanna	Guardian Bond	1806	Fauquier Co.	Probate, Box 49	1806-006
TURNER						
Turner	Ann	Will	3/10/1825	Fredericksburg, VA.	Chancery	1846-030
Turner	Anne	Guardian Bond	1805	Fauquier Co.	Probate, Box 49	1805-008
Turner	Charles C.	Guardian Appt.	7/22/1867	Fauquier Co.	Chancery	1891-011
Turner	Charles C.	Guardian Acct.	11/10/1868	Fauquier Co.	Chancery	1891-011
Turner	Charles C.	Guardian Acct.	7/27/1870	Fauquier Co.	Chancery	1891-011
Turner	Edward	Admr. Transfer	10/28/1816	Fauquier Co.	Probate, Box 50	1816-005
Turner	Edward C.	Guardian Acct.	11/10/1868	Fauquier Co.	Chancery	1891-011
Turner	Edward C.	Guardian Acct.	7/27/1870	Fauquier Co.	Chancery	1891-011
Turner	Edward C.	Guardian Acct.	5/29/1872	Fauquier Co.	Chancery	1891-011
Turner	Edward C.	Guardian Acct.	11/18/1872	Fauquier Co.	Chancery	1891-011
Turner	Edward C.	Guardian Acct.	3/1877	Fauquier Co.	Chancery	1891-011
Turner	Edward C.	Guardian Acct.	2/1874	Fauquier Co.	Chancery	1891-011
Turner	Edward C.	Guardian Acct.	7/27/1870	Fauquier Co.	Chancery	1891-011
Turner	Edward C.	Will	3/23/1891	Fauquier Co.	Chancery	1900-058
Turner	Edward C's Children	Guardian Acct.	12/1/1872	Fauquier Co.	Chancery	1891-011

Consolidated Probate Index from the Clerks Loose Papers & the Superior Court/Circuit Court Records 1759-1919

Surname	**Given Name**	**Instrument**	**Date**	**County**	**CLP Record Series**	**Index #**
TURNER (Cont.)						
Turner	Eliza R.	Guardian Acct.	11/10/1868	Fauquier Co.	Chancery	1891-011
Turner	Eliza R.	Guardian Acct.	7/27/1870	Fauquier Co.	Chancery	1891-011
Turner	Eliza R.	Guardian Acct.	2/1872	Fauquier Co.	Chancery	1891-011
Turner	Eliza R.	Guardian Acct.	11/18/1872	Fauquier Co.	Chancery	1891-011
Turner	Eliza R.	Guardian Acct.	11/30/1874	Fauquier Co.	Chancery	1891-011
Turner	Eliza R.	Guardian Acct.	3/1877	Fauquier Co.	Chancery	1891-011
Turner	Eliza R.	Guardian Acct.	6/1879	Fauquier Co.	Chancery	1891-011
Turner	Eliza R.	Guardian Acct.	4/1881	Fauquier Co.	Chancery	1891-011
Turner	J. T.	Report of Division	9/1887	Fauquier Co.	Chancery	1887-023
Turner	J. T.	Plat & Survey Of Division	9/1887	Fauquier Co.	Chancery	1887-023
Turner	John	Exors. Bond	1815	Fauquier Co.	Probate, Box 47	1815-024
Turner	Mary B.	Guardian Acct.	11/10/1868	Fauquier Co.	Chancery	1891-011
Turner	Mary B.	Guardian Acct.	7/27/1870	Fauquier Co.	Chancery	1891-011
Turner	Mary B.	Guardian Acct.	2/1872	Fauquier Co.	Chancery	1891-011
Turner	Mary B.	Guardian Acct.	5/29/1872	Fauquier Co.	Chancery	1891-011
Turner	Mary B.	Guardian Acct.	11/18/1872	Fauquier Co.	Chancery	1891-011
Turner	Mary B.	Guardian Acct.	11/20/1874	Fauquier Co.	Chancery	1891-011
Turner	Mary B.	Guardian Acct.	3/1877	Fauquier Co.	Chancery	1891-011
Turner	Mary B.	Guardian Acct.	6/1879	Fauquier Co.	Chancery	1891-011
Turner	Nathan L.	Guardian Acct.	11/10/1868	Fauquier Co.	Chancery	1891-011
Turner	Nathan L.	Guardian Acct.	7/27/1870	Fauquier Co.	Chancery	1891-011
Turner	Nathan L.	Guardian Acct.	5/29/1872	Fauquier Co.	Chancery	1891-011
Turner	Nathan L.	Guardian Acct.	11/18/1872	Fauquier Co.	Chancery	1891-011
Turner	Nathan L.	Guardian Acct.	2/1874	Fauquier Co.	Chancery	1891-011
Turner	Nathan L.	Guardian Acct.	11/30/1874	Fauquier Co.	Chancery	1891-011
Turner	Nathan L.	Guardian Acct.	3/1877	Fauquier Co.	Chancery	1891-011
Turner	Nathan L.	Guardian Acct.	6/1879	Fauquier Co.	Chancery	1891-011

Consolidated Probate Index from the Clerks Loose Papers & the Superior Court/Circuit Court Records 1759-1919

Surname	Given Name	Instrument	Date	County	CLP Record Series	Index #
TURNER (Cont.)						
Turner	Nathan L.	Guardian Acct.	4/1881	Fauquier Co.	Chancery	1891-011
Turner	Nathan L.	Guardian Acct.	3/30/1889	Fauquier Co.	Chancery	1891-011
Turner	Robert F.	Guardian Appt.	7/22/1867	Fauquier Co.	Chancery	1891-011
Turner	Robert F.	Guardian Acct.	11/10/1868	Fauquier Co.	Chancery	1891-011
Turner	Robert F.	Guardian Acct.	7/27/1870	Fauquier Co.	Chancery	1891-011
Turner	Robert F.	Guardian Acct.	5/29/1872	Fauquier Co.	Chancery	1891-011
Turner	Robert F.	Guardian Acct.	11/18/1872	Fauquier Co.	Chancery	1891-011
Turner	Robert F.	Guardian Acct.	2/1874	Fauquier Co.	Chancery	1891-011
TUTT						
Tutt	Archibald	Admr. Acct.	4/18/1836	Culpeper Co. VA.	Chancery	1866-076
TWENTYMAN						
Twentyman	Edward	Admr. Bond	1760	Fauquier Co.	Probate, Box 44	1760-008
TYLER						
Tyler	George G.	Estate Papers	1811-1824	Fauquier Co.	Probate, Box 41	1811-001 to 1824-001
Tyler	Mary	Admr. Bond	1766	Fauquier Co.	Probate, Box 44	1766-006
TYSON						
Tyson	Joseph	Admr. Bond	9/7/1858	Fauquier Co.	Probate, Box 52 Superior/Circuit Ct.	1858-009
Tyson	Joseph	Admr. Bond	4/6/1861	Fauquier Co.	Probate, Box 52 Superior/Circuit Ct.	1861-001

Consolidated Probate Index from the Clerks Loose Papers & the Superior Court/Circuit Court Records 1759-1919

Surname	Given Name	Instrument	Date	County	CLP Record Series	Index #
ULLMAN						
Ullman	Adolph	Will	9/11/1882	Fauquier Co.	Chancery	1891-048
URTON						
Urton	John	Guardian Bond	1815	Fauquier Co.	Probate, Box 49	1815-001
Urton	Minor	Guardian Bond	1815	Fauquier Co.	Probate, Box 49	1815-001
Urton	Phebe	Guardian Bond	1815	Fauquier Co.	Probate, Box 49	1815-001
Urton	Phebe	Guardian Bond	1817	Fauquier Co.	Probate, Box 49	1817-024
Urton	William	Will	3/3/1815	Fauquier Co.	Probate, Box 39	1815-001
Urton	William	Admrs. Bond	1815	Fauquier Co.	Probate, Box 47	1815-060
Urton	William	Division	1816	Fauquier Co.	Chancery	1824-019
UTTERBACK						
Utterback	Armistead	Plat & Survey Of Division	2/5/1866	Fauquier Co.	Chancery	1866-065
Utterback	Benjamin	Admr. Bond	1813	Fauquier Co.	Probate, Box 47	1813-018
Utterback	Martin	Will	7/14/1880	Fauquier Co.	Probate, Box 50 Addendum Folder	1880-001
Utterback	William	Inventory + Appraisement	8/15/1848	Fauquier Co.	Chancery	1859-045
Utterback	William	Division of Slaves	8/30/1848	Fauquier Co.	Chancery	1859-045
VANHORN						
Vanhorn	Burr W.	Will	5/28/1883	Fauquier Co.	Probate, Box 50 Addendum Folder	1883-001
VASS						
Vass	Anna E.	Will	8/18/1890	Culpeper Co. VA.	Chancery	1906-051
VIOLETT						
Violett	Ashford	Admr. Bond	1/25/1841	Fauquier Co.	Chancery	1869-023
VOWLES						
Vowles	Newton	Admr. Appt.	7/26/1875	Fauquier Co.	Chancery	1881-047
Vowles	Richard	Admr. Bond	1796	Fauquier Co.	Probate, Box 46	1796-002

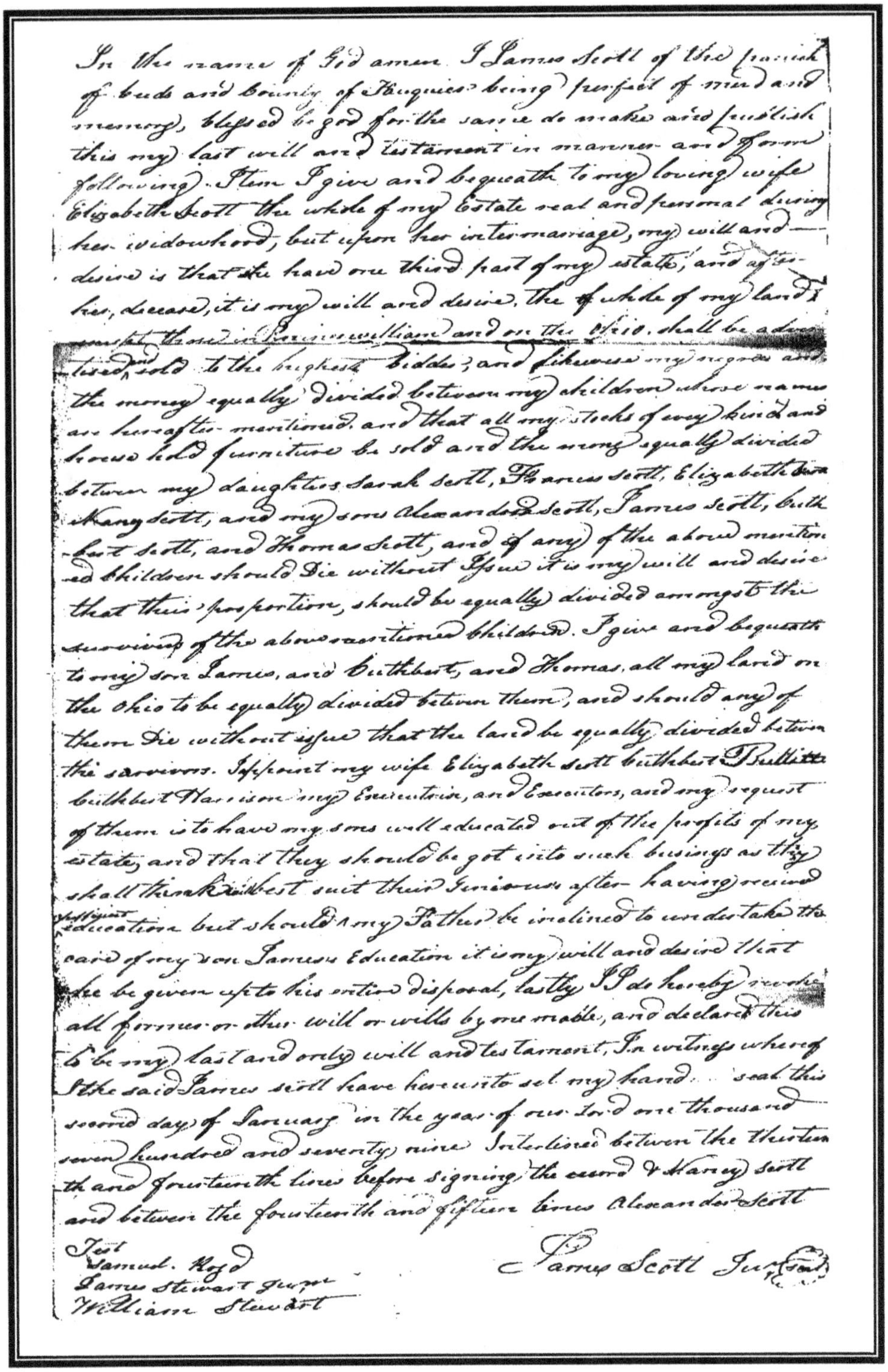
In the name of God amen I James Scott of the parish
of Leeds and County of Fauquier being perfect of mind and
memory, blessed be god for the same do make and publish
this my last will and testament in manner and form
following. Item I give and bequeath to my loving wife
Elizabeth Scott the whole of my Estate real and personal during
her widowhood, but upon her intermarriage, my will and
desire is that she have one third part of my estate, and after
her decease, it is my will and desire, the whole of my lands
except those in Prince william and on the Ohio. shall be adver-
tised and sold to the highest bidder; and likewise my negroes and
the money equally divided between my children whose names
are hereafter mentioned. and that all my stocks of every kind and
house hold furniture be sold and the money equally divided
between my daughters Sarah Scott, Frances Scott, Elizabeth Scott
Nancy Scott, and my sons Alexander Scott, James Scott, Cuthbert Scott, and Thomas Scott, and if any of the above mentioned children should Die without Issue it is my will and desire
that their proportion, should be equally divided amongst the
surviving of the above mentioned children. I give and bequeath
to my son James, and Cuthbert, and Thomas, all my land on
the Ohio to be equally divided between them, and should any of
them Die without issue that the land be equally divided between
the survivors. I appoint my wife Elizabeth Scott Cuthbert Bullitt
Cuthbert Harrison my Executrix, and Executors, and my request
of them is to have my sons well educated out of the profits of my
estate, and that they should be got into such business as they
shall think will best suit their Geniouses after having received
sufficient education but should my Father be inclined to undertake the
care of my son James's Education it is my will and desire that
he be given up to his entire disposal, lastly I do hereby revoke
all former or other will or wills by me made, and declare this
to be my last and only will and testament, In witness whereof
I the said James Scott have hereunto set my hand & seal this
second day of January in the year of our Lord one thousand
seven hundred and seventy nine Interlined between the thirteen
th and fourteenth lines before signing the word & Nancy Scott
and between the fourteenth and fifteen lines Alexander Scott

Test
Samuel. Hogg
James Stewart Junr
William Stewart

James Scott Jur (Seal)

Plate 7. Probate, Scanned Image from Box 50. Clerks Copies/Unrecorded Deeds. 1779-001. James Scott's Will.

Consolidated Probate Index from the Clerks Loose Papers & the Superior Court/Circuit Court Records 1759-1919

Surname	Given Name	Instrument	Date	County	CLP Record Series	Index #
WADDELL						
Waddell	Francis	Guardian Bond	1802	Fauquier Co.	Probate, Box 48	1802-005
WAGENER (See also Waggoner)						
Wagener	Peter	Will	10/1/1795	Fairfax Co. VA.	Chancery	1848-032
Wagener	Peter	Will	10/15/1798	Fairfax Co. VA.	Chancery	1851-002
Wagener	Sinah	Nuncupative Will	1/15/1810	Fairfax Co. VA.	Chancery	1848-032
Wagener	Sinah	Nuncupative Will	1/15/1810	Fairfax Co. VA.	Chancery	1851-002
WAGER						
Wager	H. D.	Estate committed To Sheriff	4/4/1906	Fauquier Co.	Probate, Box 56 Superior/Circuit Ct.	1906-002
Wager	John	Inventory + Appraisement	Undated	Jefferson Co. WV	Chancery	1848-011
Wager	John	Sales	11/15/1803	Jefferson Co. WV	Chancery	1848-011
Wager	John	Plat & Survey Of Division in Jefferson Co. WV	1804	Jefferson Co. WV	Chancery	1848-011
Wager	John	Admr. Acct.	2/18/1808	Jefferson Co. WV	Chancery	1848-011
Wager	John	Admr. Acct.	2/21/1808	Jefferson Co. WV	Chancery	1848-011
WAGGONER (See also Wagener)						
Waggoner	Peter	Will	10/15/1798	Fairfax Co. VA.	Probate, Box 39	1793-006
WAITE (See also Wate)						
Waite	Jane	Will	12/22/1794	Fauquier Co.	Chancery	1802-005
WALDEN						
Walden	Betsy	Will	9/223/1832	Fauquier Co.	Probate, Box 50	1832-002
Walden	Betsy	Will	9/26/1832	Fauquier Co.	Chancery	1838-002
Walden	John	Plat & Survey Of Sub-Division of Carter Run Tract	9/13/1865	Fauquier Co.	Chancery	1902-023
WALKER						
Walker	Frances	Relinquishment	1/1830	Fauquier Co.	Probate, Box 40	1830-002
Walker	Frances	Dower Allotment (in Comr. Report)	1832	Fauquier Co.	Chancery	1832-043
Walker	John	Admr. Acct.	1/28/1833	Fauquier Co.	Probate, Box 50	1833-001
Walker	Samuel	Will	12/23/1872	San Francisco, CA.	Chancery	1902-041

Consolidated Probate Index from the Clerks Loose Papers & the Superior Court/Circuit Court Records 1759-1919

Surname	Given Name	Instrument	Date	County	CLP Record Series	Index #
WALKER (Cont.)						
Walker	William	Inventory	1773	Fauquier Co.	Probate, Box 39	1773-001
WALL (See also Walls)						
Wall	Armistead	Exor. Acct.	3/13/1854	Fauquier Co.	Chancery	1855-035
WALLACE						
Wallace	Elizabeth	Will	11/30/1833	Fauquier Co.	Chancery	1868-232
Wallace	James W. M.	Will	10/31/1833	Fauquier Co.	Chancery	1838-029
Wallace	James W. M.	Will	1/28/1834	Fauquier Co.	Chancery	1853-014
Wallace	James W. M.	Division of Slaves	1/28/1834	Fauquier Co.	Chancery	1853-014
Wallace	John Robert	Will	2/1852	Fauquier Co.	Probate, Box 50	1852-001
Wallace	John Robert	Will	4/1849	Fauquier Co.	Chancery	1866-011
Wallace	John Robert	Exor. Acct. Settled	11/24/1852	Alexandria, VA.	Chancery	1866-011
Wallace	John R.	Admr. Appt.	6/9/1866	Alexandria, VA.	Chancery	1867-003
Wallace	Margaret	Will	4/20/1859	Fauquier Co.	Chancery	1869-009
Wallace	Margaret H.	Will	4/20/1859	Fauquier Co.	Probate, Box 52 Superior/Circuit Ct.	1859-004
Wallace	Margaret M.	Exor. Acct.	9/6/1859	Fauquier Co.	Probate, Box 52 Superior/Circuit Ct.	1859-007
WALLS (See also Wall)						
Walls	Sarah	Exor. Acct.	1807	Fauquier Co.	Probate, Box 46	1807-020
WALTER (See also Walters)						
Walter	William	Relinquishment	12/1818	Fauquier Co.	Probate, Box 39	1818-013
WALTERS (See also Walter)						
Walters	John	Admr. Bond	1810	Fauquier Co.	Probate, Box 47	1810-010
Walters	Nancy	Guardian Bond	1816	Fauquier Co.	Probate, Box 49	1816-007
WALTON						
Walton	Susan	Admr. Appt.	11/28/1904	Fauquier Co.	Probate, Box 55 Superior/Circuit Ct.	1904-007
WARD						
Ward	Berkeley	Will	5/28/1860	Fauquier Co.	Chancery	1888-002
Ward	Berkley	Will	5/28/1860	Fauquier Co.	Chancery	1880-047
Ward	Berkley	Appraisement	9/24/1860	Fauquier Co.	Chancery	1880-047
Ward	Berkley	Division	9/24/1860	Fauquier Co.	Chancery	1880-047

Consolidated Probate Index from the Clerks Loose Papers & the Superior Court/Circuit Court Records 1759-1919

Surname	Given Name	Instrument	Date	County	CLP Record Series	Index #
WARD (Cont.)						
Ward	Berkley	Division of Slaves	9/24/1860	Fauquier Co.	Chancery	1880-047
Ward	Berkley	Sales	10/28/1861	Fauquier Co.	Chancery	1880-047
Ward	Berkeley	Admr. Acct.	5/29/1873	Fauquier Co.	Chancery	1897-044
Ward	Berkeley	Admr. Acct.	1/27/1874	Fauquier Co.	Chancery	1897-044
Ward	Berkeley	Admr. Acct.	2/26/1878	Fauquier Co.	Chancery	1897-044
Ward	Berkeley	Admr. Acct.	4/30/1884	Fauquier Co.	Chancery	1897-044
Ward	F. G.	Appraisement	11/26/1880	Fauquier Co.	Probate, Box 54	1880-008
Ward	Henry C.	Will	10/28/1861	Fauquier Co.	Chancery	1880-047
Ward	Henry C.	Extrx. Bond	11/25/1861	Fauquier Co.	Chancery	1880-047
Ward	Henry C.	Will	10/28/1861	Fauquier Co.	Chancery	1897-048
Ward	John	Admr. Bond	4/22/1885	Fauquier Co.	Probate, Box 54 Superior/Circuit Ct.	1885-003
Ward	Martha	Will	5/18/1863	Culpeper Co. VA.	Chancery	1875-006
Ward	Martha	Will	5/18/1863	Culpeper Co. VA.	Chancery	1881-032
Ward	Martha	Will	5/18/1863	Culpeper Co. VA.	Chancery	1882-012
Ward	P. G.	Will	4/20/1880	Fauquier Co.	Probate, Box 54	1880-003
Ward	P. G.	Exor. Bond	4/20/1880	Fauquier Co.	Probate, Box 54	1880-003
WARDER						
Warder	E. A.	Report of Partition	9/1880	Fauquier Co.	Chancery	1893-032
WASHINGTON						
Washington	Augustine	Will	5/6/1743	King George Co. VA.	Land Records & Disputes	1799-011
Washington	George	Will	1/20/1800	Fairfax Co. VA.	Land Records & Disputes	1812-009
Washington	John A.	Will	10/31/1861	Fauquier Co.	Chancery	1886-041
Washington	John A.	Division	4/15/1865	Fauquier Co.	Chancery	1886-041
Washington	John A.	Will	10/31/1861	Fauquier Co.	Chancery	1886-050
Washington	John A.	Admr. Acct.	7/17/1874	Fauquier Co.	Chancery	1886-050
Washington	Mary D.	Admr. Acct.	12/19/1836	Fauquier Co.	Probate, Box 51 Superior/Circuit Ct.	1836-004

Consolidated Probate Index from the Clerks Loose Papers & the Superior Court/Circuit Court Records 1759-1919

Surname	Given Name	Instrument	Date	County	CLP Record Series	Index #
WASHINGTON (Cont.)						
Washington	Olivia H.	Will	11/22/1847	Calvert Co. MD.	Chancery	1875-074
Washington	Olivia H.	Exor. Acct.	11/13/1855	Fauquier Co.	Chancery	1875-074
Washington	Robert	Affidavit about His Lunacy	10/11/1847	Fauquier Co.	Chancery	1851-011
WATE (See also Waite)						
Wate	Ann E.	Transfer of Adm.. Of Estate	7/16/1907	Fauquier Co.	Probate, Box 56 Superior/Circuit Ct.	1907-010
WATERHOUSE						
Waterhouse	Charles	Admr. Bond	1793	Fauquier Co.	Probate, Box 46	1793-001
WATKIN (See also Watkins)						
Watkin	William	Admtrx. Bond	10/5/1841	Fauquier Co.	Probate, Box 51 Superior/Circuit Ct.	1841-001
Watkin	William	Inventory + Appraisement	10/4/1842	Fauquier Co.	Probate, Box 51 Superior/Circuit Ct.	1842-001
Watkin	William	Admtrx. Acct.	5/1842	Fauquier Co.	Probate, Box 51 Superior/Circuit Ct.	1842-001
Watkin	William	Estate Acct.	10/3/1843	Fauquier Co.	Probate, Box 51 Superior/Circuit Ct.	1843-002
WATKINS (See also Watkin)						
Watkins	Jane	Will	3/24/1845	Fauquier Co.	Chancery	1859-025
Watkins	Jane	Will	3/24/1845	Fauquier Co.	Chancery	1869-052
Watkins	Jane	Admr. Appt.	9/29/1852	Fauquier Co.	Chancery	1869-052
Watkins	Jane	Will	3/24/1848	Fauquier Co.	Chancery	1877-026
Watkins	William	Admr. Bond	5/18/1841	Fauquier Co.	Chancery	1854-037
Watkins	William	Admr. Acct.	5/4/1842	Fauquier Co.	Chancery	1854-037
Watkins	William	Inventory + Appraisement	10/4/1842	Fauquier Co.	Chancery	1854-037
WATTS						
Watts	Bennett	Guardian Bond	1770	Fauquier Co.	Probate, Box 48	1770-002
Watts	Bennett	Guardian Bond	1773	Fauquier Co.	Probate, Box 48	1773-001
Watts	Bennett	Guardian Bond	1775	Fauquier Co.	Probate, Box 48	1775-003
Watts	Francis	Admr. Bond	1770	Fauquier Co.	Probate, Box 44	1770-004
Watts	Mary	Guardian Bond	1770	Fauquier Co.	Probate, Box 44	1770-002

Consolidated Probate Index from the Clerks Loose Papers & the Superior Court/Circuit Court Records 1759-1919

Surname	Given Name	Instrument	Date	County	CLP Record Series	Index #
WATTS (Cont.)						
Watts	Mary	Guardian Bond	1783	Fauquier Co.	Probate, Box 48	1783-002
Watts	Mason	Guardian Bond	1770	Fauquier Co.	Probate, Box 48	1770-002
Watts	Molly	Guardian Bond	1778	Fauquier Co.	Probate, Box 48	1778-005
Watts	Peggy Ann	Guardian Bond	1761	Fauquier Co.	Probate, Box 48	1761-001
Watts	Thomas	Admtrx. Bond	1769	Fauquier Co.	Probate, Box 44	1761-001
WAUGH						
Waugh	Mary	Will	3/27/1749	Stafford Co. VA.	Land Records & Disputes	1811-015
Waugh	Mary	Will	3/1758	Stafford Co. VA.	Land Records & Disputes	1769-001
Waugh	Tabitha	Will	4/9/1868	Fauquier Co.	Probate, Box 53	1868-001
Waugh	Tabitha	Exor. Bond	4/9/1868	Fauquier Co.	Probate, Box 53	1868-001
Waugh	Tabitha	Admr. Acct.	12/9/1877	Fauquier Co.	Probate, Box 54	1877-007
WAY						
Way	Emily	Guardian Bond	1816	Fauquier Co.	Probate, Box 49	1816-006
Way	Henry	Admr. Bond	1815	Fauquier Co.	Probate, Box 47	1815-035
Way	Mary	Renunciation	1815	Fauquier Co.	Probate, Box 39	1815-035
WEAVER						
Weaver	Charles	Plat & Survey Of Division	10/1873	Fauquier Co.	Chancery	1876-060
Weaver	Christina	Division of Dower Allotment (Extract)	4/4/1903	Fauquier Co.	Chancery	1906-021
Weaver	Jacob	Admr. Bond	10/5/1841	Fauquier Co.	Probate, Box 51 Superior/Circuit Ct.	1841-002
Weaver	Jacob	Inventory + Appraisement	10/4/1842	Fauquier Co.	Probate, Box 51 Superior/Circuit Ct.	1842-003
Weaver	Jacob	Sales	10/4/1842	Fauquier Co.	Probate, Box 51 Superior/Circuit Ct.	1842-004
Weaver	Jacob	Admr. Bond	10/3/1843	Fauquier Co.	Probate, Box 51 Superior/Circuit Ct.	1843-004
Weaver	Jacob	Estate Acct.	5/10/1844	Fauquier Co.	Probate, Box 51 Superior/Circuit Ct.	1844-001
Weaver	Jacob	Admr. Acct.	5/5/1846	Fauquier Co.	Probate, Box 51 Superior/Circuit Ct.	1846-003

Consolidated Probate Index from the Clerks Loose Papers & the Superior Court/Circuit Court Records 1759-1919

Surname	Given Name	Instrument	Date	County	CLP Record Series	Index #
WEAVER (Cont.)						
Weaver	Jacob	Admr. Acct.	5/2/1848	Fauquier Co.	Probate, Box 51 Superior/Circuit Ct.	1848-004
Weaver	Jacob	Admr. Acct.	10/8/1850	Fauquier Co.	Probate, Box 52 Superior/Circuit Ct.	1850-007
Weaver	Jacob	Report of Division Of Slaves	4/27/1841	Fauquier Co.	Chancery	1842-071
Weaver	Jacob	Report of Division	10/28/1842	Fauquier Co.	Chancery	1842-071
Weaver	Jacob	Plat & Survey Of Division	10/28/1842	Fauquier Co.	Chancery	1842-071
Weaver	Jacob	Admr. Bond	10/3/1843	Fauquier Co.	Chancery	1846-054
Weaver	Jacob	Admr. Bond	10/3/1843	Fauquier Co.	Chancery	1848-028
Weaver	Jacob	Admr. Bond	5/4/1844	Fauquier Co.	Chancery	1888-040
Weaver	Jacob	Admr. Acct.	4/6/1870	Fauquier Co.	Probate, Box 53 Superior/Circuit Ct.	1870-001
Weaver	Jacob	Admr. Bond	12/16/1874	Fauquier Co.	Probate, Box 53 Superior/Circuit Ct.	1874-010
Weaver	James	Exor. Bond	1814	Fauquier Co.	Probate, Box 47	1814-005
Weaver	James	Division of Slaves	4/1/1843	Fauquier Co.	Chancery	1842-058
Weaver	Janet C.	Will	10/29/1895	Fauquier Co.	Chancery	1896-032
Weaver	Joseph	Report of Division	12/23/1852	Fauquier Co.	Chancery	1855-087
Weaver	Joseph	Plat & Survey Of Division	12/23/1852	Fauquier Co.	Chancery	1855-087
Weaver	Oscar	Heirs	8/26/1873	Fauquier Co.	Chancery	1871-095
Weaver	Samuel	Admtrx. Acct.	11/25/1835	Fauquier Co.	Probate, Box 50	1833-003
Weaver	Samuel	Admr. Bond	6/21/1831	Fauquier Co.	Chancery	1867-004
Weaver	Samuel	Admr. Acct.	9/1835	Fauquier Co.	Chancery	1867-004
Weaver	Samuel	Survey of 1837 Division (Abstract)	10/16/1902	Fauquier Co.	Chancery	1906-021
Weaver	Samuel	1837 Division of Slaves (Abstract)	10/16/1902	Fauquier Co.	Chancery	1906-021
Weaver	Samuel Estate	Plat & Survey of Dower Allotment	12/23/1869	Fauquier Co.	Chancery	1906-021

Consolidated Probate Index from the Clerks Loose Papers & the Superior Court/Circuit Court Records 1759-1919

Surname	**Given Name**	**Instrument**	**Date**	**County**	**CLP Record Series**	**Index #**
WEAVER (Cont.)						
Weaver	Sarah	Plat & Survey Of Division	3/15/1879	Fauquier Co.	Chancery	1890-026
Weaver	Tilman	Will	3/27/1760	Fauquier Co.	Chancery	1811-046
Weaver	Tilman	Will	3/27/1760	Fauquier Co.	Probate, Box 39	1759-001
Weaver	Tilman	Exors. Bond	1760	Fauquier Co.	Probate, Box 44	1760-001
Weaver	Tilman	Inventory of Slaves	5/22/1809	Fauquier Co.	Chancery	1888-040
Weaver	Tilman	Curator Acct.	5/22/1809	Fauquier Co.	Chancery	1888-040
Weaver	Tilman	Will	5/22/1809	Fauquier Co.	Chancery	1888-040
Weaver	Tilman	Exors. Bond	1809	Fauquier Co.	Probate, Box 47	1809-020
Weaver	William	Admr. Bond	10/3/1843	Fauquier Co.	Probate, Box 51 Superior/Circuit Ct.	1843-003
Weaver	William	Inventory + Appraisement	10/14/1844	Fauquier Co.	Probate, Box 51	1844-003
Weaver	William	Sales	10/14/1844	Fauquier Co.	Probate, Box 51 Superior/Circuit Ct.	1844-004
Weaver	William	Admr. Acct.	5/5/1846	Fauquier Co.	Probate, Box 51 Superior/Circuit Ct.	1846-002
Weaver	William	Admr. Acct.	5/2/1848	Fauquier Co.	Probate, Box 51 Superior/Circuit Ct.	1848-002
Weaver	William	Admr. Acct.	10/8/1850	Fauquier Co.	Probate, Box 52 Superior/Circuit Ct.	1850-006
Weaver	William	Admr. Bond	10/3/1843	Fauquier Co.	Chancery	1846-054
Weaver	William	Report of Division Of 52 Slaves	12/26/1843	Fauquier Co.	Chancery	1848-073
Weaver	William	Report of Division	4/16/1844	Fauquier Co.	Chancery	1848-073
Weaver	William	Plat & Survey Of Division	4/16/1844	Fauquier Co.	Chancery	1848-073
Weaver	William	Report of Division Of Slaves	12/26/1843	Fauquier Co.	Chancery	1898-032
Weaver	William	Inventory + Appraisement (Extract)	1/16/1866	Fauquier Co.	Chancery	1898-032

Consolidated Probate Index from the Clerks Loose Papers & the Superior Court/Circuit Court Records 1759-1919

Surname	Given Name	Instrument	Date	County	CLP Record Series	Index #
WEAVER (Cont.)						
Weaver	William S.	Plat & Survey of Division of Kettle Run Tract	Undated	Fauquier Co.	Chancery	1902-007
WEBB						
Webb	John	Extrx. Bond	1778	Fauquier Co.	Probate, Box 45	1778-008
Webb	John	Exor. Bond	1778	Fauquier Co.	Probate, Box 45	1778-018
Webb	John	Guardian Bond	1778	Fauquier Co.	Probate, Box 48	1778-008
Webb	John F.	Plat & Survey Of Division	2/28/1901	Fauquier Co.	Chancery	1903-045
Webb	Priscilla	Guardian Bond	1770	Fauquier Co.	Probate, Box 48	1770-002
Webb	Priscilla	Guardian Bond	1778	Fauquier Co.	Probate, Box 48	1778-008
Webb	Williamson	Guardian Bond	1778	Fauquier Co.	Probate, Box 48	1778-008
WEEDON						
Weedon	Eliza	Guardian Bond	1817	Fauquier Co.	Probate, Box 49	1817-019
Weedon	Elizabeth	Guardian Bond	1817	Fauquier Co.	Probate, Box 49	1817-019
Weedon	John	Admr. Bond	1776	Fauquier Co.	Probate, Box 44	1776-001
Weedon	Nancy Drummond	Plat & Survey Of Dower Allotment	4/5/1872	Fauquier Co.	Chancery	1878-002
WEEKS						
Weeks	Mary	Admr. Acct.	9/8/1888	Fauquier Co.	Probate, Box 54 Superior/Circuit Ct.	1888-002
Weeks	Mary	Admr. Acct.	4/6/1897	Fauquier Co.	Probate, Box 54 Superior/Circuit Ct.	1897-002
Weeks	Virginia	Admr. Appt.	3/5/1909	Fauquier Co.	Probate, Box 56 Superior/Circuit Ct.	1909-005
WEIR						
Weir	Sarah	Will	2/25/1901	Fauquier Co.	Chancery	1907-012
WELCH						
Welch	Alexander	Will	4/1834	Fauquier Co.	Chancery	1836-019
Welch	Alexander	Will	4/29/1834	Fauquier Co.	Chancery	1838-013
Welch	James	Will	4/27/1837	Fauquier Co.	Chancery	1843-062
Welch	Joseph	Will	1/15/1750/51	Pr. Wm. Co. VA.	Land Records & Disputes	1767-003

Consolidated Probate Index from the Clerks Loose Papers & the Superior Court/Circuit Court Records 1759-1919

Surname	Given Name	Instrument	Date	County	CLP Record Series	Index #
WELCH (Cont.)						
Welch	Sarah	Will	8/26/1751	Pr. Wm. Co. VA.	Land Records & Disputes	1767-003
Welch	Sarah	Exor. Acct.	2/23/1756	Pr. Wm. Co. VA.	Land Records & Disputes	1767-003
Welch	Sylvester	Will	10/28/1833	Fauquier Co.	Chancery	1843-062
Welch	Sylvester	Will	5/1834	Fauquier Co.	Chancery	1867-005
Welch	Sylvester Sr.	Will	5/1834	Fauquier Co.	Chancery	1836-038
Welch	Sylvester Sr.	Division of Slaves	1/27/1836	Fauquier Co.	Chancery	1836-038
WEST						
West	James	Admr. Bond	7/3/1780	Fauquier Co.	Chancery	1809-063
West	James	Admr. Acct. Settled	1780	Fauquier Co.	Chancery	1809-063
West	Richard	Report of Partition	5/5/1902	Fauquier Co.	Chancery	1907-038
West	Richard	Plat & Survey Of Partition	5/5/1902	Fauquier Co.	Chancery	1907-038
West	Silas M.	Appraisement	3/30/1836	Fauquier Co.	Probate, Box 50	1835-001
WHARTON						
Wharton	William	Will (Extract)	8/16/1858	Culpeper Co. VA.	Chancery	1894-082
WHEATLEY (See also Whitley)						
Wheatley	Ann C.	Admr. Bond	10/4/1851	Fauquier Co.	Probate, Box 52 Superior/Circuit Ct.	1851-012
Wheatley	Honor	Guardian Bond	1771	Fauquier Co.	Probate, Box 48	1771-004
Wheatley	James	Admr. Acct. Settled	1795	Fauquier Co.	Chancery	1811-027
Wheatley	James	Division	4/25/1795	Fauquier Co.	Chancery	1811-027
Wheatley	James	Inventory + Appraisement	4/27/1795	Fauquier Co.	Chancery	1868-210
Wheatley	James	Inventory of Slaves	Undated	Fauquier Co.	Chancery	1868-210
Wheatley	James	Report of Division Of Slaves	4/27/1795	Fauquier Co.	Chancery	1868-210
Wheatley	James	Admr. Acct.	1/20/1798	Fauquier Co.	Chancery	1868-210
Wheatley	James	Guardian Bond	1811	Fauquier Co.	Probate, Box 49	1811-012

Consolidated Probate Index from the Clerks Loose Papers & the Superior Court/Circuit Court Records 1759-1919

Surname	Given Name	Instrument	Date	County	CLP Record Series	Index #
WHEATLEY (Cont.)						
Wheatley	John	Inventory + Appraisement	6/27/1796	Fauquier Co.	Chancery	1868-210
Wheatley	John	Admr. Bond	1808	Fauquier Co.	Probate, Box 46	1808-015
Wheatley	John L.	Admr. Bond	1806	Fauquier Co.	Probate, Box 46	1806-003
Wheatley	Joseph	Guardian Bond	1762	Fauquier Co.	Probate, Box 48	1762-003
Wheatley	Joseph	Admr. Acct.	12/28/1795	Fauquier Co.	Chancery	1868-210
Wheatley	Joseph	Admr. Acct.	3/1799	Fauquier Co.	Chancery	1868-210
Wheatley	Joseph	Division	6/4/1799	Fauquier Co.	Chancery	1868-210
Wheatley	Joseph	Sales	10/23/1820	Fauquier Co.	Chancery	1868-210
Wheatley	Landon	Guardian Bond	1804	Fauquier Co.	Probate, Box 48	1804-005
Wheatley	Shadrach	Guardian Bond	1811	Fauquier Co.	Probate, Box 49	1811-012
Wheatley	Thornton	Guardian Bond	1808	Fauquier Co.	Probate, Box 49	1808-007
Wheatley	William	Guardian Bond	1796	Fauquier Co.	Probate, Box 48	1796-003
WHITE						
White	Arian	Guardian Bond	1813	Fauquier Co.	Probate, Box 49	1813-006
White	Armistead	Guardian Bond	1812	Fauquier Co.	Probate, Box 49	1812-001
White	C. B.	Appraisement of Real Estate	8/31/1854	Fauquier Co.	Probate, Box 52 Superior/Circuit Ct.	1854-002
White	Caroline	Appraisement of Real Estate	Undated	Fauquier Co.	Chancery	1872-041
White	Caroline B.	Will	4/5/1853	Fauquier Co.	Probate, Box 52 Superior/Circuit Ct.	1853-003
White	Caroline Battaile	Will	4/5/1853	Fauquier Co.	Chancery	1888-002
White	Eliza	Dower Allotment	11/5/1881	Fauquier Co.	Chancery	1883-035
White	James W.	Guardian Bond	1813	Fauquier Co.	Probate, Box 49	1813-006
White	John	Exor. Bond	1806	Fauquier Co.	Probate, Box 49	1806-030
White	John	Will	6/28/1841	Fauquier Co.	Chancery	1872-045
White	John	Exor. Acct.	11/1843	Fauquier Co.	Probate, Box 40	1843-005
White	Margaret	Guardian Bond	1817	Fauquier Co.	Probate, Box 49	1817-023

Consolidated Probate Index from the Clerks Loose Papers & the Superior Court/Circuit Court Records 1759-1919

Surname	Given Name	Instrument	Date	County	CLP Record Series	Index #
WHITE (Cont.)						
White	Nancy	Guardian Bond	1812	Fauquier Co.	Probate, Box 49	1812-001
White	Nancy	Guardian Bond	1814	Fauquier Co.	Probate, Box 49	1814-004
White	Pleasant	Exors. Bond	1769	Fauquier Co.	Probate, Box 44	1769-001
White	William	Statements about His Death	5/1796	Fauquier Co.	Chancery	1808-024
White	William	Will	10/1804	Fauquier Co.	Probate, Box 40	1823-002
White	William	Court Order to Settle Admr. Acct.	9/1805	Fauquier Co.	Chancery	1808-024
White	William	Guardian Bond	1817	Fauquier Co.	Probate, Box 49	1817-008
White	William	Guardian Bond	Undated	Fauquier Co.	Probate, Box 49	No Date- 001
WHITEFORD						
Whiteford	Robert	Admr. Bond	1804	Fauquier Co.	Probate, Box 46	1804-001
WHITESCARVER						
Whitescarver	Catharine O.	Will	12/26/1859	Fauquier Co.	Chancery	1881-002
Whitescarver	George H.	Will	9/25/1865	Fauquier Co.	Chancery	1871-013
WHITING						
Whiting	Meta H.	Trustee Appt.	12/4/1908	Fauquier Co.	Probate, Box 56 Superior/Circuit Ct.	1908-018
WHITLEY (See also Wheatley)						
Whitley	John	Admtrx. Bond	1815	Fauquier Co.	Probate, Box 47	1816-032
Whitley	Susan	Will	1/26/1846	Fauquier Co.	Chancery	1855-030
Whitley	Susan	Admr. Bond	2/23/1846	Fauquier Co.	Chancery	1855-030
WIATT						
Wiatt	John	Guardian Bond	1763	Fauquier Co.	Probate, Box 47	1763-002
WICKLIFF						
Wickliff	David Jr.	Admr. Bond	1812	Fauquier Co.	Probate, Box 47	1812-019
WIGGINTON						
Wigginton	Benjamin	Sales	11/15/1827	Culpeper Co. VA.	Chancery	1833-027
Wigginton	Benjamin	Inventory + Appraisement	8/18/1828	Culpeper Co. VA.	Chancery	1833-027
Wigginton	Benjamin	Division of Slaves	12/15/1828	Fauquier Co.	Chancery	1833-027
Wigginton	Benjamin	Admr. Acct.	2/21/1829	Culpeper Co. VA.	Chancery	1833-027

Consolidated Probate Index from the Clerks Loose Papers & the Superior Court/Circuit Court Records 1759-1919

Surname	Given Name	Instrument	Date	County	CLP Record Series	Index #
WIGGINTON (Cont.)						
Wigginton	Benjamin	Admr. Acct.	9/21/1829	Culpeper Co. VA.	Chancery	1833-027
Wigginton	Benjamin	Admr. Acct.	1829	Fauquier Co.	Chancery	1833-027
Wigginton	Benjamin	Division of Slaves	3/15/1830	Culpeper Co. VA.	Chancery	1833-027
Wigginton	Benjamin	Admr. Acct.	1832	Culpeper Co. VA.	Chancery	1833-027
WILLIAMS						
Williams	---- [No Name Found]	Report of Division	2/14/1902	Fauquier Co.	Chancery	1902-038
Williams	---- [No Name Found]	Plat & Survey Of Division	2/14/1902	Fauquier Co.	Chancery	1902-038
Williams	Elijah	Admtrx. Bond	1815	Fauquier Co.	Probate, Box 47	1815-056
Williams	George	Will	4/10/1750	Stafford Co. VA.	Chancery	1807-041
Williams	George	Exors. Bond	1786	Fauquier co.	Probate, Box 45	1786-004
Williams	Henry H.	Will	12/17/1873	Baltimore, MD.	Chancery	1874-001
Williams	Jacob T.	Admr. Bond	1813	Fauquier Co.	Probate, Box 47	1813-013
Williams	Jane	Guardian Bond	1808	Fauquier Co.	Probate, Box 49	1808-005
Williams	Mary	Admr. Acct.	1/1828	Fauquier Co.	Chancery	1839-064
Williams	Mary H.	Admr. Acct.	1/1827	Fauquier Co.	Chancery	1839-064
Williams	Mary H.	Admr. Acct.	2/21/1828	Fauquier Co.	Chancery	1839-064
Williams	Mary H.	Admr. Acct.	Undated	Fauquier Co.	Chancery	1839-064
Williams	Mary H.	Admr. Acct.	1/27/1830	Fauquier Co.	Chancery	1839-064
Williams	Mary H.	Admr. Acct.	3/23/1839	Fauquier Co.	Chancery	1839-064
Williams	Mary H.	Admr. Acct.	4/23/1839	Fauquier Co.	Chancery	1839-064
WILLIAMSON						
Williamson	George E.	Report of Division	4/1880	Fauquier Co.	Chancery	1887-041
Williamson	George E.	Plat & Survey Of Division	4/1880	Fauquier Co.	Chancery	1887-041
WILLIS						
Willis	Joel	Will	12/7/1793	Delaware Co. PA.	Chancery	1804-051
Willis	John	Will	8/26/1850	Fauquier Co.	Chancery	1872-066
Willis	John	Exor. Bond	8/26/1850	Fauquier Co.	Chancery	1872-066

Consolidated Probate Index from the Clerks Loose Papers & the Superior Court/Circuit Court Records 1759-1919

Surname	Given Name	Instrument	Date	County	CLP Record Series	Index #
WILLIS (Cont.)						
Willis	John	Sales	12/27/1850	Fauquier Co.	Chancery	1872-066
Willis	John P.	Will	8/26/1850	Fauquier Co.	Chancery	1852-063
Willis	John P.	Sales	8/9/1860	Fauquier Co.	Probate, Box 50	1850-001
Willis	Mabel	Guardian Appt.	9/9/1895	Fauquier Co.	Chancery	1903-049
Willis	Sarah	Admr. Bond	9/13/1832	Fauquier Co.	Probate, Box 51	1832-001
WILLOUGHBY						
Willoughby	John	Admr. Bond	1782	Fauquier Co.	Probate, Box 45	1782-018
WILSON						
Wilson	----- [No Name Found]	Guardian Bond	1802	Fauquier Co.	Probate, Box 49	1802-002
Wilson	Alice C.	Will	1/26/1874	Fauquier Co.	Chancery	1894-033
Wilson	Archibald	Will	11/29/1849	Fauquier Co.	Chancery	1854-008
Wilson	Archibald	Will	11/29/1855	Fauquier Co.	Chancery	1889-043
Wilson	Henry	Will	6/23/1817	Fauquier Co.	Probate, Box 50	1817-005
Wilson	Wesley	Guardian Bond	1810	Fauquier Co.	Probate, Box 49	1810-014
WINDSOR						
Windsor	Charity	Renunciation	1809	Fauquier Co.	Probate, Box 39	1809-012
Windsor	Joseph	Admr. Bond	1809	Fauquier Co.	Probate, Box 47	1809-012
WINES						
Wines	James	Admr. Appt.	9/27/1909	Fauquier Co.	Probate, Box 56 Superior/Circuit Ct.	1909-015
WINGFIELD						
Wingfield	John J.	Will	4/23/1866	Fauquier Co.	Chancery	1880-016
Wingfield	John J.	Will	4/23/1866	Fauquier Co.	Chancery	1886-059
Wingfield	John J.	Exor. Bond	7/23/1866	Fauquier Co.	Chancery	1886-059
Wingfield	John J.	Inventory	2/26/1866	Fauquier Co.	Chancery	1886-059
WINN						
Winn	Elizabeth	Guardian Bond	1817	Fauquier Co.	Probate, Box 49	1817-025
Winn	Isham	Guardian Bond	1817	Fauquier Co.	Probate, Box 49	1817-025
Winn	John H.	Exors. Bond	1815	Fauquier Co.	Probate, Box 47	1815-016
Winn	John W.	Exor. Bond	5/22/1815	Fauquier Co.	Chancery	1839-017

Consolidated Probate Index from the Clerks Loose Papers & the Superior Court/Circuit Court Records 1759-1919

Surname	Given Name	Instrument	Date	County	CLP Record Series	Index #
WINN (Cont.)						
Winn	John W.	Inventory + Appraisement	8/28/1815	Fauquier Co.	Chancery	1839-017
Winn	John W.	Sales	11/16/1815	Fauquier Co.	Chancery	1839-017
Winn	John W.	Exor. Acct.	6/23/1823	Fauquier Co.	Chancery	1839-017
Winn	John W.	Will	5/22/1815	Fauquier Co.	Chancery	1859-035
Winn	Mary	Guardian Bond	1817	Fauquier Co.	Probate, Box 49	1817-025
Winn	Minor	Exors. Bond	1778	Fauquier Co.	Probate, Box 45	1778-016
Winn	Minor	Exor. Bond	1813	Fauquier Co.	Probate, Box 47	1813-005
Winn	Minor	Exor. Bond	1813	Fauquier Co.	Probate, Box 47	1813-007
Winn	Minor	Exor. Bond	1816	Fauquier Co.	Probate, Box 47	1816-001
Winn	Minor	Guardian Bond	1817	Fauquier Co.	Probate, Box 49	1817-025
Winn	Minor	Sales	11/27/1815	Fauquier Co.	Probate, Box 50	1813-001
Winn	Minor	Will	5/22/1815	Fauquier Co.	Chancery	1839-017
Winn	Minor	Exor. Acct.	2/1816	Fauquier Co.	Chancery	1839-017
Winn	Minor	Exor. Acct.	3/1/1825	Fauquier Co.	Chancery	1839-017
Winn	Minor	Will	10/25/1813	Fauquier Co.	Chancery	1855-032
Winn	Minor	Sales	11/27/1815	Fauquier Co.	Chancery	1855-032
Winn	Minor	Exor. Acct.	3/1/1825	Fauquier Co.	Chancery	1855-032
Winn	Minor	Will	10/25/1813	Fauquier Co.	Chancery	1859-035
Winn	Minor (Capt.)	Estate Papers	Undated	Fauquier Co.	Probate, Box 39	1818-014
Winn	Minor (Capt.)	Exor. Acct.	2/1816	Fauquier Co.	Probate, Box 39	1818-014
Winn	Thomas	Guardian Bond	1817	Fauquier Co.	Probate, Box 49	1817-025
Winn	William	Guardian bond	1817	Fauquier Co.	Probate, Box 49	1817-025
WINSTON						
Winston	Hamilton B.	Will	2/28/1885	Fauquier Co.	Chancery	1886-028
WISER						
Wiser	Thomas	Heirs	1/24/1859	Fauquier Co.	Military Records	1859-001

Consolidated Probate Index from the Clerks Loose Papers & the Superior Court/Circuit Court Records 1759-1919

Surname	Given Name	Instrument	Date	County	CLP Record Series	Index #
WITHERS						
Withers	Andrew F.	Guardian Appt.	8/18/1840	Fauquier Co.	Chancery	1859-021
Withers	Andrew F.	Guardian Appt.	8/18/1840	Fairfax Co. VA.	Chancery	1859-021
Withers	Augustine	Division of Slaves	3/15/1826	Fairfax Co. VA.	Probate, Box 50	1826-001
Withers	Catharine E.	Guardian Appt.	8/25/1857	Fauquier Co.	Chancery	1899-026
Withers	Catharine E.	Guardian Acct.	9/4/1867	Fauquier Co.	Probate, Box 53 Superior/Circuit Ct.	1867-002
Withers	Catharine E.	Guardian Acct.	9/10/1868	Fauquier Co.	Probate, Box 53 Superior/Circuit Ct.	1868-004
Withers	Eliza	Inventory + Appraisement	5/1768	Stafford Co. VA.	Chancery	1789-011
Withers	Elizabeth S.	Guardian Appt.	8/18/1840	Fauquier Co.	Chancery	1859-021
Withers	Elizabeth S.	Guardian Appt.	8/18/1840	Fairfax Co. VA.	Chancery	1859-021
Withers	Enoch K.	Extrx. Bond	1813	Fauquier Co.	Probate, Box 47	1813-001
Withers	George Washington	Guardian Bond	1784	Fauquier Co.	Probate, Box 44	1784-006
Withers	Horatio Chinn	Will	5/30/1840	Fauquier Co.	Chancery	1859-021
Withers	Horatio C.	Guardian Appt.	4/19/1840	Fairfax Co. VA.	Chancery	1859-021
Withers	Horatio C.	Guardian Appt.	4/19/1841	Fairfax Co. VA.	Chancery	1859-021
Withers	Horatio C.	Will	5/30/1840	Fauquier Co.	Chancery	1872-041
Withers	J. H.	Admr. Accts.	9/26/1858	Fauquier Co.	Chancery	1866-058
Withers	J. H.	Admr. Acct.	6/27/1859	Fauquier Co.	Chancery	1866-058
Withers	James	Will	6/1/1746	Stafford Co. VA.	Chancery	1794-018
Withers	James	Inventory + Appraisement	5/1768	Stafford Co. VA.	Chancery	1789-011
Withers	James	Will	1/26/1784	Fauquier Co.	Chancery	1791-023
Withers	James	Will	1/9/1784	Fauquier Co.	Chancery	1816-042
Withers	James	Exors. Bond	1784	Fauquier Co.	Probate, Box 45	1784-012
Withers	James	List of Property + Land in KY, given to daughter Caty	5/24/1801	Fauquier Co.	Land Records & Disputes	1801-013
Withers	James	Will	12/26/1808	Fauquier Co.	Chancery	1837-025

Consolidated Probate Index from the Clerks Loose Papers & the Superior Court/Circuit Court Records 1759-1919

Surname	Given Name	Instrument	Date	County	CLP Record Series	Index #
WITHERS (Cont.)						
Withers	James	Exor. Bond	1808	Fauquier Co.	Probate, Box 46	1808-002
Withers	James	Admr. Appt.	5/27/1828	Fauquier Co.	Chancery	1837-025
Withers	James	Heirs	1/1832	Fauquier Co.	Chancery	1837-025
Withers	Jesse	Guardian Acct.	9/4/1867	Fauquier Co.	Probate, Box 53 Superior/Circuit Ct.	1867-002
Withers	Jesse	Report of Division	12/16/1882	Fauquier Co.	Chancery	1892-032
Withers	Jesse	Plat & Survey Of Division	12/16/1882	Fauquier Co.	Chancery	1892-032
Withers	Jesse H.	Guardian Acct.	9/10/1868	Fauquier co.	Probate, Box 53 Superior/Circuit Ct.	1868-003
Withers	Jesse H.	Guardian Acct.	4/15/1869	Fauquier Co.	Probate, Box 53 Superior/Circuit Ct.	1869-005
Withers	Jesse H.	Guardian Bond	12/14/1865	Fauquier Co.	Chancery	1865-006
Withers	Jesse H.	Guardian Appt.	12/14/1865	Fauquier Co.	Chancery	1866-058
Withers	Jesse H.	Admr. Appt.	10/28/1856	Fauquier Co.	Chancery	1866-058
Withers	Jesse H.	Admr. Bond	10/28/1856	Fauquier Co.	Chancery	1866-058
Withers	Jesse H.	Admr. Bond	9/25/1860	Fauquier Co.	Chancery	1866-058
Withers	Jesse H.	Admr. Acct.	1/28/1861	Fauquier Co.	Chancery	1866-058
Withers	Jesse H.	Admr. Acct.	10/27/1862	Fauquier Co.	Chancery	1866-058
Withers	Jesse H.	Guardian Appt.	8/25/1857	Fauquier Co.	Chancery	1899-026
Withers	Jesse H.	Survey of Lot # 2 From Division of Great Run Tract (Extract)	4/15/1878	Fauquier Co.	Chancery	1902-021
Withers	Jesse H.	Division of Great Run Tract (Extract)	10/19/1865	Fauquier Co.	Chancery	1902-050
Withers	Jesse H. (Col.)	Report of Division	9/17/1857	Fauquier Co.	Chancery	1899-026
Withers	Jesse H. (Col.)	Plat & Survey Of Division	9/17/1857	Fauquier Co.	Chancery	1899-026
Withers	John	Will	9/1/1794	Stafford Co. VA.	Chancery	1815-041
Withers	Lewis	Division	1/29/1823	Fauquier Co.	Chancery	1823-027

Consolidated Probate Index from the Clerks Loose Papers & the Superior Court/Circuit Court Records 1759-1919

Surname	Given Name	Instrument	Date	County	CLP Record Series	Index #
WITHERS (Cont.)						
Withers	Margaret Hord	Plat & Survey Of Division of "Knox Hill"	4/22/1874	Fauquier Co.	Chancery	1902-026
Withers	Patsy	Guardian Bond	1805	Fauquier Co.	Probate, Box 49	1806-006
Withers	Sallie	Guardian Acct.	9/7/1870	Fauquier Co.	Probate, Box 53 Superior/Circuit Ct.	1870-004
Withers	Sallie A.	Guardian Acct.	9/4/1867	Fauquier Co.	Probate, Box 53 Superior/Circuit Ct.	1867-002
Withers	Sallie A.	Guardian Acct.	4/15/1869	Fauquier Co.	Probate, Box 53 Superior/Circuit Ct.	1869-005
Withers	Sallie A.	Guardian Acct.	9/7/1870	Fauquier Co.	Probate, Box 53 Superior/Circuit Ct.	1870-004
Withers	Sallie A.	Guardian Appt.	12/14/1865	Fauquier Co.	Chancery	1866-058
Withers	Sallie A.	Guardian Appt.	12/14/1865	Fauquier Co.	Chancery	1902-050
Withers	Samuel Melville	Guardian Appt.	8/25/1857	Fauquier Co.	Chancery	1899-026
Withers	Susanna	Guardian Appt.	6/18/1840	Fairfax Co. VA.	Chancery	1859-021
Withers	Thomas	Heirs	1832	Fauquier Co.	Chancery	1832-074
Withers	Thomas T.	Guardian Appt.	8/25/1857	Fauquier Co.	Chancery	1899-026
Withers	Thomas T.	Will	3/27/1865	Baltimore, MD.	Chancery	1874-052
Withers	Thomas T.	Will	3/27/1865	Fauquier Co.	Chancery	1897-039
Withers	Thomas T.	Exor. Acct.	12/4/1872	Fauquier Co.	Chancery	1897-039
Withers	William	Will	1/23/1804	Fauquier Co.	Probate, Box 50	1803-003
WOOD						
Wood	John	Report of Division	4/10/1875	Fauquier Co.	Chancery	1892-016
Wood	John	Plat & Survey	4/10/1875	Fauquier Co.	Chancery	1892-016
Wood	Robert	Admr. Bond	1763	Fauquier Co.	Probate, Box 44	1763-004
Wood	Robert	Admr. Acct. Settled	6/1765	Fauquier Co.	Probate, Box 39	1765-001
Wood	Samuel	Admtrx. Bond	1777	Fauquier Co.	Probate, Box 44	1777-002

Consolidated Probate Index from the Clerks Loose Papers & the Superior Court/Circuit Court Records 1759-1919

Surname	Given Name	Instrument	Date	County	CLP Record Series	Index #
WOODSIDE (See also Woodsides)						
Woodside	William	Plat & Survey Of Division	Undated	Fauquier Co.	Chancery	1824-029
WOODSIDES (See also Woodside)						
Woodsides	Sally	Guardian Bond	1813	Fauquier Co.	Probate, Box 49	1815-029
Woodsides	William	Guardian Bond	1813	Fauquier Co.	Probate, Box 49	1815-029
Woodsides	William	Admr. Bond	1815	Fauquier Co.	Probate, Box 47	1815-045
WOODWARD						
Woodward	Luke	Report of Division	9/1885	Fauquier Co.	Chancery	1888-050
Woodward	Luke	Plat & Survey Of Division	9/1885	Fauquier Co.	Chancery	1888-050
WRIGHT						
Wright	James	Exors. Bond	1760	Fauquier Co.	Probate, Box 44	1760-002
Wright	James	Admr. Bond	1810	Fauquier Co.	Probate, Box 47	1810-006
Wright	James	Admr. Bond	1812	Fauquier Co.	Probate, Box 47	1812-008
Wright	William B.	Will	7/23/1855	Fauquier Co.	Chancery	1866-059
Wright	William B.	Will	7/23/1855	Fauquier Co.	Chancery	1871-014
Wright	William B.	Will	7/23/1855	Fauquier Co.	Chancery	1877-021
WYAT (See also Wyatt, Wiatt)						
Wyat	William	Admtrx. Bond	1761	Fauquier Co.	Probate, Box 44	1761-007
WYATT (See also Wyat, Wiatt)						
Wyatt	Conquest	Exor. Bond	1815	Fauquier Co.	Probate, Box 47	1815-013
WYCOFF (See also Wykoff)						
Wycoff	Abraham	Will	7/24/1815	Fauquier Co.	Chancery	1868-227
WYER						
Wyer	Ann E.	Admr. Appt.	2/18/1905	Fauquier Co.	Probate, Box 55 Superior/Circuit Ct.	1905-005
WYKOFF (See also Wycoff)						
Wykoff	Nicholas	Admtrx. Bond	1797	Fauquier Co.	Probate, Box 46	1797-007
YATES						
Yates	J. W.	Admr. Appt.	5/12/1908	Fauquier Co.	Probate, Box 56 Superior/Circuit Ct.	1908-010
Yates	Lincie R.	Renunciation	5/12/1908	Fauquier Co.	Probate, Box 56 Superior/Circuit Ct.	1908-010

www.ingramcontent.com/pod-product-compliance
Lightning Source LLC
Chambersburg PA
CBHW081146230426
43664CB00018B/2825